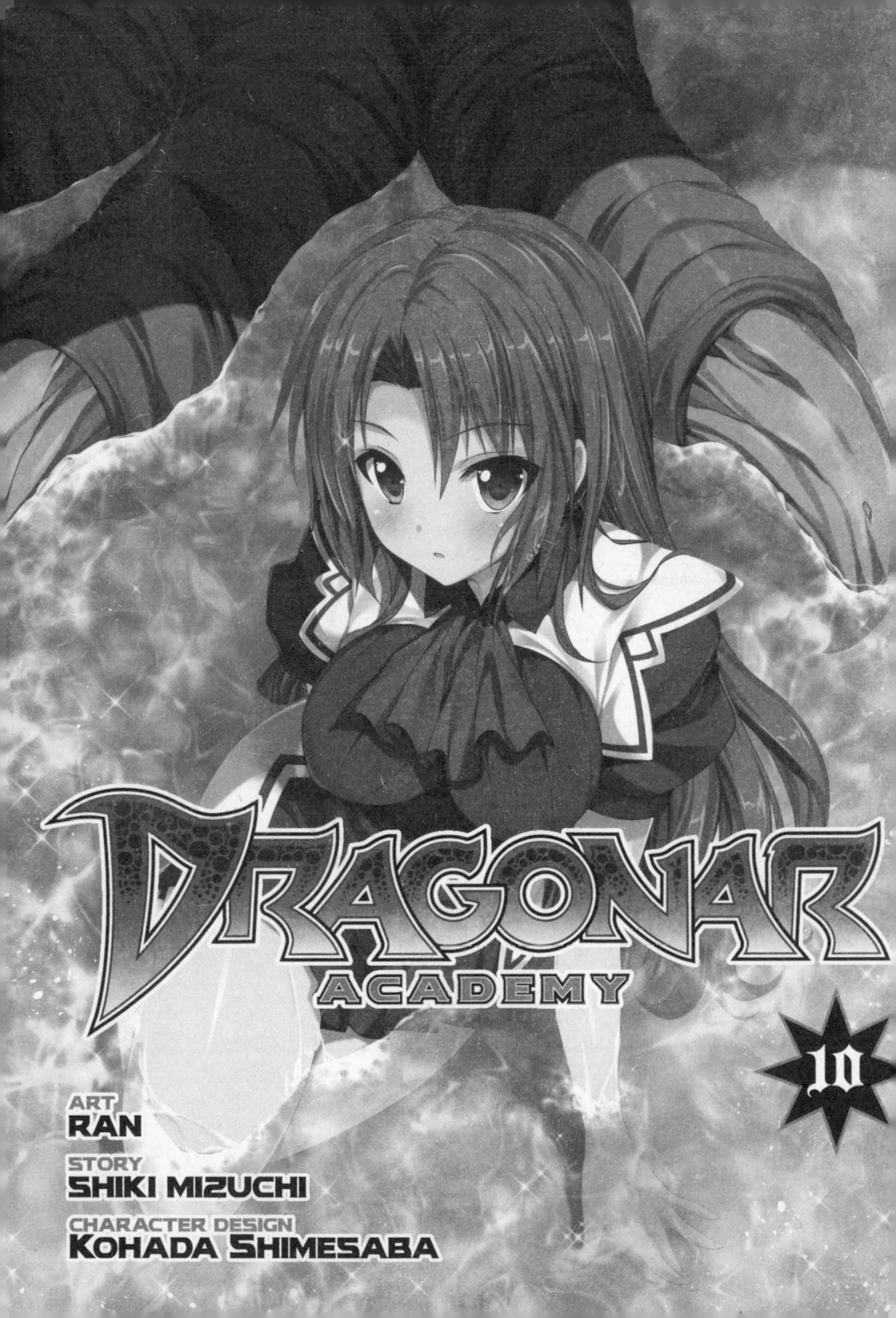
DRAGONAR
ACADEMY
10
ART
RAN
STORY
SHIKI MIZUCHI
CHARACTER DESIGN
KOHADA SHIMESABA

DRAGONAR ACADEMY
THE STORY SO FAR

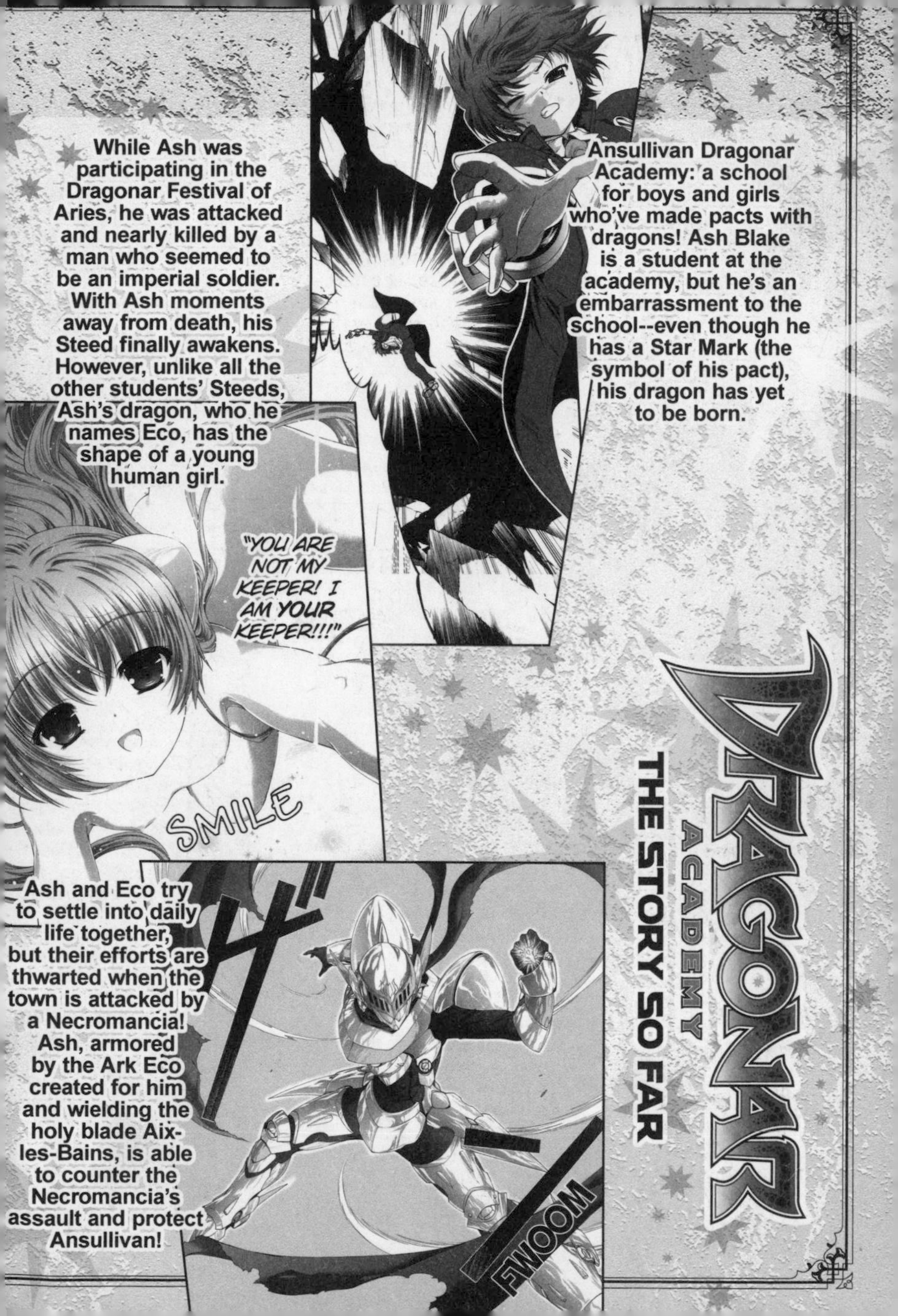

Ansullivan Dragonar Academy: a school for boys and girls who've made pacts with dragons! Ash Blake is a student at the academy, but he's an embarrassment to the school--even though he has a Star Mark (the symbol of his pact), his dragon has yet to be born.
While Ash was participating in the Dragonar Festival of Aries, he was attacked and nearly killed by a man who seemed to be an imperial soldier. With Ash moments away from death, his Steed finally awakens. However, unlike all the other students' Steeds, Ash's dragon, who he names Eco, has the shape of a young human girl.
"YOU ARE NOT MY KEEPER! I AM YOUR KEEPER!!!"
SMILE
Ash and Eco try to settle into daily life together, but their efforts are thwarted when the town is attacked by a Necromancia! Ash, armored by the Ark Eco created for him and wielding the holy blade Aix-les-Bains, is able to counter the Necromancia's assault and protect Ansullivan!
FWOOM

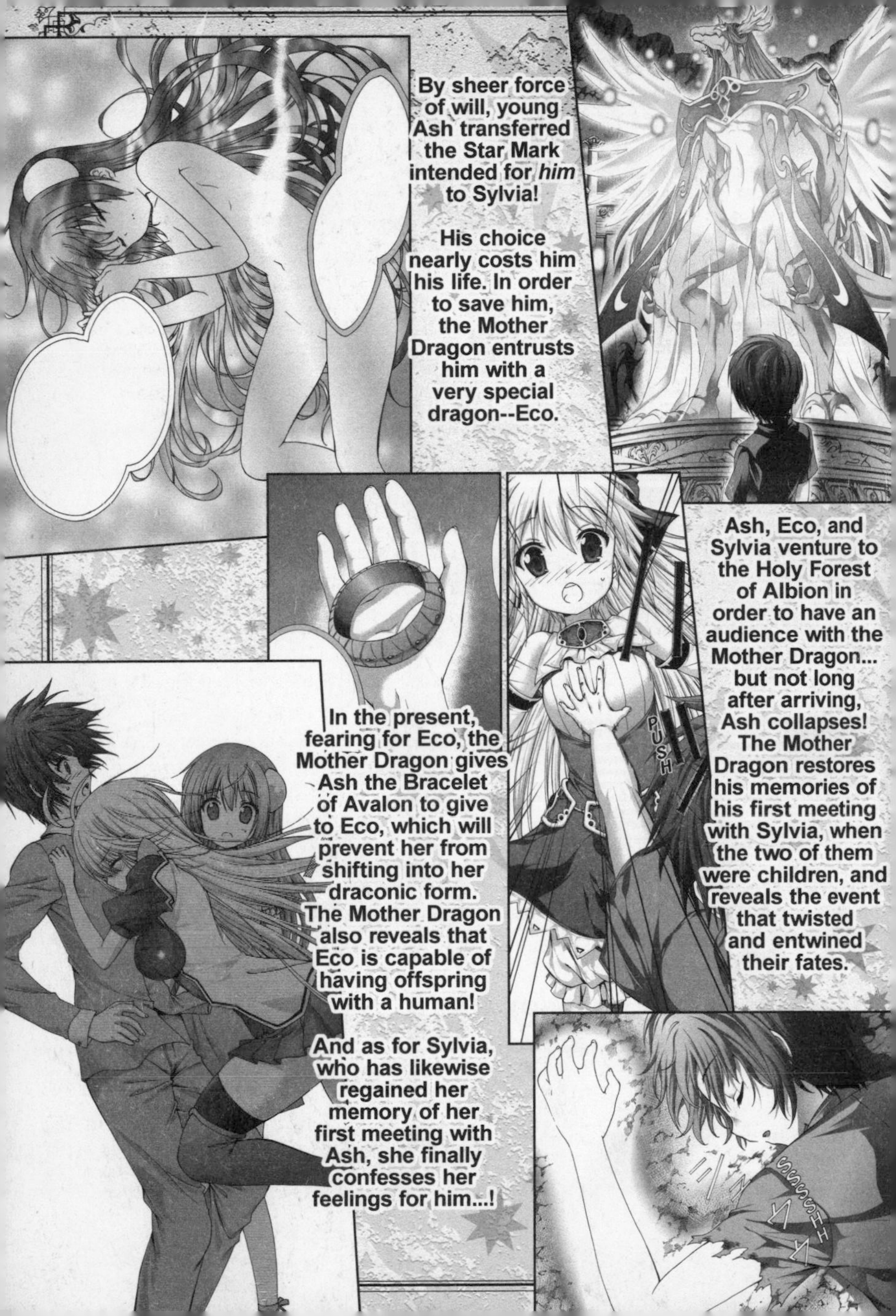
By sheer force of will, young Ash transferred the Star Mark intended for *him* to Sylvia!
His choice nearly costs him his life. In order to save him, the Mother Dragon entrusts him with a very special dragon--Eco.
Ash, Eco, and Sylvia venture to the Holy Forest of Albion in order to have an audience with the Mother Dragon... but not long after arriving, Ash collapses! The Mother Dragon restores his memories of his first meeting with Sylvia, when the two of them were children, and reveals the event that twisted and entwined their fates.
PUSH
In the present, fearing for Eco, the Mother Dragon gives Ash the Bracelet of Avalon to give to Eco, which will prevent her from shifting into her draconic form. The Mother Dragon also reveals that Eco is capable of having offspring with a human!
And as for Sylvia, who has likewise regained her memory of her first meeting with Ash, she finally confesses her feelings for him...!

SEVEN SEAS ENTERTAINMENT PRESENTS

DRAGONAR ACADEMY
VOLUME 10

art by **RAN** / story by **SHIKI MIZUCHI** / character design by **KOHADA SHIMESABA**

TRANSLATION
Nan Rymer

ADAPTATION
Libby Mitchell

LETTERING AND LAYOUT
Paweł Szczęszek

COVER DESIGN
Nicky Lim

PROOFREADER
Lee Otter

PRODUCTION MANAGER
Lissa Pattillo

EDITOR-IN-CHIEF
Adam Arnold

PUBLISHER
Jason DeAngelis

ISBN: 978-1-626922-70-9

Printed in Canada

First Printing: August 2016

10 9 8 7 6 5 4 3 2 1

FOLLOW US ONLINE: *www.gomanga.com*

READING DIRECTIONS

This book reads from *right to left*, Japanese style.
If this is your first time reading manga, you start
reading from the top right panel on each page and
take it from there. If you get lost, just follow the
numbered diagram here. It may seem backwards at
first, but you'll get the hang of it! Have fun!!

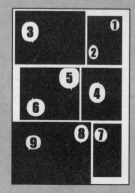

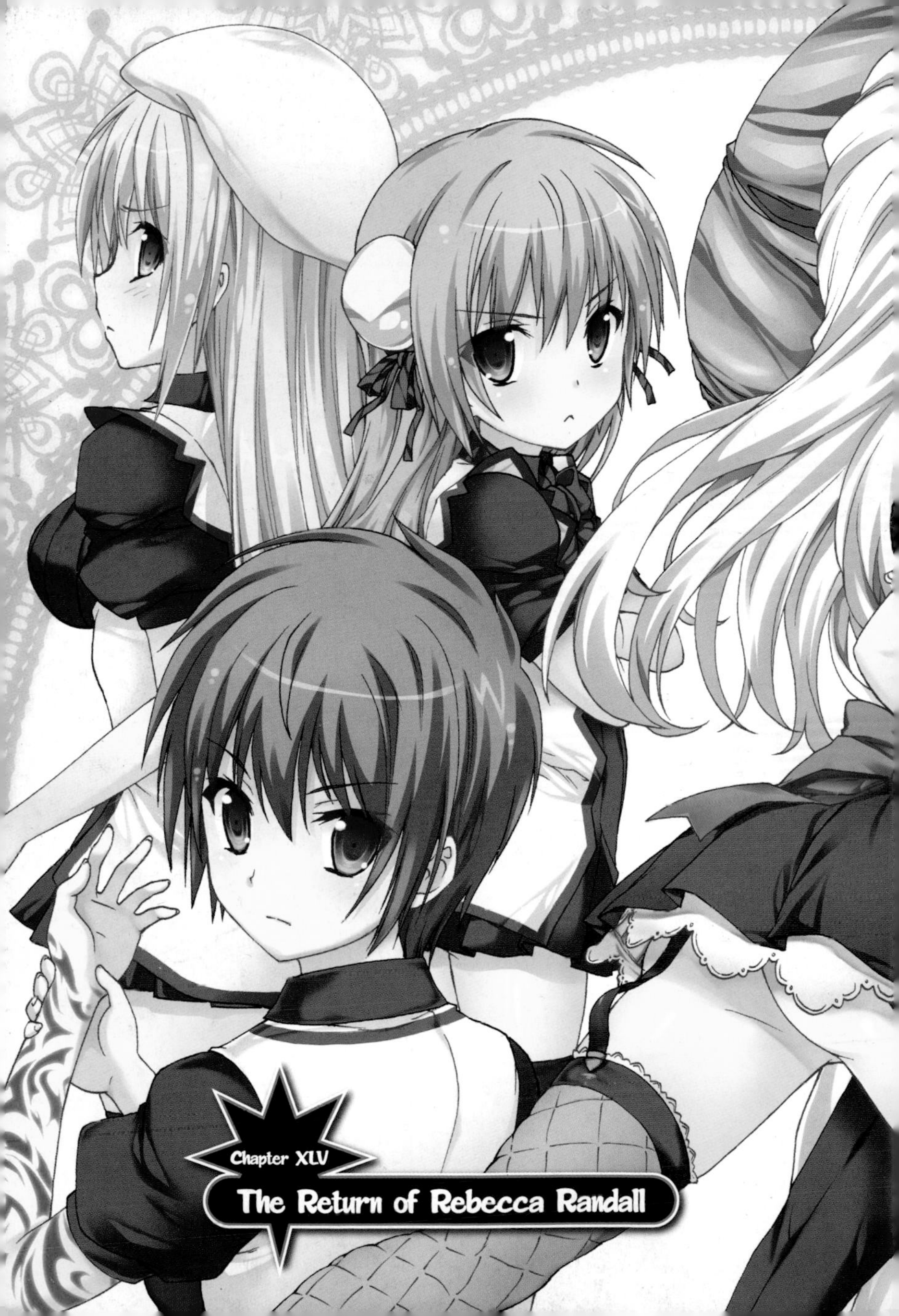
Chapter XLV
The Return of Rebecca Randall

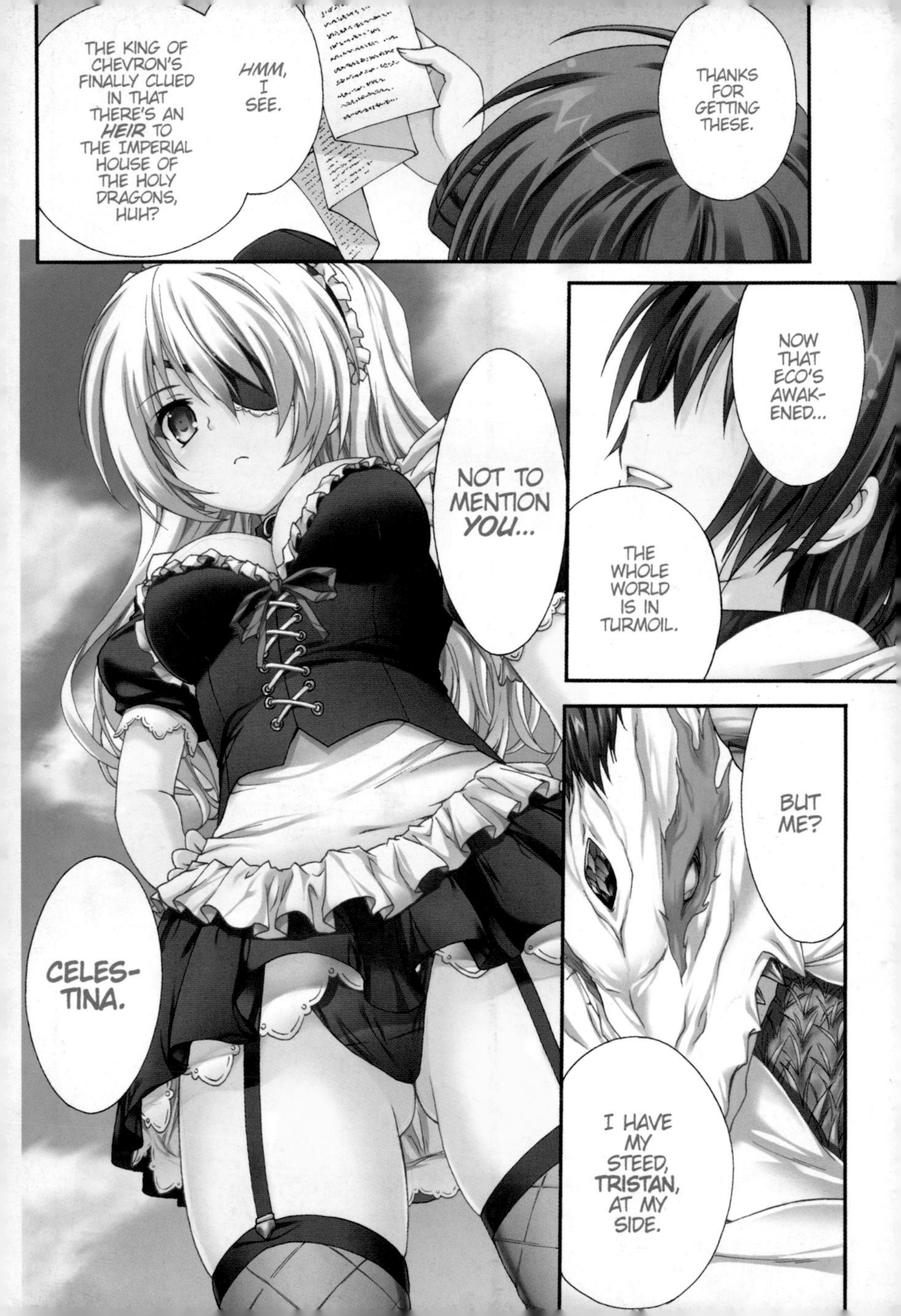

THANKS FOR GETTING THESE.
HMM, I SEE.
THE KING OF CHEVRON'S FINALLY CLUED IN THAT THERE'S AN **HEIR** TO THE IMPERIAL HOUSE OF THE HOLY DRAGONS, HUH?
NOW THAT ECO'S AWAK-ENED...
THE WHOLE WORLD IS IN TURMOIL.
BUT ME?
I HAVE MY STEED, **TRISTAN,** AT MY SIDE.
NOT TO MENTION **YOU...**
CELES-TINA.

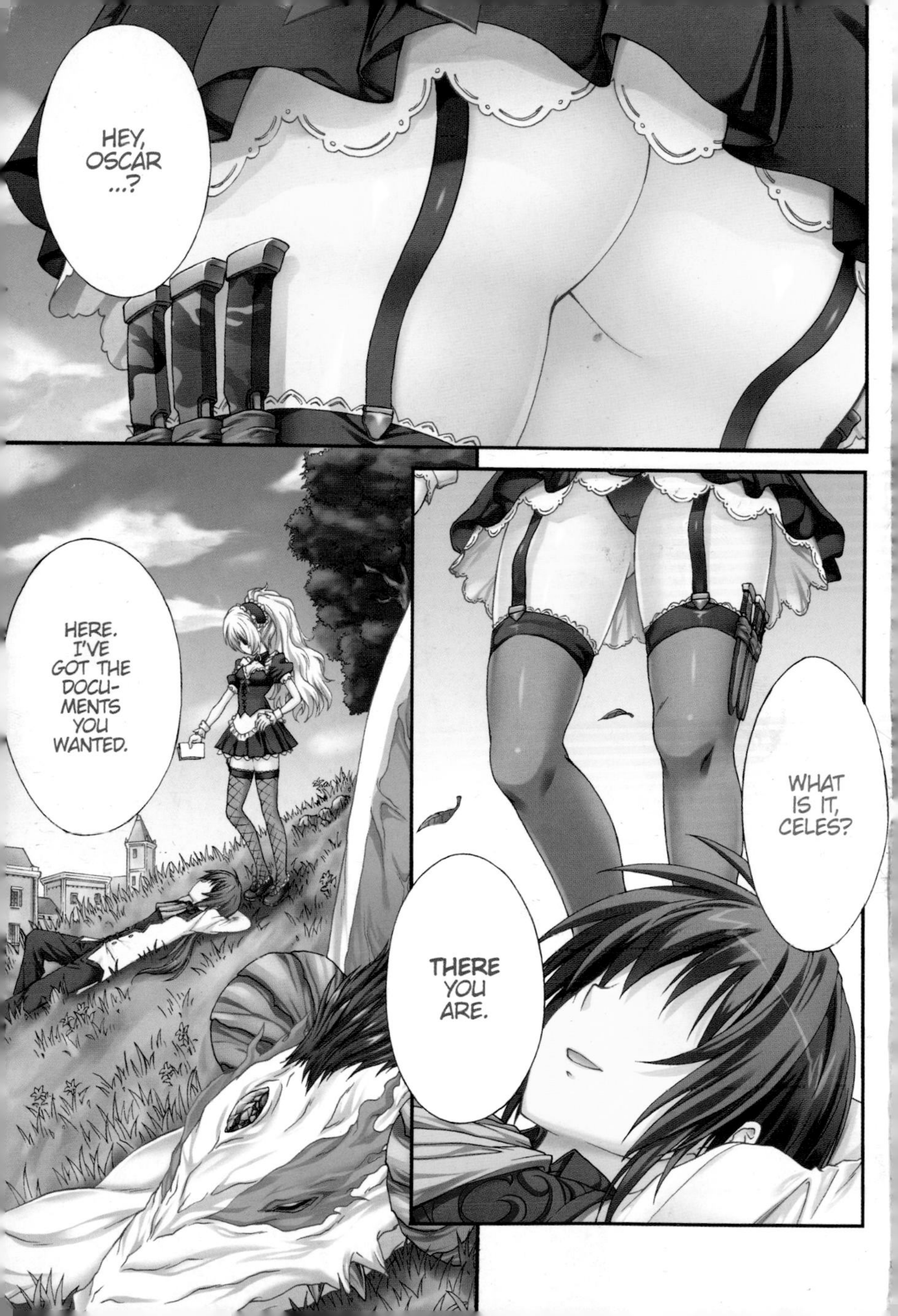
HEY, OSCAR ...?
WHAT IS IT, CELES?
THERE YOU ARE.
HERE. I'VE GOT THE DOCUMENTS YOU WANTED.

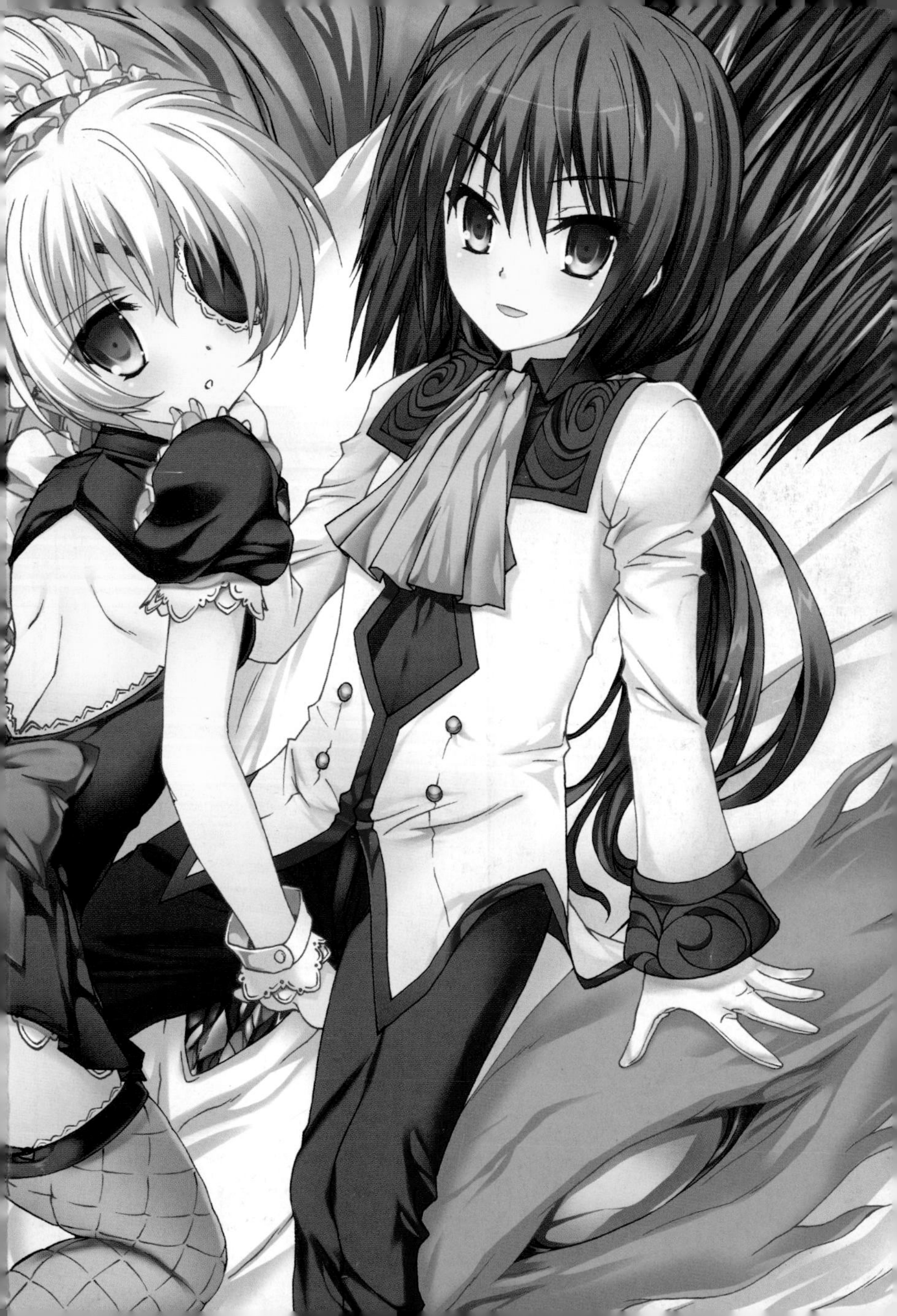

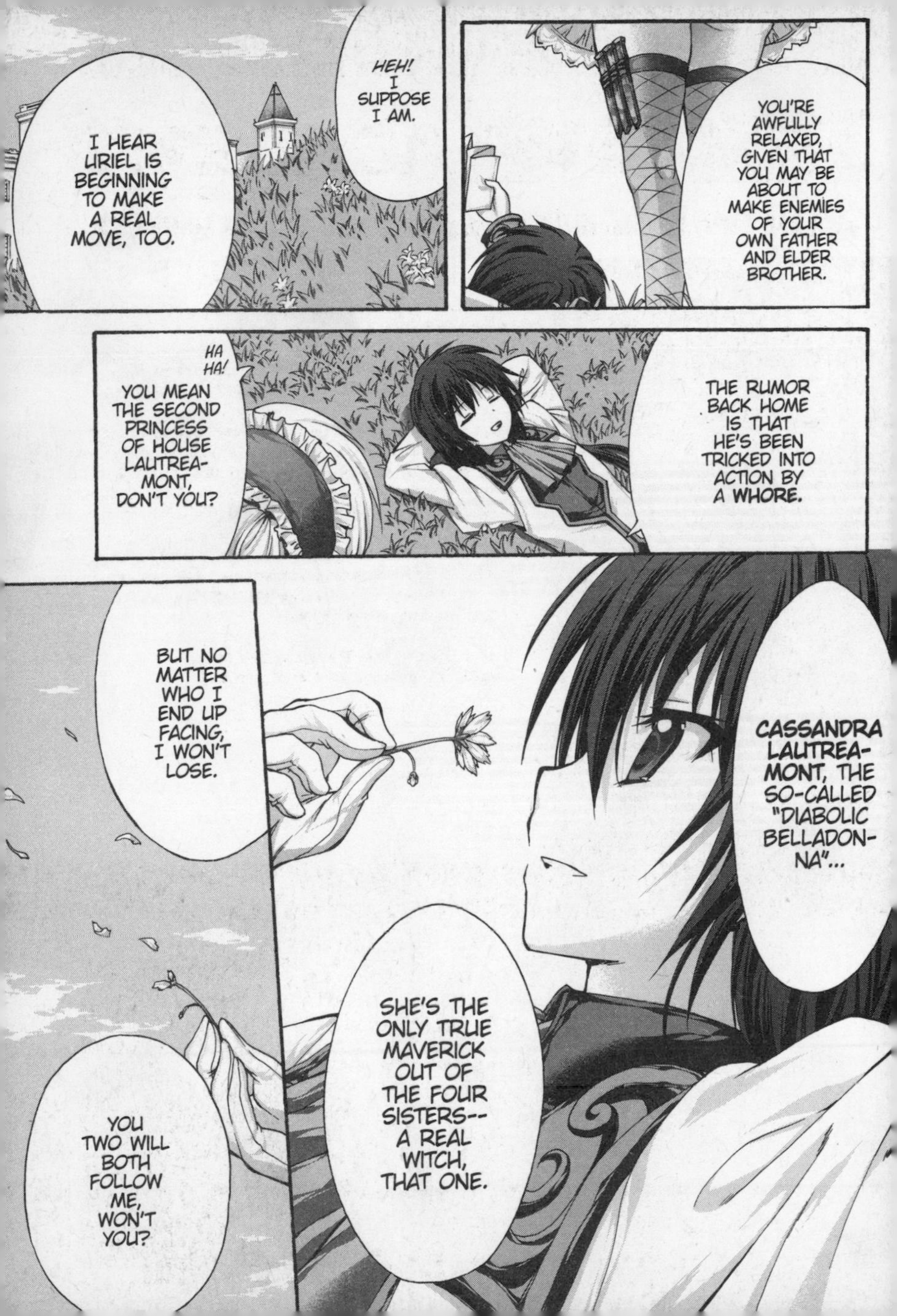
YOU'RE AWFULLY RELAXED, GIVEN THAT YOU MAY BE ABOUT TO MAKE ENEMIES OF YOUR OWN FATHER AND ELDER BROTHER.
HEH! I SUPPOSE I AM.
I HEAR URIEL IS BEGINNING TO MAKE A REAL MOVE, TOO.
THE RUMOR BACK HOME IS THAT HE'S BEEN TRICKED INTO ACTION BY A **WHORE.**
HA HA!
YOU MEAN THE SECOND PRINCESS OF HOUSE LAUTREA-MONT, DON'T YOU?
CASSANDRA LAUTREA-MONT, THE SO-CALLED "DIABOLIC BELLADON-NA"...
SHE'S THE ONLY TRUE MAVERICK OUT OF THE FOUR SISTERS-- A REAL WITCH, THAT ONE.
BUT NO MATTER WHO I END UP FACING, I WON'T LOSE.
YOU TWO WILL BOTH FOLLOW ME, WON'T YOU?

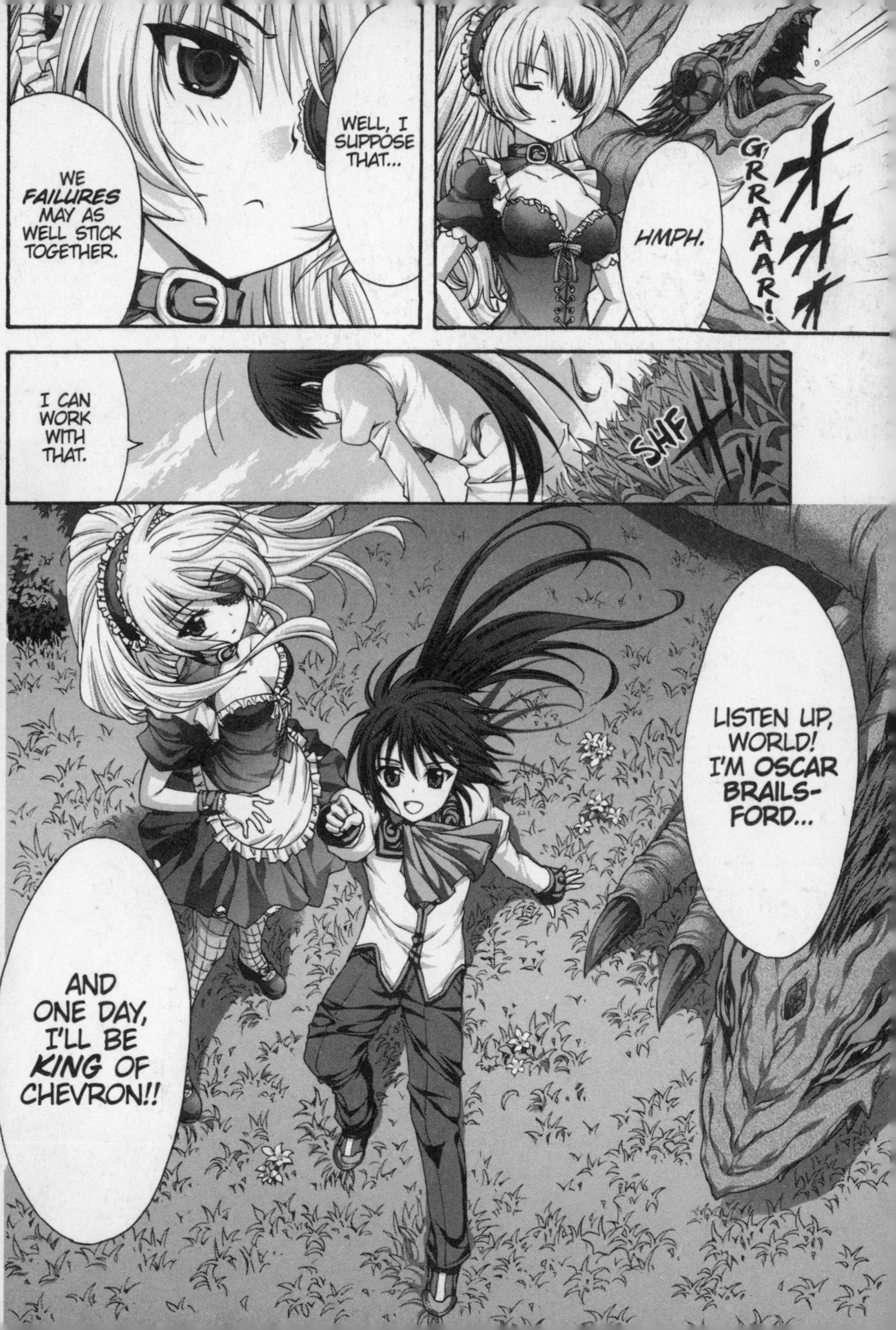
GRRAAAR!
HMPH.
WELL, I SUPPOSE THAT...
WE *FAILURES* MAY AS WELL STICK TOGETHER.
SHF
I CAN WORK WITH THAT.
LISTEN UP, WORLD! I'M OSCAR BRAILS-FORD...
AND ONE DAY, I'LL BE *KING* OF CHEVRON!!

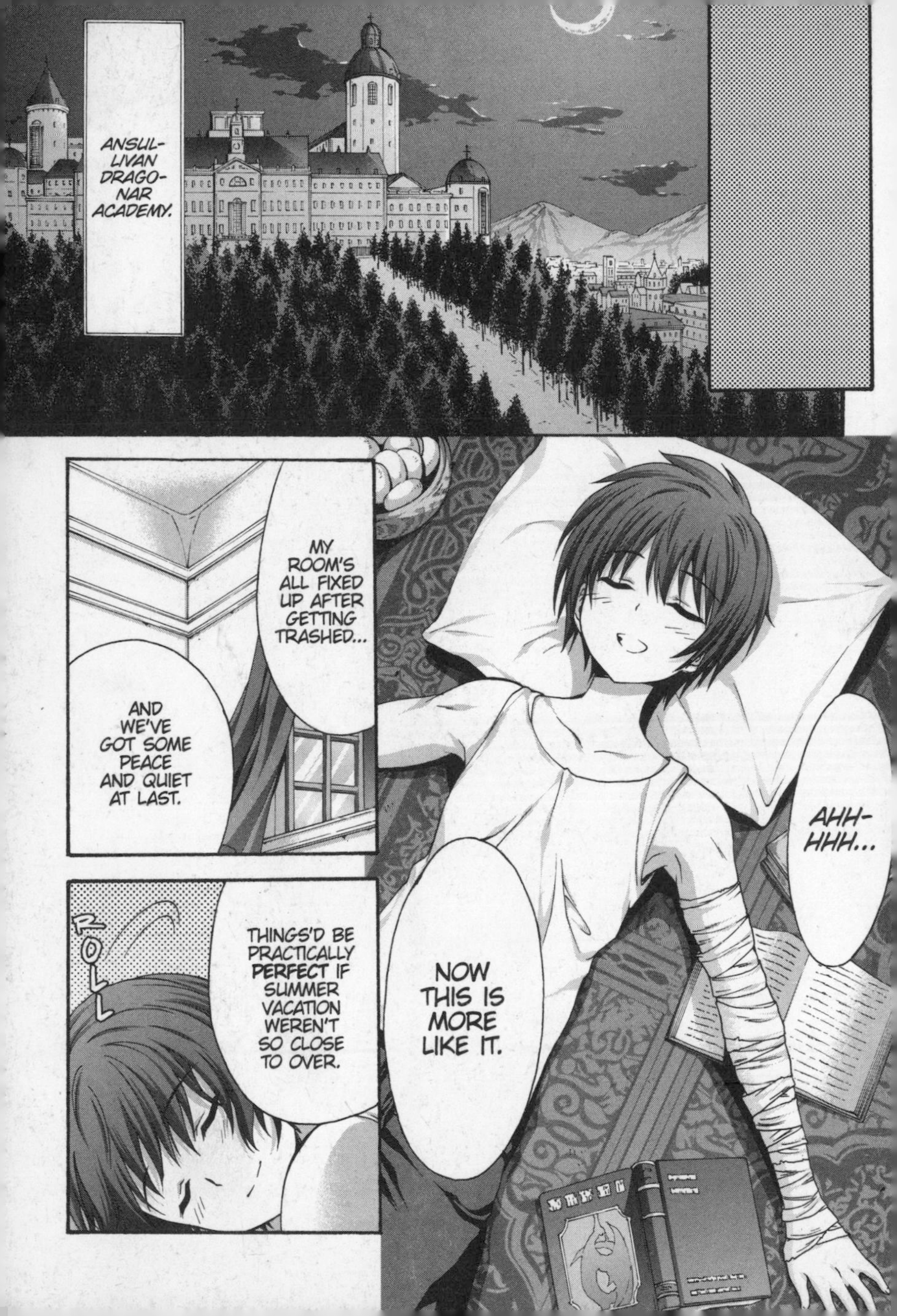
ANSUL-LIVAN DRAGO-NAR ACADEMY.
AHH-HHH...
NOW THIS IS MORE LIKE IT.
MY ROOM'S ALL FIXED UP AFTER GETTING TRASHED...
AND WE'VE GOT SOME PEACE AND QUIET AT LAST.
ROLL
THINGS'D BE PRACTICALLY PERFECT IF SUMMER VACATION WEREN'T SO CLOSE TO OVER.

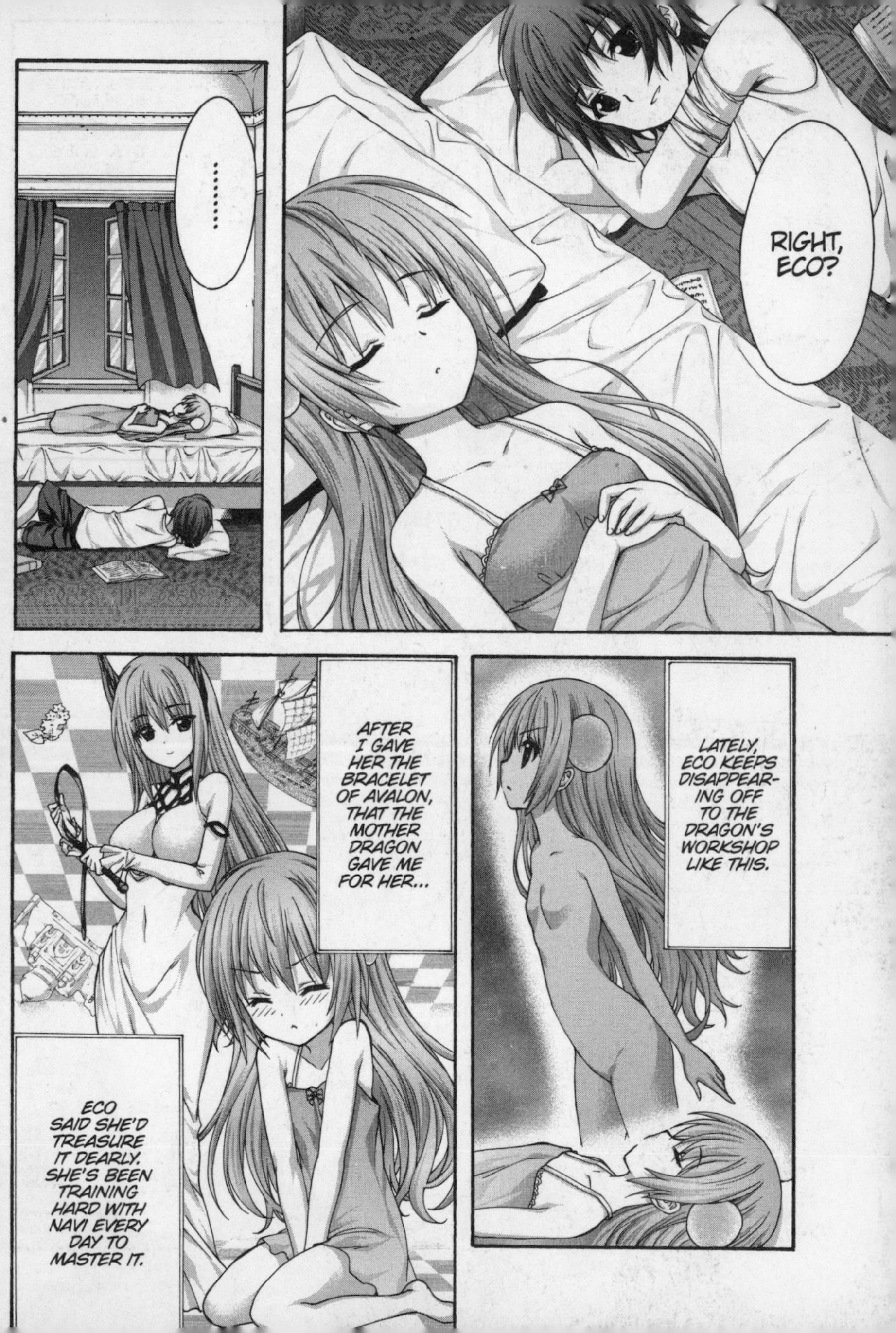

RIGHT, ECO?
......
LATELY, ECO KEEPS DISAPPEARING OFF TO THE DRAGON'S WORKSHOP LIKE THIS.
AFTER I GAVE HER THE BRACELET OF AVALON, THAT THE MOTHER DRAGON GAVE ME FOR HER...
ECO SAID SHE'D TREASURE IT DEARLY. SHE'S BEEN TRAINING HARD WITH NAVI EVERY DAY TO MASTER IT.

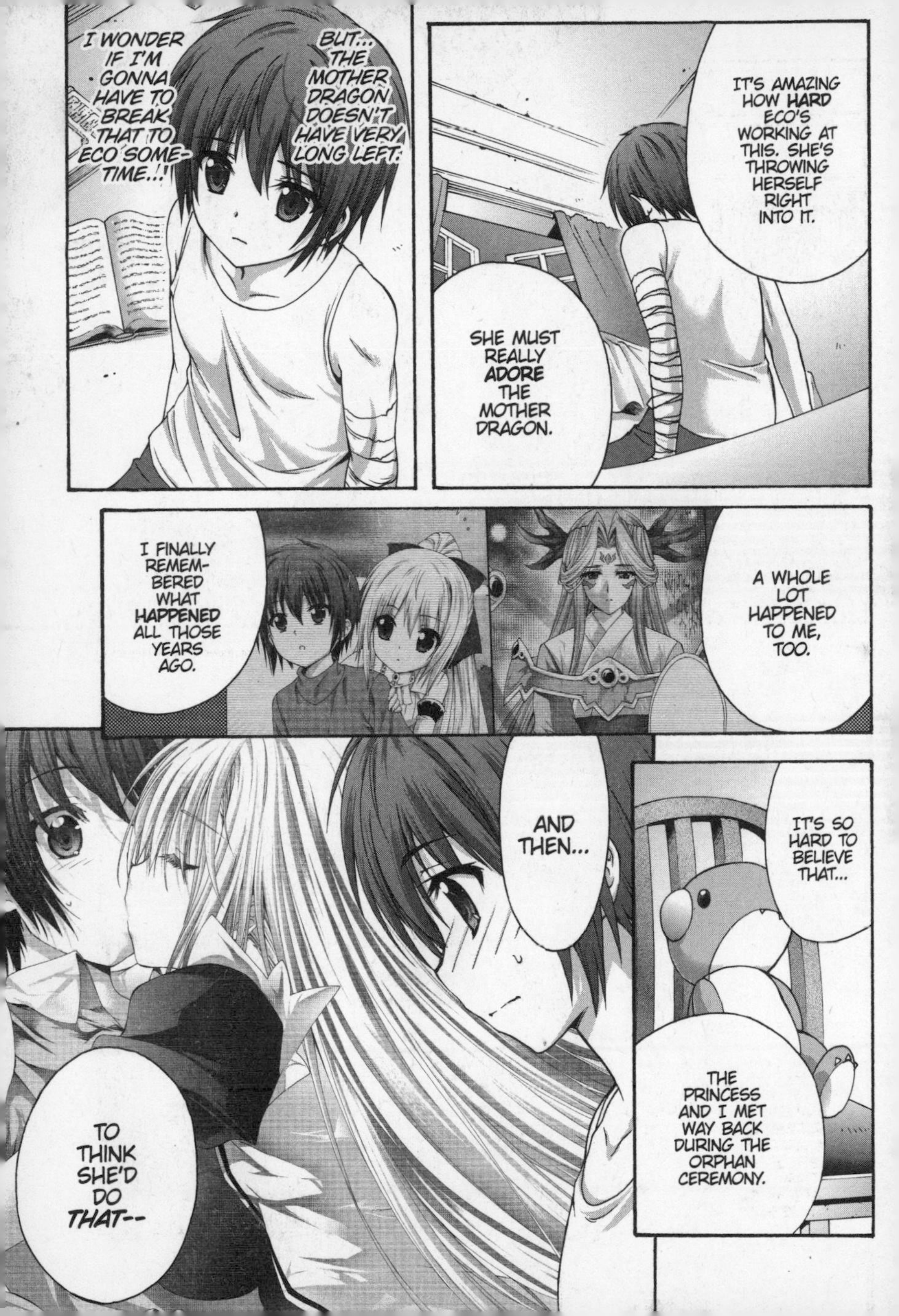
IT'S AMAZING HOW HARD ECO'S WORKING AT THIS. SHE'S THROWING HERSELF RIGHT INTO IT.
SHE MUST REALLY ADORE THE MOTHER DRAGON.
BUT... THE MOTHER DRAGON DOESN'T HAVE VERY LONG LEFT.
I WONDER IF I'M GONNA HAVE TO BREAK THAT TO ECO SOMETIME...!
A WHOLE LOT HAPPENED TO ME, TOO.
I FINALLY REMEMBERED WHAT HAPPENED ALL THOSE YEARS AGO.
IT'S SO HARD TO BELIEVE THAT...
THE PRINCESS AND I MET WAY BACK DURING THE ORPHAN CEREMONY.
AND THEN...
TO THINK SHE'D DO THAT--

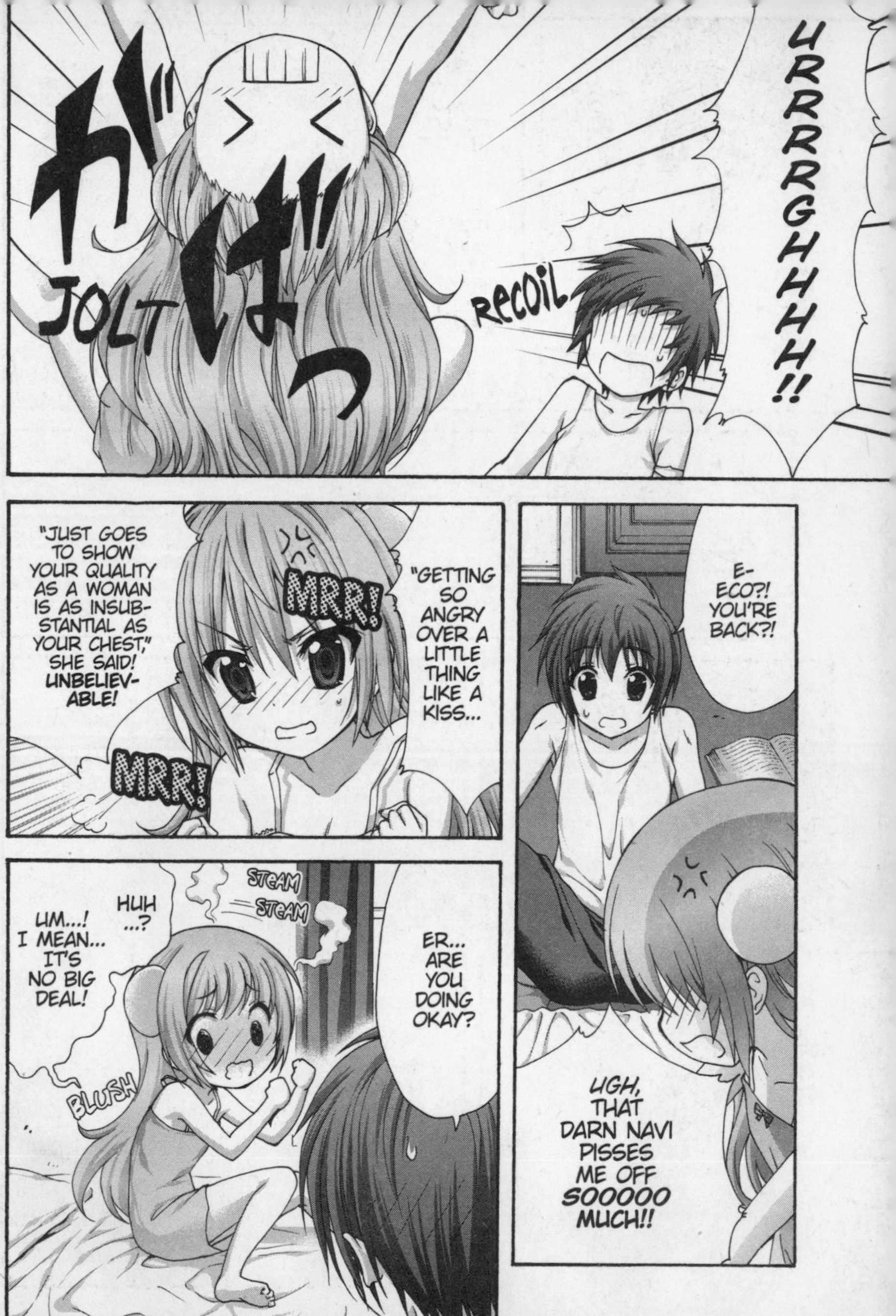
URRRRGHHHHH!!
RECOIL
わ゛ば゛っ
JOLT
E-ECO?! YOU'RE BACK?!
UGH, THAT DARN NAVI PISSES ME OFF SOOOOO MUCH!!
"GETTING SO ANGRY OVER A LITTLE THING LIKE A KISS...
MRR!
"JUST GOES TO SHOW YOUR QUALITY AS A WOMAN IS AS INSUB-STANTIAL AS YOUR CHEST," SHE SAID! UNBELIEV-ABLE!
MRR!
ER... ARE YOU DOING OKAY?
STEAM
STEAM
HUH ...?
UM...! I MEAN... IT'S NO BIG DEAL!
BLUSH
...

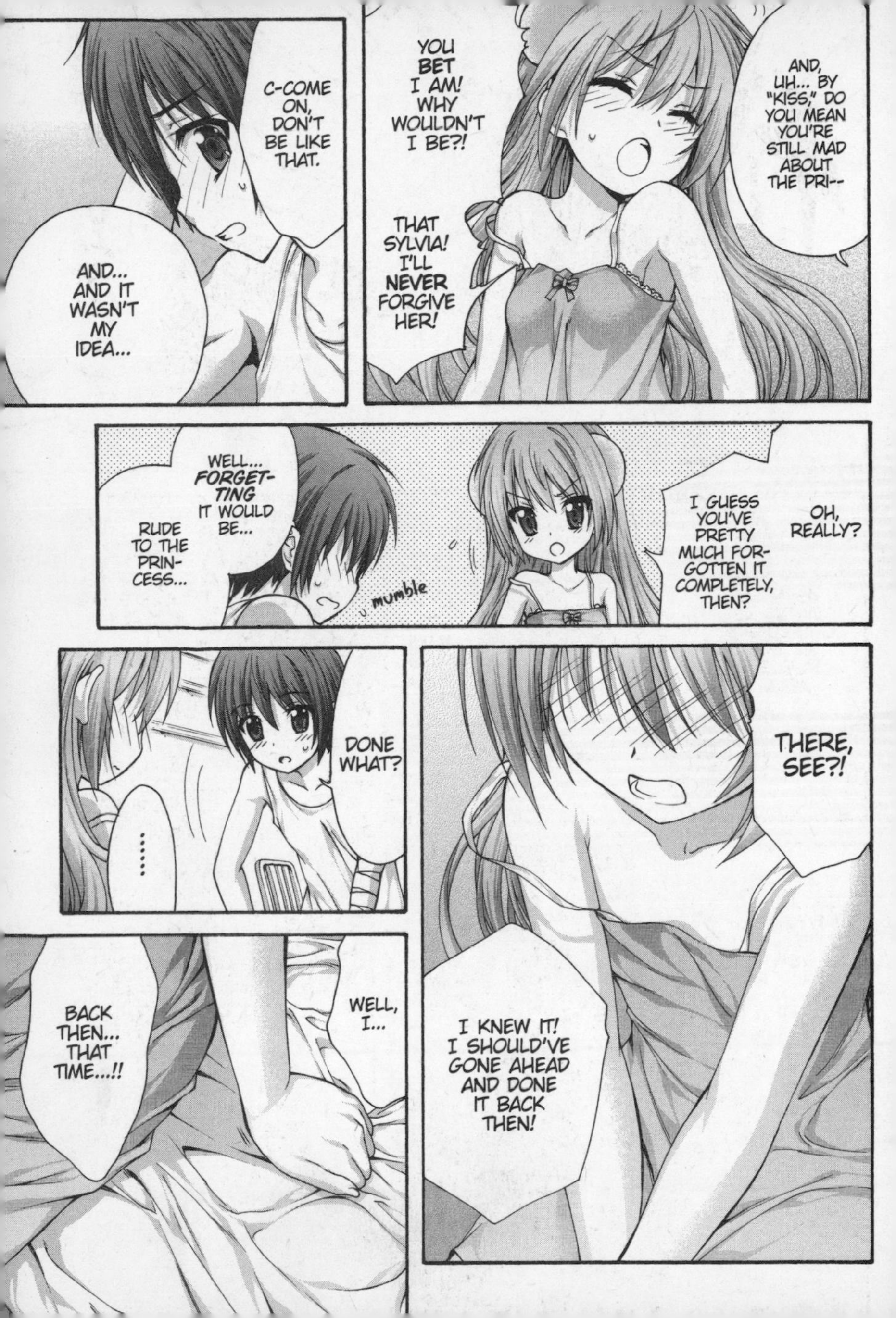

AND, UH... BY "KISS," DO YOU MEAN YOU'RE STILL MAD ABOUT THE PRI--
YOU BET I AM! WHY WOULDN'T I BE?!
THAT SYLVIA! I'LL NEVER FORGIVE HER!
C-COME ON, DON'T BE LIKE THAT.
AND... AND IT WASN'T MY IDEA...
OH, REALLY?
I GUESS YOU'VE PRETTY MUCH FOR-GOTTEN IT COMPLETELY, THEN?
WELL... FORGET-TING IT WOULD BE...
RUDE TO THE PRIN-CESS...
mumble
THERE, SEE?!
I KNEW IT! I SHOULD'VE GONE AHEAD AND DONE IT BACK THEN!
DONE WHAT?
......
WELL, I...
BACK THEN... THAT TIME...!!

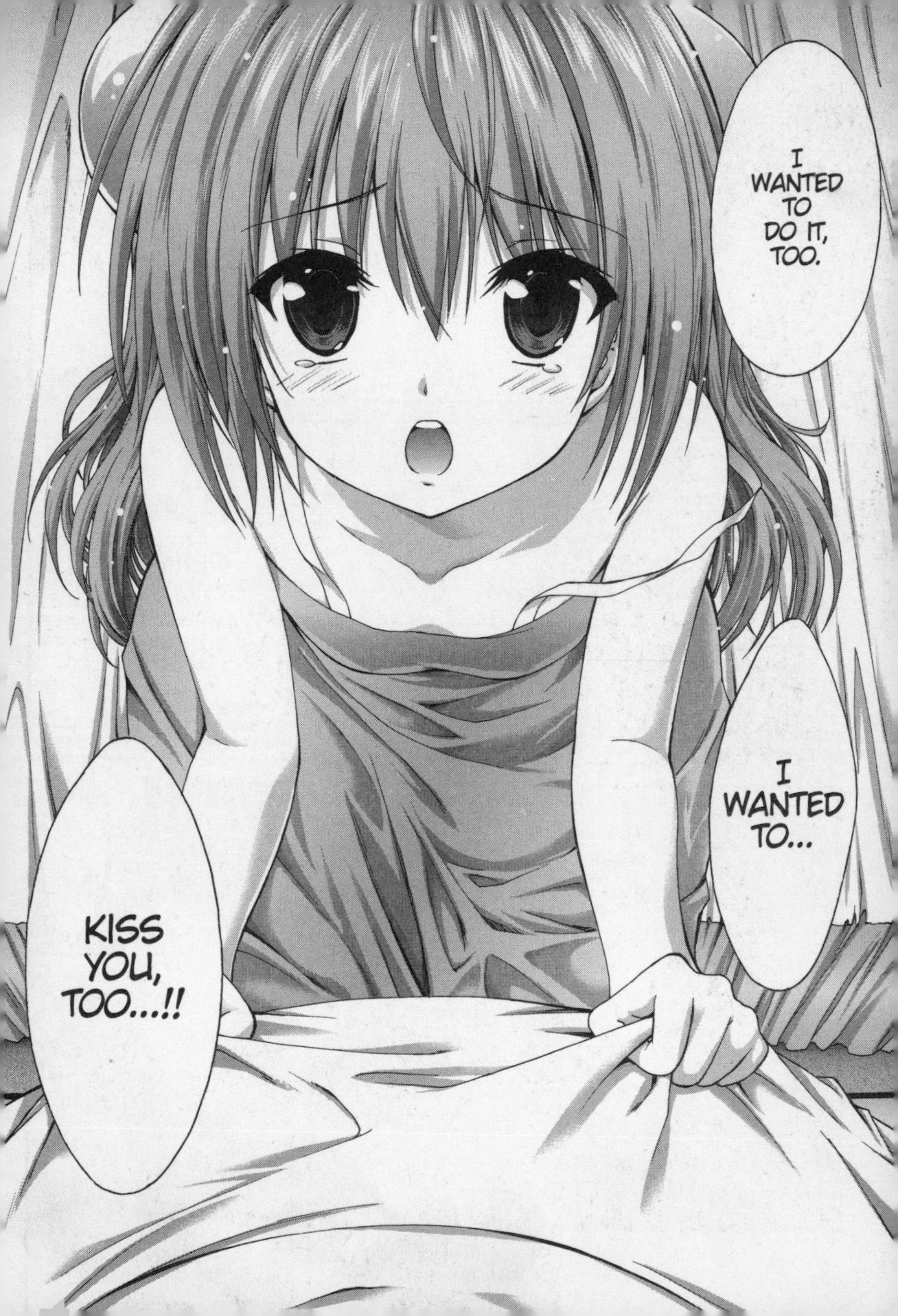
I WANTED TO DO IT, TOO.
I WANTED TO...
KISS YOU, TOO...!!

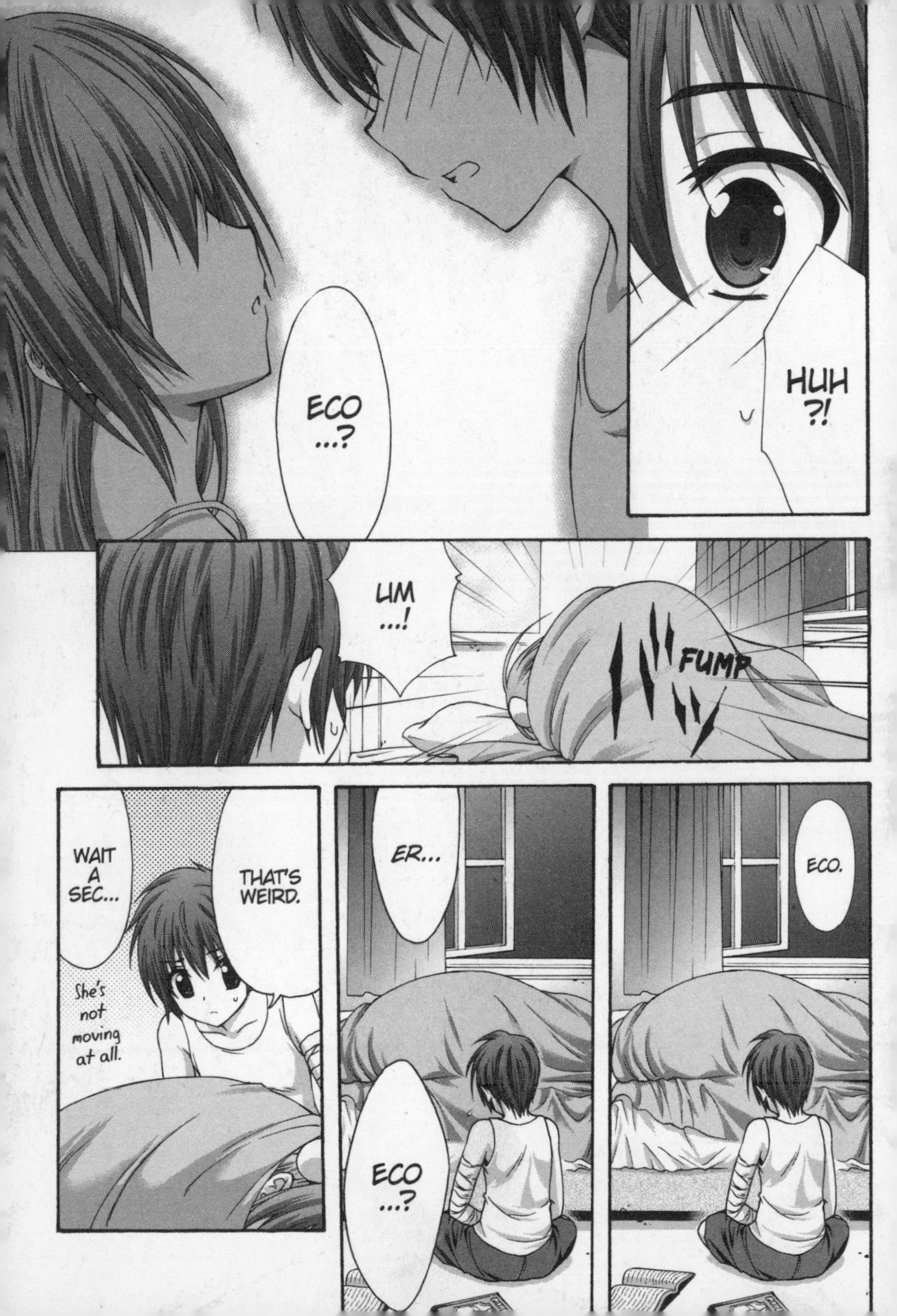
HUH ?!
ECO ...?
UM ...!
FUMP
ECO.
ER...
ECO ...?
THAT'S WEIRD.
WAIT A SEC...
She's not moving at all.

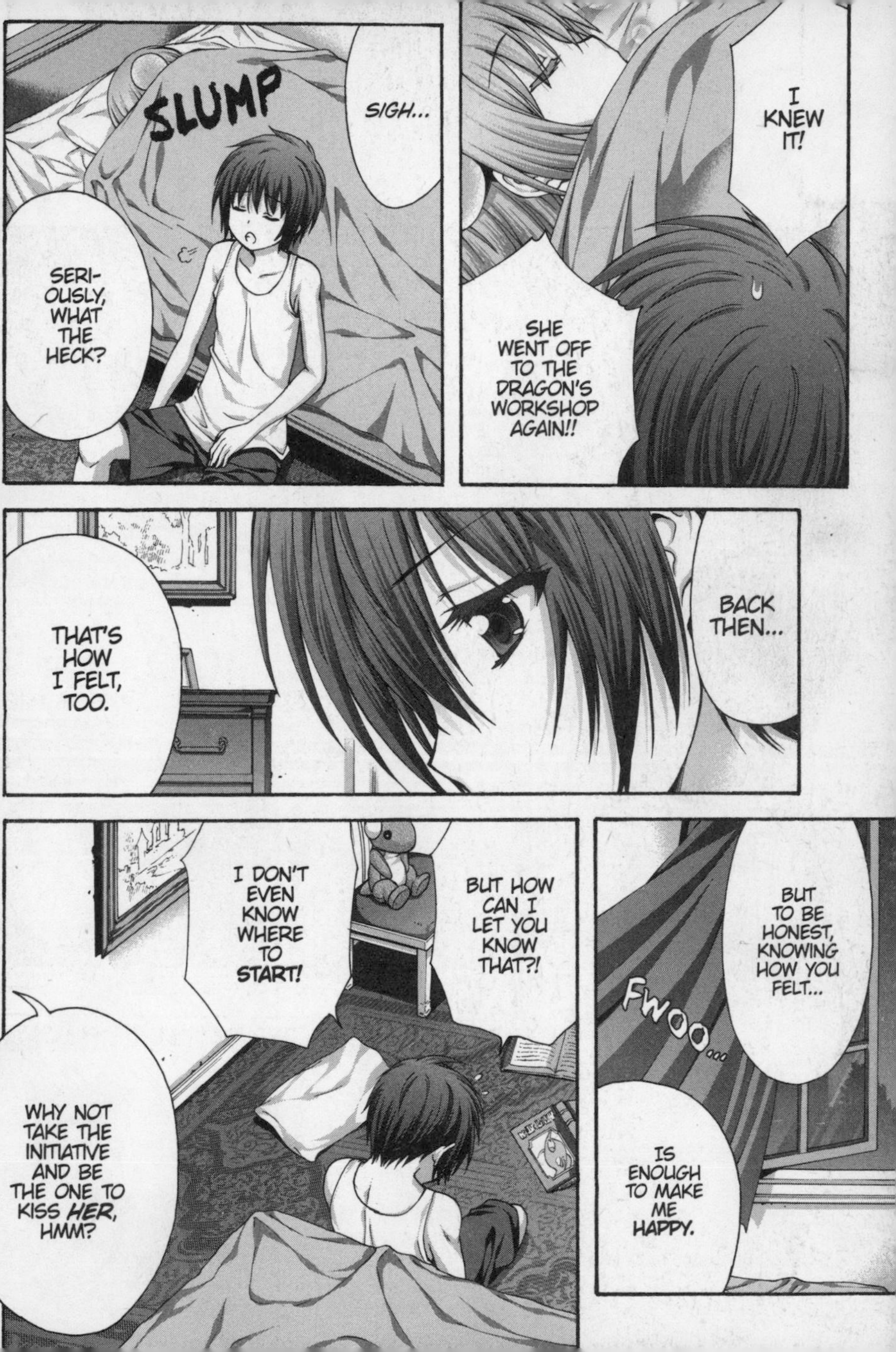
I KNEW IT!
SHE WENT OFF TO THE DRAGON'S WORKSHOP AGAIN!!
SIGH...
SLUMP
SERI-OUSLY, WHAT THE HECK?
BACK THEN...
THAT'S HOW I FELT, TOO.
BUT TO BE HONEST, KNOWING HOW YOU FELT...
FWOO...
IS ENOUGH TO MAKE ME HAPPY.
BUT HOW CAN I LET YOU KNOW THAT?!
I DON'T EVEN KNOW WHERE TO START!
WHY NOT TAKE THE INITIATIVE AND BE THE ONE TO KISS HER, HMM?

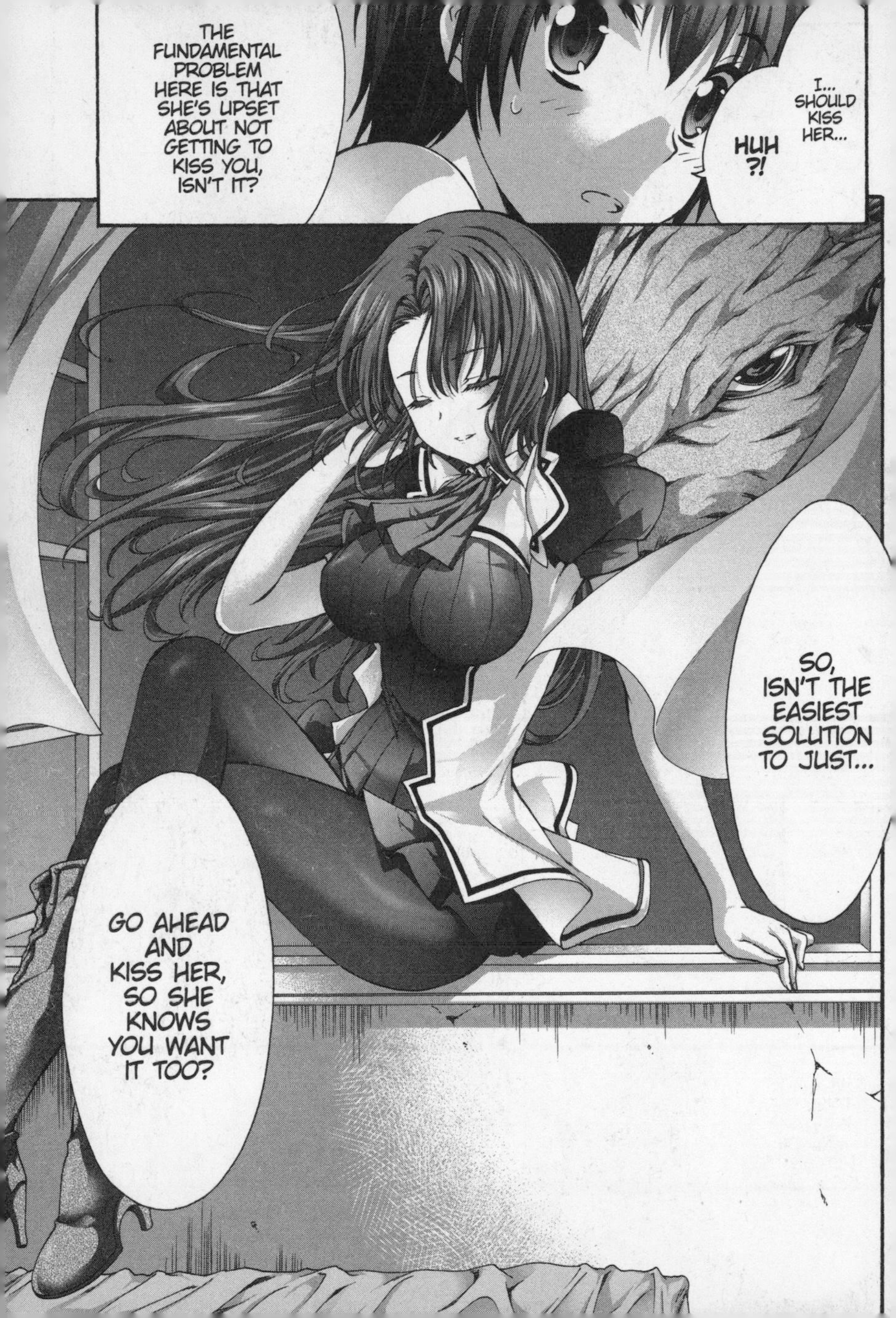
I... SHOULD KISS HER...
HUH?!
THE FUNDAMENTAL PROBLEM HERE IS THAT SHE'S UPSET ABOUT NOT GETTING TO KISS YOU, ISN'T IT?
SO, ISN'T THE EASIEST SOLUTION TO JUST...
GO AHEAD AND KISS HER, SO SHE KNOWS YOU WANT IT TOO?

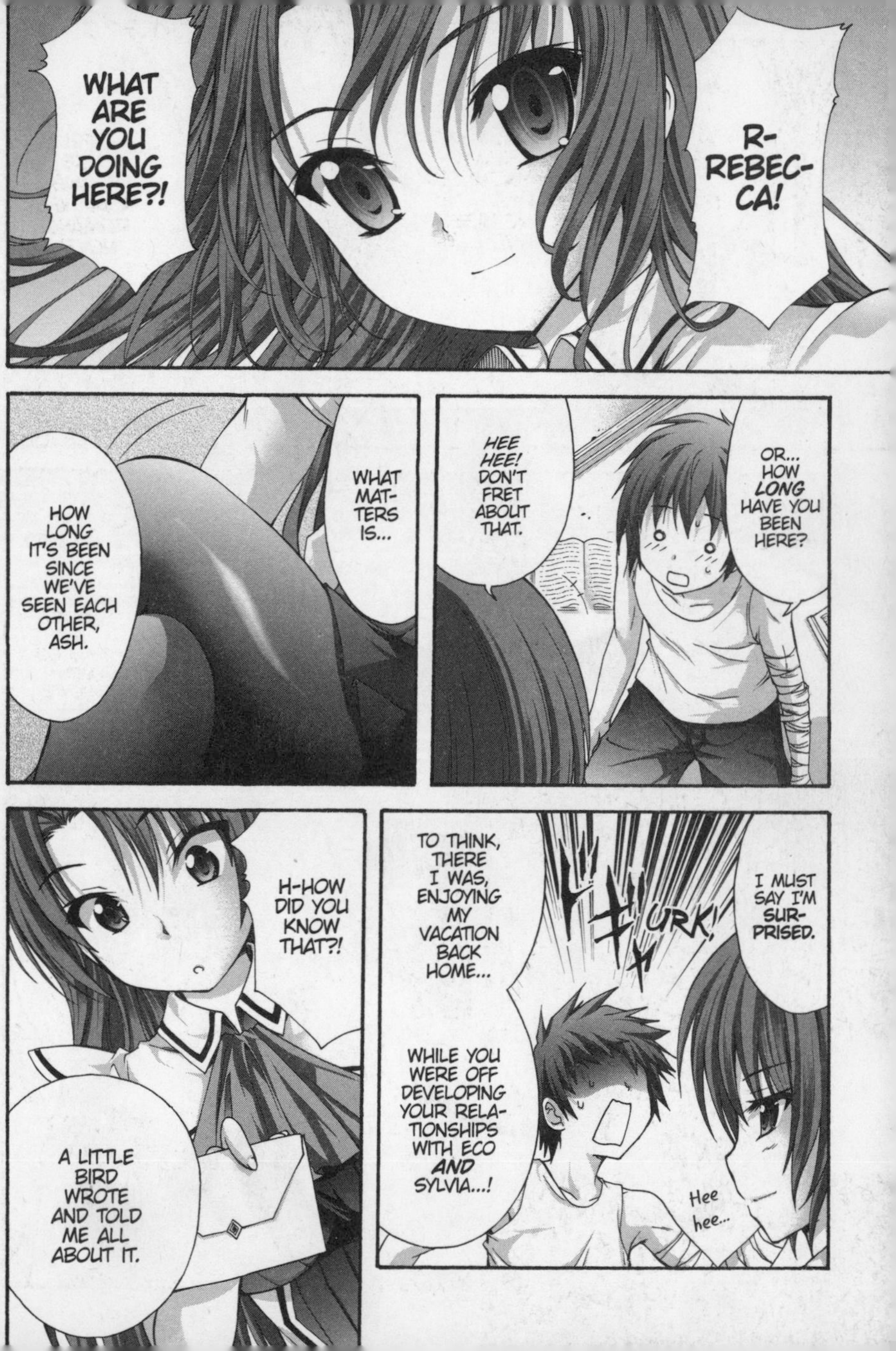
R-REBECCA!
WHAT ARE YOU DOING HERE?!
OR... HOW LONG HAVE YOU BEEN HERE?
HEE HEE! DON'T FRET ABOUT THAT.
WHAT MATTERS IS...
HOW LONG IT'S BEEN SINCE WE'VE SEEN EACH OTHER, ASH.
I MUST SAY I'M SURPRISED.
URK!
TO THINK, THERE I WAS, ENJOYING MY VACATION BACK HOME...
WHILE YOU WERE OFF DEVELOPING YOUR RELATIONSHIPS WITH ECO AND SYLVIA...!
Hee hee...
H-HOW DID YOU KNOW THAT?!
A LITTLE BIRD WROTE AND TOLD ME ALL ABOUT IT.

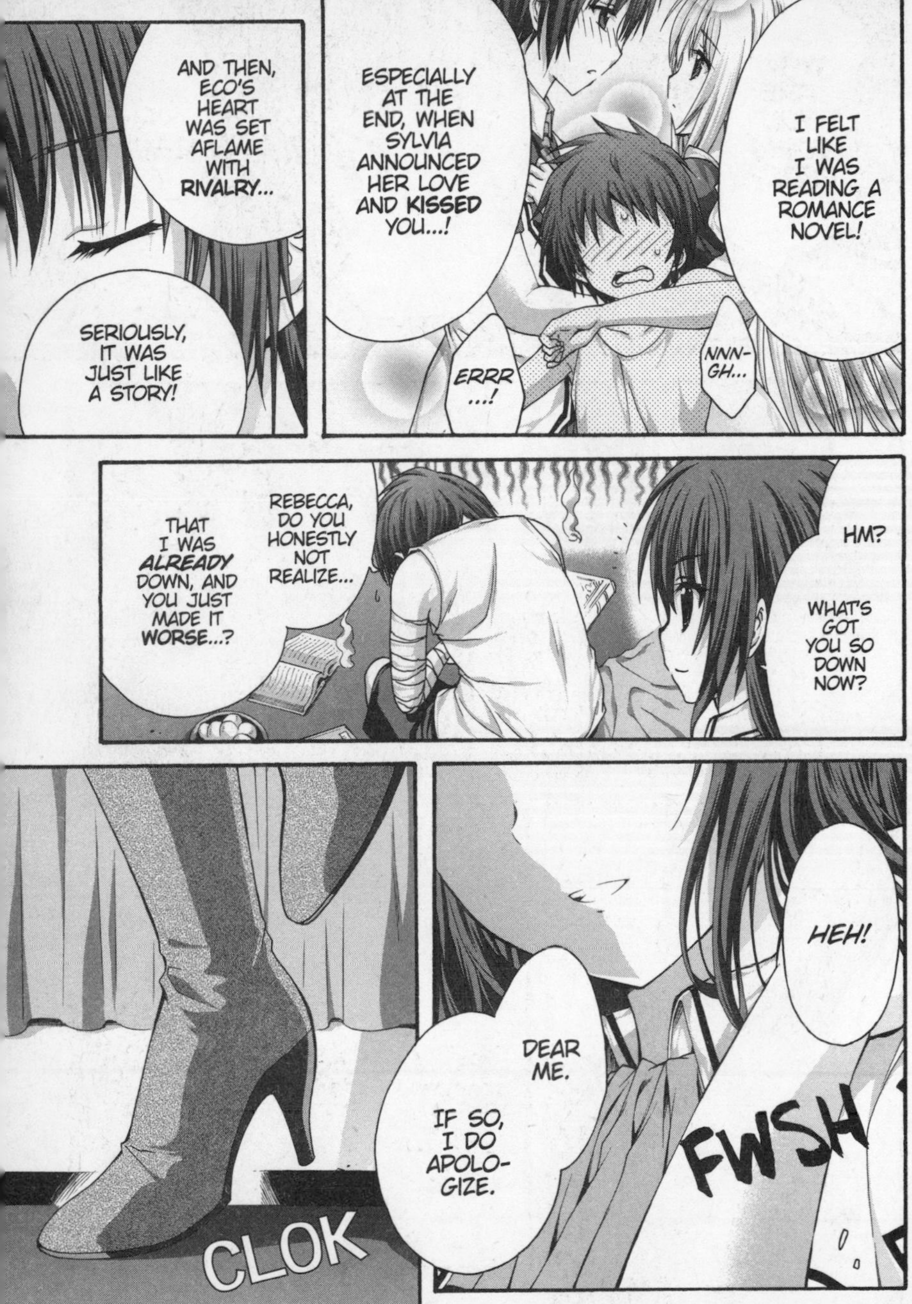
I FELT LIKE I WAS READING A ROMANCE NOVEL!
NNNGH...
ESPECIALLY AT THE END, WHEN SYLVIA ANNOUNCED HER LOVE AND KISSED YOU...!
ERRR...!
AND THEN, ECO'S HEART WAS SET AFLAME WITH RIVALRY...
SERIOUSLY, IT WAS JUST LIKE A STORY!
HM?
WHAT'S GOT YOU SO DOWN NOW?
REBECCA, DO YOU HONESTLY NOT REALIZE...
THAT I WAS ALREADY DOWN, AND YOU JUST MADE IT WORSE...?
HEH!
DEAR ME.
IF SO, I DO APOLOGIZE.
FWSH
CLOK

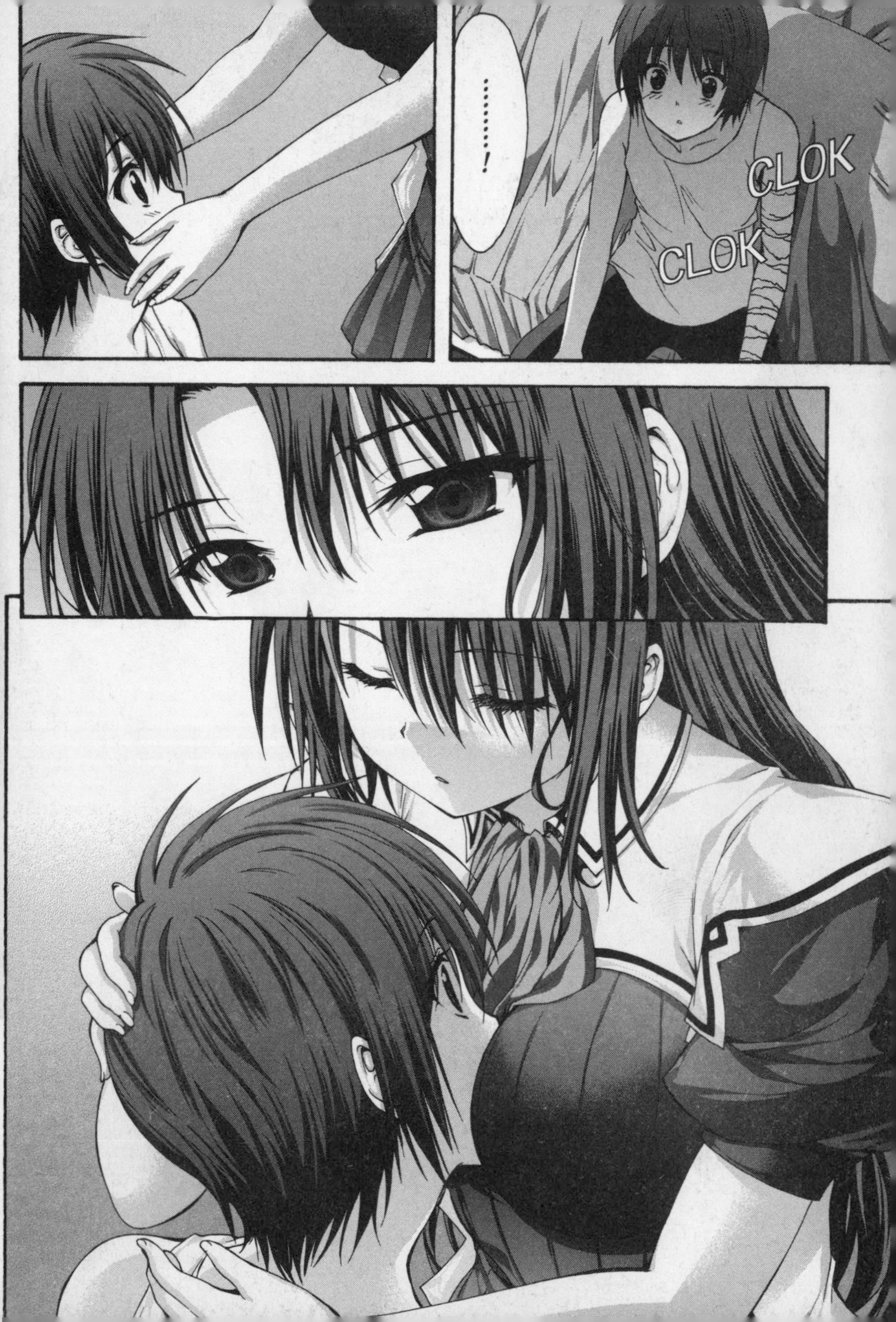
......!
CLOK
CLOK

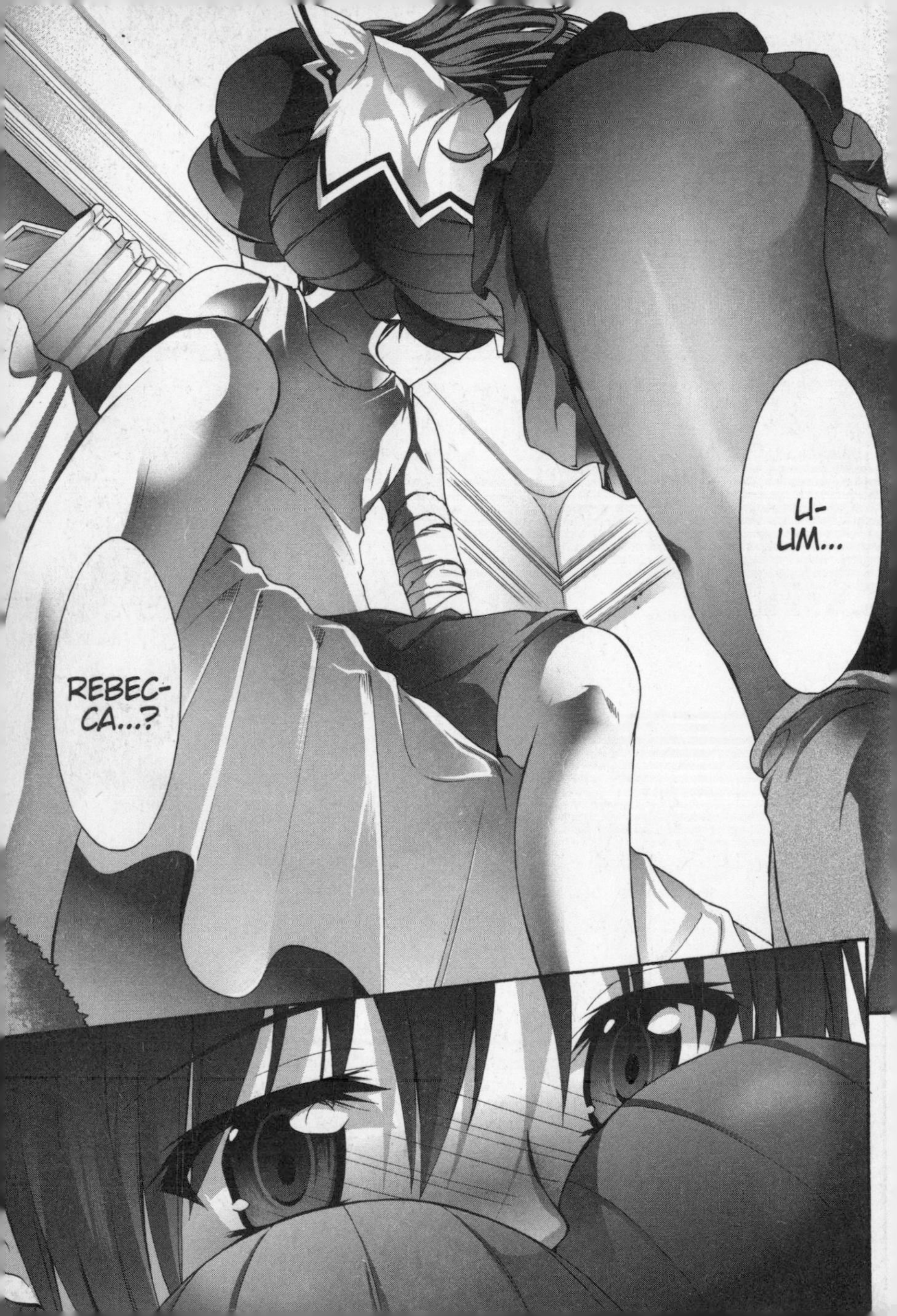
U-UM...
REBEC-CA...?

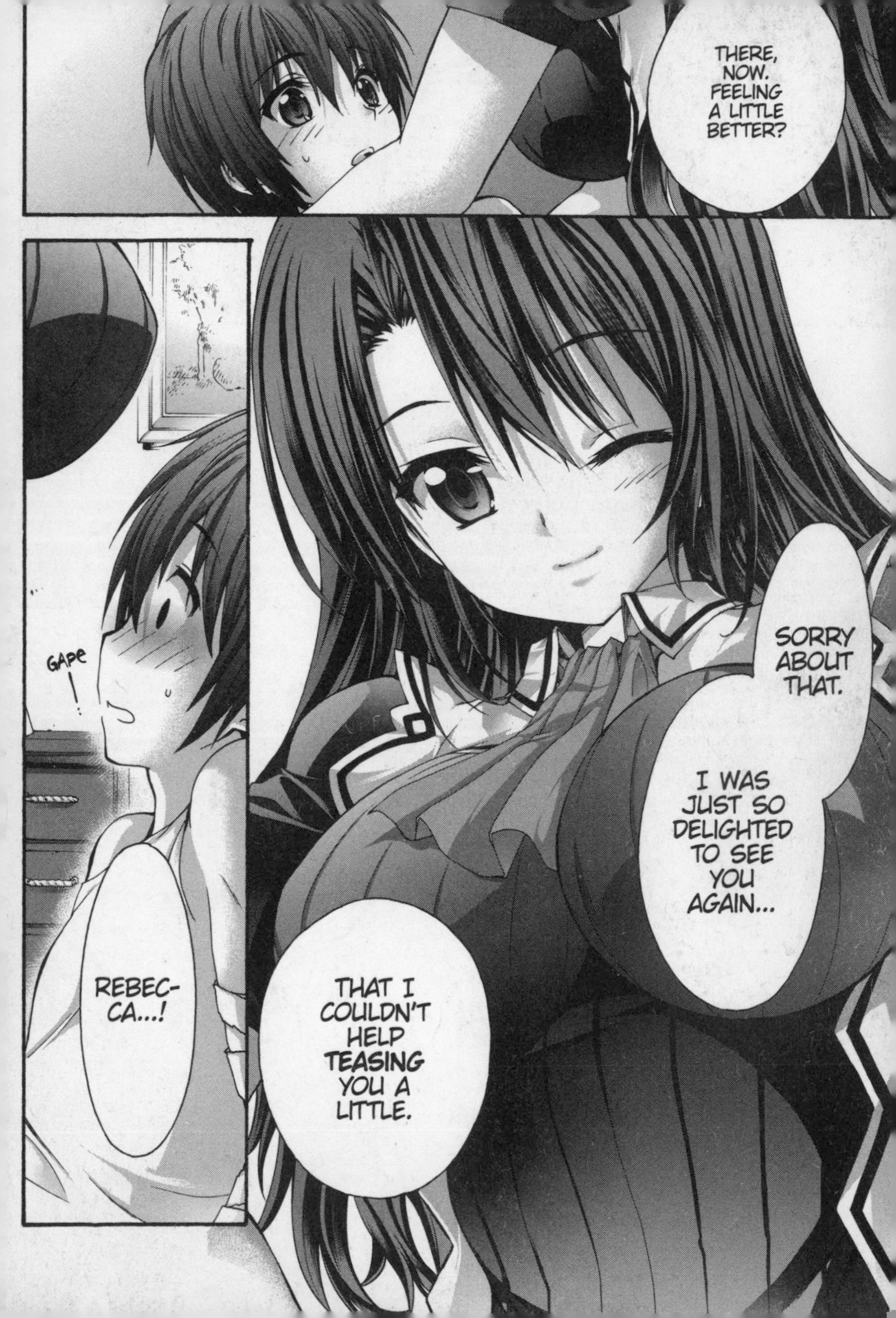
THERE, NOW. FEELING A LITTLE BETTER?
SORRY ABOUT THAT.
I WAS JUST SO DELIGHTED TO SEE YOU AGAIN...
THAT I COULDN'T HELP TEASING YOU A LITTLE.
GAPE
REBEC-CA...!

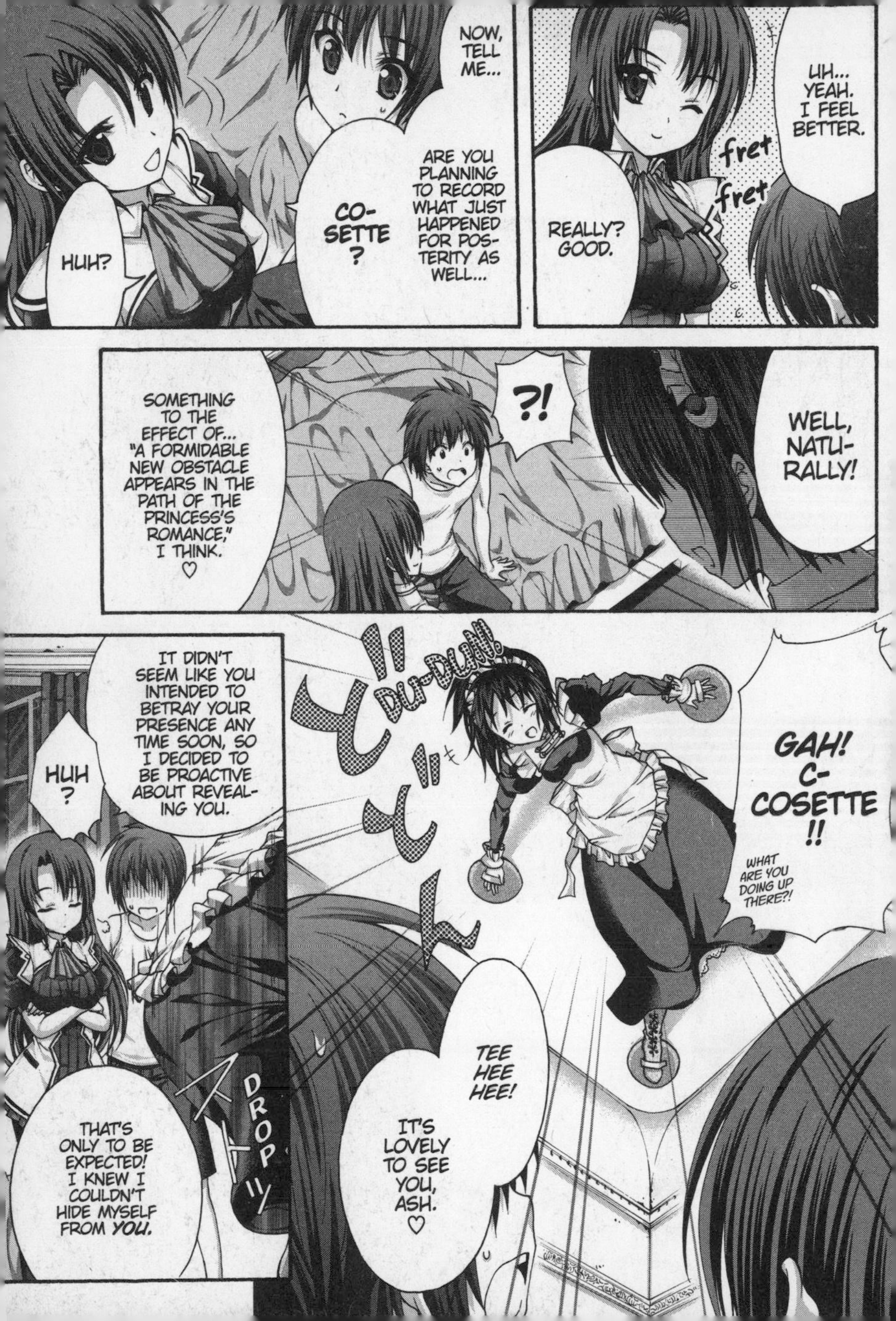
UH... YEAH. I FEEL BETTER.
fret fret
REALLY? GOOD.
NOW, TELL ME...
ARE YOU PLANNING TO RECORD WHAT JUST HAPPENED FOR POSTERITY AS WELL...
CO-SETTE?
HUH?
WELL, NATU-RALLY!
?!
SOMETHING TO THE EFFECT OF... "A FORMIDABLE NEW OBSTACLE APPEARS IN THE PATH OF THE PRINCESS'S ROMANCE," I THINK. ♡
GAH! C-COSETTE!!
WHAT ARE YOU DOING UP THERE?!
DU-DUN!!
TEE HEE HEE!
IT'S LOVELY TO SEE YOU, ASH. ♡
IT DIDN'T SEEM LIKE YOU INTENDED TO BETRAY YOUR PRESENCE ANY TIME SOON, SO I DECIDED TO BE PROACTIVE ABOUT REVEALING YOU.
HUH?
DROP
THAT'S ONLY TO BE EXPECTED! I KNEW I COULDN'T HIDE MYSELF FROM ***YOU***.

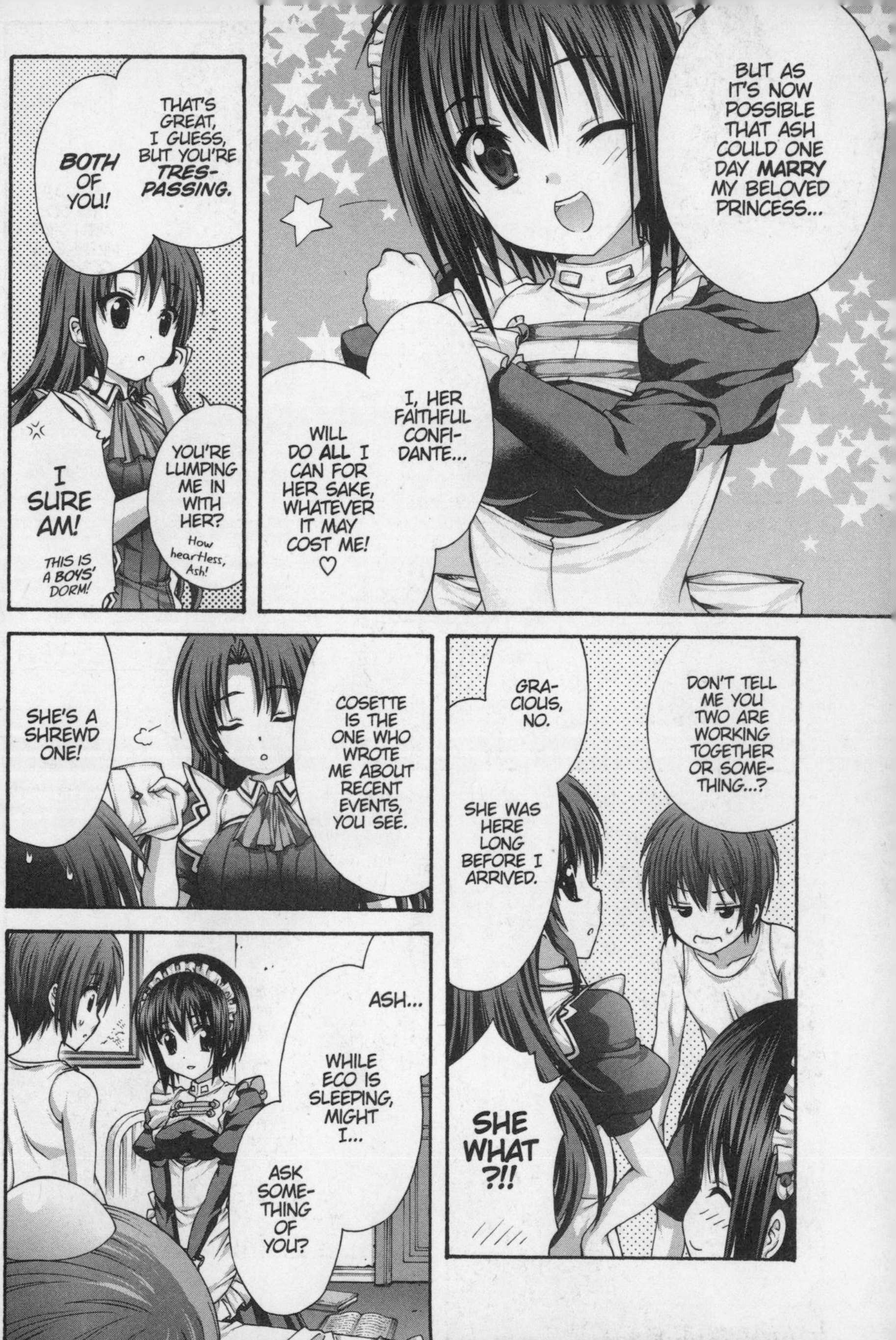
BUT AS IT'S NOW POSSIBLE THAT ASH COULD ONE DAY MARRY MY BELOVED PRINCESS...
I, HER FAITHFUL CONFIDANTE...
WILL DO ALL I CAN FOR HER SAKE, WHATEVER IT MAY COST ME! ♡
THAT'S GREAT, I GUESS, BUT YOU'RE TRESPASSING.
BOTH OF YOU!
YOU'RE LUMPING ME IN WITH HER?
How heartless, Ash!
I SURE AM!
THIS IS A BOYS' DORM!
DON'T TELL ME YOU TWO ARE WORKING TOGETHER OR SOMETHING...?
GRACIOUS, NO.
SHE WAS HERE LONG BEFORE I ARRIVED.
SHE WHAT?!!
COSETTE IS THE ONE WHO WROTE ME ABOUT RECENT EVENTS, YOU SEE.
SHE'S A SHREWD ONE!
ASH...
WHILE ECO IS SLEEPING, MIGHT I...
ASK SOMETHING OF YOU?

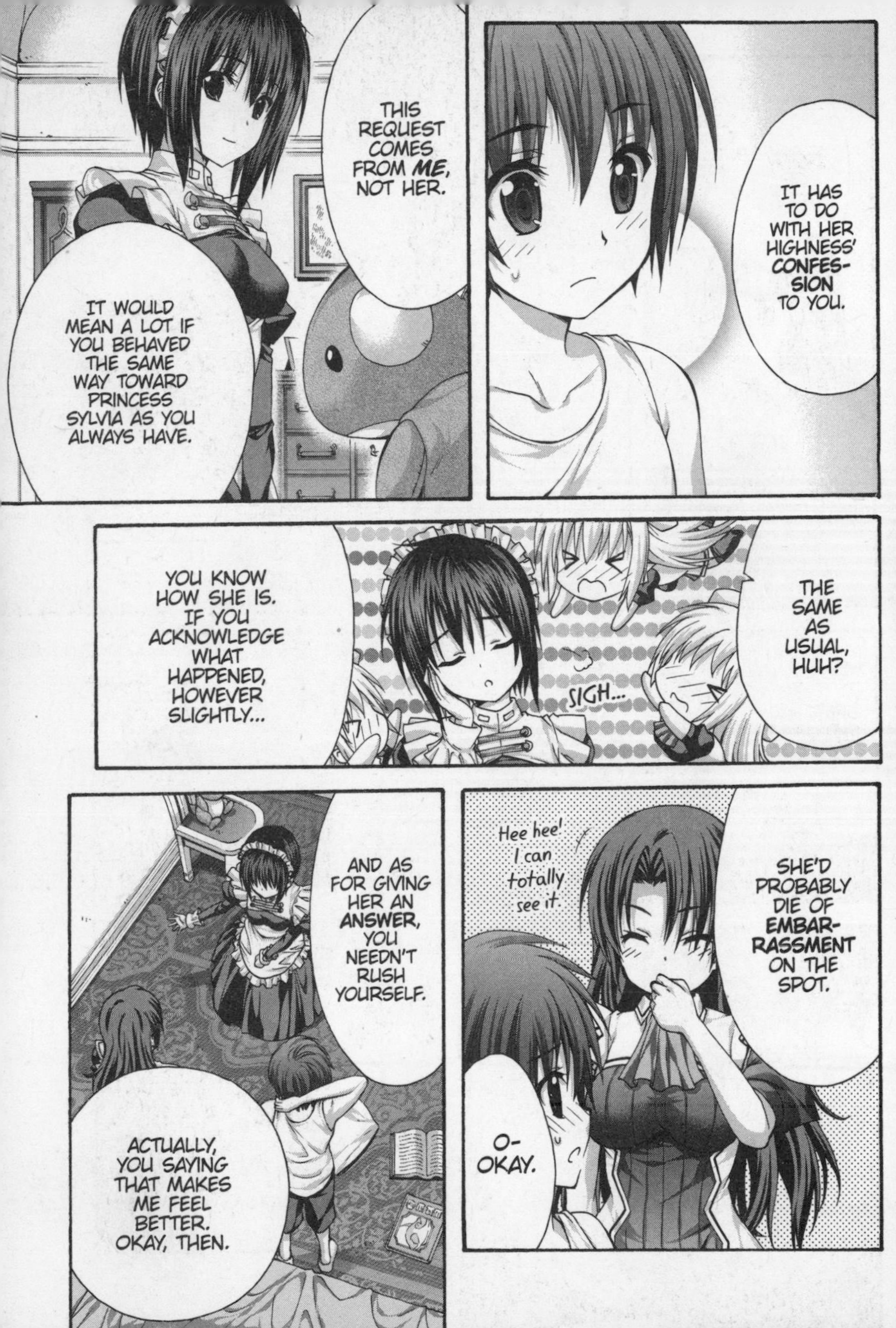
IT HAS TO DO WITH HER HIGHNESS' CONFESSION TO YOU.
THIS REQUEST COMES FROM ME, NOT HER.
IT WOULD MEAN A LOT IF YOU BEHAVED THE SAME WAY TOWARD PRINCESS SYLVIA AS YOU ALWAYS HAVE.
THE SAME AS USUAL, HUH?
SIGH...
YOU KNOW HOW SHE IS. IF YOU ACKNOWLEDGE WHAT HAPPENED, HOWEVER SLIGHTLY...
SHE'D PROBABLY DIE OF EMBARRASSMENT ON THE SPOT.
Hee hee! I can totally see it.
O-OKAY.
AND AS FOR GIVING HER AN ANSWER, YOU NEEDN'T RUSH YOURSELF.
ACTUALLY, YOU SAYING THAT MAKES ME FEEL BETTER. OKAY, THEN.

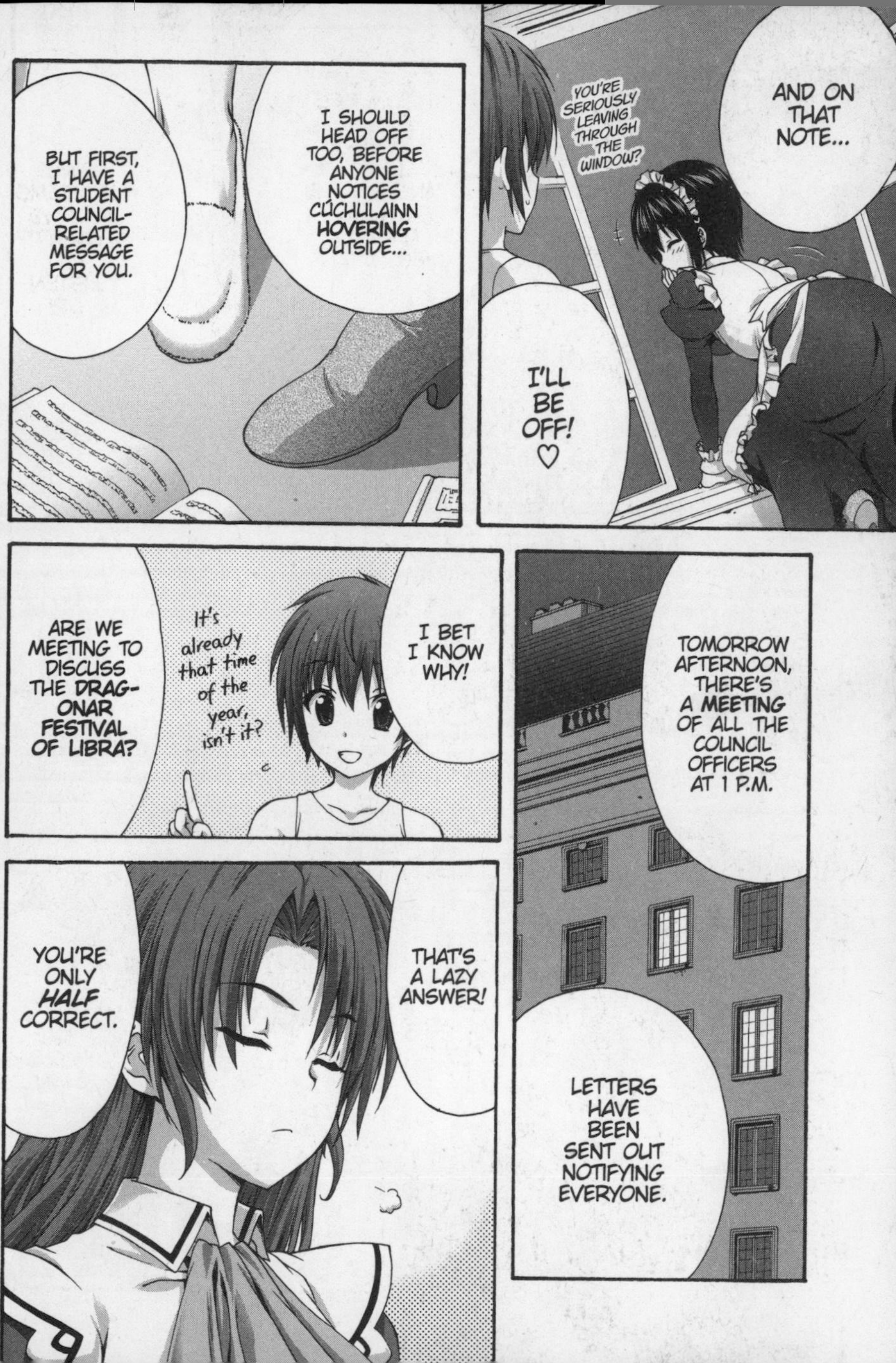
AND ON THAT NOTE...
YOU'RE SERIOUSLY LEAVING THROUGH THE WINDOW?
I'LL BE OFF! ♡
I SHOULD HEAD OFF TOO, BEFORE ANYONE NOTICES CÚCHULAINN HOVERING OUTSIDE...
BUT FIRST, I HAVE A STUDENT COUNCIL-RELATED MESSAGE FOR YOU.
TOMORROW AFTERNOON, THERE'S A MEETING OF ALL THE COUNCIL OFFICERS AT 1 P.M.
LETTERS HAVE BEEN SENT OUT NOTIFYING EVERYONE.
I BET I KNOW WHY!
It's already that time of the year, isn't it?
ARE WE MEETING TO DISCUSS THE DRAG-ONAR FESTIVAL OF LIBRA?
THAT'S A LAZY ANSWER!
YOU'RE ONLY HALF CORRECT.

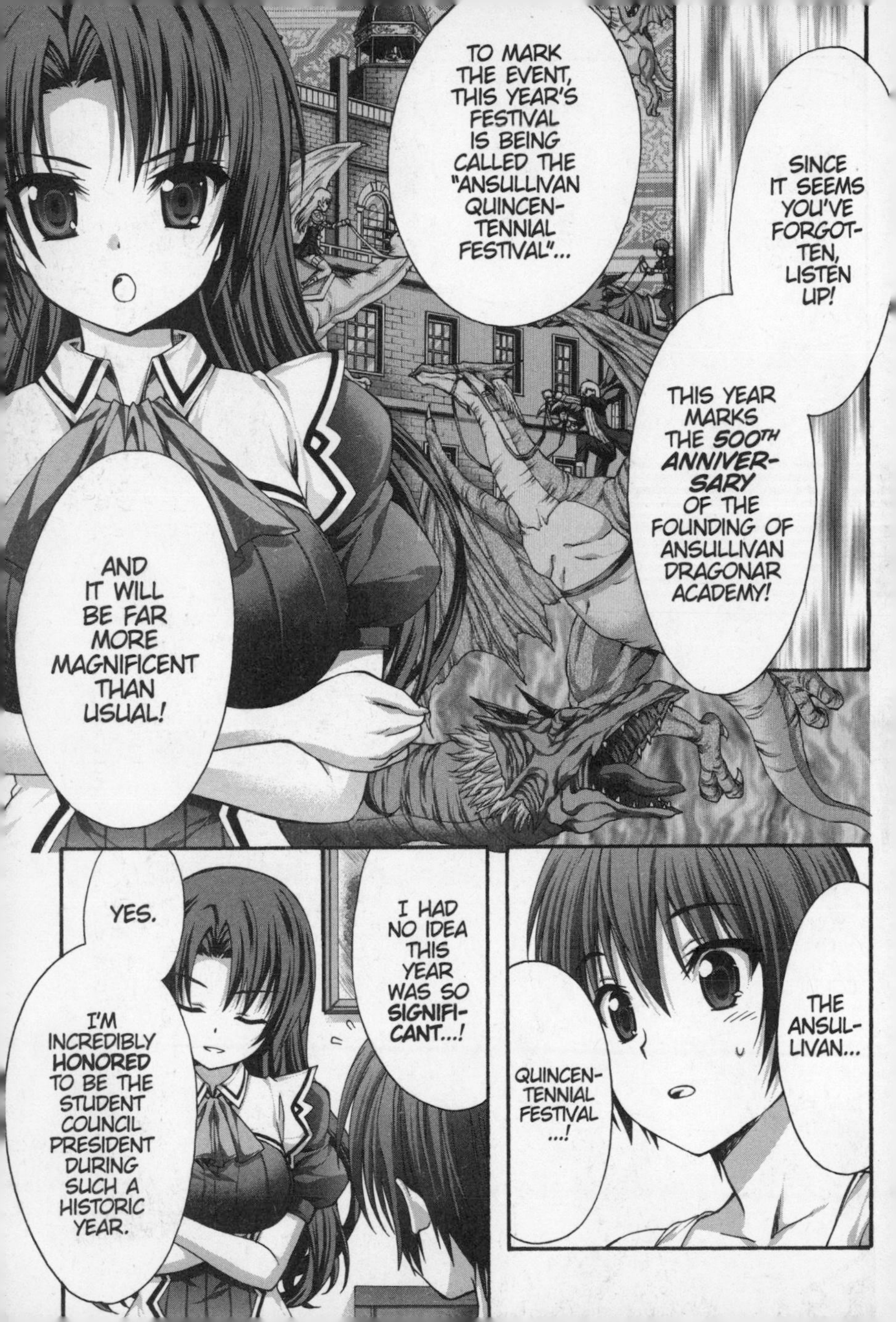
SINCE IT SEEMS YOU'VE FORGOTTEN, LISTEN UP!
THIS YEAR MARKS THE 500TH ANNIVERSARY OF THE FOUNDING OF ANSULLIVAN DRAGONAR ACADEMY!
TO MARK THE EVENT, THIS YEAR'S FESTIVAL IS BEING CALLED THE "ANSULLIVAN QUINCENTENNIAL FESTIVAL"...
AND IT WILL BE FAR MORE MAGNIFICENT THAN USUAL!
THE ANSULLIVAN...
QUINCENTENNIAL FESTIVAL ...!
I HAD NO IDEA THIS YEAR WAS SO SIGNIFICANT...!
YES.
I'M INCREDIBLY HONORED TO BE THE STUDENT COUNCIL PRESIDENT DURING SUCH A HISTORIC YEAR.

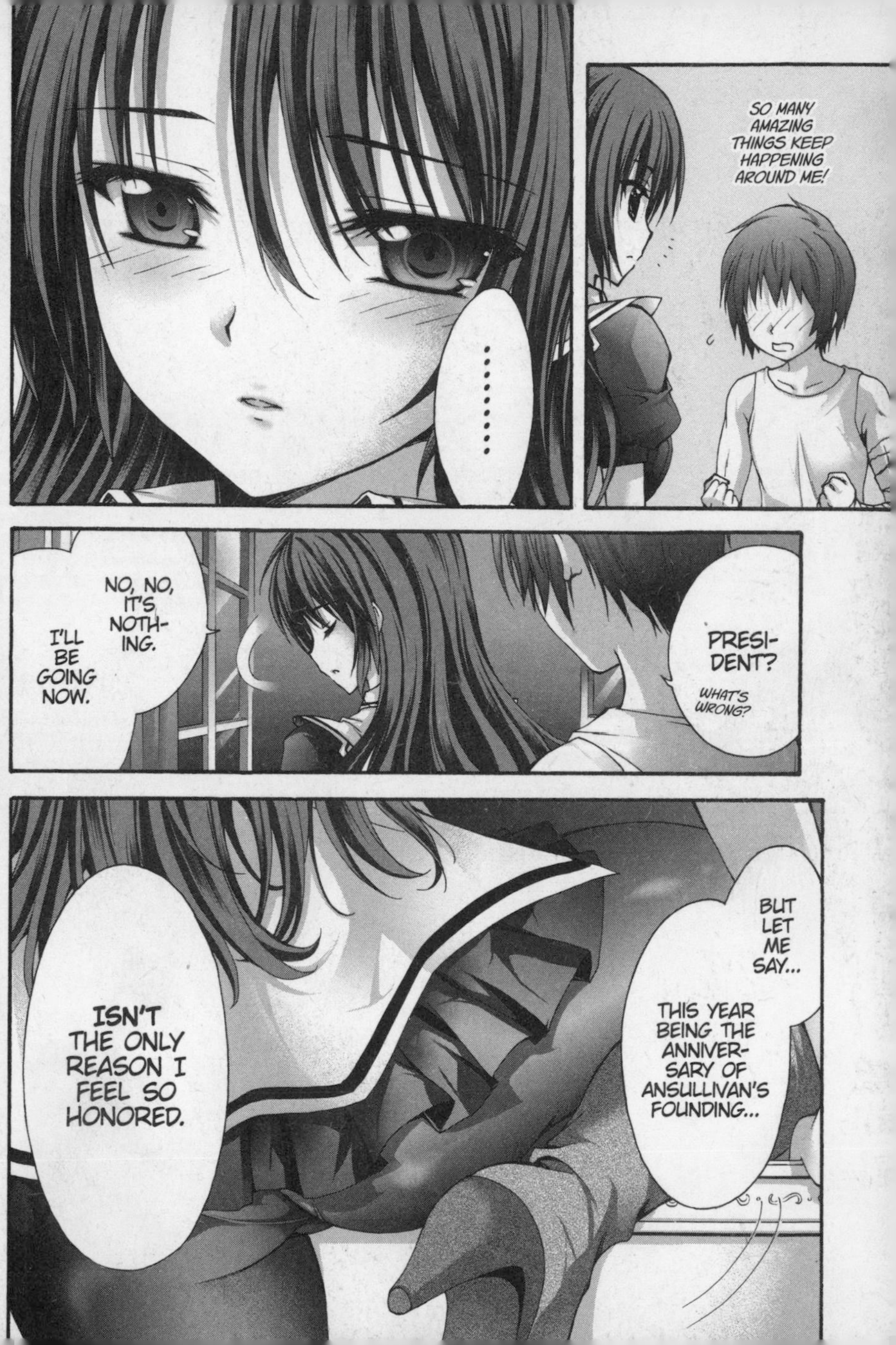
SO MANY AMAZING THINGS KEEP HAPPENING AROUND ME!
....
PRESI-DENT?
WHAT'S WRONG?
NO, NO, IT'S NOTH-ING.
I'LL BE GOING NOW.
BUT LET ME SAY...
THIS YEAR BEING THE ANNIVER-SARY OF ANSULLIVAN'S FOUNDING...
ISN'T THE ONLY REASON I FEEL SO HONORED.

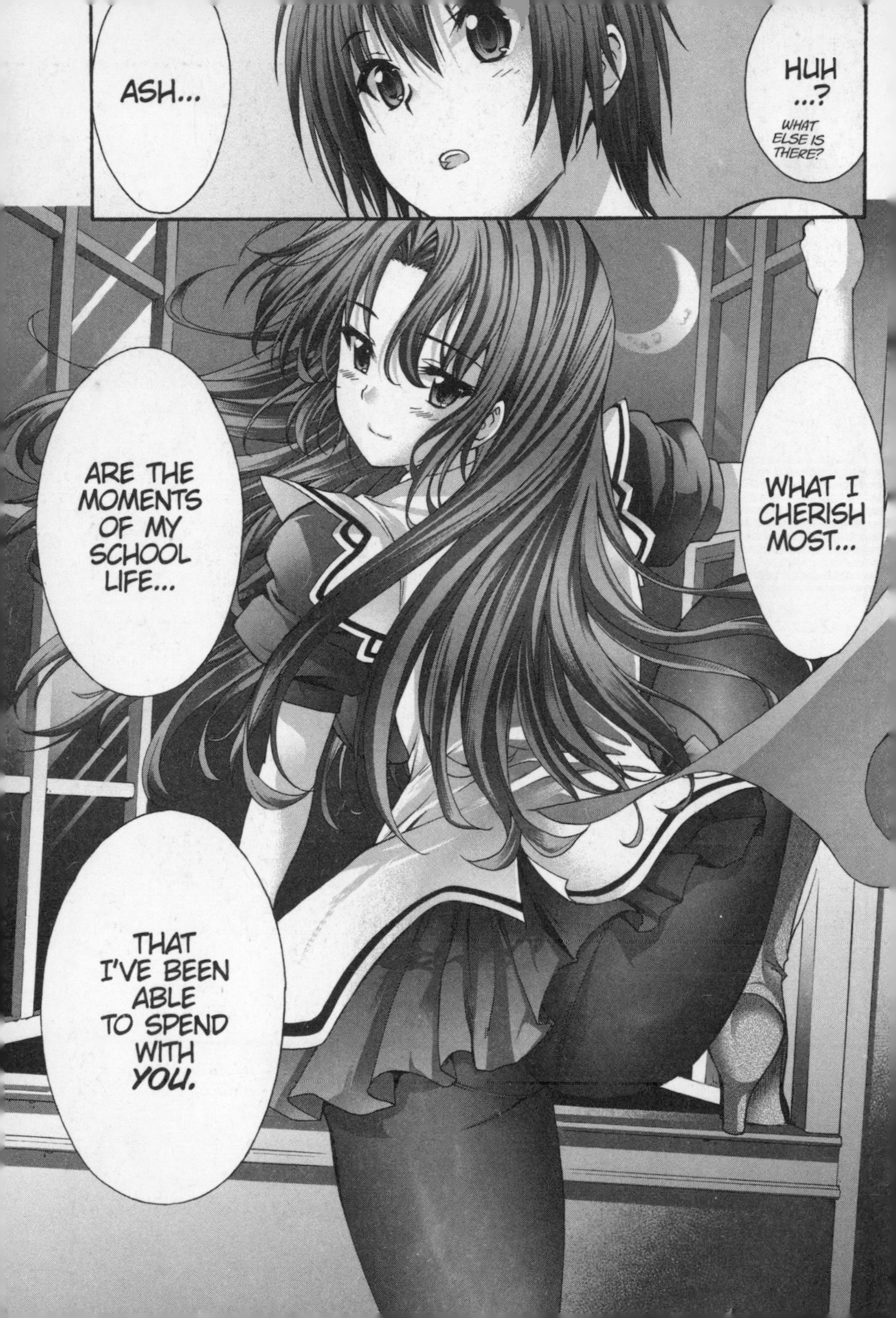
HUH ...?
WHAT ELSE IS THERE?
ASH...
WHAT I CHERISH MOST...
ARE THE MOMENTS OF MY SCHOOL LIFE...
THAT I'VE BEEN ABLE TO SPEND WITH YOU.

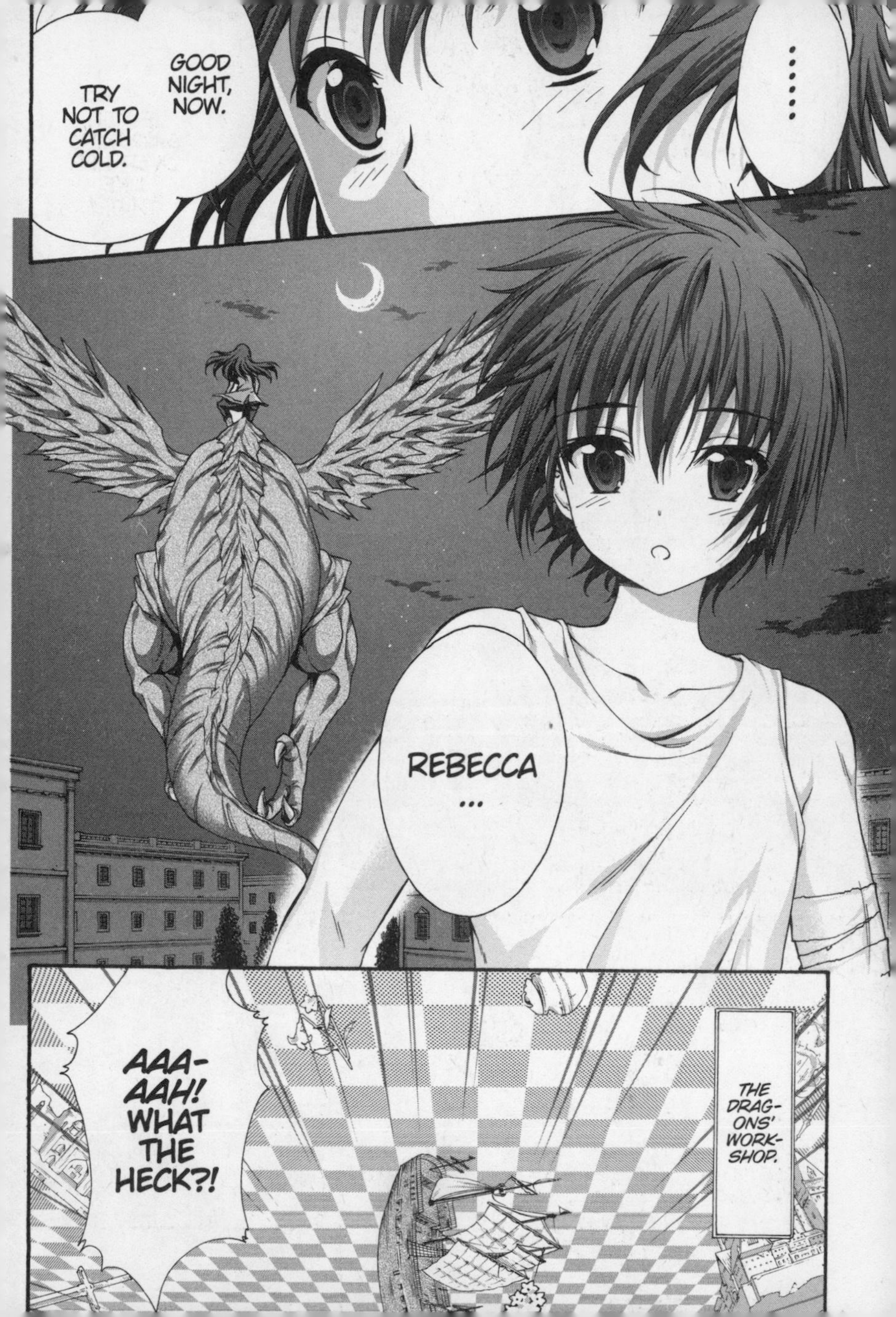
......
GOOD NIGHT, NOW.
TRY NOT TO CATCH COLD.
REBECCA ...
THE DRAG-ONS' WORK-SHOP.
AAA-AAH! WHAT THE HECK?!

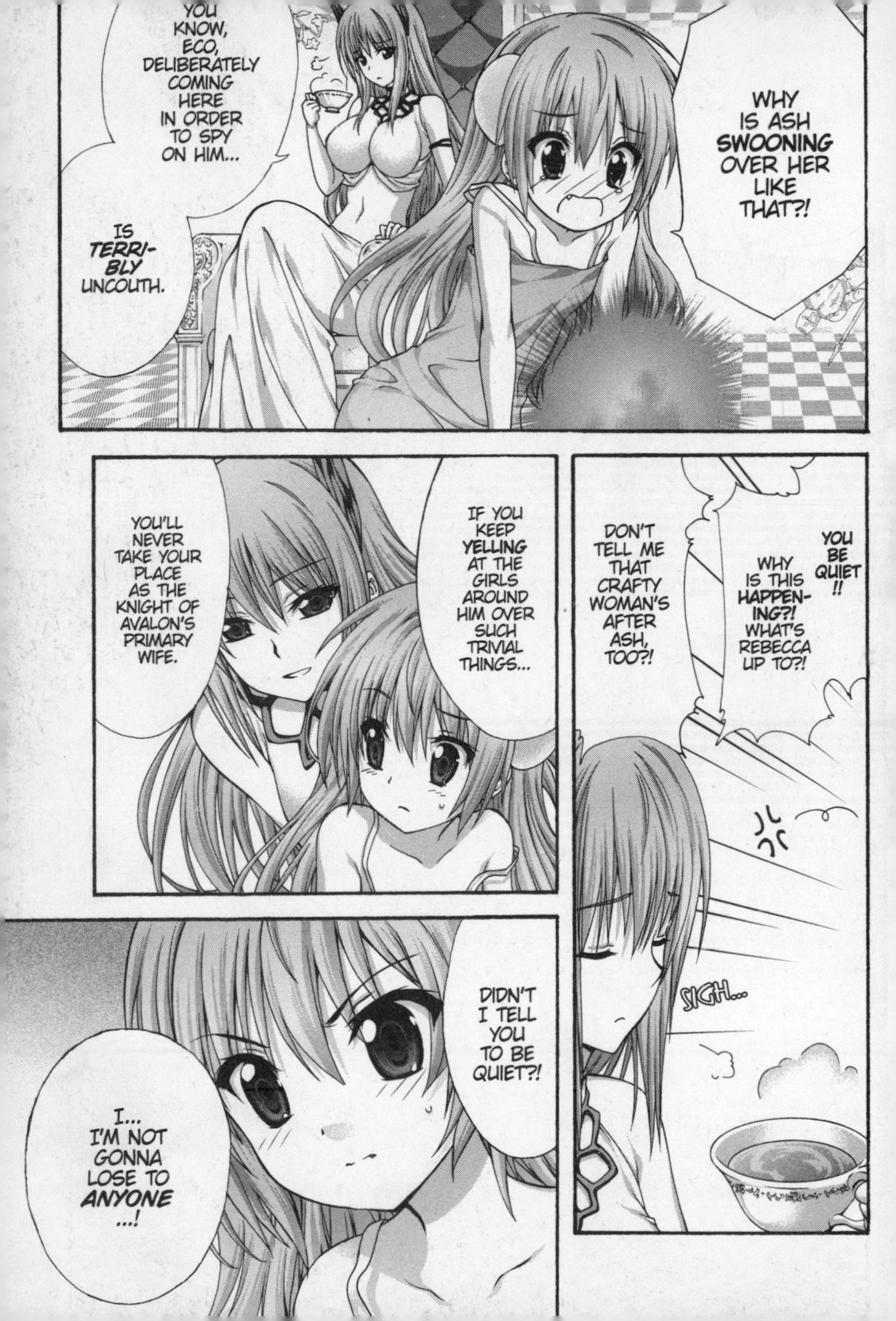
WHY IS ASH SWOONING OVER HER LIKE THAT?!
YOU KNOW, ECO, DELIBERATELY COMING HERE IN ORDER TO SPY ON HIM...
IS TERRIBLY UNCOUTH.
YOU BE QUIET!!
WHY IS THIS HAPPENING?! WHAT'S REBECCA UP TO?!
DON'T TELL ME THAT CRAFTY WOMAN'S AFTER ASH, TOO?!
SIGH...
IF YOU KEEP YELLING AT THE GIRLS AROUND HIM OVER SUCH TRIVIAL THINGS...
YOU'LL NEVER TAKE YOUR PLACE AS THE KNIGHT OF AVALON'S PRIMARY WIFE.
DIDN'T I TELL YOU TO BE QUIET?!
I... I'M NOT GONNA LOSE TO ANYONE ...!

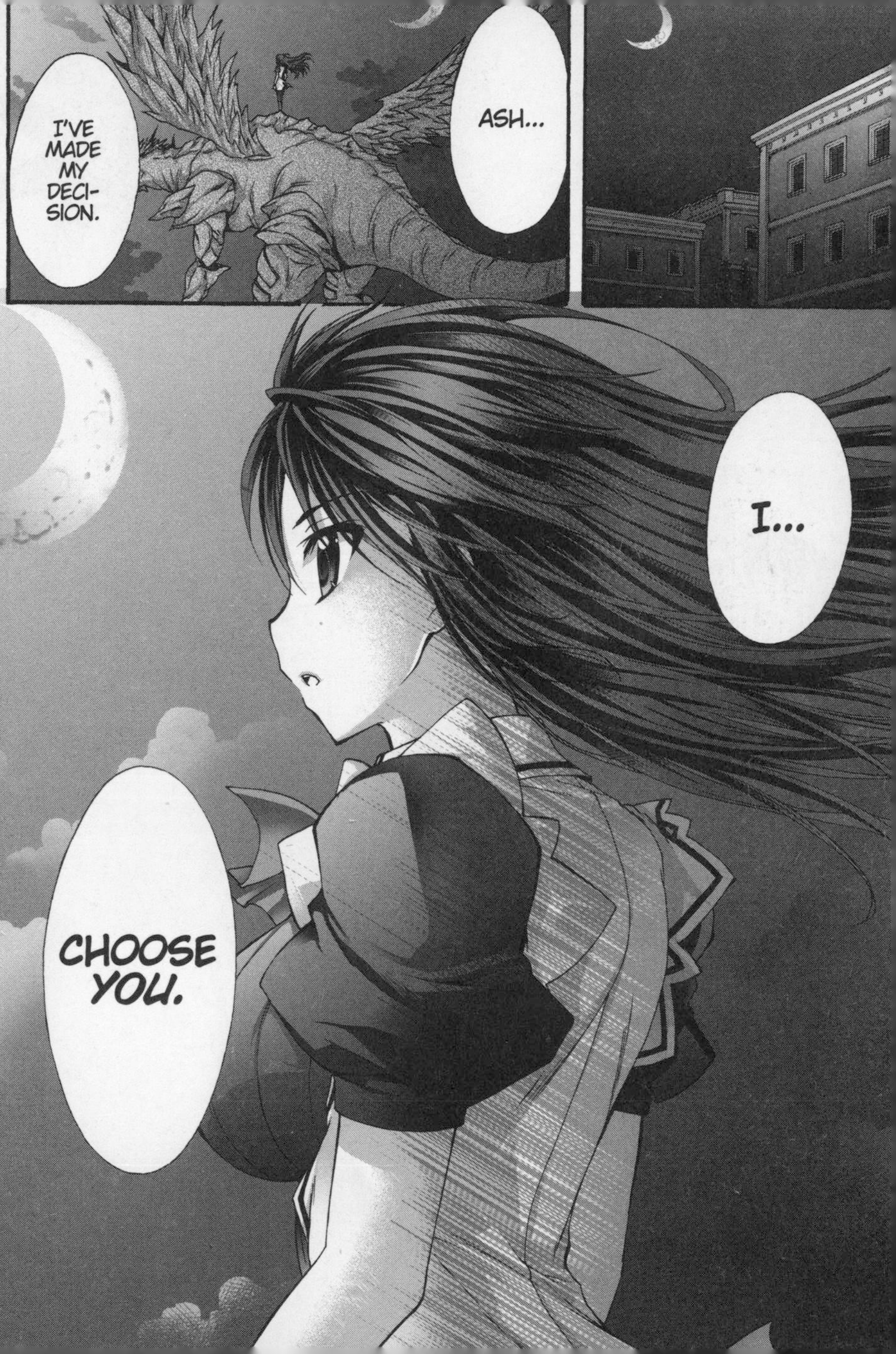
ASH...
I'VE MADE MY DECISION.
I...
CHOOSE YOU.

DRAGONAR
ACADEMY

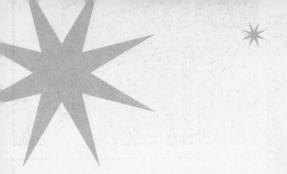

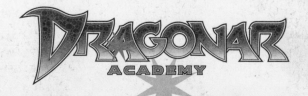

星刻の竜騎士

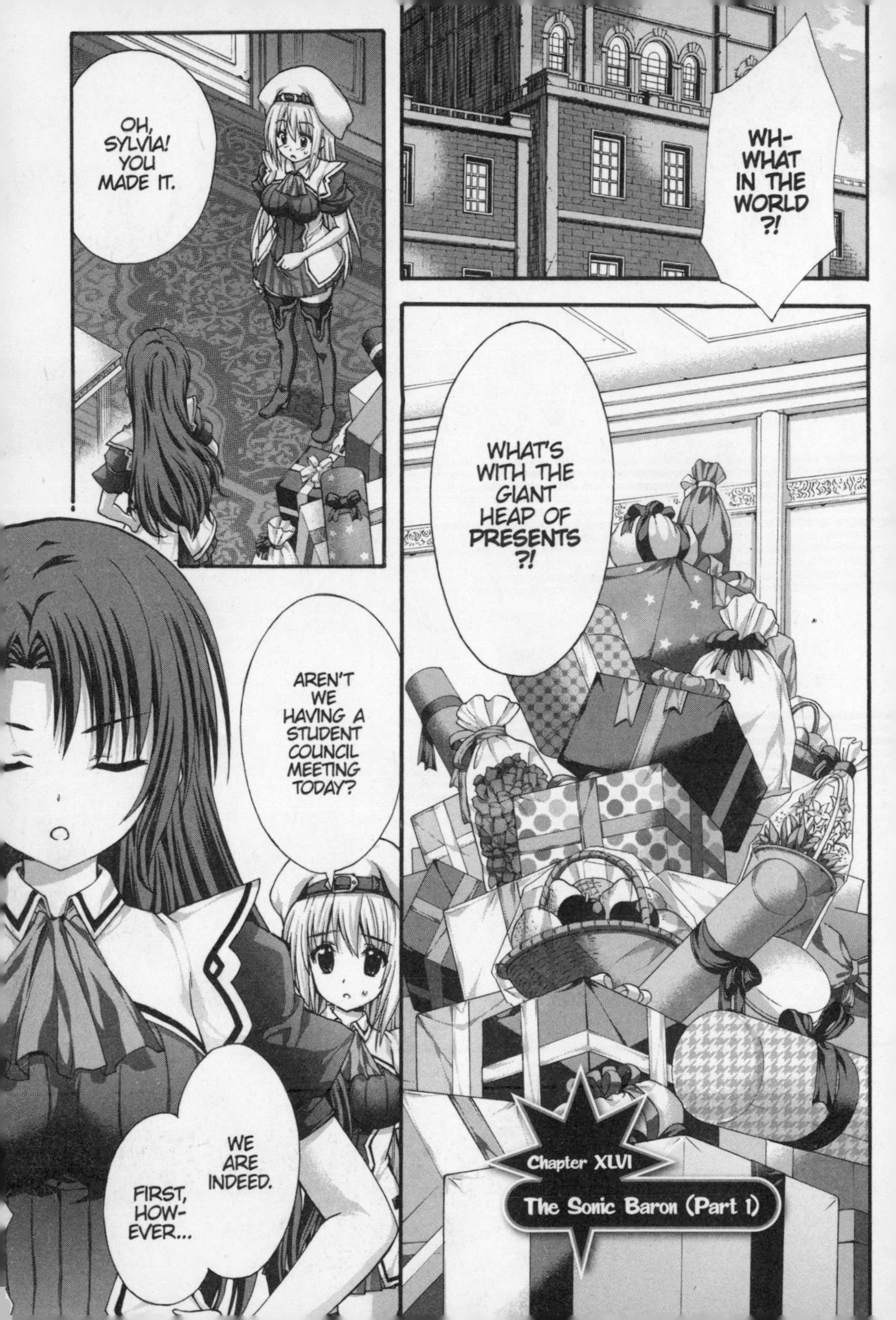
WH-WHAT IN THE WORLD?!
WHAT'S WITH THE GIANT HEAP OF PRESENTS?!
Chapter XLVI
The Sonic Baron (Part 1)
OH, SYLVIA! YOU MADE IT.
AREN'T WE HAVING A STUDENT COUNCIL MEETING TODAY?
WE ARE INDEED.
FIRST, HOWEVER...

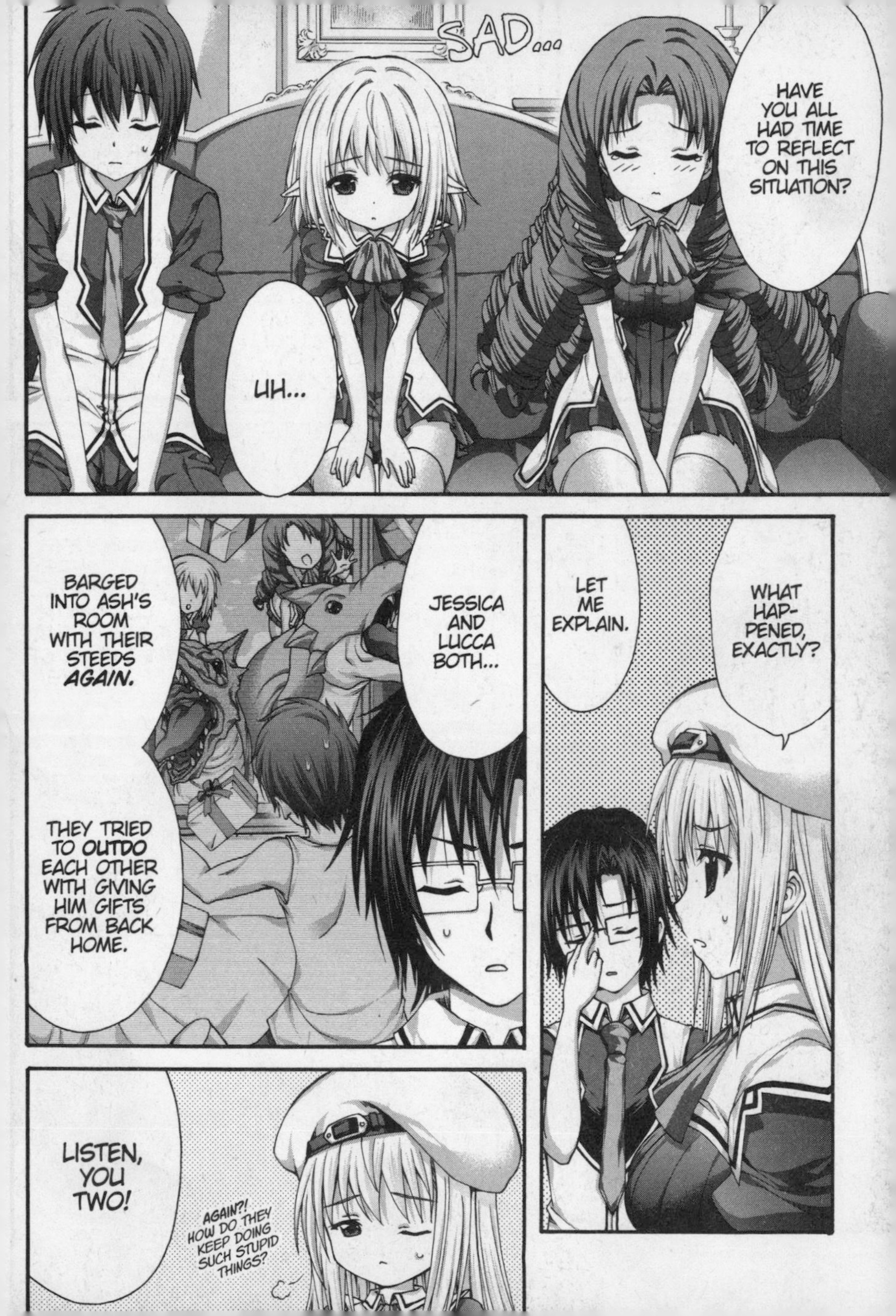
HAVE YOU ALL HAD TIME TO REFLECT ON THIS SITUATION?
SAD...
UH...
WHAT HAP-PENED, EXACTLY?
LET ME EXPLAIN.
JESSICA AND LUCCA BOTH...
BARGED INTO ASH'S ROOM WITH THEIR STEEDS AGAIN.
THEY TRIED TO OUTDO EACH OTHER WITH GIVING HIM GIFTS FROM BACK HOME.
LISTEN, YOU TWO!
AGAIN?! HOW DO THEY KEEP DOING SUCH STUPID THINGS?

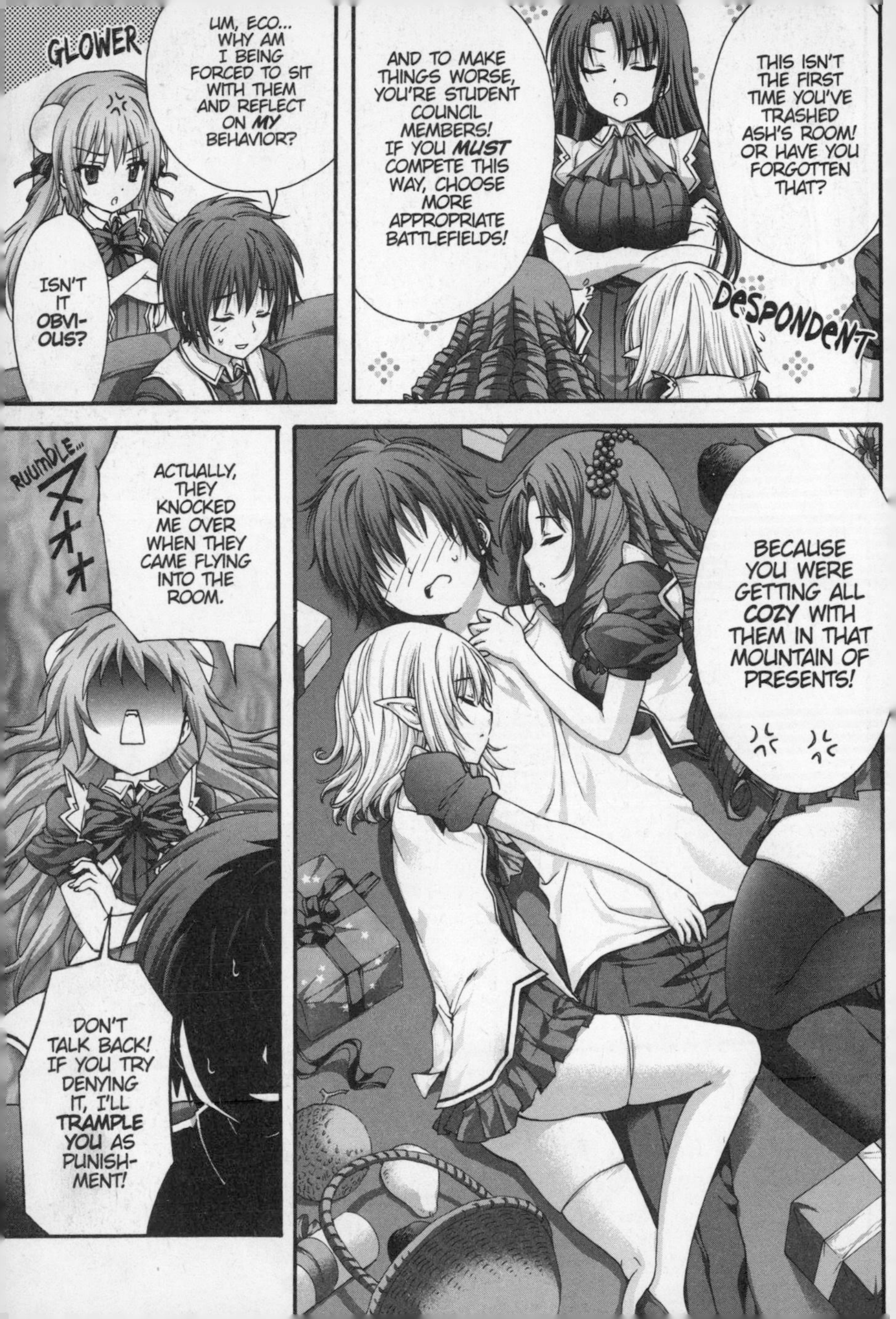
THIS ISN'T THE FIRST TIME YOU'VE TRASHED ASH'S ROOM! OR HAVE YOU FORGOTTEN THAT?
AND TO MAKE THINGS WORSE, YOU'RE STUDENT COUNCIL MEMBERS! IF YOU MUST COMPETE THIS WAY, CHOOSE MORE APPROPRIATE BATTLEFIELDS!
DESPONDENT
GLOWER
UM, ECO... WHY AM I BEING FORCED TO SIT WITH THEM AND REFLECT ON MY BEHAVIOR?
ISN'T IT OBVIOUS?
BECAUSE YOU WERE GETTING ALL COZY WITH THEM IN THAT MOUNTAIN OF PRESENTS!
RUUMBLE...
ACTUALLY, THEY KNOCKED ME OVER WHEN THEY CAME FLYING INTO THE ROOM.
DON'T TALK BACK! IF YOU TRY DENYING IT, I'LL TRAMPLE YOU AS PUNISHMENT!

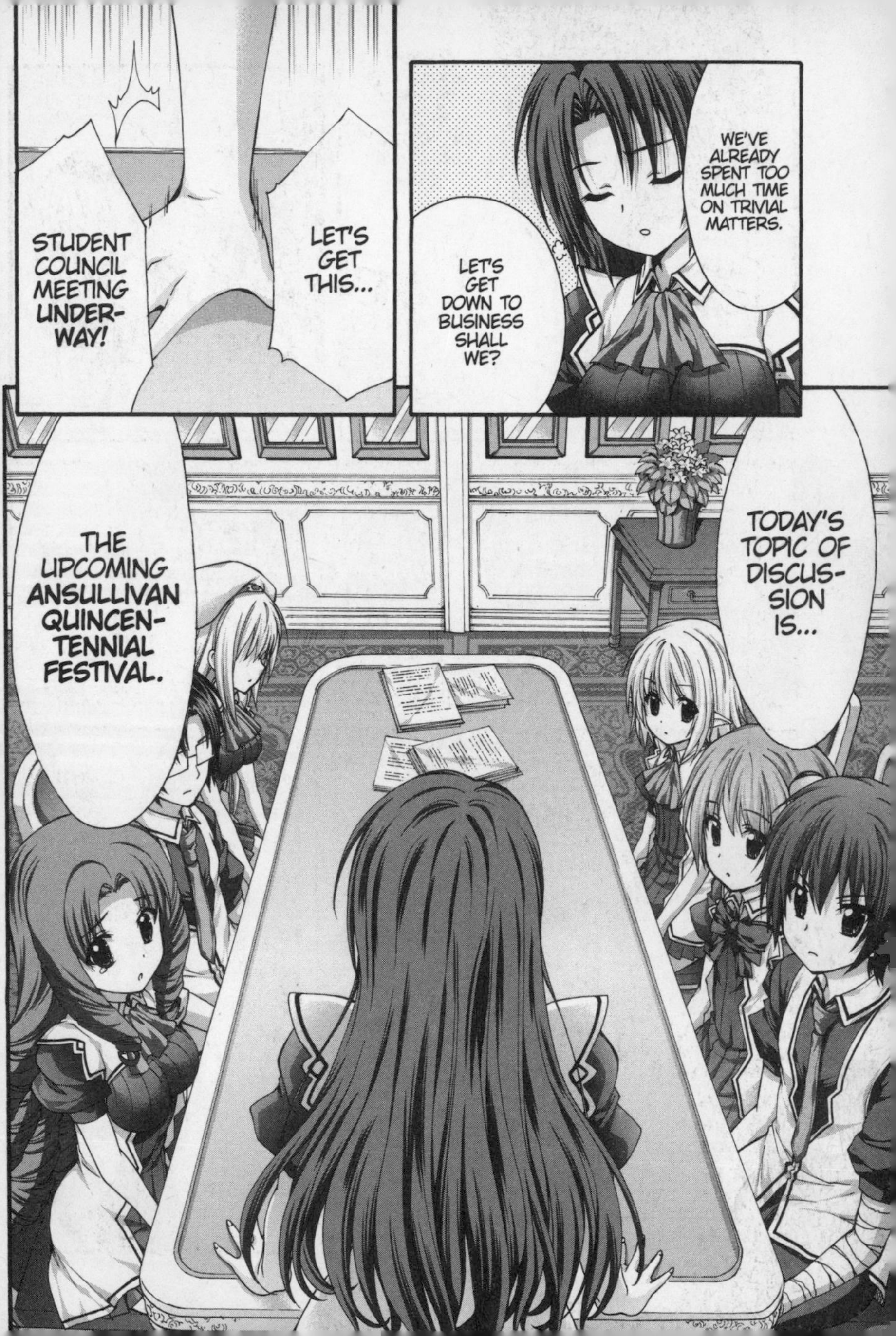
WE'VE ALREADY SPENT TOO MUCH TIME ON TRIVIAL MATTERS.
LET'S GET DOWN TO BUSINESS SHALL WE?
LET'S GET THIS...
STUDENT COUNCIL MEETING UNDER-WAY!
TODAY'S TOPIC OF DISCUS-SION IS...
THE UPCOMING ANSULLIVAN QUINCEN-TENNIAL FESTIVAL.

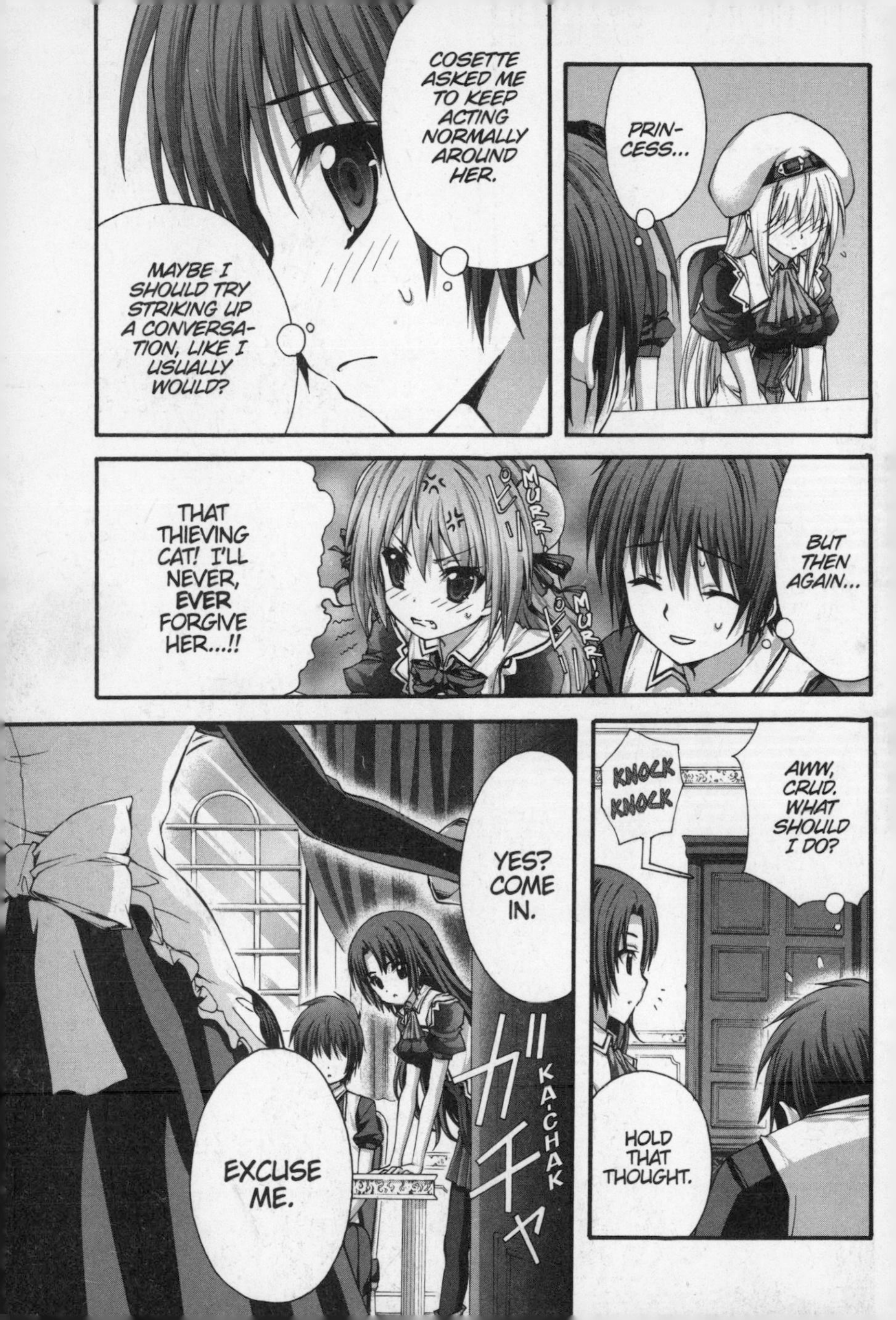
PRIN-CESS...
COSETTE ASKED ME TO KEEP ACTING NORMALLY AROUND HER.
MAYBE I SHOULD TRY STRIKING UP A CONVERSATION, LIKE I USUALLY WOULD?
BUT THEN AGAIN...
MURR MURR
THAT THIEVING CAT! I'LL NEVER, EVER FORGIVE HER...!!
AWW, CRUD. WHAT SHOULD I DO?
KNOCK KNOCK
HOLD THAT THOUGHT.
YES? COME IN.
KA-CHAK
EXCUSE ME.

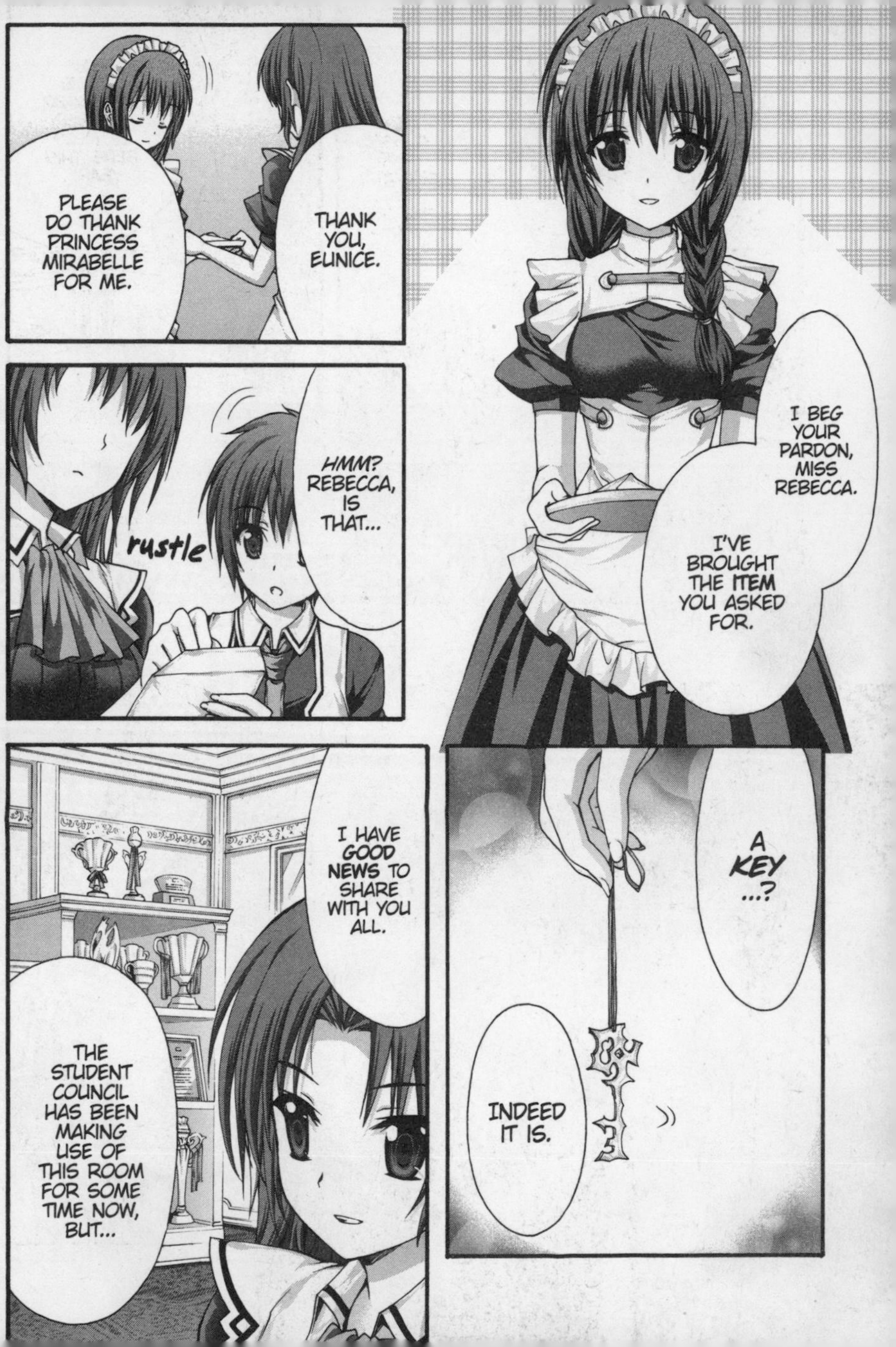
I BEG YOUR PARDON, MISS REBECCA.
I'VE BROUGHT THE ITEM YOU ASKED FOR.
THANK YOU, EUNICE.
PLEASE DO THANK PRINCESS MIRABELLE FOR ME.
HMM? REBECCA, IS THAT...
rustle
A KEY ...?
INDEED IT IS.
I HAVE GOOD NEWS TO SHARE WITH YOU ALL.
THE STUDENT COUNCIL HAS BEEN MAKING USE OF THIS ROOM FOR SOME TIME NOW, BUT...

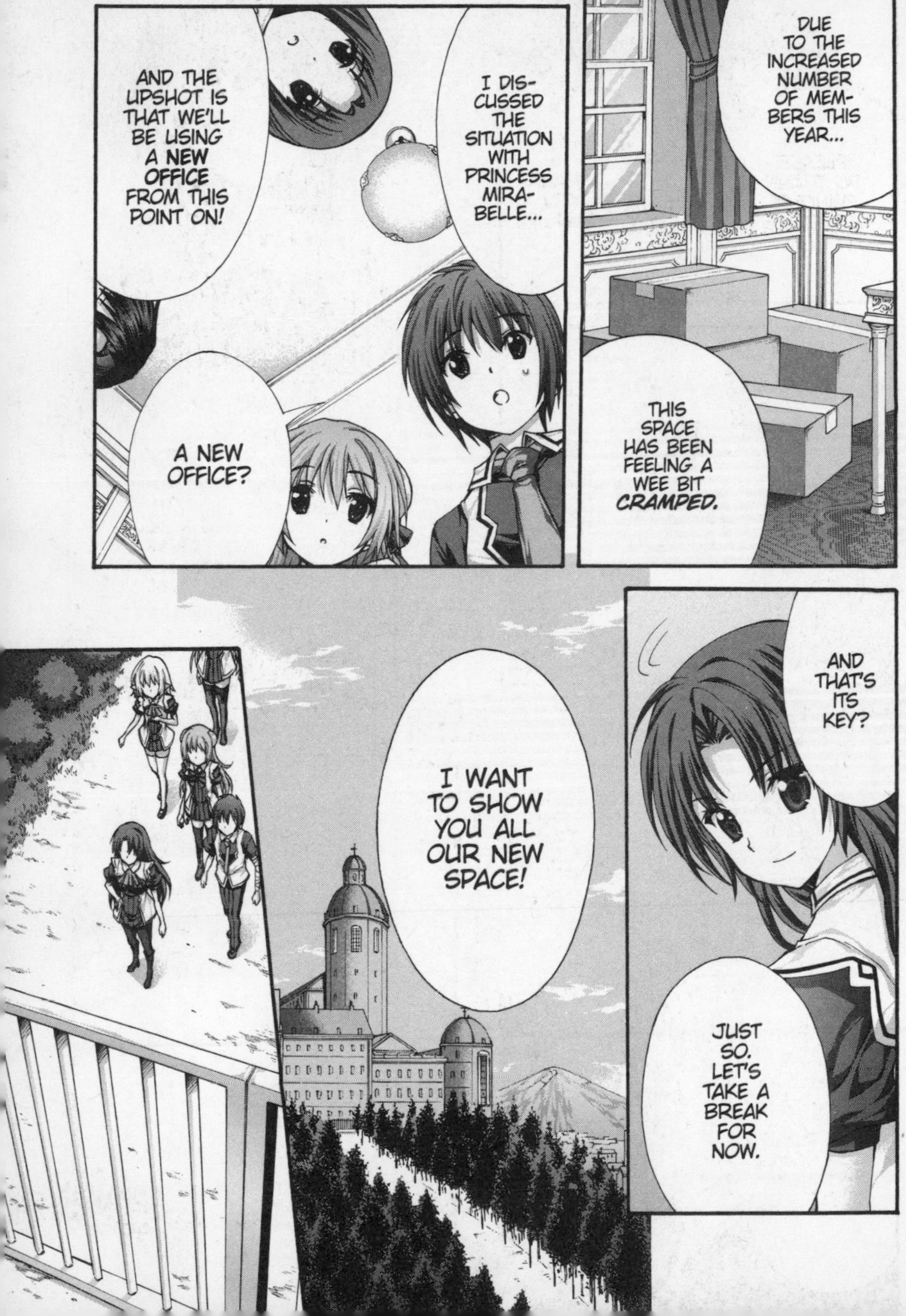
DUE TO THE INCREASED NUMBER OF MEMBERS THIS YEAR...
THIS SPACE HAS BEEN FEELING A WEE BIT CRAMPED.
I DISCUSSED THE SITUATION WITH PRINCESS MIRABELLE...
AND THE UPSHOT IS THAT WE'LL BE USING A NEW OFFICE FROM THIS POINT ON!
A NEW OFFICE?
AND THAT'S ITS KEY?
JUST SO. LET'S TAKE A BREAK FOR NOW.
I WANT TO SHOW YOU ALL OUR NEW SPACE!

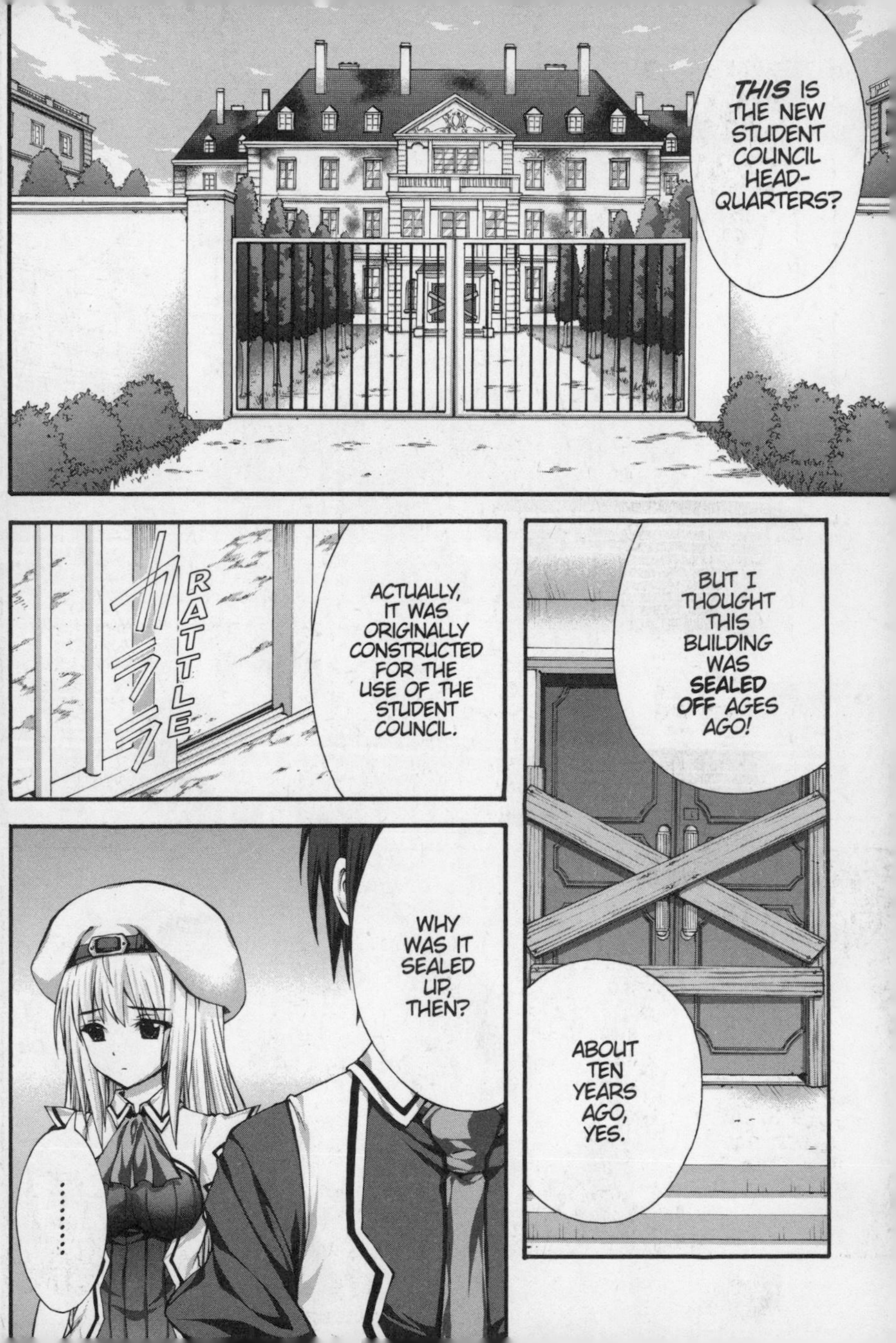
THIS IS THE NEW STUDENT COUNCIL HEAD-QUARTERS?
BUT I THOUGHT THIS BUILDING WAS SEALED OFF AGES AGO!
ABOUT TEN YEARS AGO, YES.
ACTUALLY, IT WAS ORIGINALLY CONSTRUCTED FOR THE USE OF THE STUDENT COUNCIL.
RATTLE
WHY WAS IT SEALED UP, THEN?
....

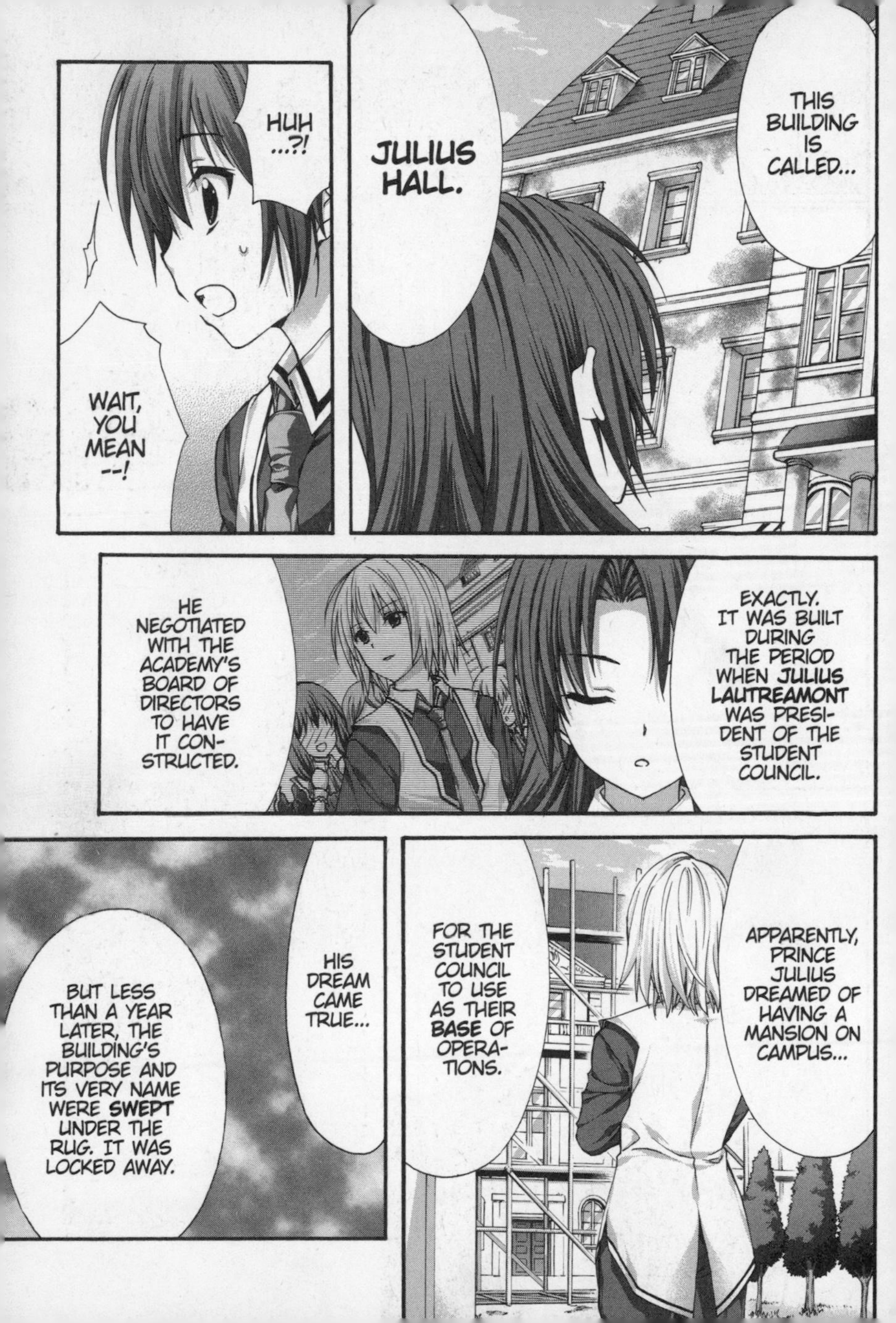
THIS BUILDING IS CALLED...
JULIUS HALL.
HUH ...?!
WAIT, YOU MEAN --!
EXACTLY. IT WAS BUILT DURING THE PERIOD WHEN JULIUS LAUTREAMONT WAS PRESIDENT OF THE STUDENT COUNCIL.
HE NEGOTIATED WITH THE ACADEMY'S BOARD OF DIRECTORS TO HAVE IT CONSTRUCTED.
APPARENTLY, PRINCE JULIUS DREAMED OF HAVING A MANSION ON CAMPUS...
FOR THE STUDENT COUNCIL TO USE AS THEIR BASE OF OPERATIONS.
HIS DREAM CAME TRUE...
BUT LESS THAN A YEAR LATER, THE BUILDING'S PURPOSE AND ITS VERY NAME WERE SWEPT UNDER THE RUG. IT WAS LOCKED AWAY.

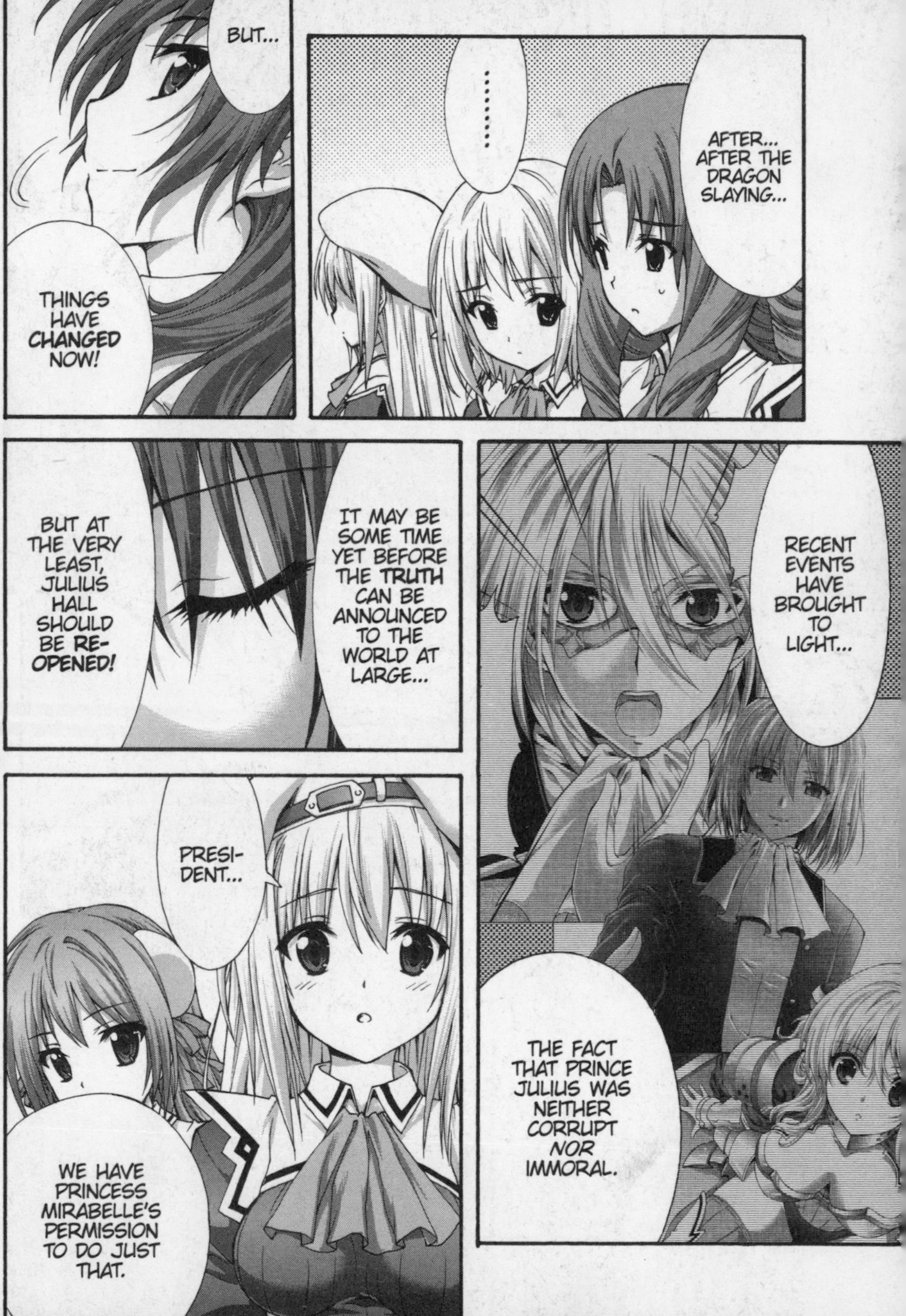
AFTER... AFTER THE DRAGON SLAYING...
......
BUT...
THINGS HAVE CHANGED NOW!
RECENT EVENTS HAVE BROUGHT TO LIGHT...
THE FACT THAT PRINCE JULIUS WAS NEITHER CORRUPT NOR IMMORAL.
IT MAY BE SOME TIME YET BEFORE THE TRUTH CAN BE ANNOUNCED TO THE WORLD AT LARGE...
BUT AT THE VERY LEAST, JULIUS HALL SHOULD BE RE-OPENED!
PRESIDENT...
WE HAVE PRINCESS MIRABELLE'S PERMISSION TO DO JUST THAT.

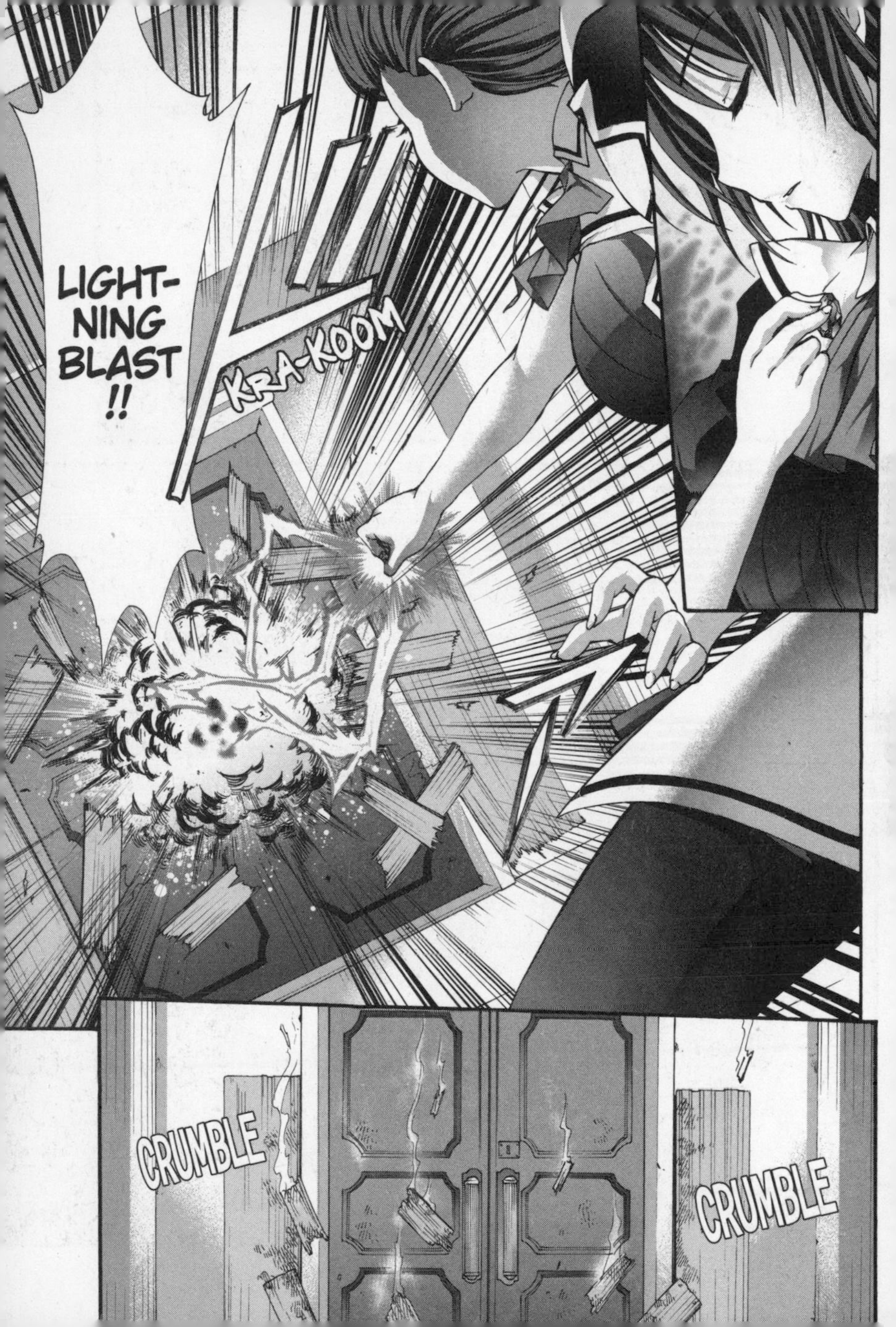
KRA-KOOM
LIGHTNING BLAST!!
CRUMBLE
CRUMBLE

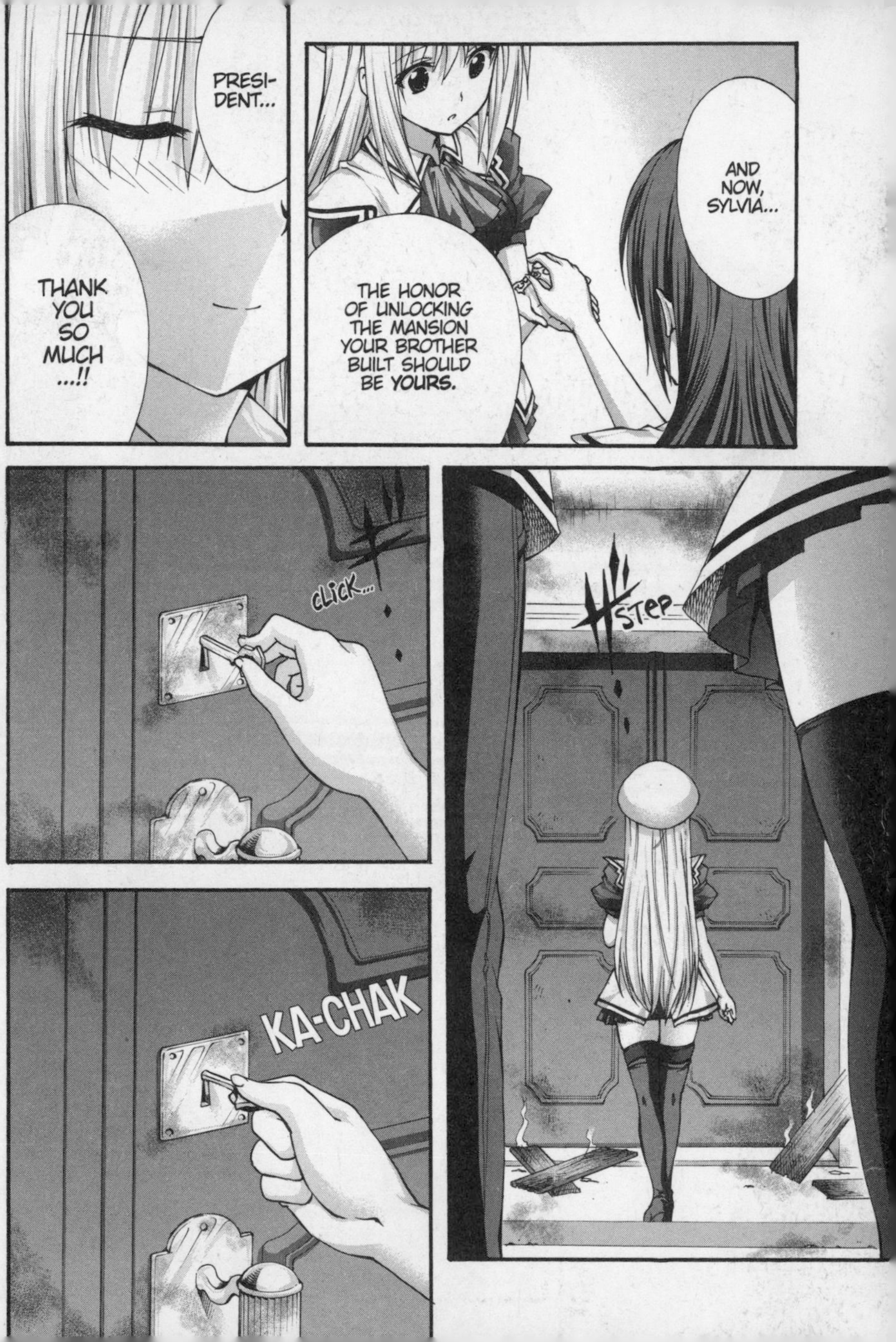
AND NOW, SYLVIA...
THE HONOR OF UNLOCKING THE MANSION YOUR BROTHER BUILT SHOULD BE YOURS.
PRESI-DENT...
THANK YOU SO MUCH ...!!
STEP
CLICK...
KA-CHAK

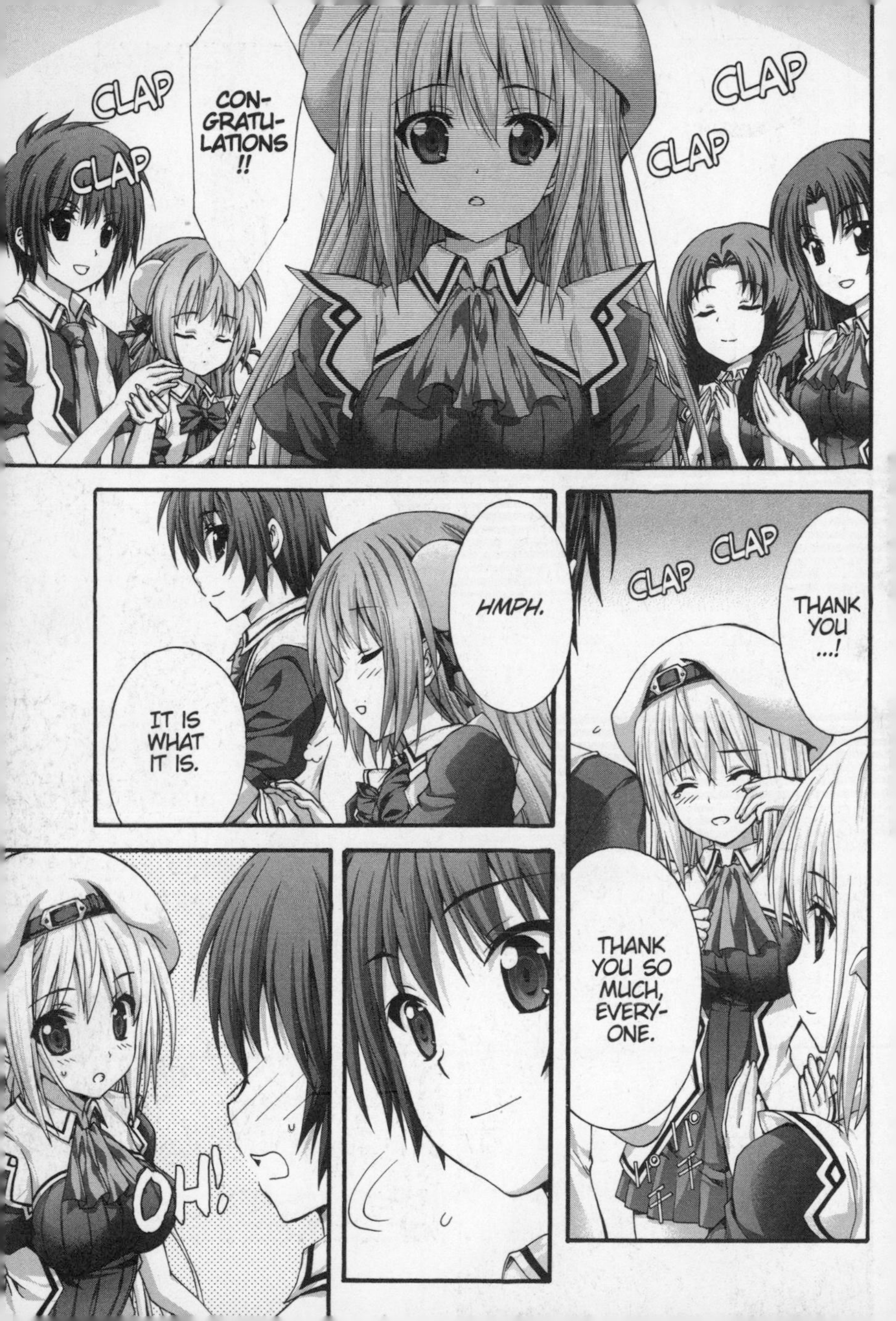
CLAP
CLAP
CON-GRATULATIONS!!
CLAP
CLAP
CLAP CLAP
THANK YOU ...!
THANK YOU SO MUCH, EVERYONE.
HMPH.
IT IS WHAT IT IS.
OH!

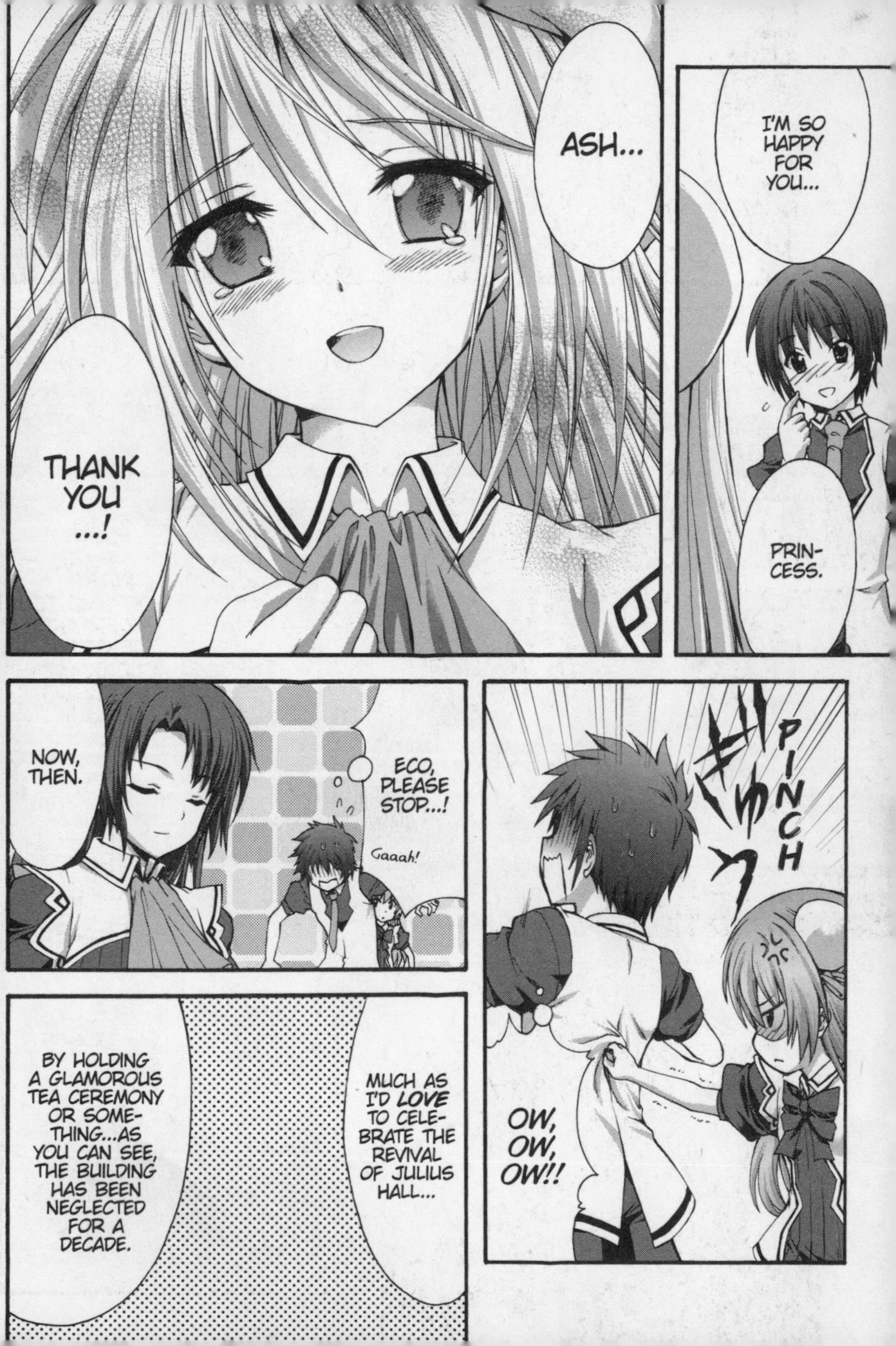
I'M SO HAPPY FOR YOU...
PRIN-CESS.
ASH...
THANK YOU ...!
PINCH
OW, OW, OW!!
NOW, THEN.
ECO, PLEASE STOP...!
Gaaah!
MUCH AS I'D *LOVE* TO CELE-BRATE THE REVIVAL OF JULIUS HALL...
BY HOLDING A GLAMOROUS TEA CEREMONY OR SOME-THING...AS YOU CAN SEE, THE BUILDING HAS BEEN NEGLECTED FOR A DECADE.

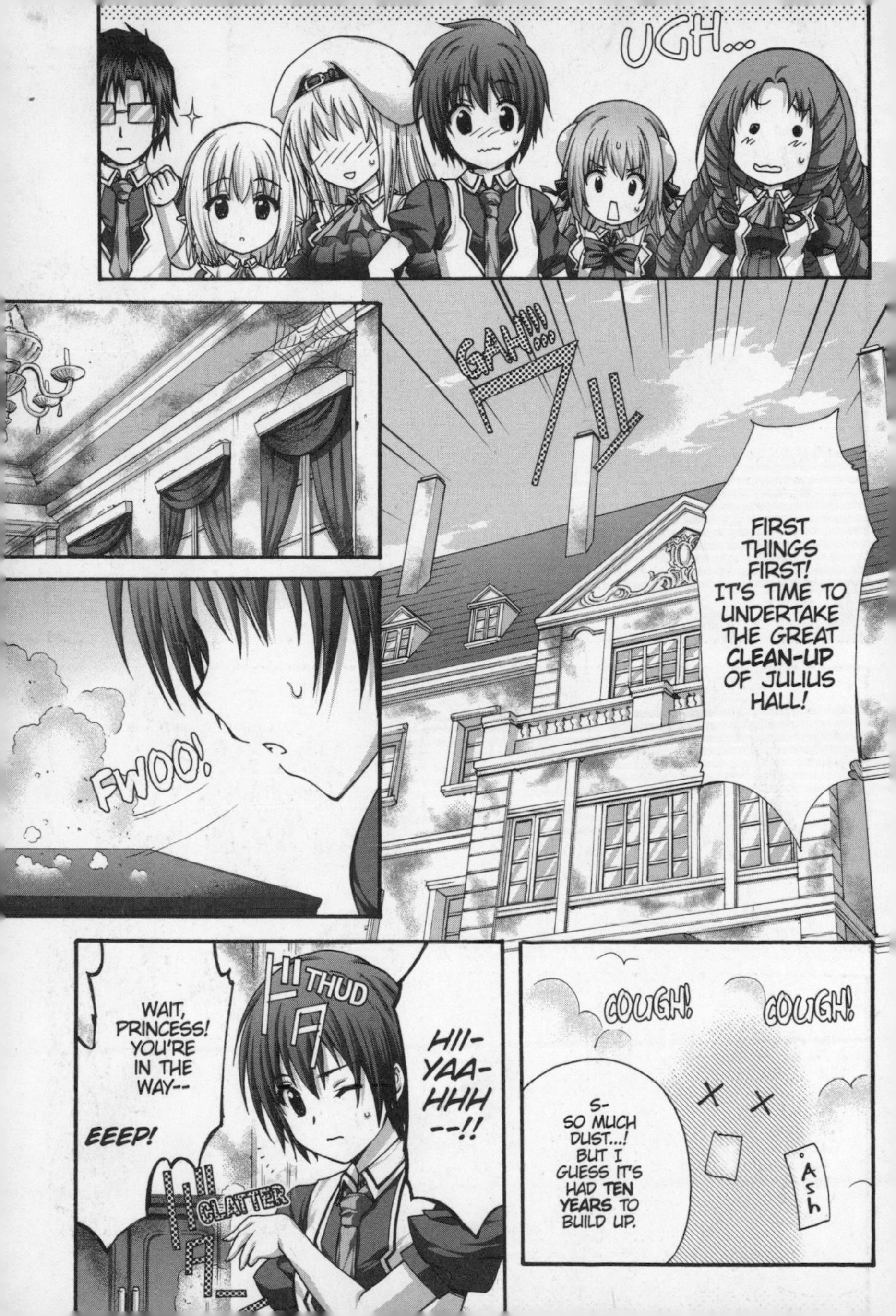
UGH...
GAH!!...
FIRST THINGS FIRST! IT'S TIME TO UNDERTAKE THE GREAT CLEAN-UP OF JULIUS HALL!
FWOO!
COUGH!
COUGH!
S- SO MUCH DUST...! BUT I GUESS IT'S HAD TEN YEARS TO BUILD UP.
Ash
THUD
HII-YAA-HHH--!!
WAIT, PRINCESS! YOU'RE IN THE WAY--
EEEP!
CLATTER

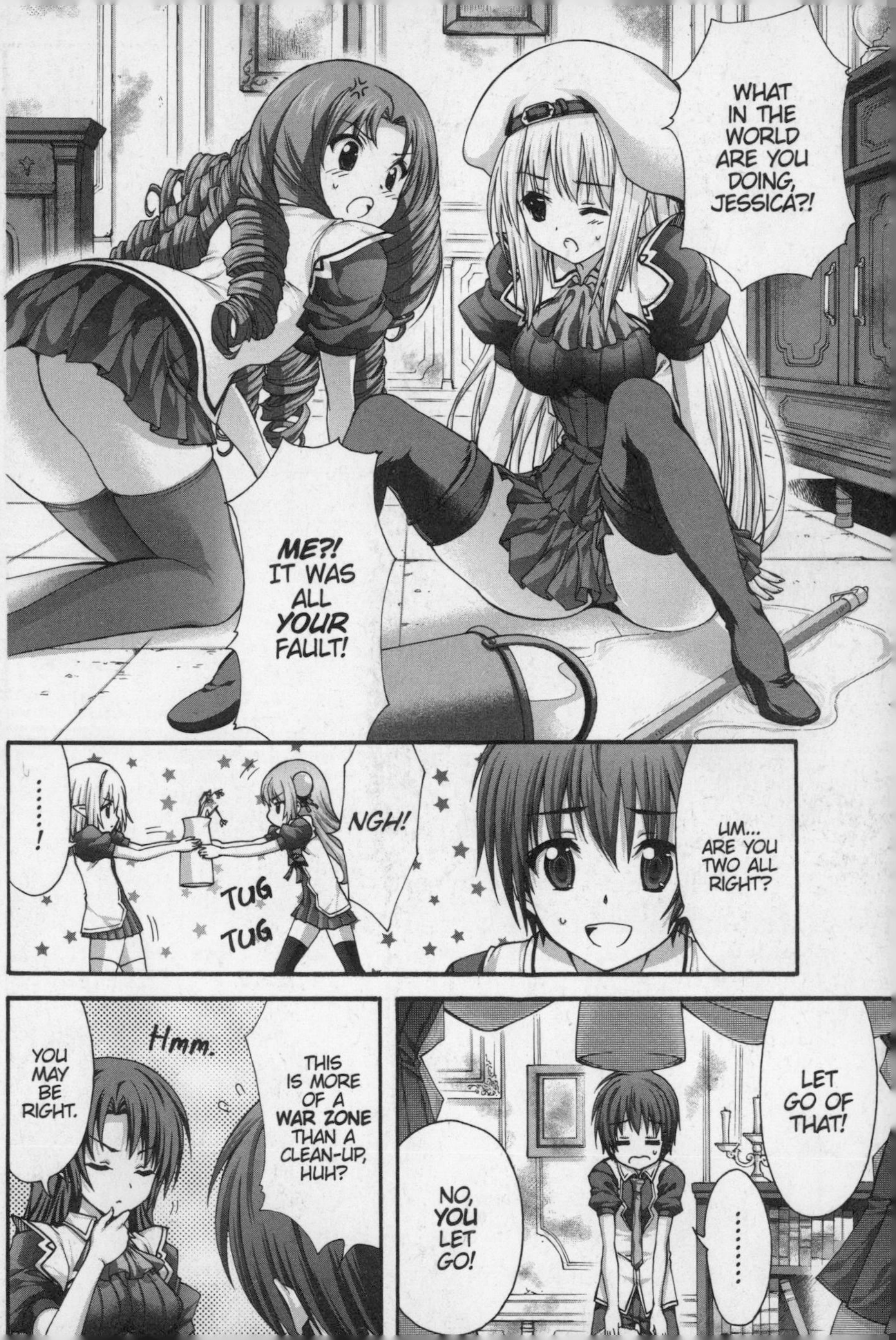
WHAT IN THE WORLD ARE YOU DOING, JESSICA?!
ME?! IT WAS ALL YOUR FAULT!
UM... ARE YOU TWO ALL RIGHT?
NGH!
TUG TUG
......!
LET GO OF THAT!
......
NO, YOU LET GO!
THIS IS MORE OF A WAR ZONE THAN A CLEAN-UP, HUH?
Hmm.
YOU MAY BE RIGHT.

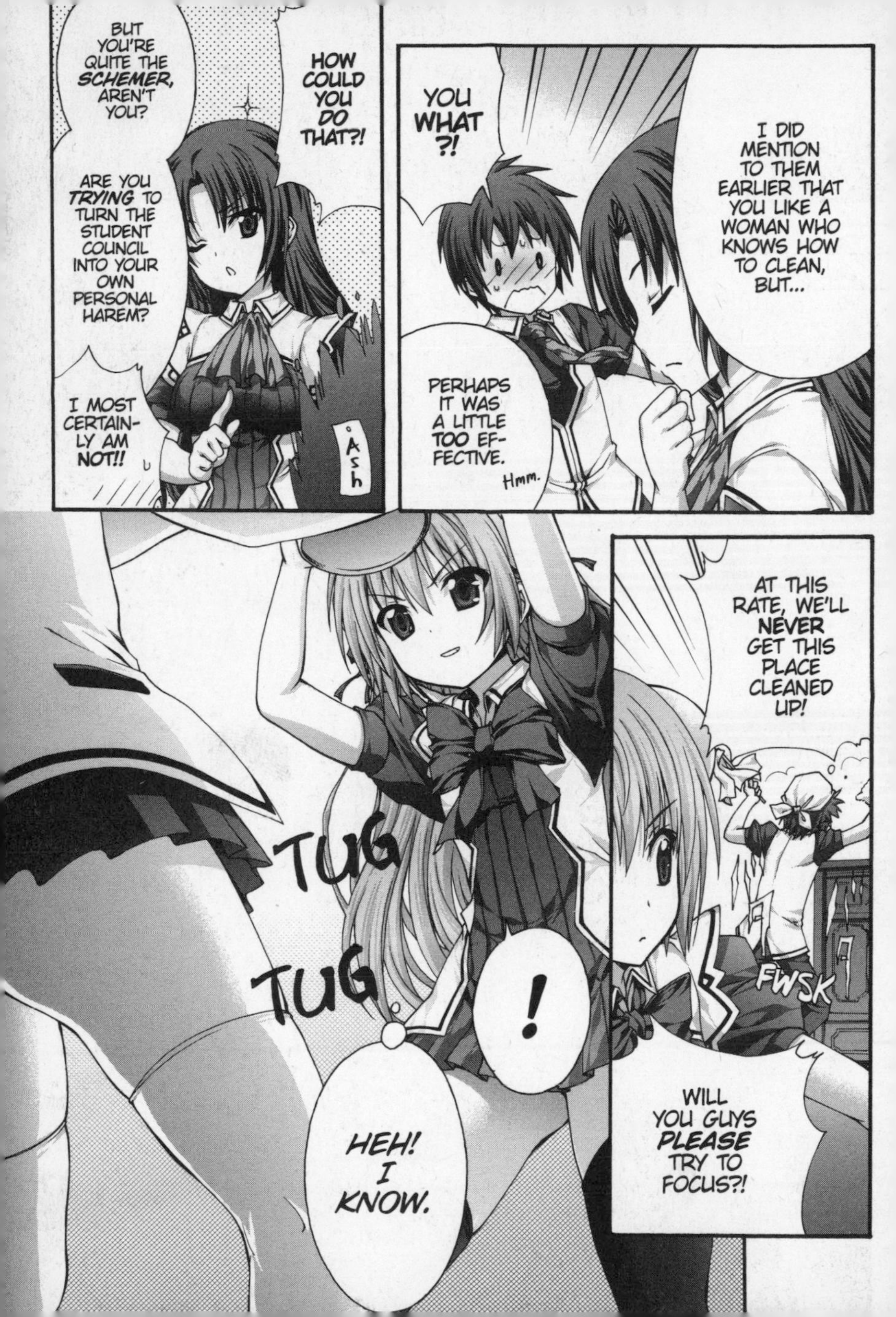

I DID MENTION TO THEM EARLIER THAT YOU LIKE A WOMAN WHO KNOWS HOW TO CLEAN, BUT...
YOU WHAT?!
PERHAPS IT WAS A LITTLE TOO EFFECTIVE.
Hmm.
HOW COULD YOU DO THAT?!
BUT YOU'RE QUITE THE SCHEMER, AREN'T YOU?
ARE YOU TRYING TO TURN THE STUDENT COUNCIL INTO YOUR OWN PERSONAL HAREM?
I MOST CERTAINLY AM NOT!!
Ash
AT THIS RATE, WE'LL NEVER GET THIS PLACE CLEANED UP!
FWSK
WILL YOU GUYS PLEASE TRY TO FOCUS?!
TUG
TUG
!
HEH! I KNOW.

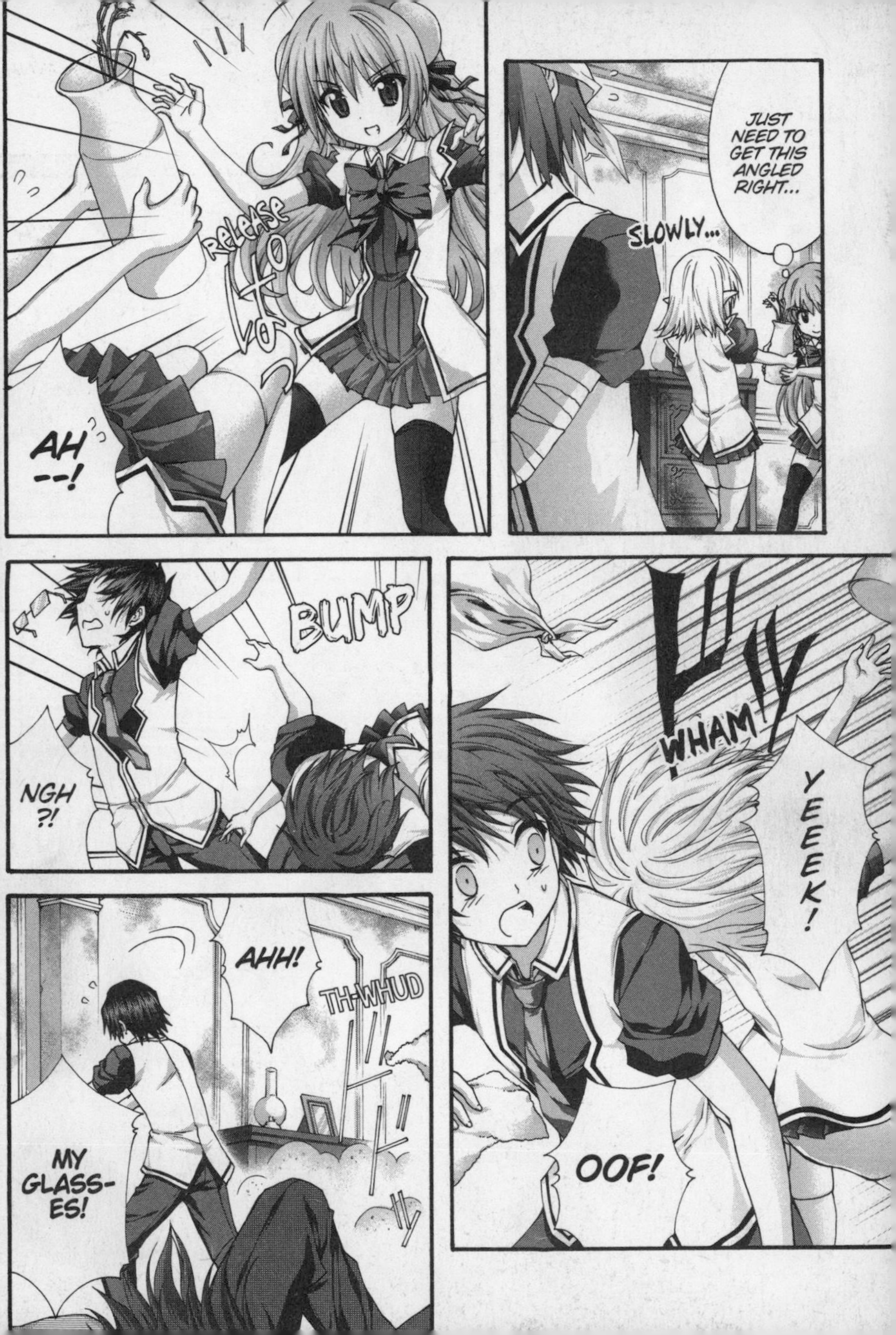
JUST NEED TO GET THIS ANGLED RIGHT...
SLOWLY...
RELEASE
AH --!
WHAM
YEEEK!
OOF!
BUMP
NGH ?!
AHH!
TH-WHUD
MY GLASS-ES!

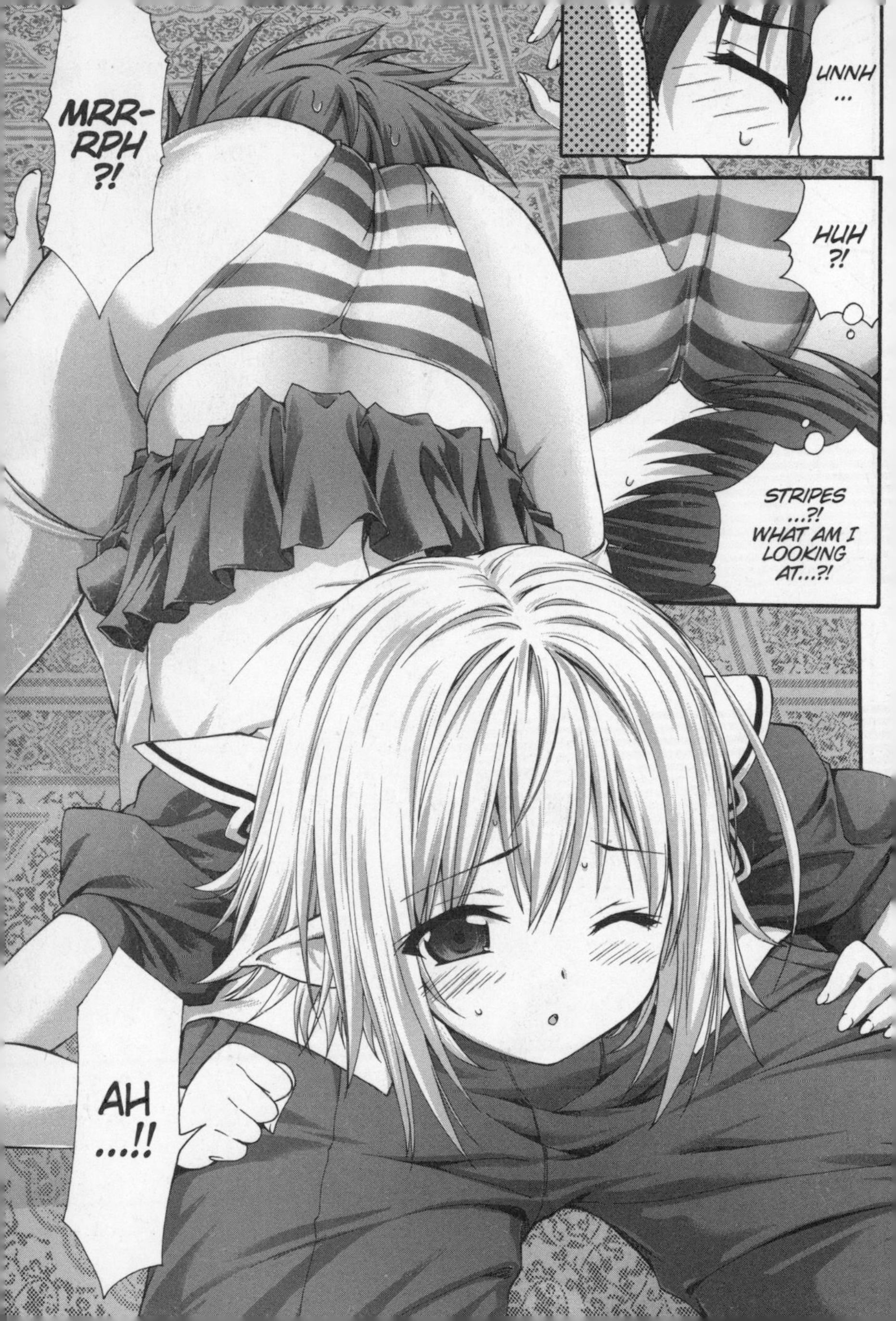
UNNH ...
HUH ?!
STRIPES ...?! WHAT AM I LOOKING AT...?!
MRR-RPH ?!
AH ....!!

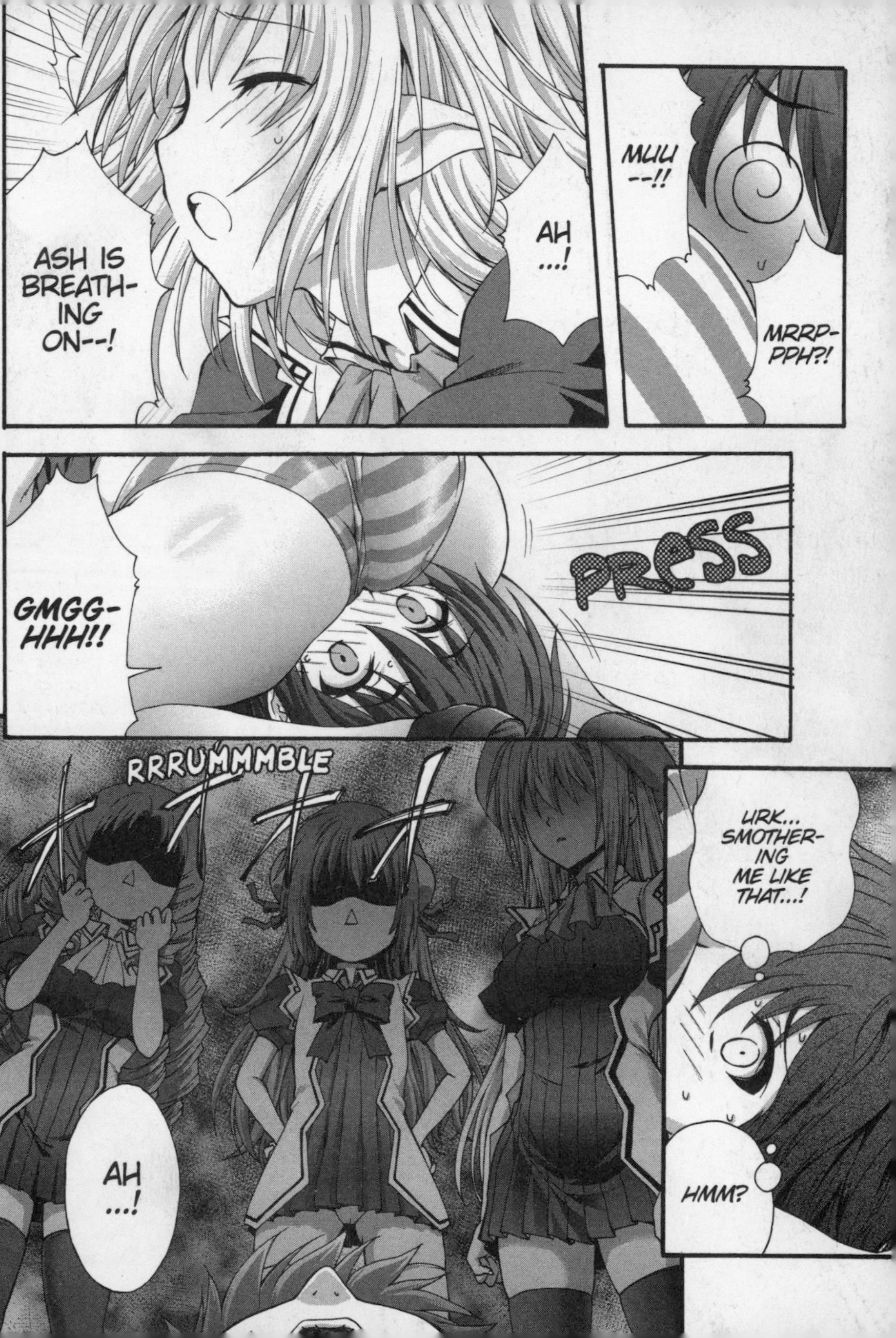
MUU--!!
MRRP-PPH?!
AH...!
ASH IS BREATHING ON--!
PRESS
GMGG-HHH!!
URK... SMOTHERING ME LIKE THAT...!
HMM?
RRRUMMMBLE
AH...!

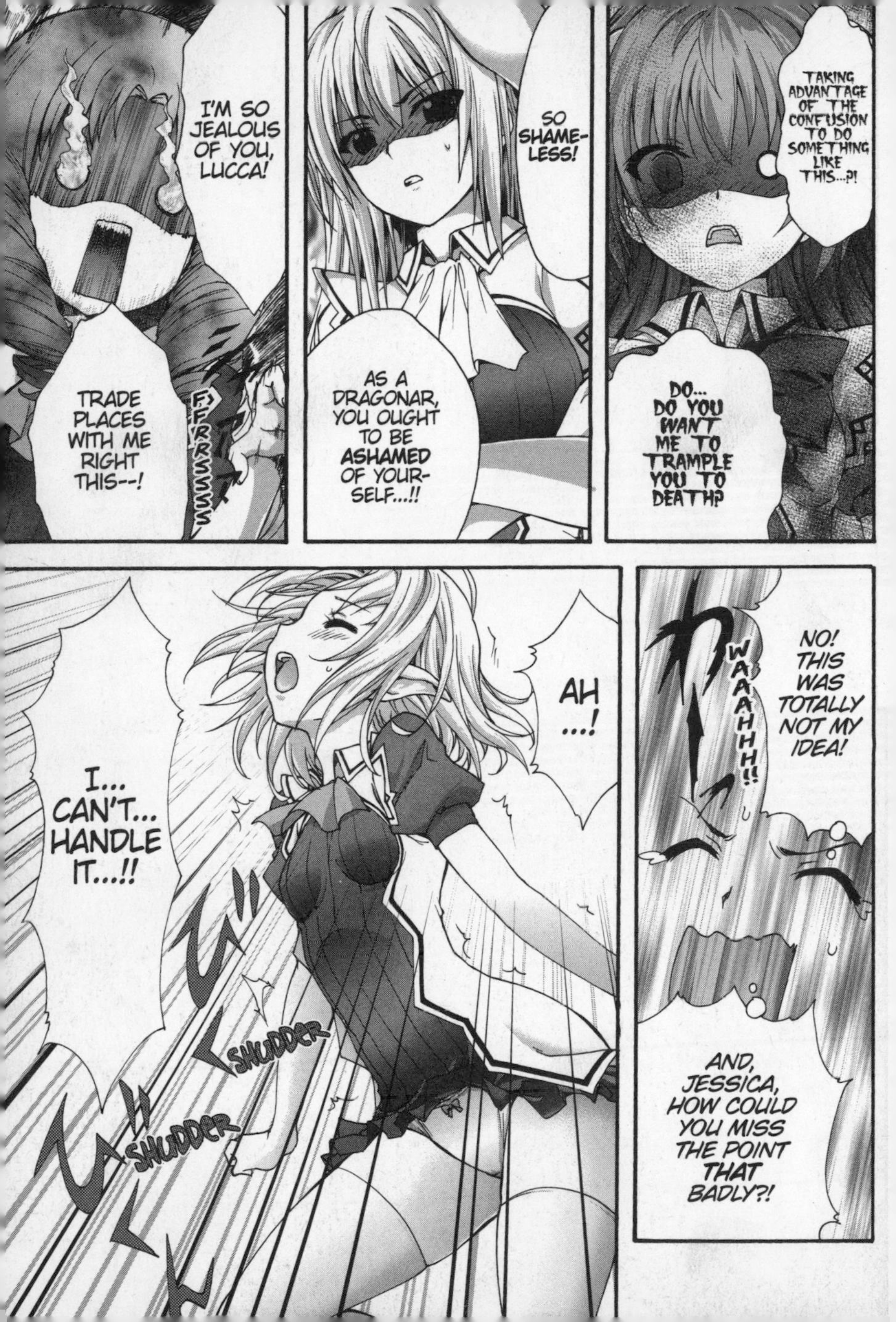
TAKING ADVANTAGE OF THE CONFUSION TO DO SOMETHING LIKE THIS...?!
DO... DO YOU WANT ME TO TRAMPLE YOU TO DEATH?
SO SHAME-LESS!
AS A DRAGONAR, YOU OUGHT TO BE ASHAMED OF YOUR-SELF...!!
I'M SO JEALOUS OF YOU, LUCCA!
FFRRSSSS
TRADE PLACES WITH ME RIGHT THIS--!
NO! THIS WAS TOTALLY NOT MY IDEA!
WAAAHHH!!
AND, JESSICA, HOW COULD YOU MISS THE POINT THAT BADLY?!
AH...!
I... CAN'T... HANDLE IT...!!
SHUDDER
SHUDDER

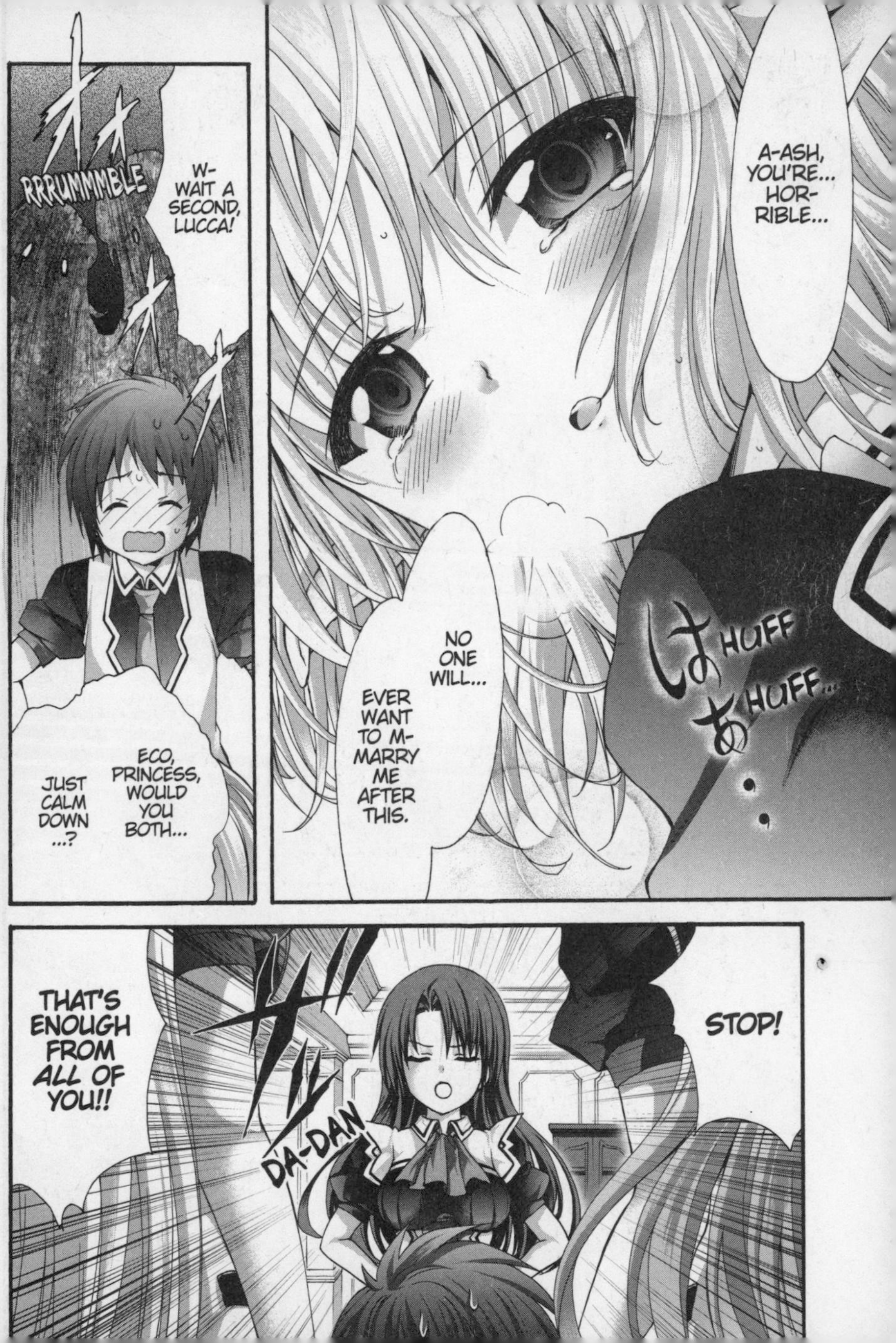
A-ASH, YOU'RE... HOR-RIBLE...
NO ONE WILL...
EVER WANT TO M-MARRY ME AFTER THIS.
はあ HUFF HUFF...
RRRUMMMBLE
W-WAIT A SECOND, LUCCA!
ECO, PRINCESS, WOULD YOU BOTH...
JUST CALM DOWN ...?
STOP!
THAT'S ENOUGH FROM ALL OF YOU!!
DA-DAN

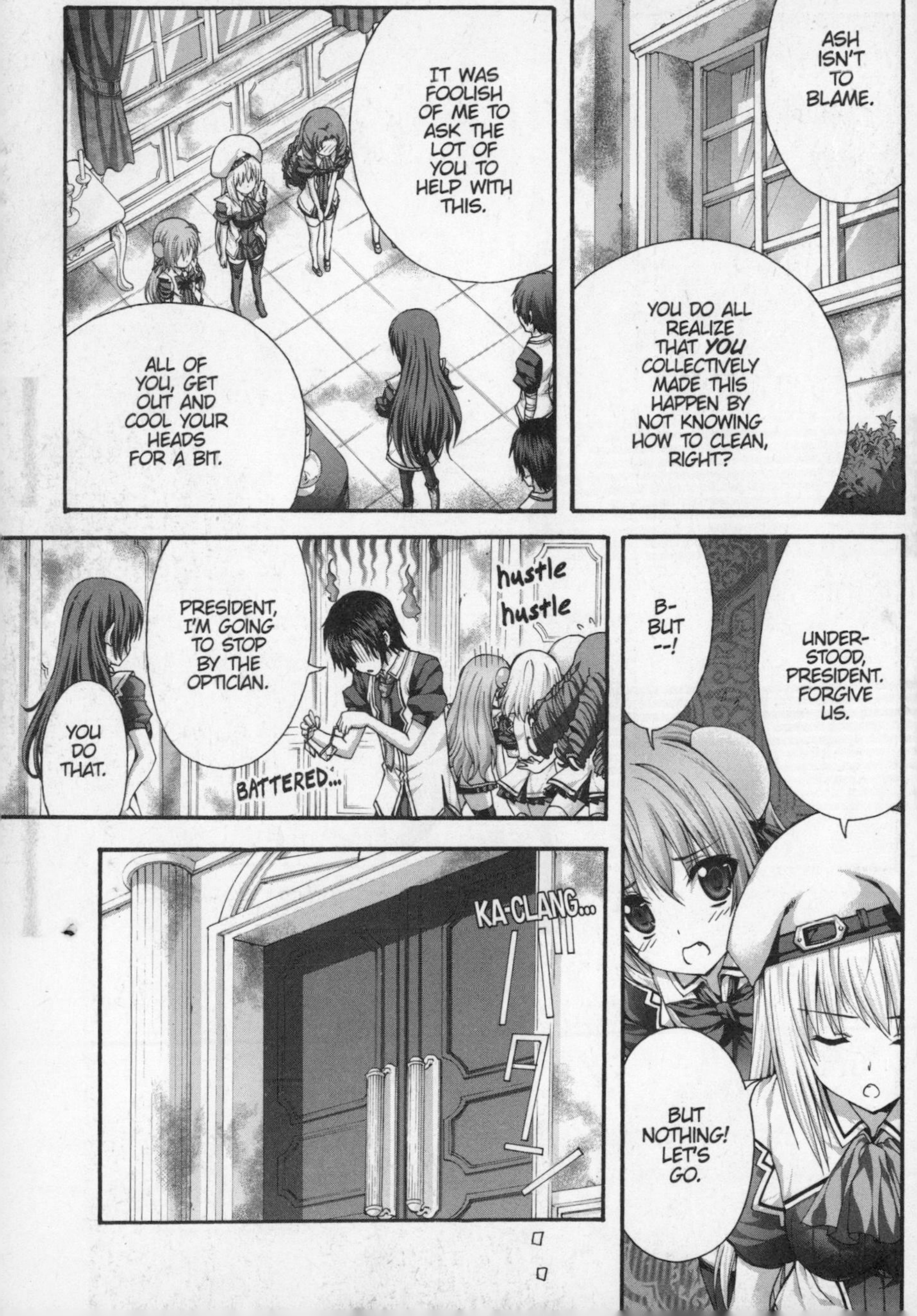
ASH ISN'T TO BLAME.
YOU DO ALL REALIZE THAT *YOU* COLLECTIVELY MADE THIS HAPPEN BY NOT KNOWING HOW TO CLEAN, RIGHT?
IT WAS FOOLISH OF ME TO ASK THE LOT OF YOU TO HELP WITH THIS.
ALL OF YOU, GET OUT AND COOL YOUR HEADS FOR A BIT.
UNDER-STOOD, PRESIDENT. FORGIVE US.
B-BUT --!
BUT NOTHING! LET'S GO.
hustle hustle
PRESIDENT, I'M GOING TO STOP BY THE OPTICIAN.
YOU DO THAT.
BATTERED...
KA-CLANG...

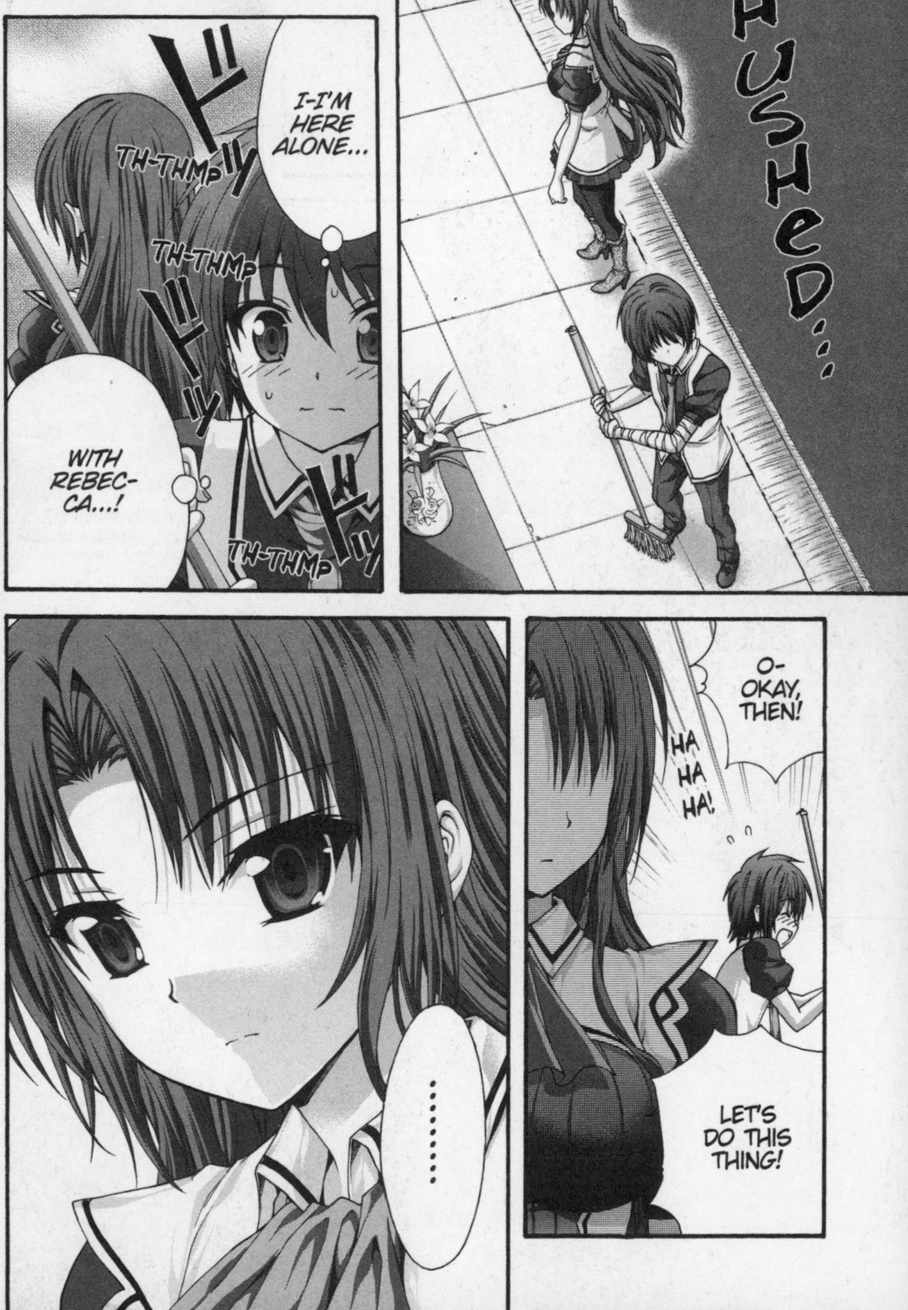
HUSHED...
I-I'M HERE ALONE...
TH-THMP
TH-THMP
TH-THMP
WITH REBEC-CA...!
O-OKAY, THEN!
HA HA HA!
LET'S DO THIS THING!
....

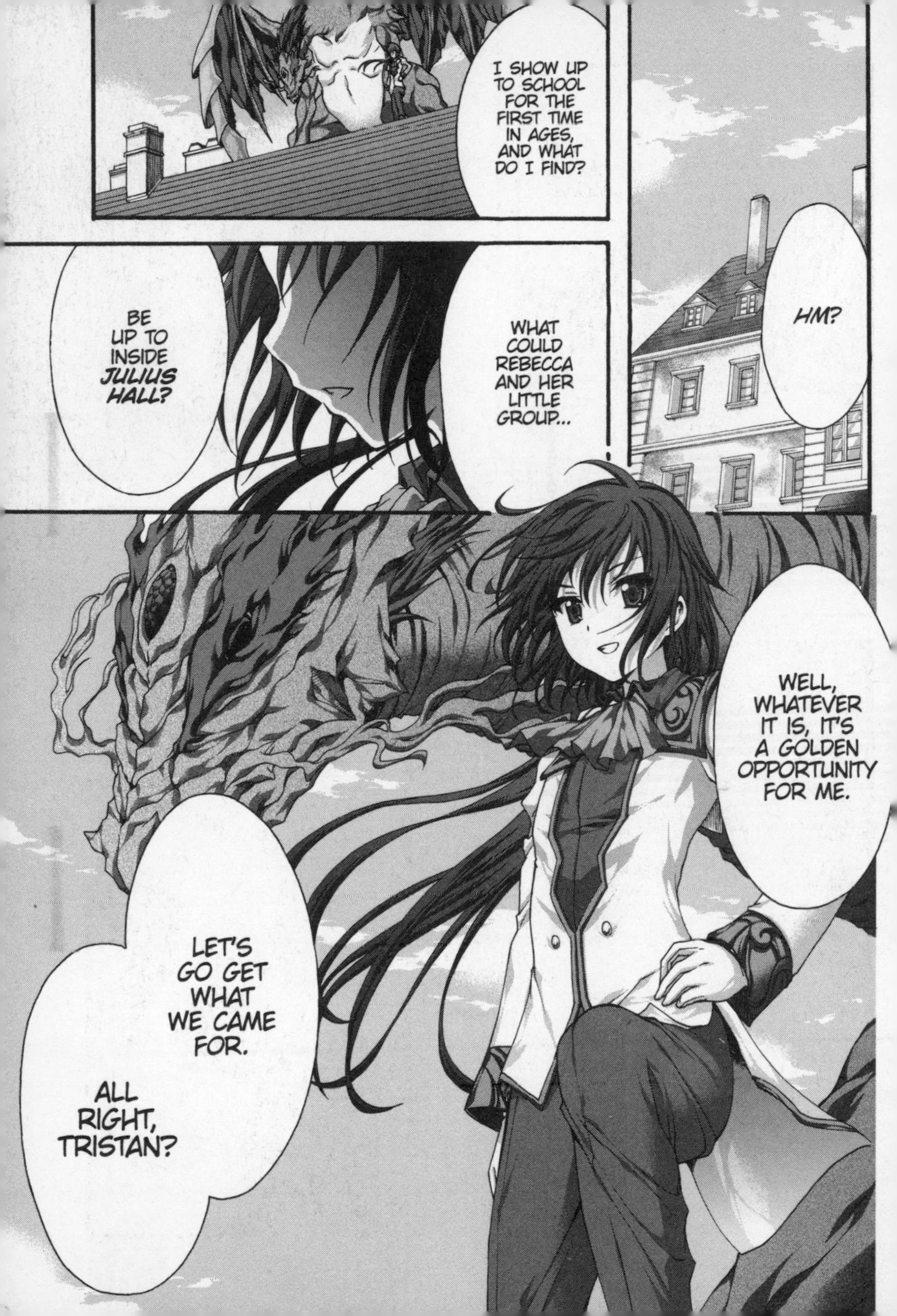
HM?
I SHOW UP TO SCHOOL FOR THE FIRST TIME IN AGES, AND WHAT DO I FIND?
WHAT COULD REBECCA AND HER LITTLE GROUP...
BE UP TO INSIDE *JULIUS HALL?*
WELL, WHATEVER IT IS, IT'S A GOLDEN OPPORTUNITY FOR ME.
LET'S GO GET WHAT WE CAME FOR.
ALL RIGHT, TRISTAN?

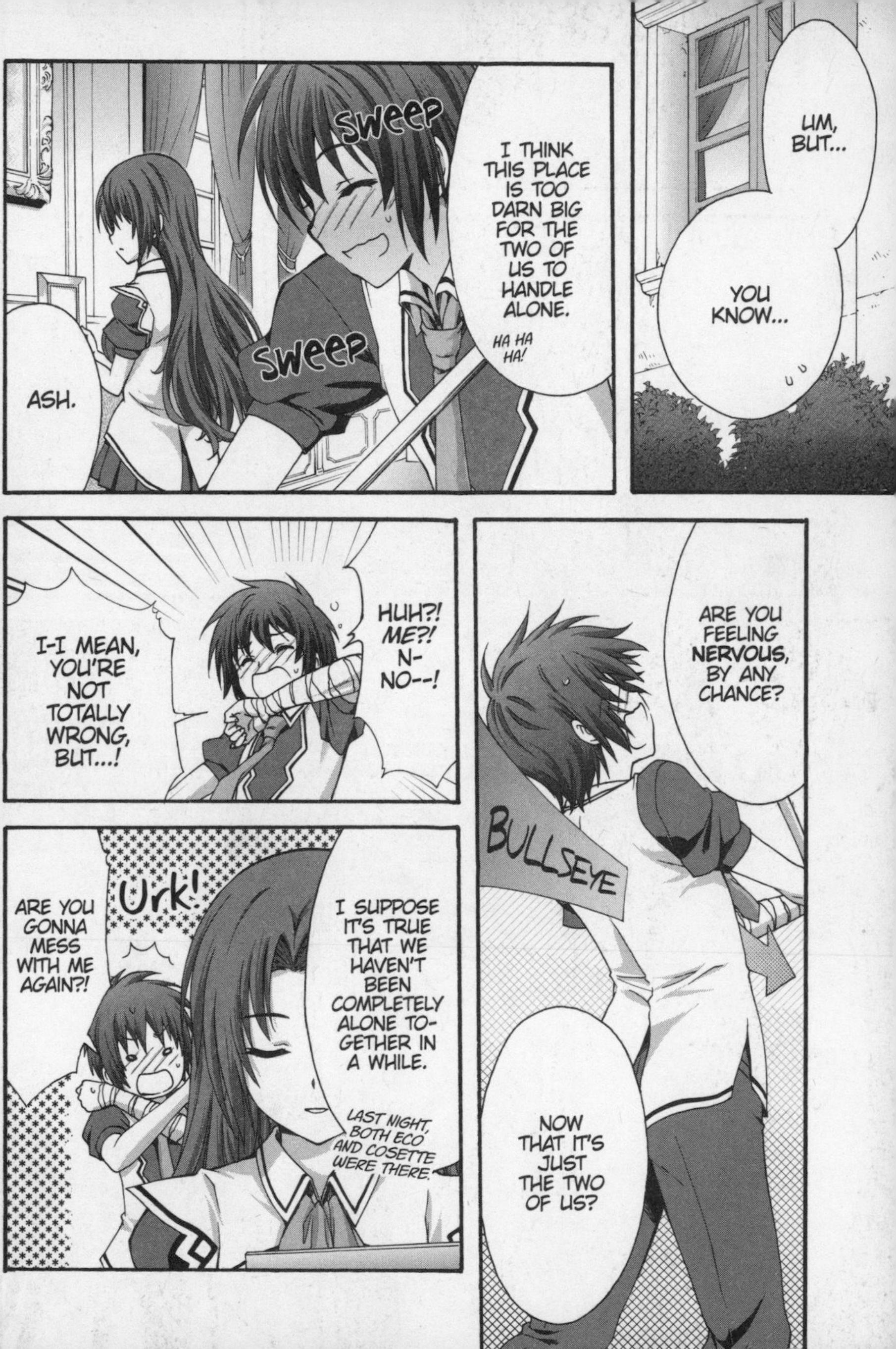
UM, BUT...
YOU KNOW...
SWEEP
I THINK THIS PLACE IS TOO DARN BIG FOR THE TWO OF US TO HANDLE ALONE.
HA HA HA!
SWEEP
ASH.
ARE YOU FEELING NERVOUS, BY ANY CHANCE?
BULLSEYE
NOW THAT IT'S JUST THE TWO OF US?
HUH?! ME?! N-NO--!
I-I MEAN, YOU'RE NOT TOTALLY WRONG, BUT...!
I SUPPOSE IT'S TRUE THAT WE HAVEN'T BEEN COMPLETELY ALONE TO-GETHER IN A WHILE.
LAST NIGHT, BOTH ECO AND COSETTE WERE THERE.
Urk!
ARE YOU GONNA MESS WITH ME AGAIN?!

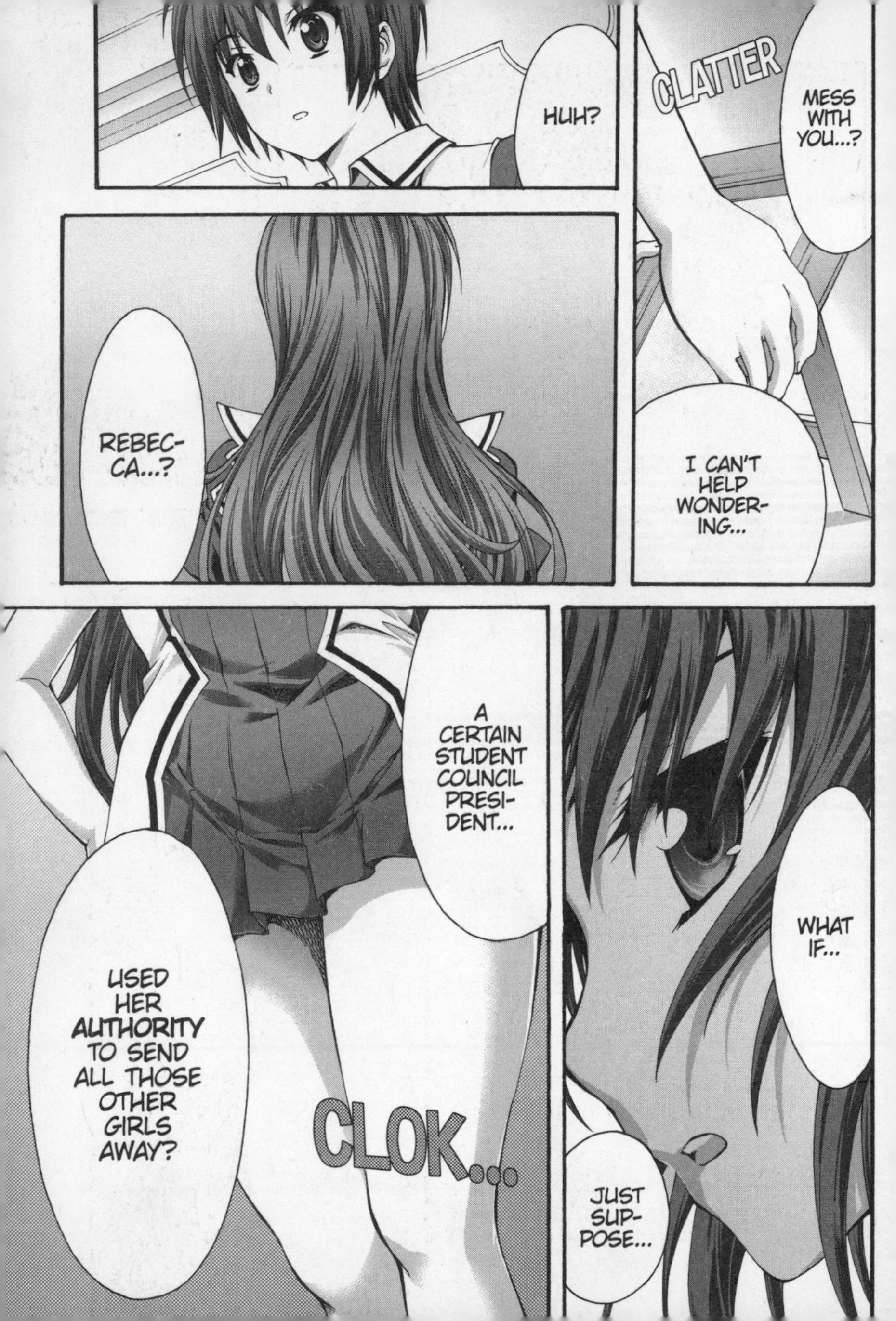
CLATTER
MESS WITH YOU...?
I CAN'T HELP WONDER-ING...
HUH?
REBEC-CA...?
WHAT IF...
JUST SUP-POSE...
A CERTAIN STUDENT COUNCIL PRESI-DENT...
USED HER AUTHORITY TO SEND ALL THOSE OTHER GIRLS AWAY?
CLOK...

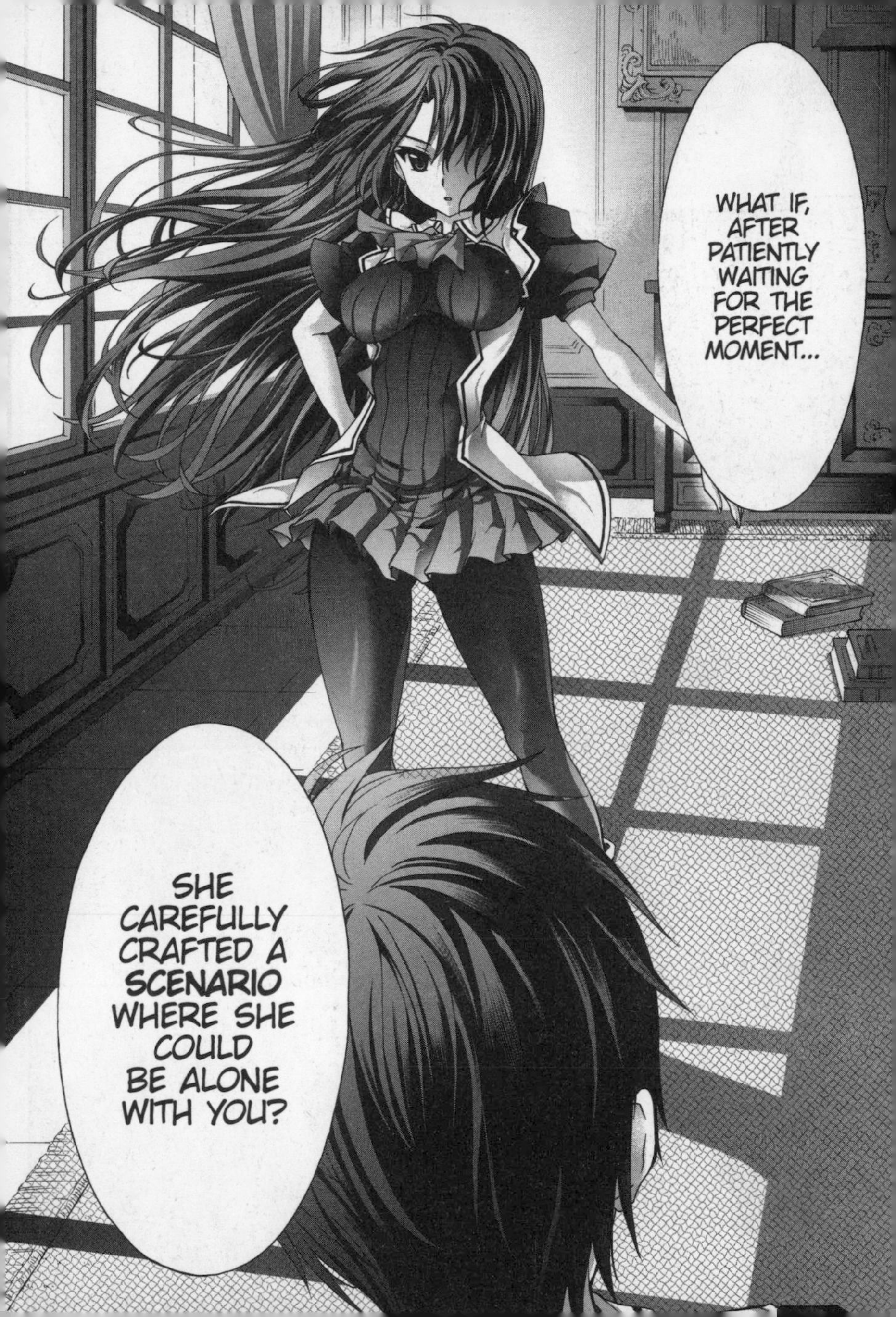
WHAT IF, AFTER PATIENTLY WAITING FOR THE PERFECT MOMENT...
SHE CAREFULLY CRAFTED A SCENARIO WHERE SHE COULD BE ALONE WITH YOU?

WHAT I'M SAYING IS... I'M NO DIFFERENT FROM THE OTHERS.

WHA--?

I'M NOT JUST A STERN AUTHORITY FIGURE, ASH.

I'M ALSO A **WOMAN.**

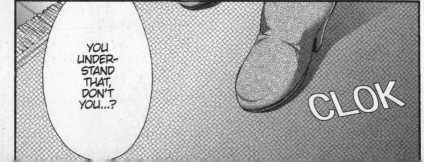

YOU UNDERSTAND THAT, DON'T YOU...?

CLOK

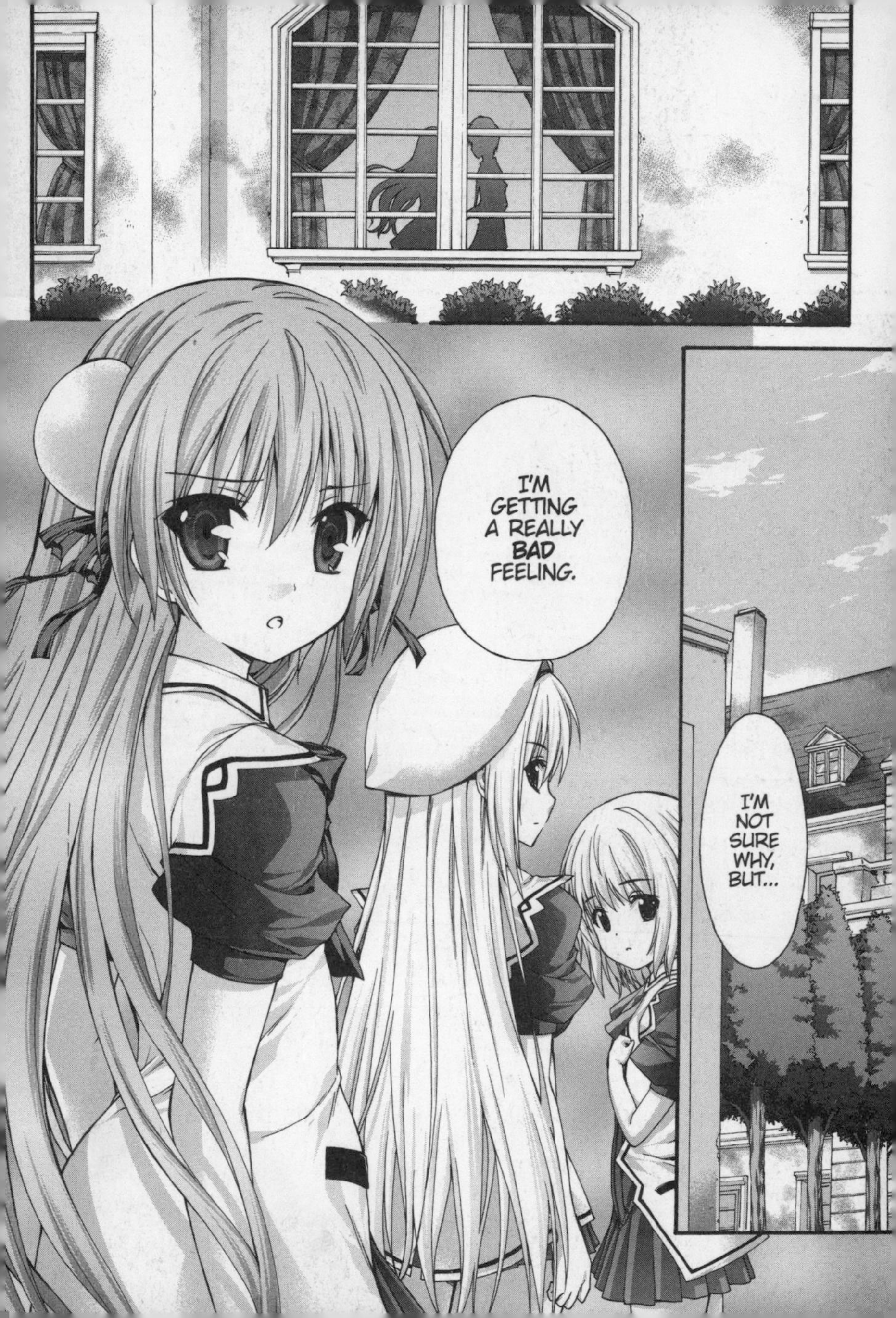
I'M NOT SURE WHY, BUT...
I'M GETTING A REALLY BAD FEELING.

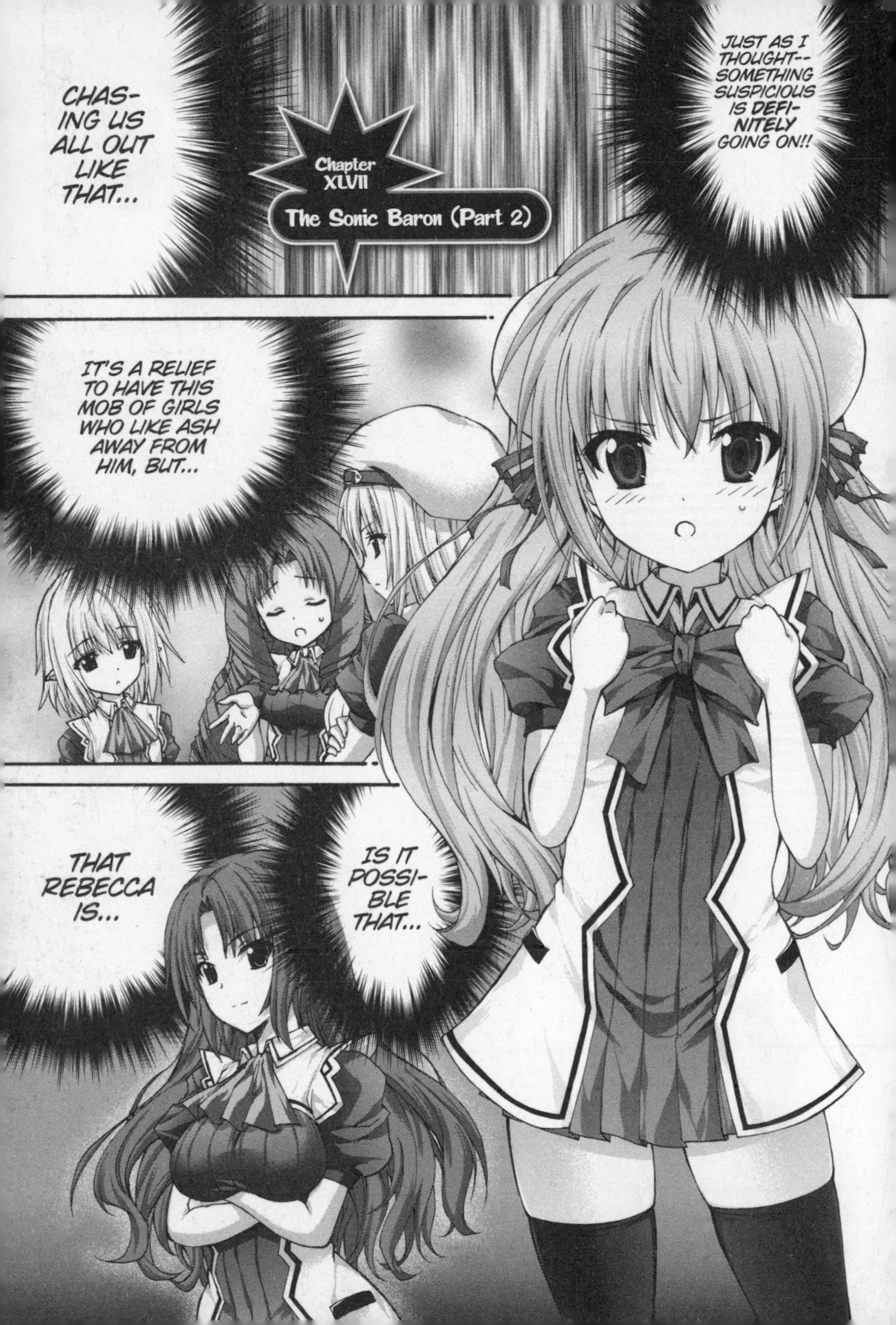
JUST AS I THOUGHT-- SOMETHING SUSPICIOUS IS DEFINITELY GOING ON!!
Chapter XLVII
The Sonic Baron (Part 2)
CHASING US ALL OUT LIKE THAT...
IT'S A RELIEF TO HAVE THIS MOB OF GIRLS WHO LIKE ASH AWAY FROM HIM, BUT...
IS IT POSSIBLE THAT...
THAT REBECCA IS...

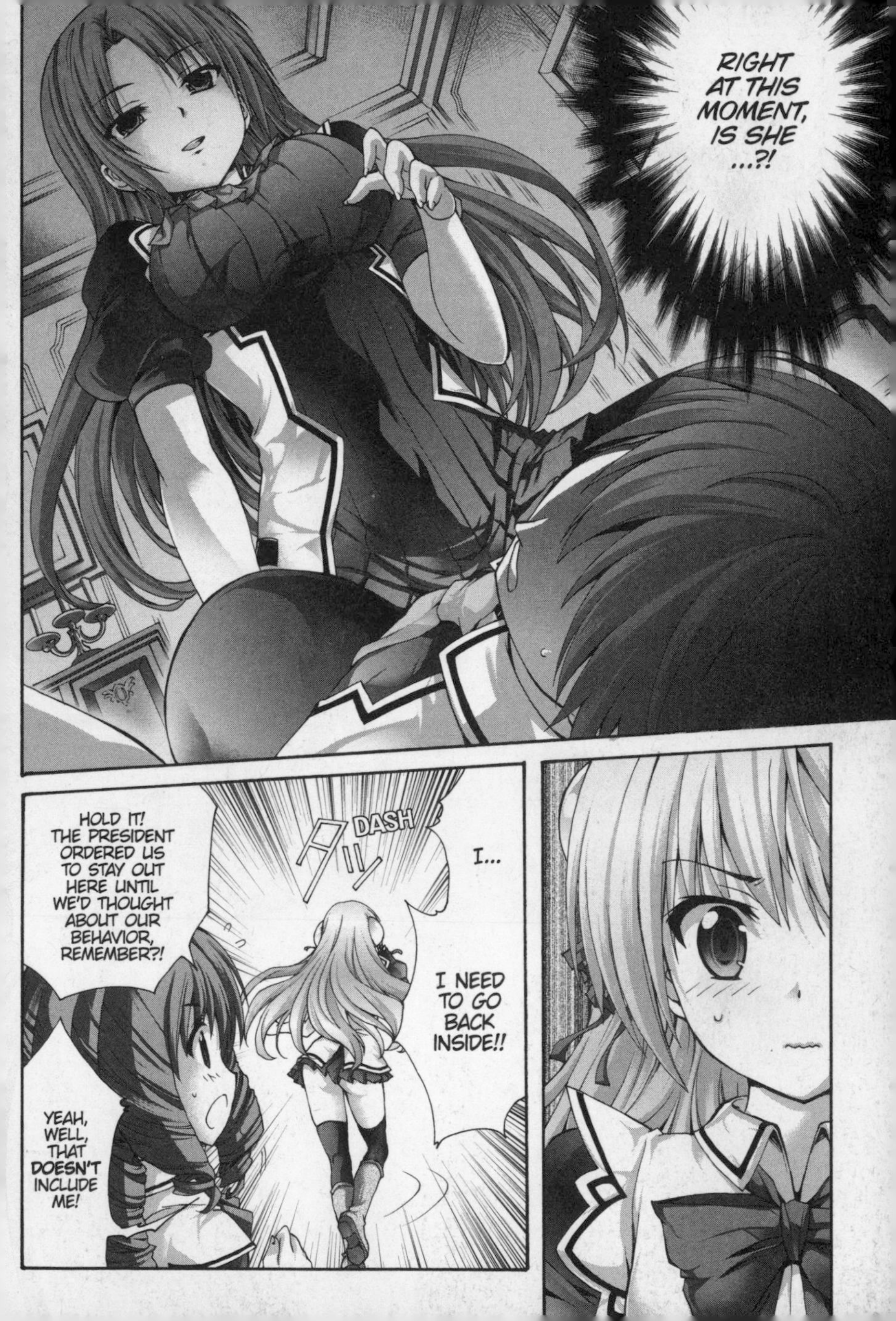
RIGHT AT THIS MOMENT, IS SHE ...?!
I...
I NEED TO GO BACK INSIDE!!
DASH
HOLD IT! THE PRESIDENT ORDERED US TO STAY OUT HERE UNTIL WE'D THOUGHT ABOUT OUR BEHAVIOR, REMEMBER?!
YEAH, WELL, THAT DOESN'T INCLUDE ME!

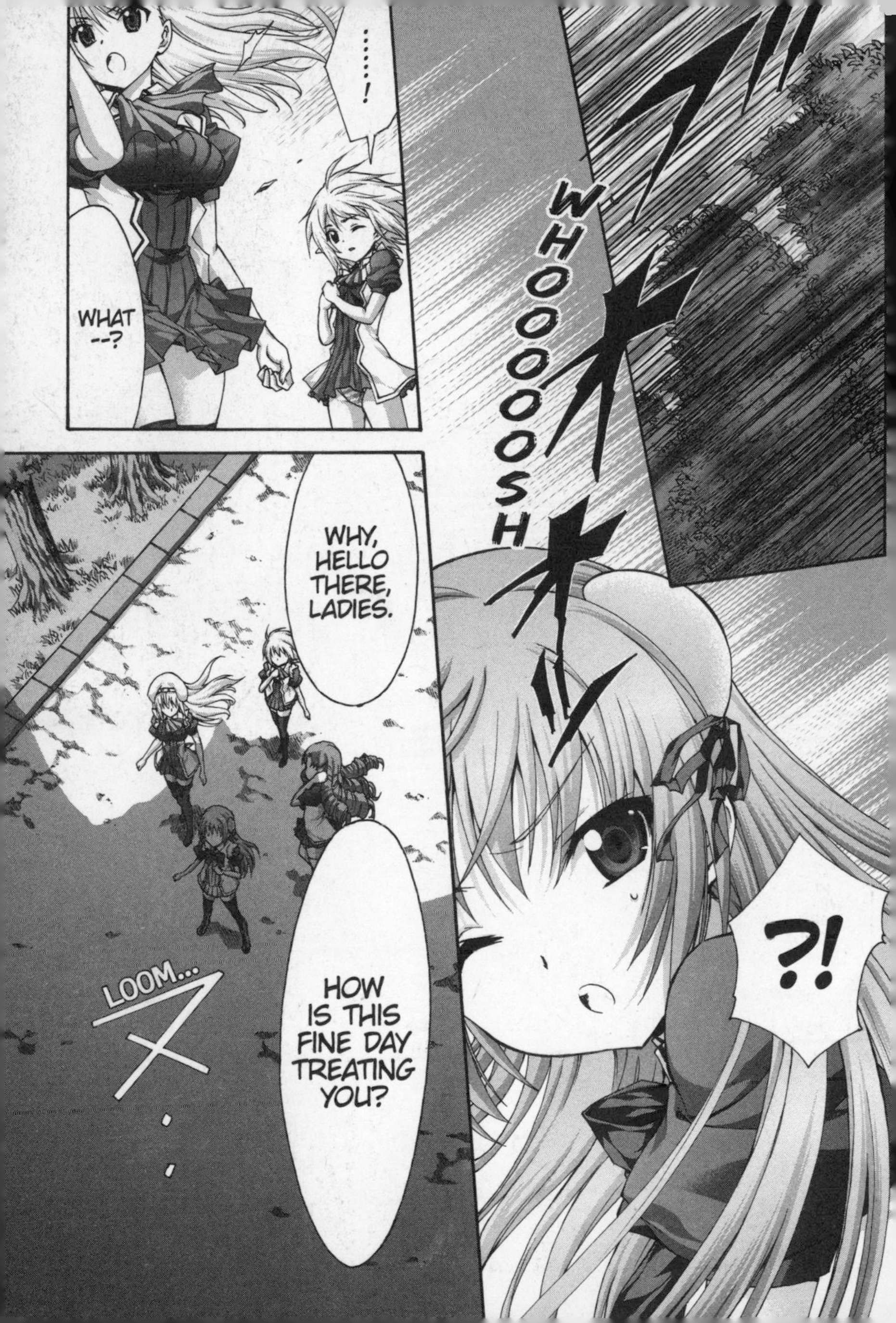
WHOOOOOSH
?!
......!
WHAT --?
WHY, HELLO THERE, LADIES.
HOW IS THIS FINE DAY TREATING YOU?
LOOM...

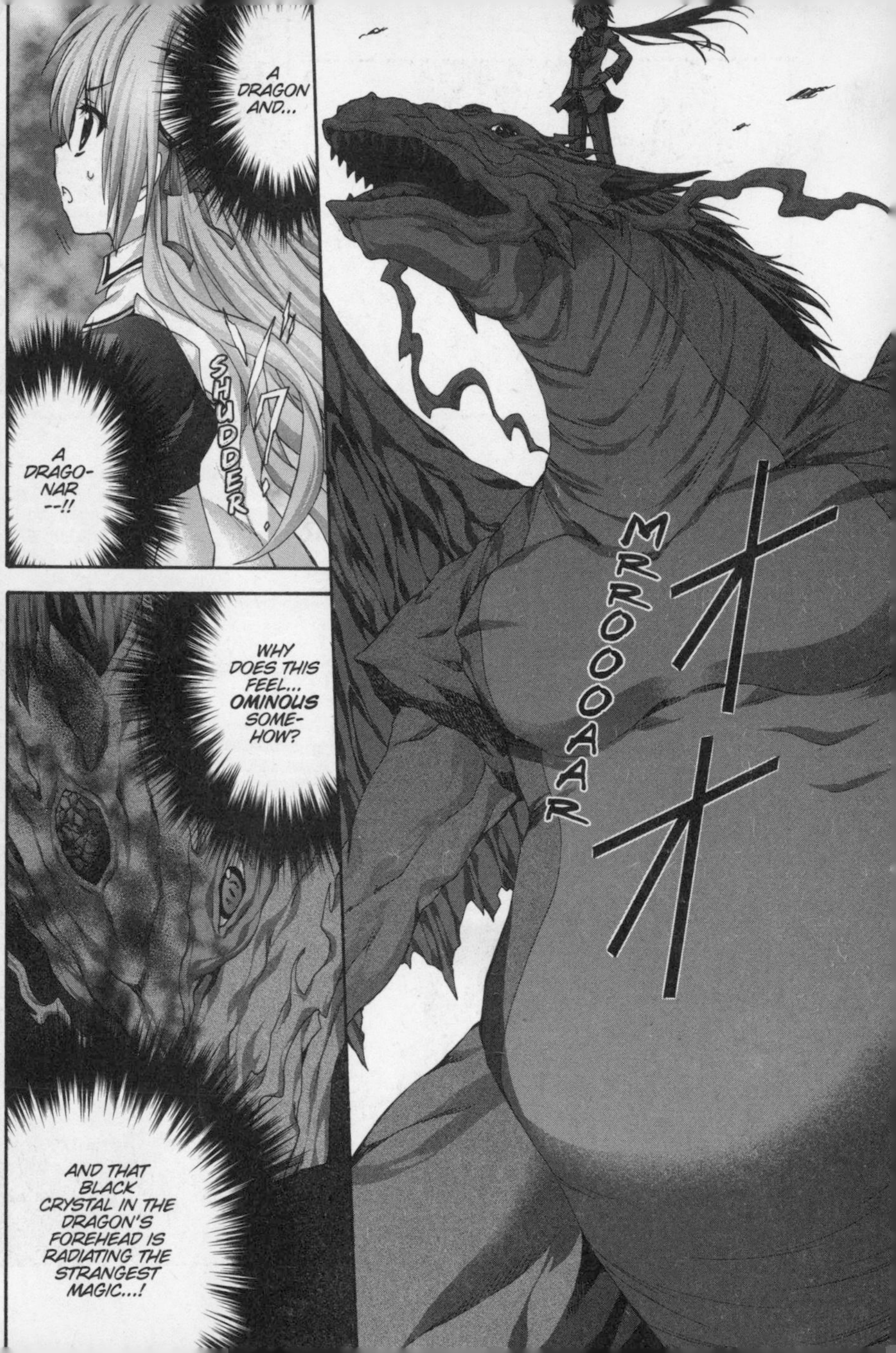
MRROOOOAAR
A DRAGON AND...
SHUDDER
A DRAGO-NAR--!!
WHY DOES THIS FEEL... OMINOUS SOMEHOW?
AND THAT BLACK CRYSTAL IN THE DRAGON'S FOREHEAD IS RADIATING THE STRANGEST MAGIC...!

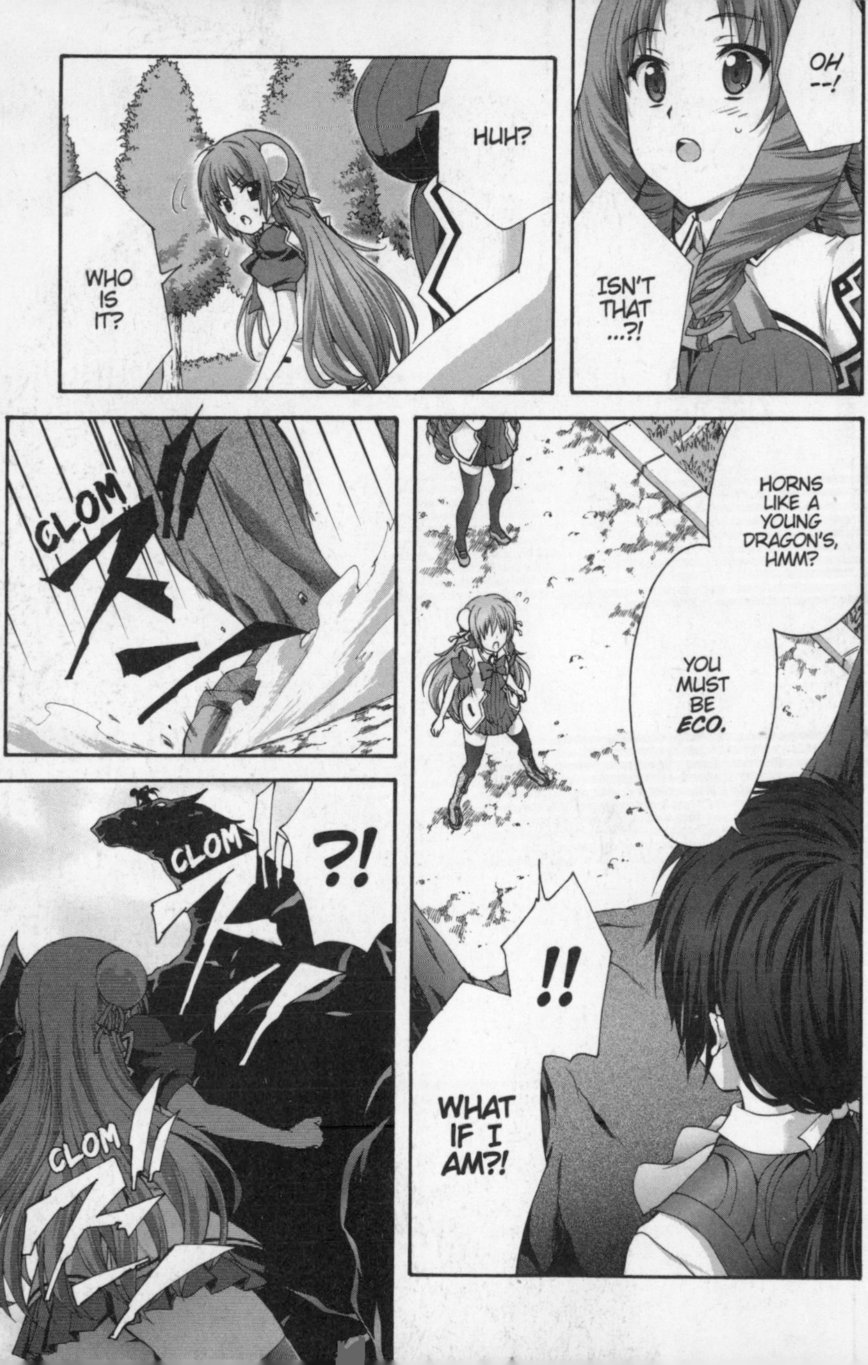
OH --!
ISN'T THAT ...?!
HUH?
WHO IS IT?
HORNS LIKE A YOUNG DRAGON'S, HMM?
YOU MUST BE ECO.
!!
WHAT IF I AM?!
CLOM
CLOM
?!
CLOM

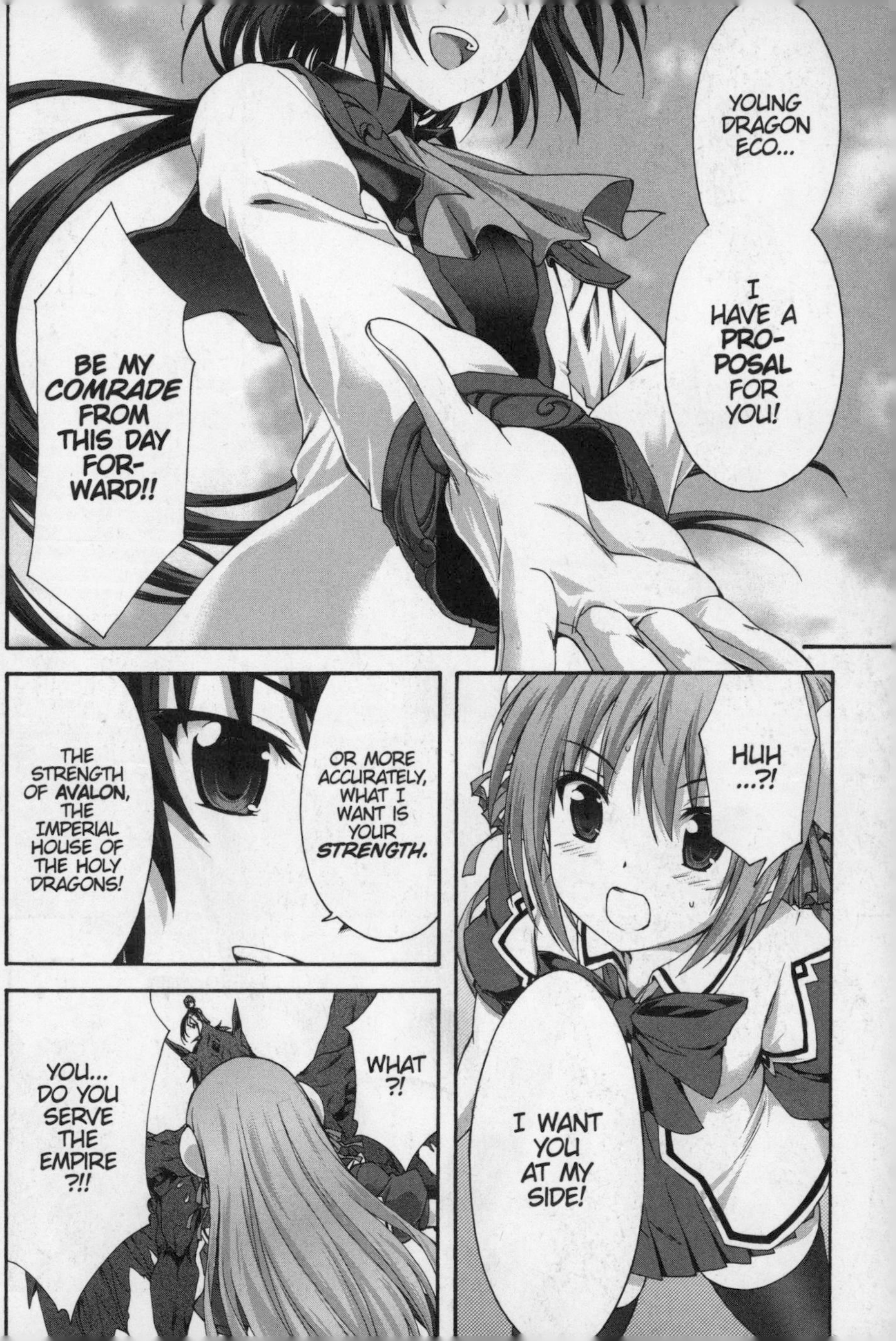
YOUNG DRAGON ECO...
I HAVE A PROPOSAL FOR YOU!
BE MY COMRADE FROM THIS DAY FORWARD!!
HUH ...?!
I WANT YOU AT MY SIDE!
OR MORE ACCURATELY, WHAT I WANT IS YOUR STRENGTH.
THE STRENGTH OF AVALON, THE IMPERIAL HOUSE OF THE HOLY DRAGONS!
WHAT ?!
YOU... DO YOU SERVE THE EMPIRE ?!!

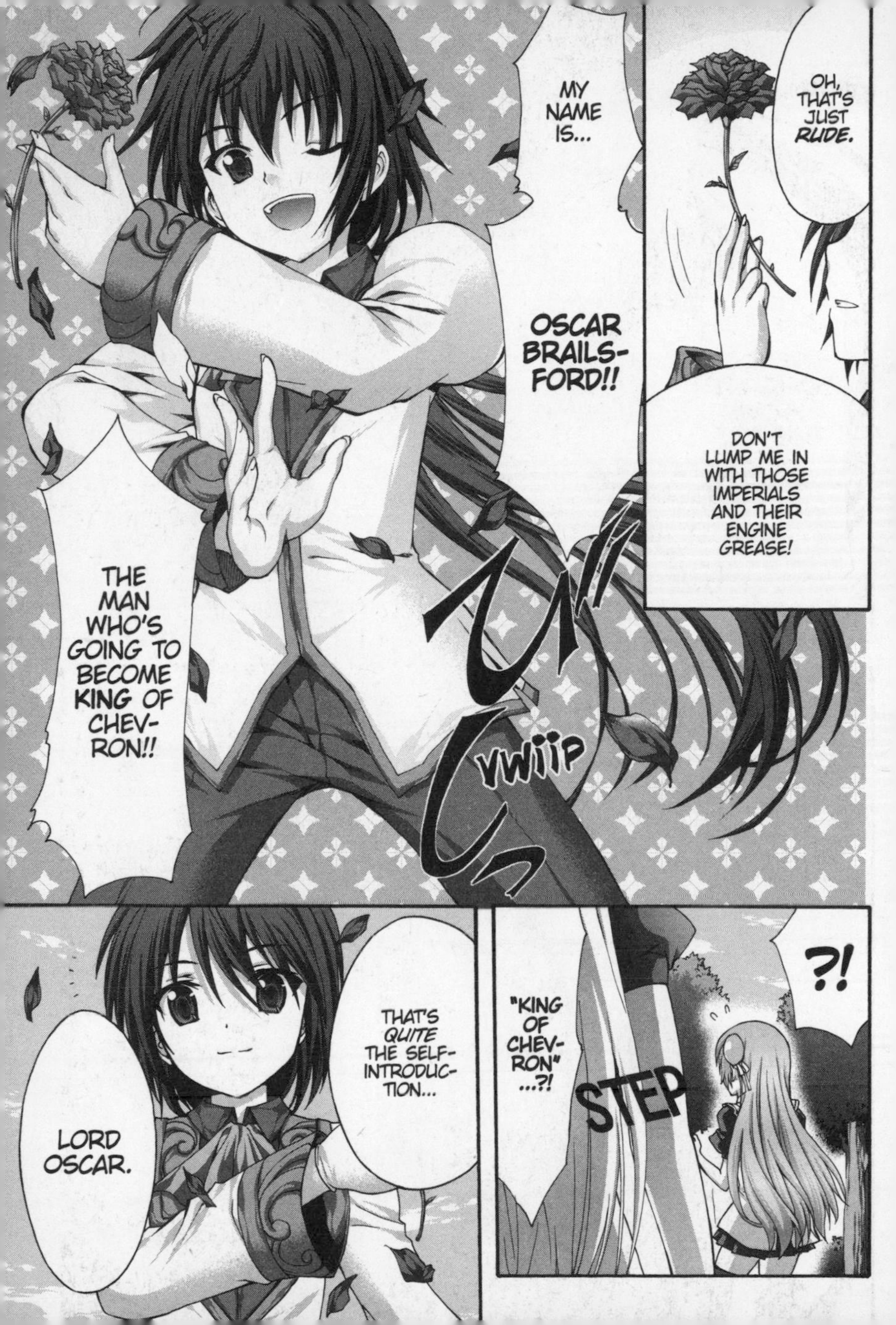
OH, THAT'S JUST *RUDE.*
DON'T LUMP ME IN WITH THOSE IMPERIALS AND THEIR ENGINE GREASE!
MY NAME IS...
OSCAR BRAILS-FORD!!
THE MAN WHO'S GOING TO BECOME **KING** OF CHEV-RON!!
VWIIP
?!
"KING OF CHEV-RON" ...?!
STEP
THAT'S *QUITE* THE SELF-INTRODUC-TION...
LORD OSCAR.

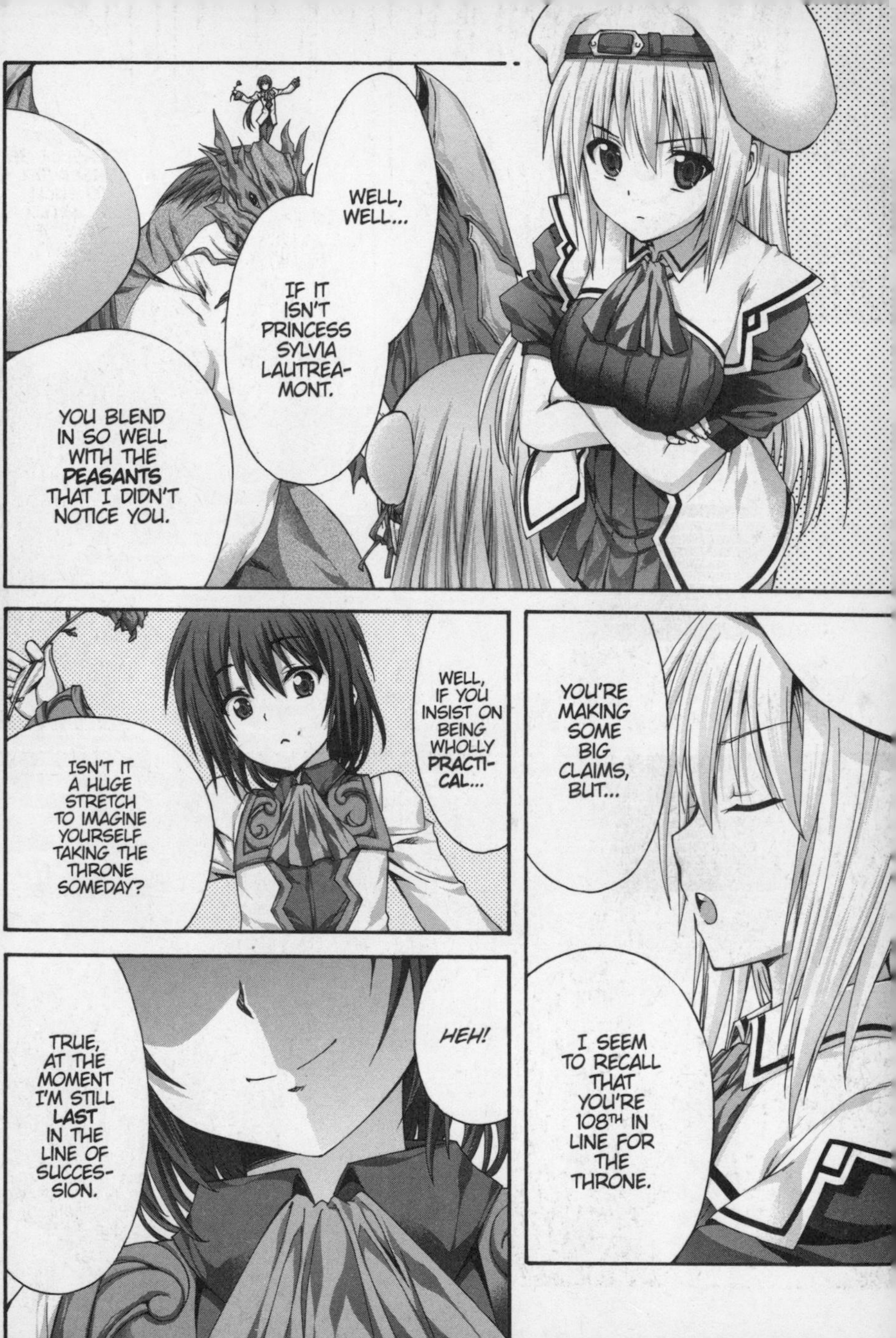
WELL, WELL...
IF IT ISN'T PRINCESS SYLVIA LAUTREAMONT.
YOU BLEND IN SO WELL WITH THE **PEASANTS** THAT I DIDN'T NOTICE YOU.
YOU'RE MAKING SOME BIG CLAIMS, BUT...
I SEEM TO RECALL THAT YOU'RE 108TH IN LINE FOR THE THRONE.
WELL, IF YOU INSIST ON BEING WHOLLY **PRACTICAL...**
ISN'T IT A HUGE STRETCH TO IMAGINE YOURSELF TAKING THE THRONE SOMEDAY?
HEH!
TRUE, AT THE MOMENT I'M STILL **LAST** IN THE LINE OF SUCCESSION.

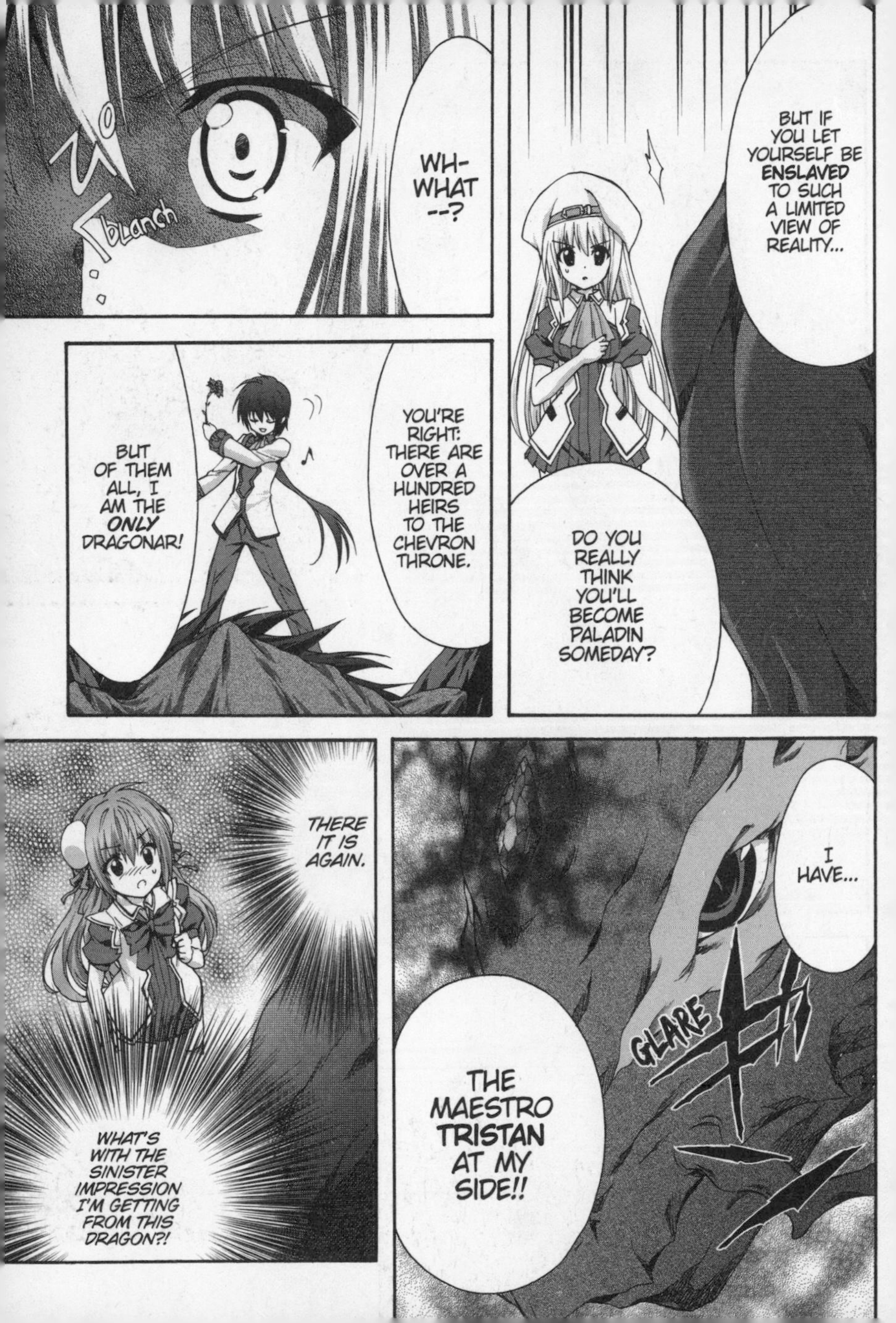
BUT IF YOU LET YOURSELF BE ENSLAVED TO SUCH A LIMITED VIEW OF REALITY...
DO YOU REALLY THINK YOU'LL BECOME PALADIN SOMEDAY?
WH-WHAT--?
blanch
YOU'RE RIGHT: THERE ARE OVER A HUNDRED HEIRS TO THE CHEVRON THRONE.
BUT OF THEM ALL, I AM THE ONLY DRAGONAR!
I HAVE...
THE MAESTRO TRISTAN AT MY SIDE!!
GLARE
THERE IT IS AGAIN.
WHAT'S WITH THE SINISTER IMPRESSION I'M GETTING FROM THIS DRAGON?!

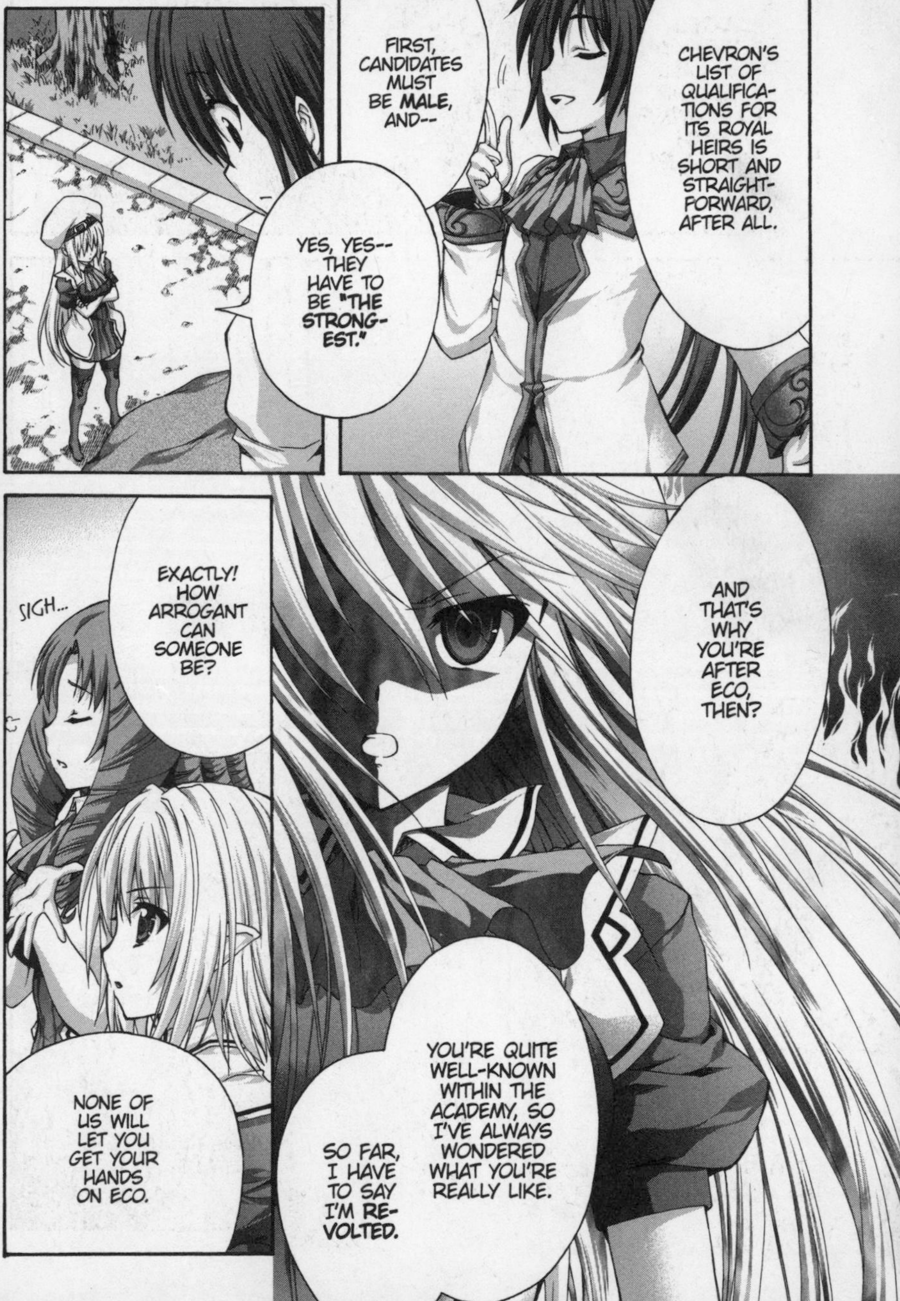
CHEVRON'S LIST OF QUALIFICA-TIONS FOR ITS ROYAL HEIRS IS SHORT AND STRAIGHT-FORWARD, AFTER ALL.
FIRST, CANDIDATES MUST BE MALE, AND--
YES, YES--THEY HAVE TO BE "THE STRONG-EST."
AND THAT'S WHY YOU'RE AFTER ECO, THEN?
YOU'RE QUITE WELL-KNOWN WITHIN THE ACADEMY, SO I'VE ALWAYS WONDERED WHAT YOU'RE REALLY LIKE.
SO FAR, I HAVE TO SAY I'M RE-VOLTED.
EXACTLY! HOW ARROGANT CAN SOMEONE BE?
SIGH...
NONE OF US WILL LET YOU GET YOUR HANDS ON ECO.

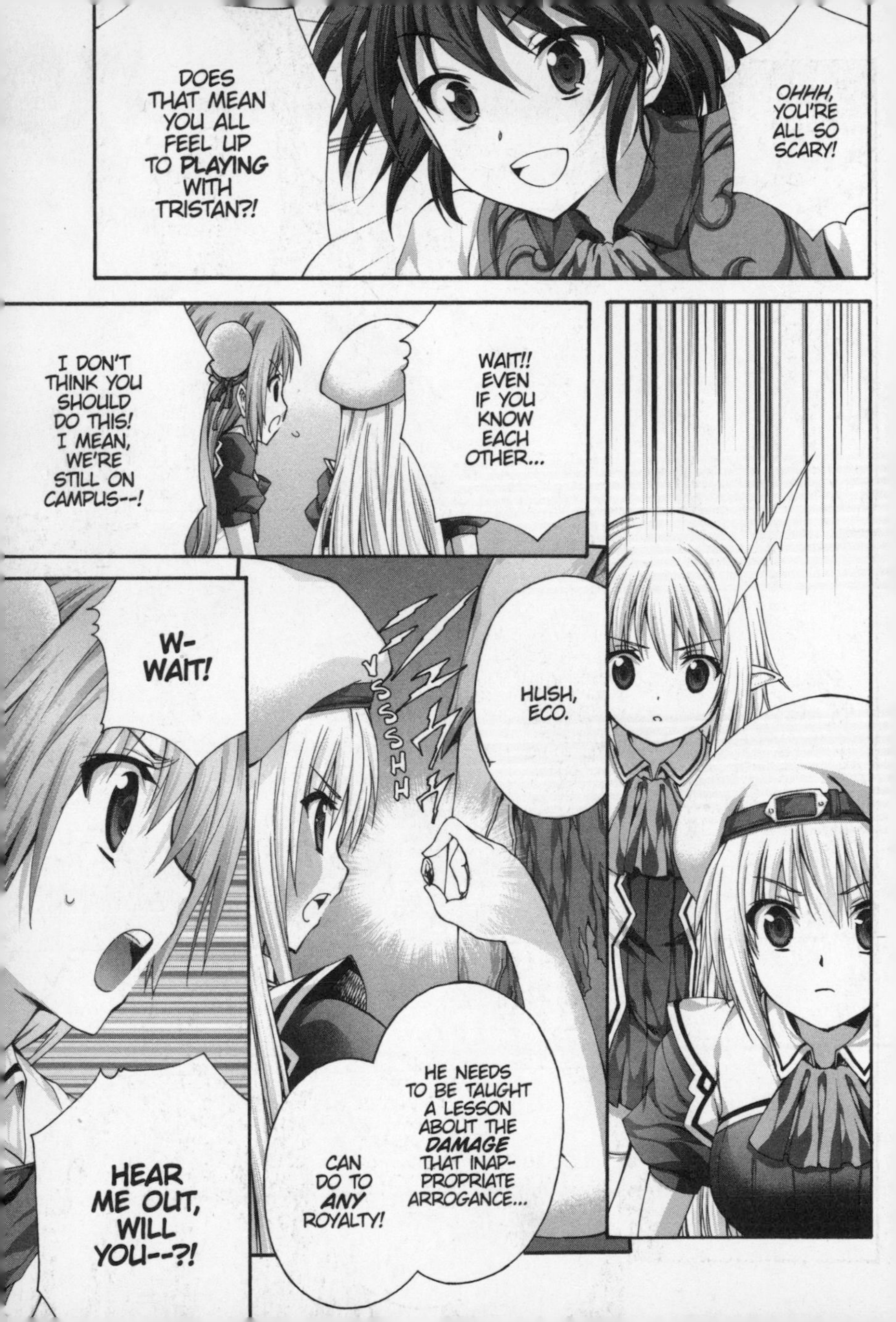
OHHH, YOU'RE ALL SO SCARY!
DOES THAT MEAN YOU ALL FEEL UP TO PLAYING WITH TRISTAN?!
WAIT!! EVEN IF YOU KNOW EACH OTHER...
I DON'T THINK YOU SHOULD DO THIS! I MEAN, WE'RE STILL ON CAMPUS--!
SSSHH
HUSH, ECO.
HE NEEDS TO BE TAUGHT A LESSON ABOUT THE DAMAGE THAT INAPPROPRIATE ARROGANCE...
CAN DO TO ANY ROYALTY!
W-WAIT!
HEAR ME OUT, WILL YOU--?!

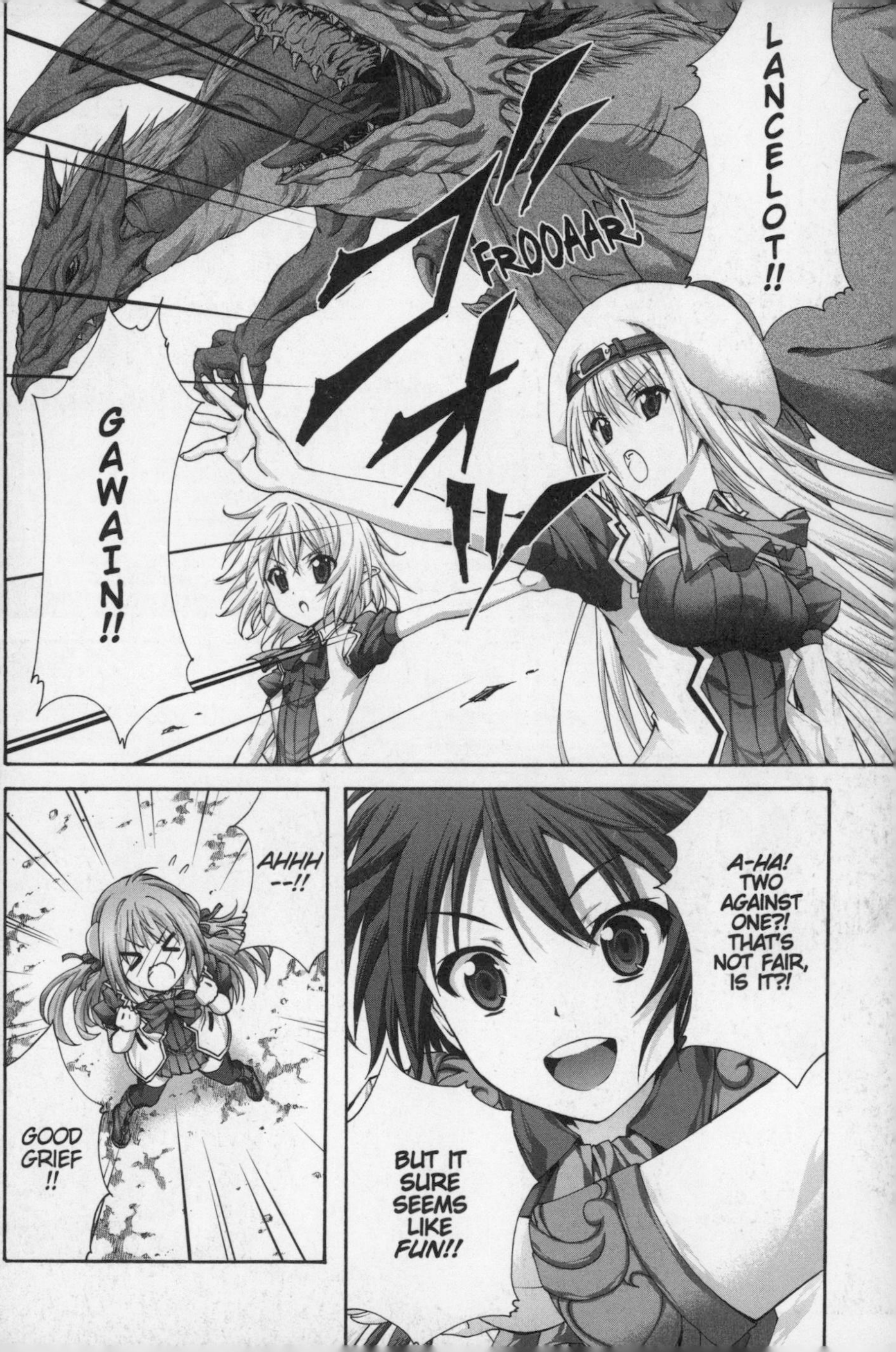
LANCELOT!!
FROOAAR!
GAWAIN!!
A-HA! TWO AGAINST ONE?! THAT'S NOT FAIR, IS IT?!
BUT IT SURE SEEMS LIKE FUN!!
AHHH--!!
GOOD GRIEF!!

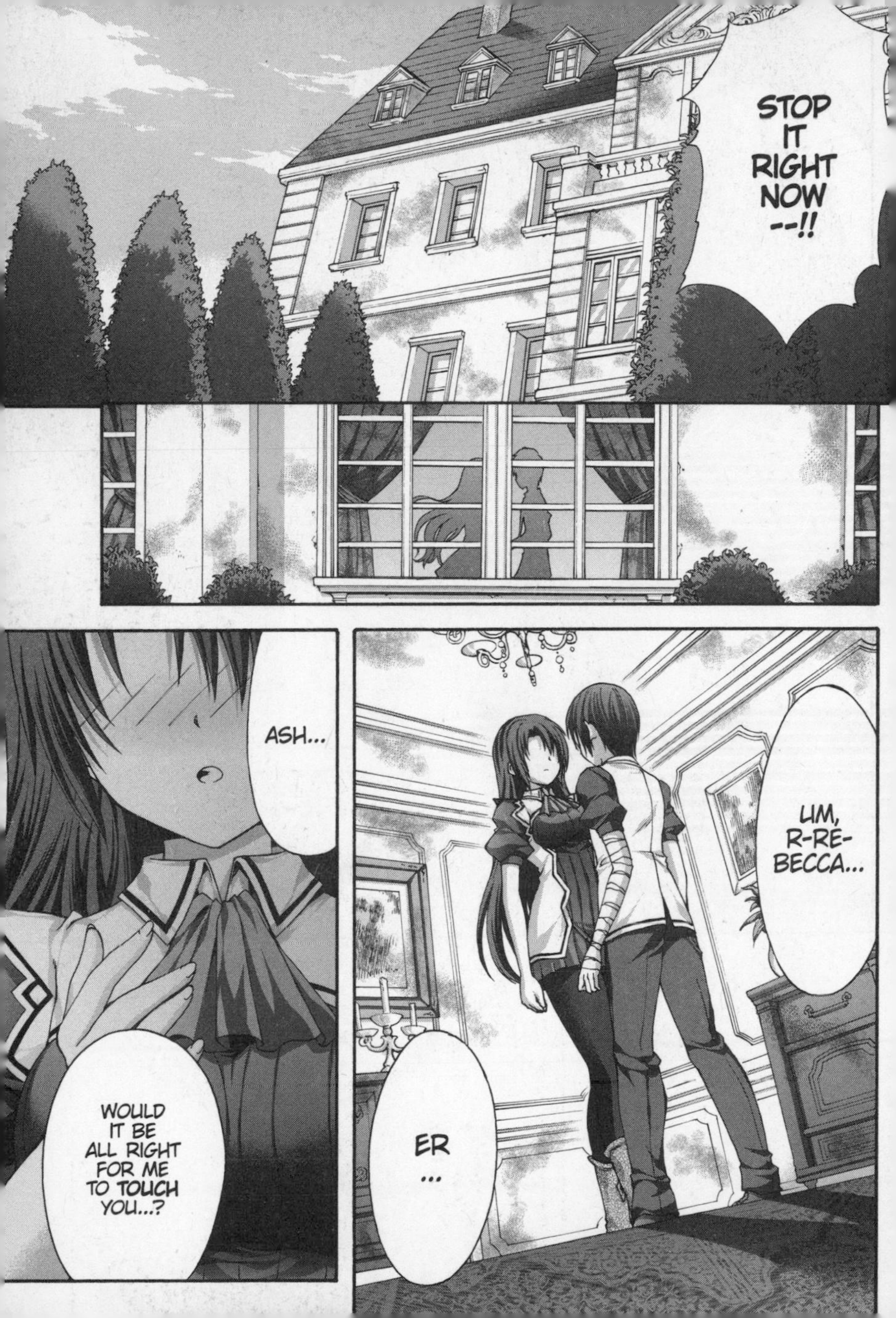
STOP IT RIGHT NOW --!!
UM, R-RE-BECCA...
ER ...
ASH...
WOULD IT BE ALL RIGHT FOR ME TO TOUCH YOU...?

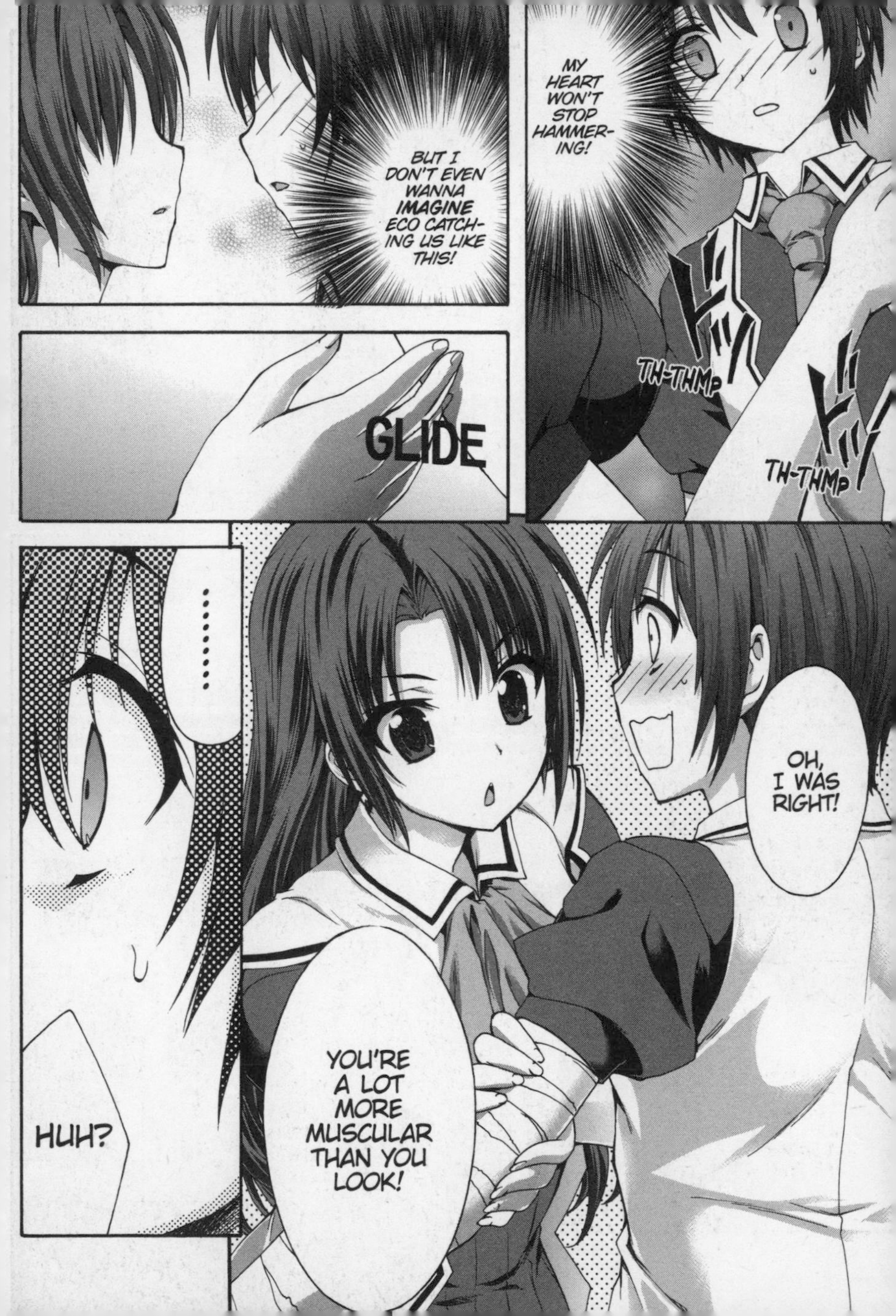
MY HEART WON'T STOP HAMMER-ING!
TH-THMP
TH-THMP
BUT I DON'T EVEN WANNA IMAGINE ECO CATCH-ING US LIKE THIS!
GLIDE
OH, I WAS RIGHT!
YOU'RE A LOT MORE MUSCULAR THAN YOU LOOK!
......
HUH?

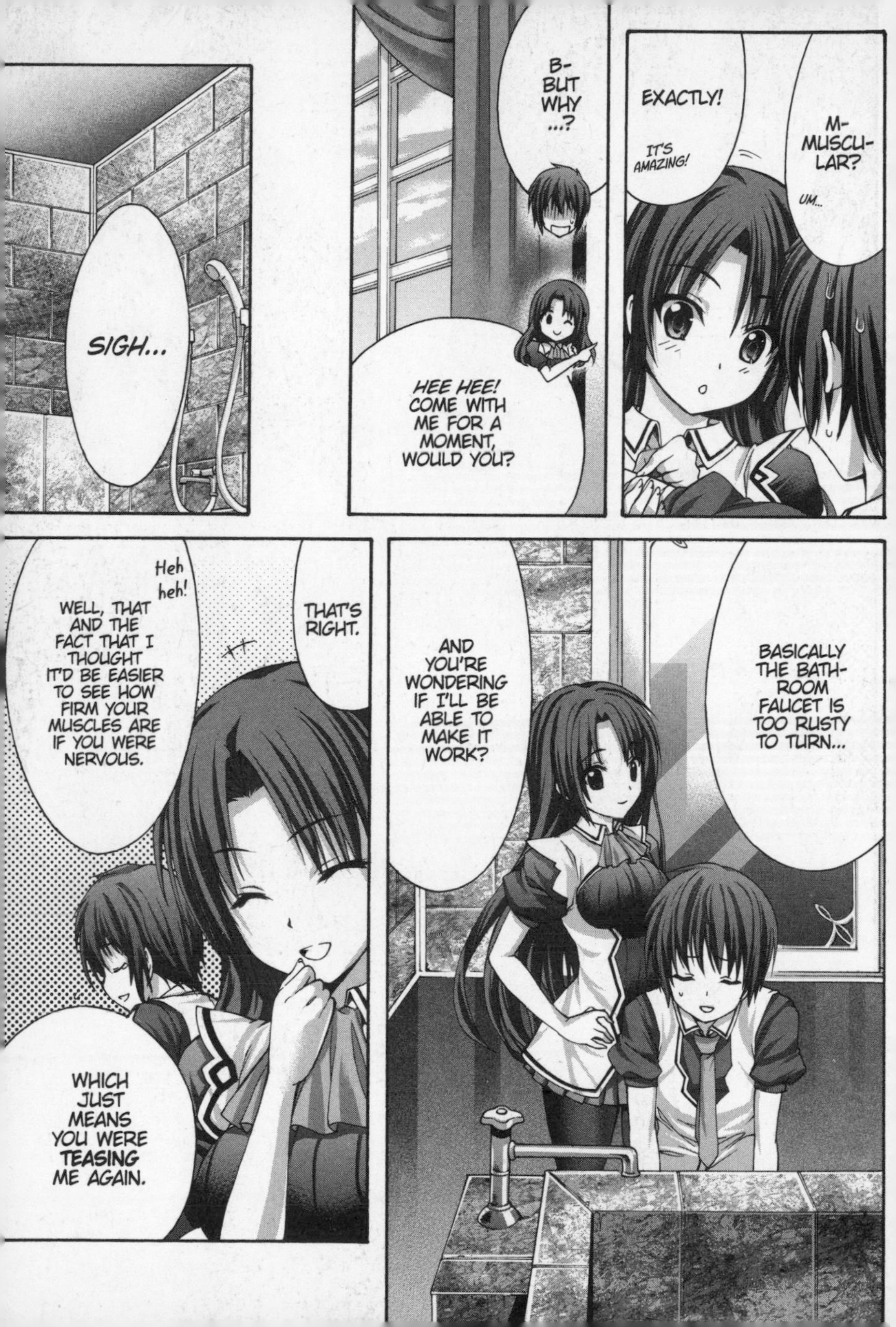
M-MUSCULAR?
UM...
EXACTLY!
IT'S AMAZING!
B-BUT WHY...?
HEE HEE! COME WITH ME FOR A MOMENT, WOULD YOU?
SIGH...
BASICALLY THE BATH-ROOM FAUCET IS TOO RUSTY TO TURN...
AND YOU'RE WONDERING IF I'LL BE ABLE TO MAKE IT WORK?
THAT'S RIGHT.
Heh heh!
WELL, THAT AND THE FACT THAT I THOUGHT IT'D BE EASIER TO SEE HOW FIRM YOUR MUSCLES ARE IF YOU WERE NERVOUS.
WHICH JUST MEANS YOU WERE TEASING ME AGAIN.

TH-THMP

TH-THMP

UH-HUH!

READY?

HERE, I'LL HELP TOO.

BETWEEN US WE SHOULD BE ABLE TO TURN IT.

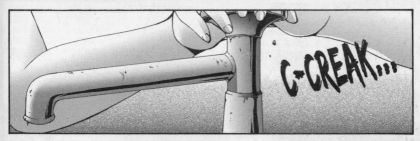

C~CREAK....

WE DID IT!!

YEAH!

TWIST

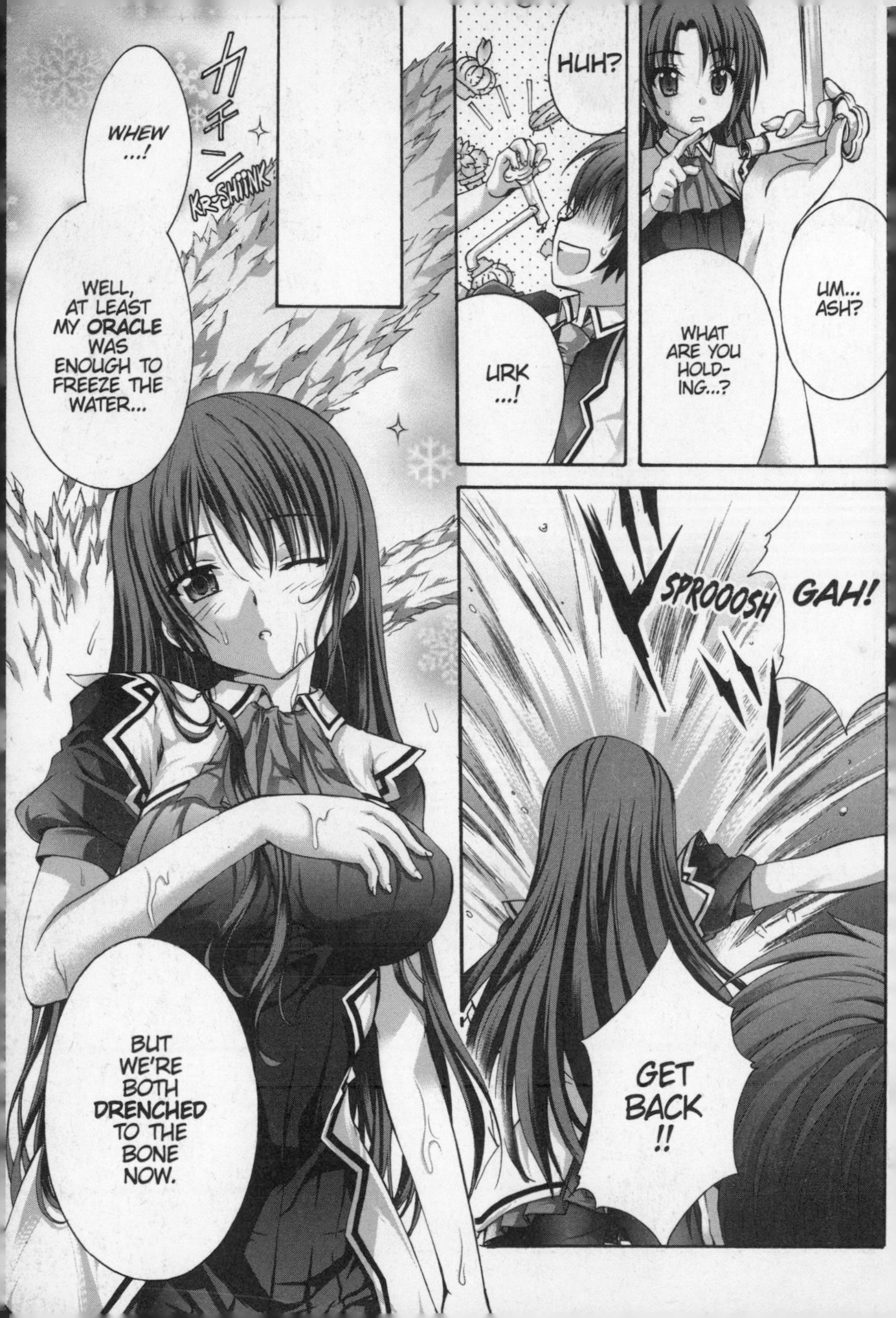
UM... ASH?
WHAT ARE YOU HOLDING...?
HUH?
URK ...!
SPROOOSH
GAH!
GET BACK !!
カチーン
KR-SHIIINK
WHEW ...!
WELL, AT LEAST MY ORACLE WAS ENOUGH TO FREEZE THE WATER...
BUT WE'RE BOTH DRENCHED TO THE BONE NOW.

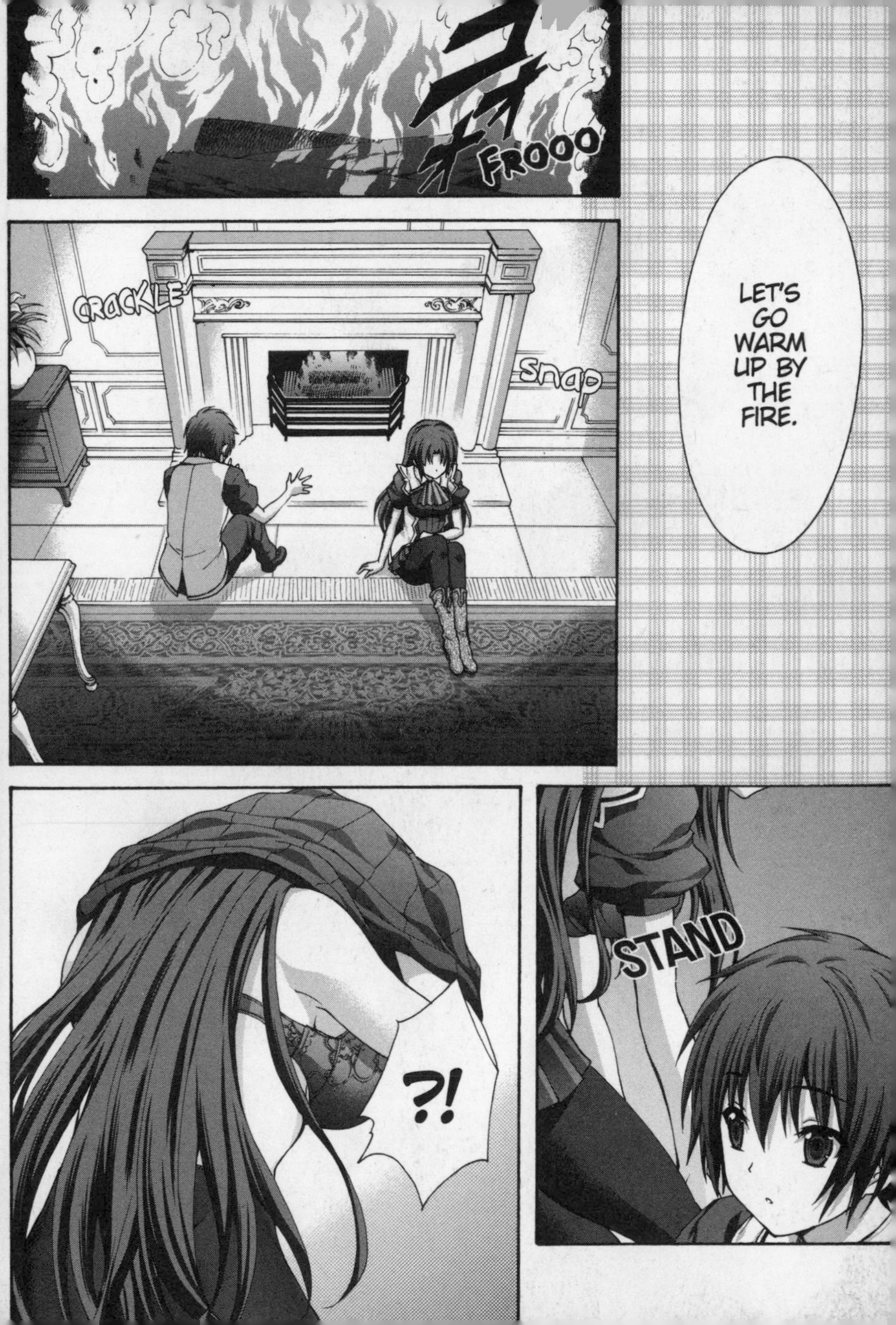
LET'S GO WARM UP BY THE FIRE.
FROOO
CRACKLE
snap
STAND
?!

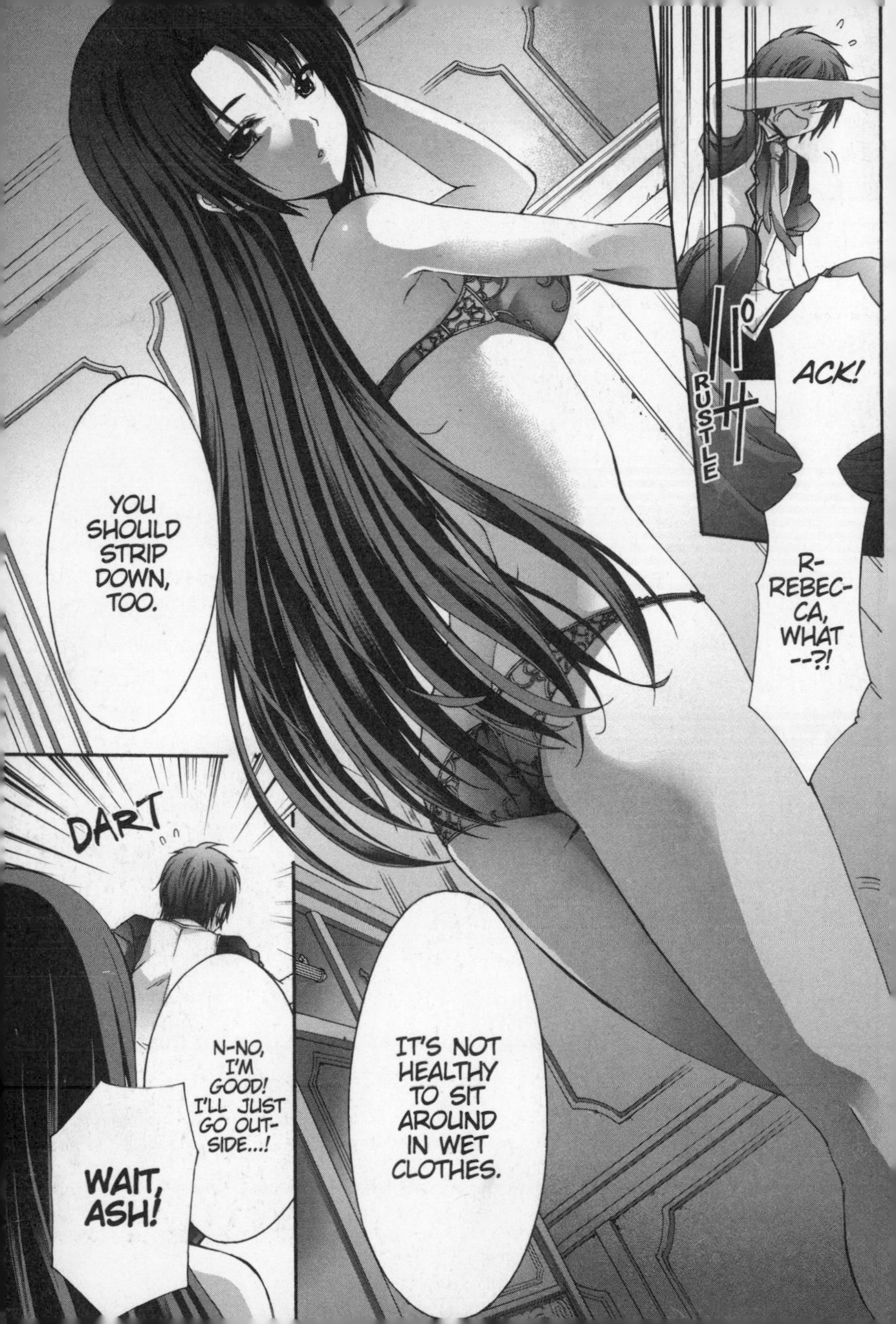
ACK!
RUSTLE
R-REBECCA, WHAT--?!
YOU SHOULD STRIP DOWN, TOO.
IT'S NOT HEALTHY TO SIT AROUND IN WET CLOTHES.
DART
N-NO, I'M GOOD! I'LL JUST GO OUT-SIDE...!
WAIT, ASH!

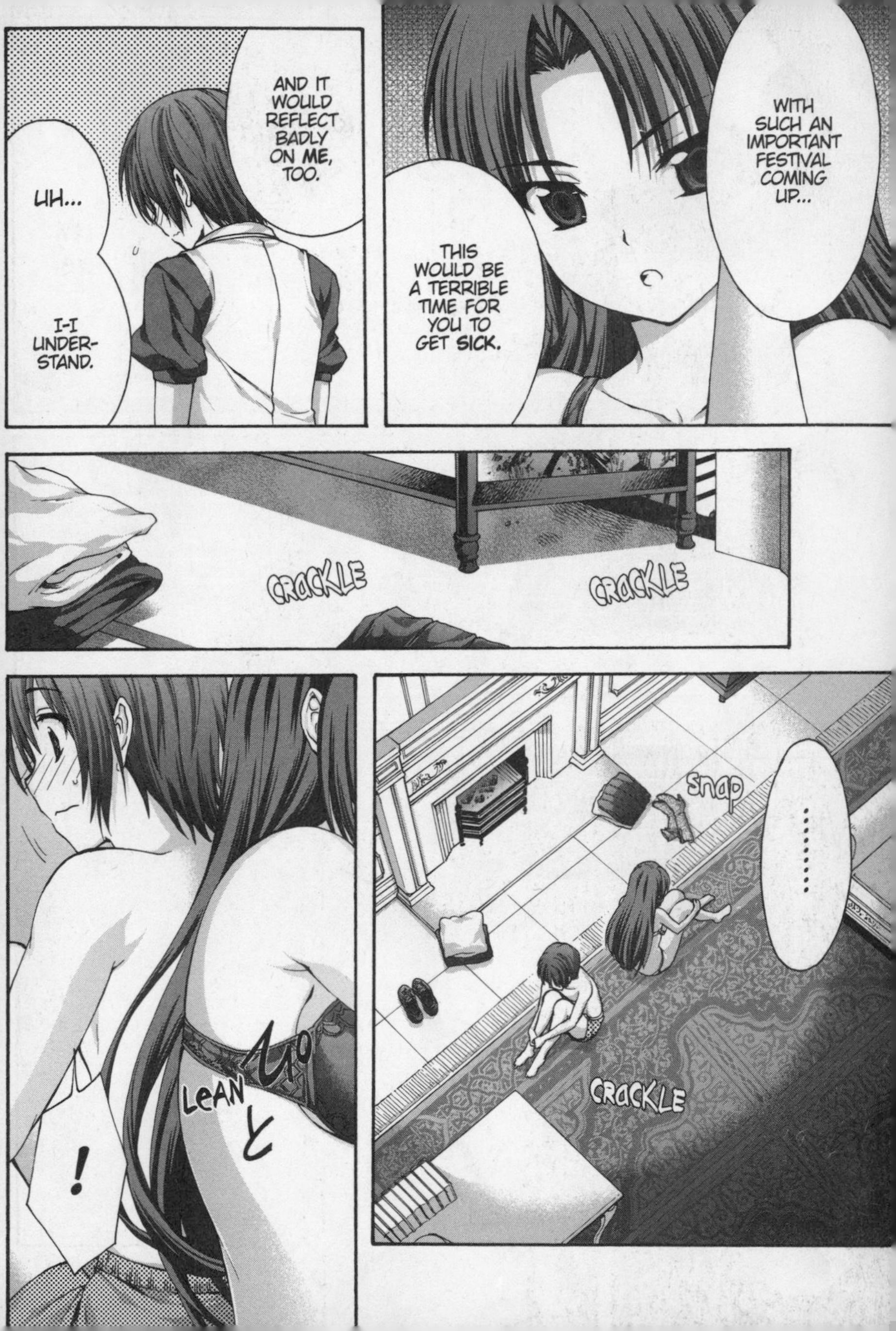
WITH SUCH AN IMPORTANT FESTIVAL COMING UP...
THIS WOULD BE A TERRIBLE TIME FOR YOU TO GET SICK.
AND IT WOULD REFLECT BADLY ON ME, TOO.
UH...
I-I UNDER-STAND.
CRACKLE
CRACKLE
......
Snap
CRACKLE
LeAN
と
!

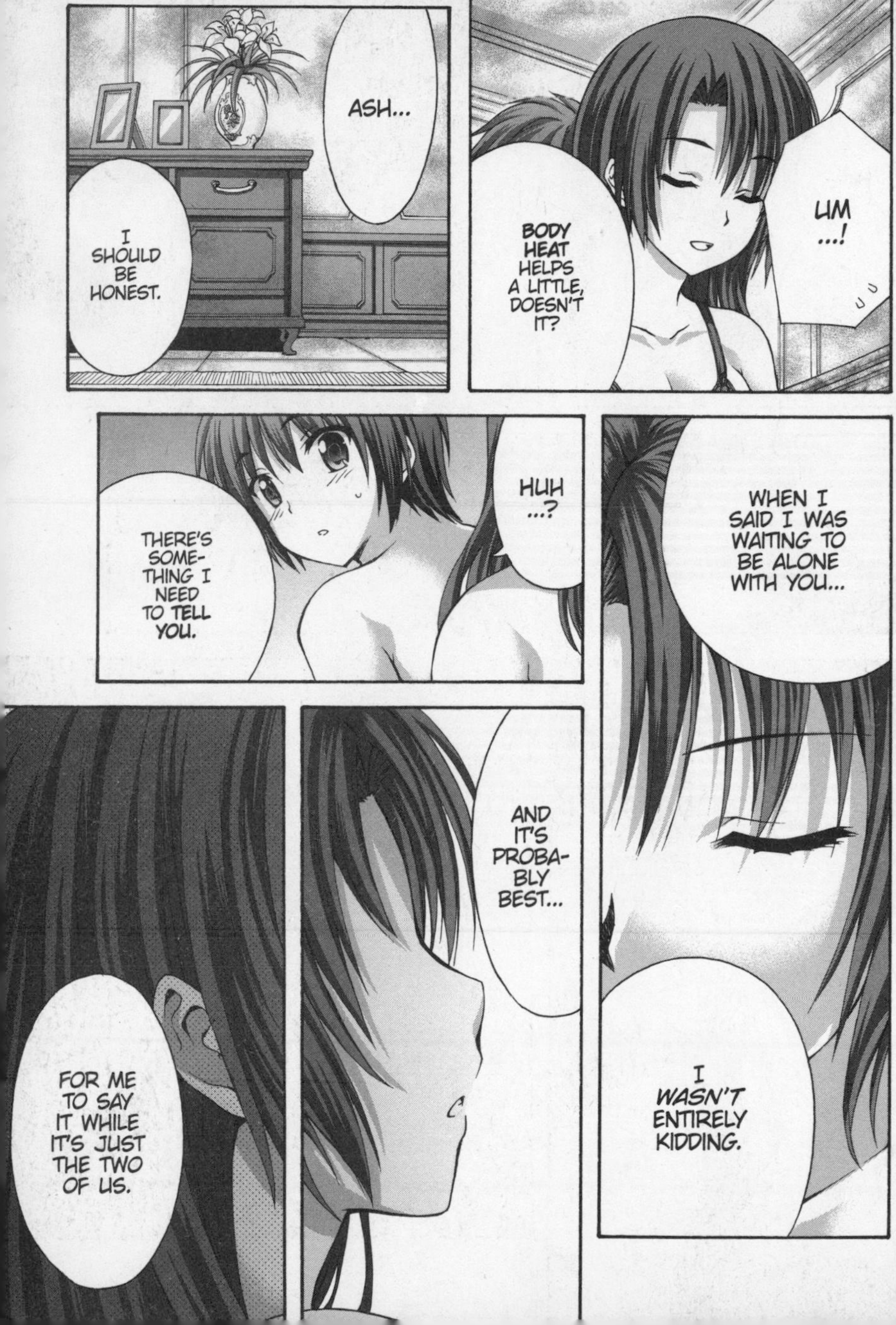
BODY HEAT HELPS A LITTLE, DOESN'T IT?
UM ...!
ASH...
I SHOULD BE HONEST.
WHEN I SAID I WAS WAITING TO BE ALONE WITH YOU...
I *WASN'T* ENTIRELY KIDDING.
HUH ...?
THERE'S SOMETHING I NEED TO TELL YOU.
AND IT'S PROBABLY BEST...
FOR ME TO SAY IT WHILE IT'S JUST THE TWO OF US.

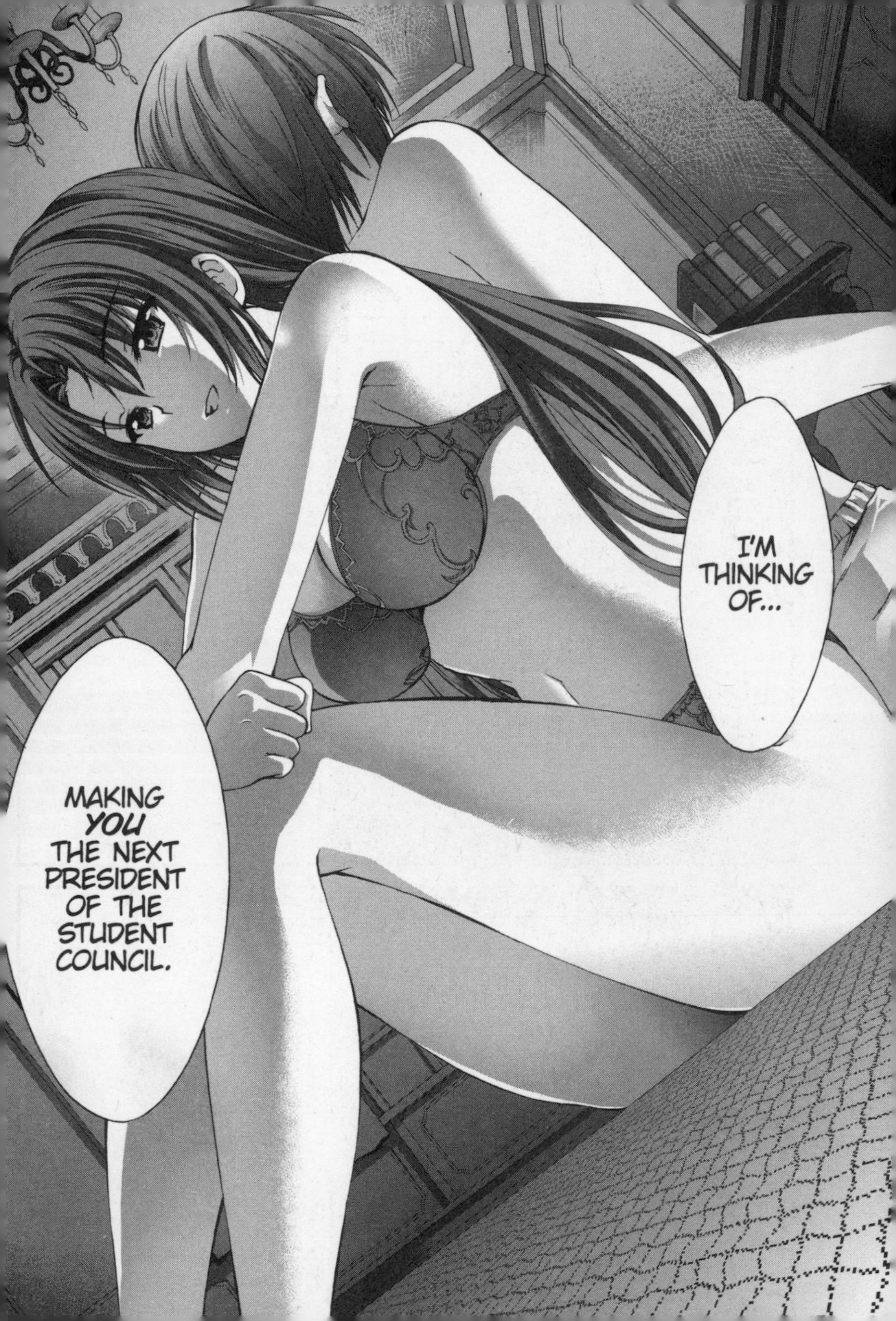
I'M THINKING OF...
MAKING *YOU* THE NEXT PRESIDENT OF THE STUDENT COUNCIL.

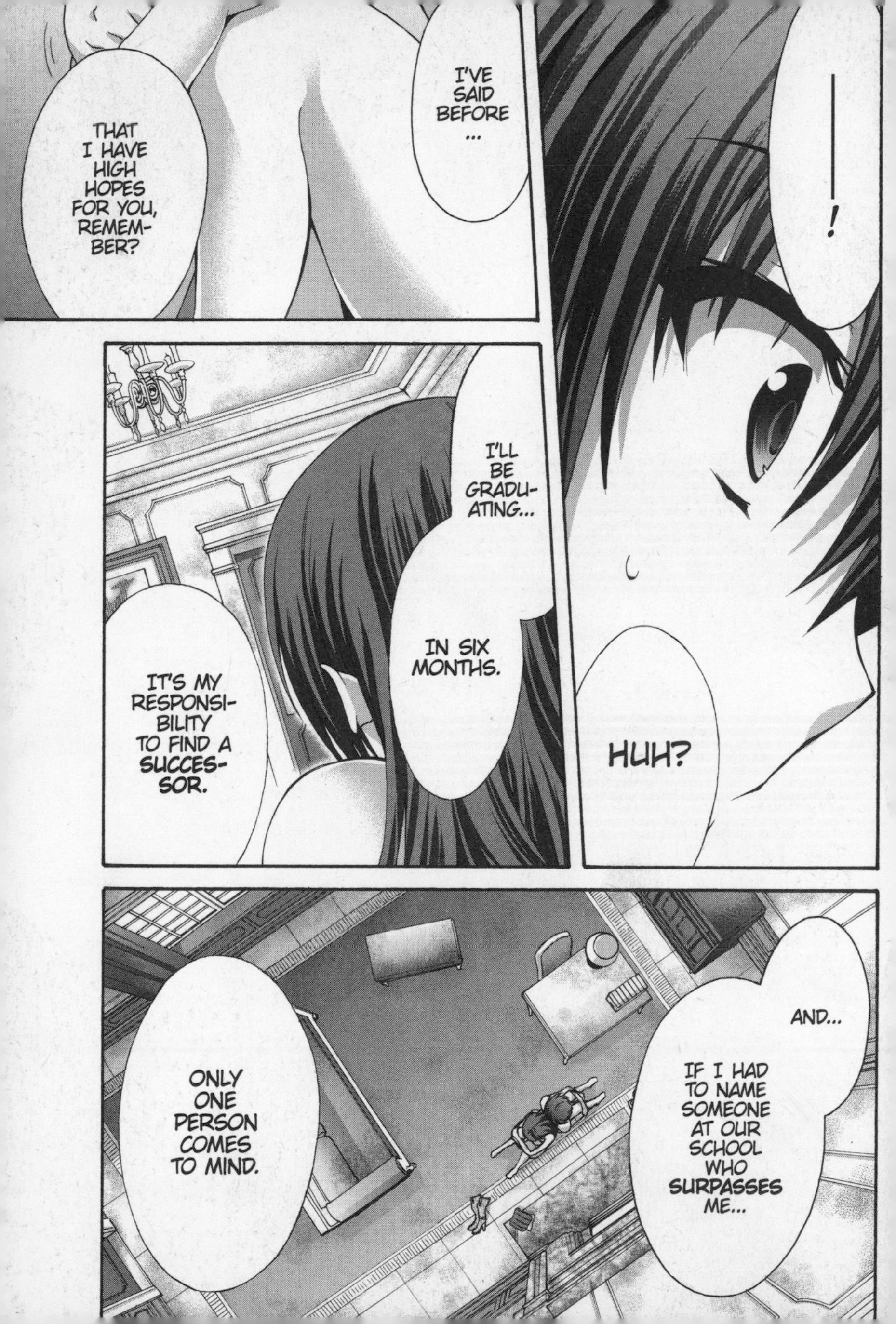
—!
HUH?
I'VE SAID BEFORE...
THAT I HAVE HIGH HOPES FOR YOU, REMEMBER?
I'LL BE GRADUATING...
IN SIX MONTHS.
IT'S MY RESPONSIBILITY TO FIND A SUCCESSOR.
AND...
IF I HAD TO NAME SOMEONE AT OUR SCHOOL WHO SURPASSES ME...
ONLY ONE PERSON COMES TO MIND.

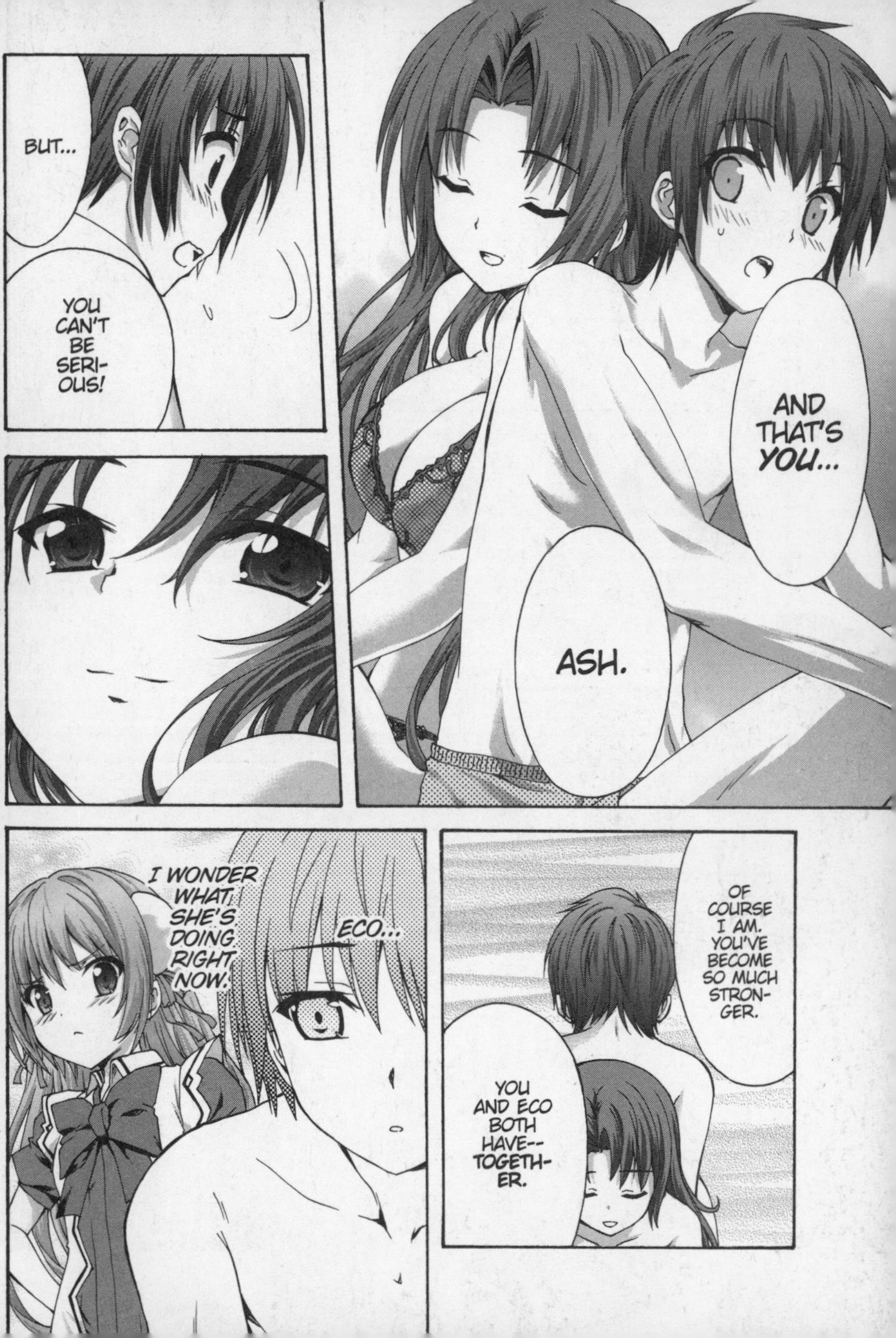
AND THAT'S YOU...
ASH.
BUT...
YOU CAN'T BE SERIOUS!
OF COURSE I AM. YOU'VE BECOME SO MUCH STRONGER.
YOU AND ECO BOTH HAVE--TOGETHER.
ECO...
I WONDER WHAT SHE'S DOING RIGHT NOW.

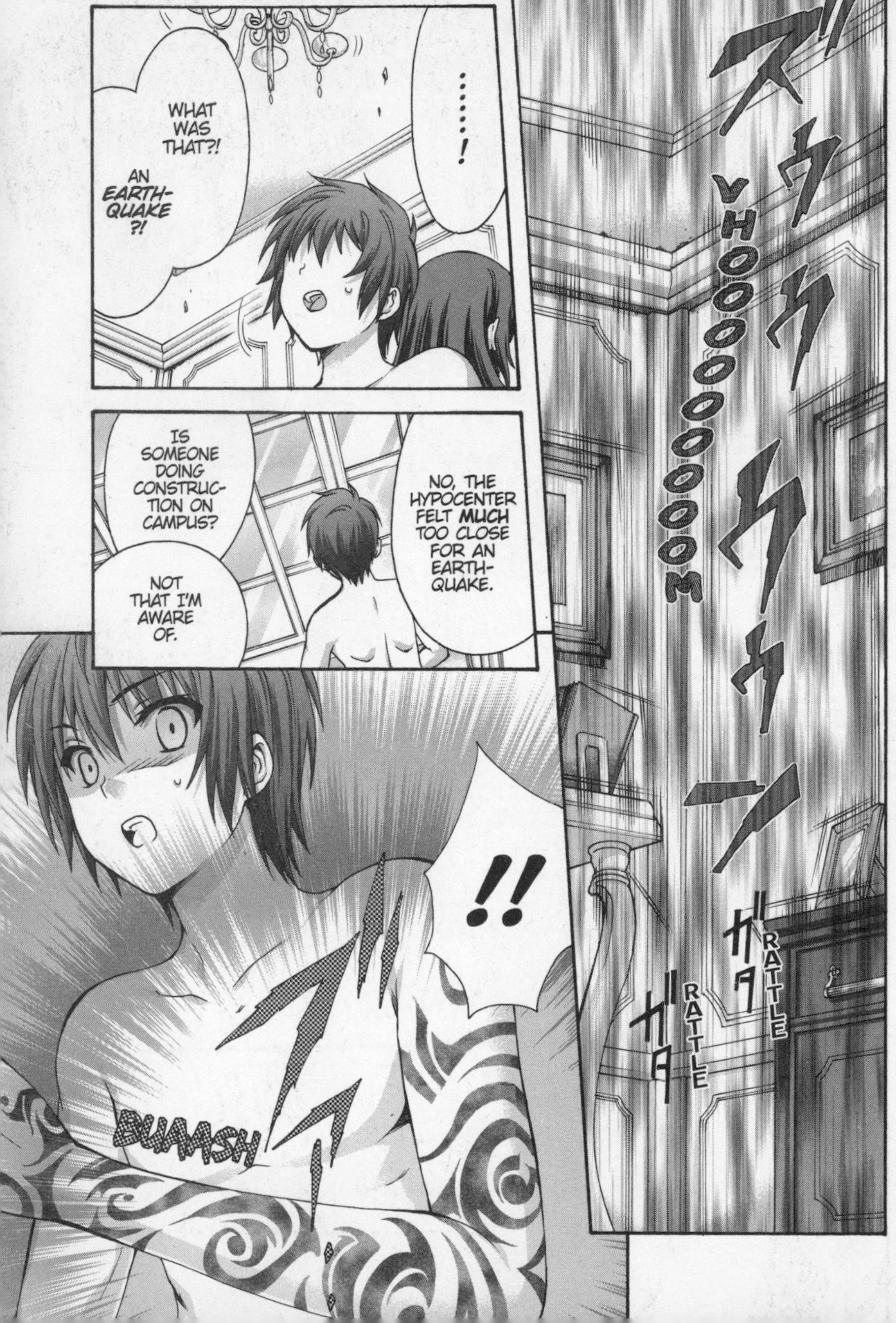
VHOOOOOOOOOOOOM
RATTLE
RATTLE
......!
WHAT WAS THAT?!
AN EARTH-QUAKE?!
NO, THE HYPOCENTER FELT MUCH TOO CLOSE FOR AN EARTH-QUAKE.
IS SOMEONE DOING CONSTRUC-TION ON CAMPUS?
NOT THAT I'M AWARE OF.
!!
BUAASH

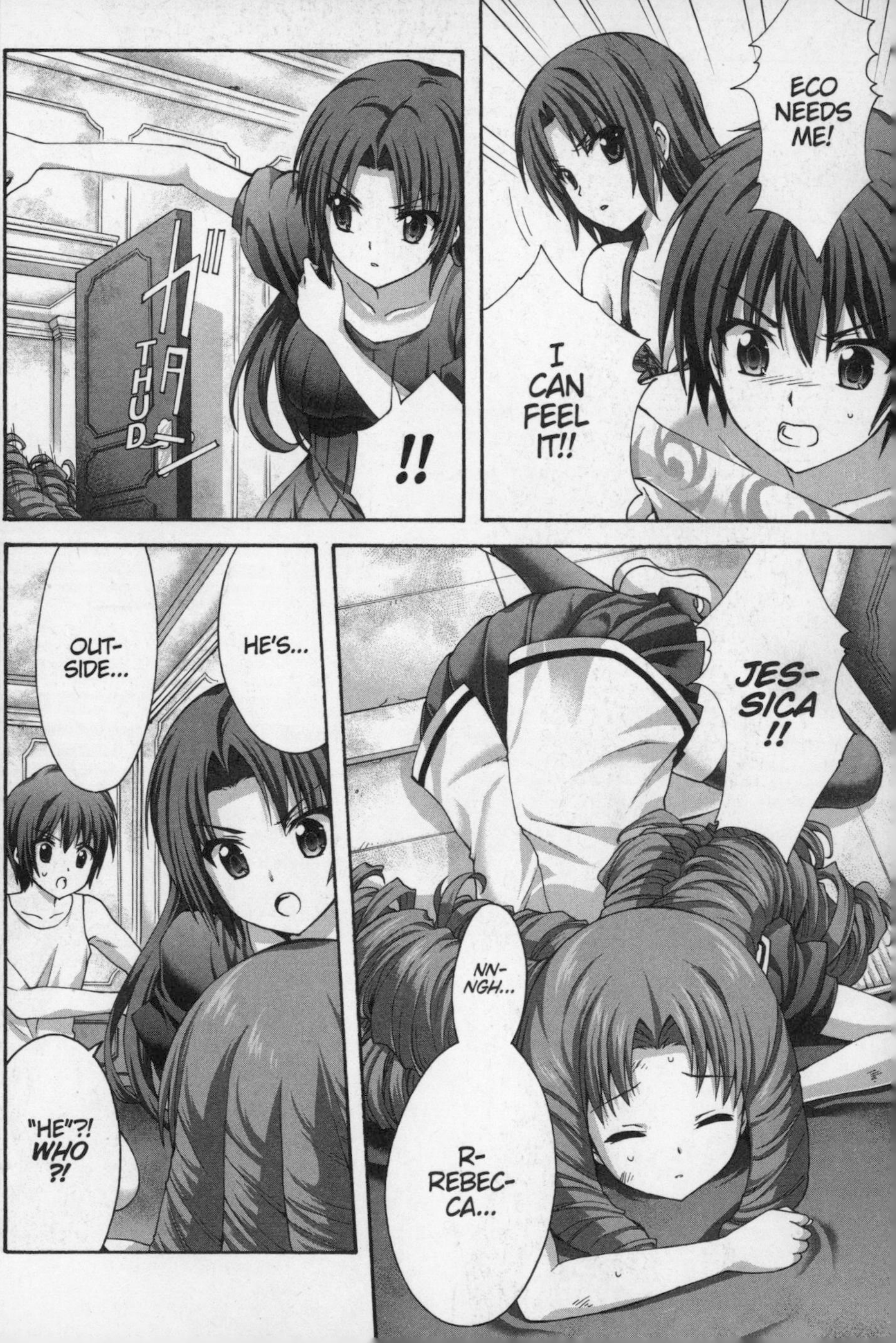
ECO NEEDS ME!
I CAN FEEL IT!!
THUD
!!
JES-SICA!!
NN-NGH...
R-REBEC-CA...
HE'S...
OUT-SIDE...
"HE"?! WHO?!

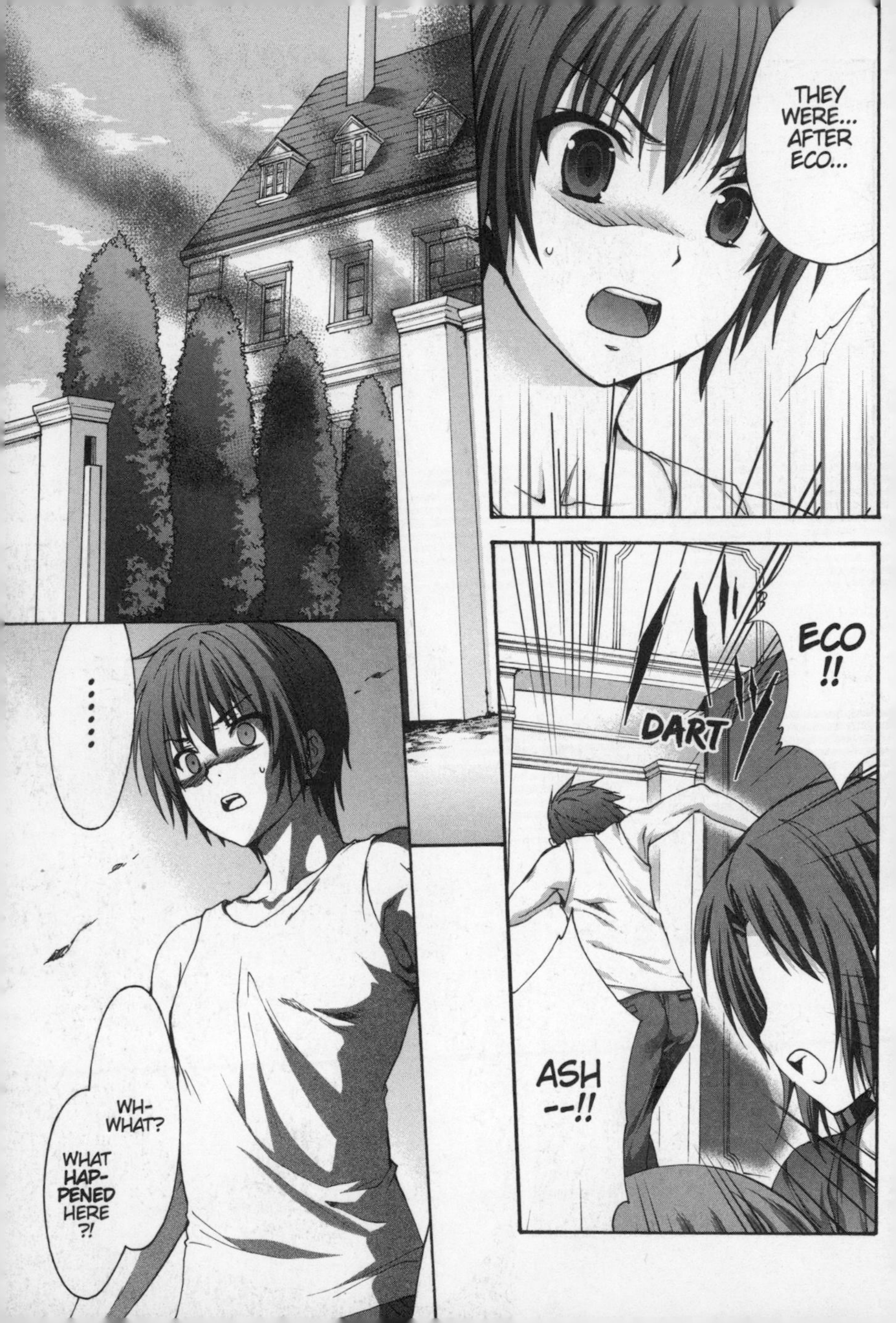
THEY WERE... AFTER ECO...
ECO!!
DART
ASH--!!
......
WH- WHAT?
WHAT HAP-PENED HERE?!

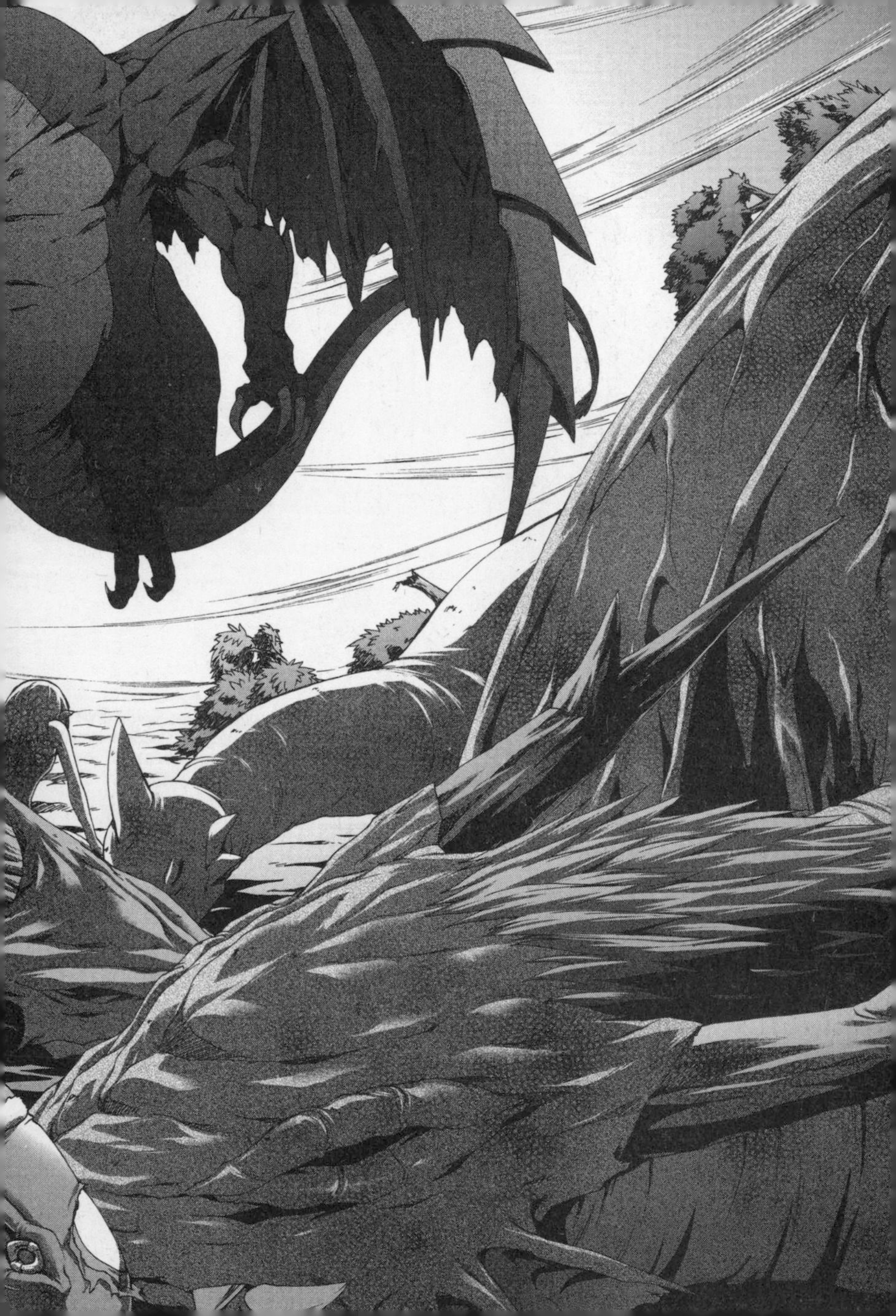

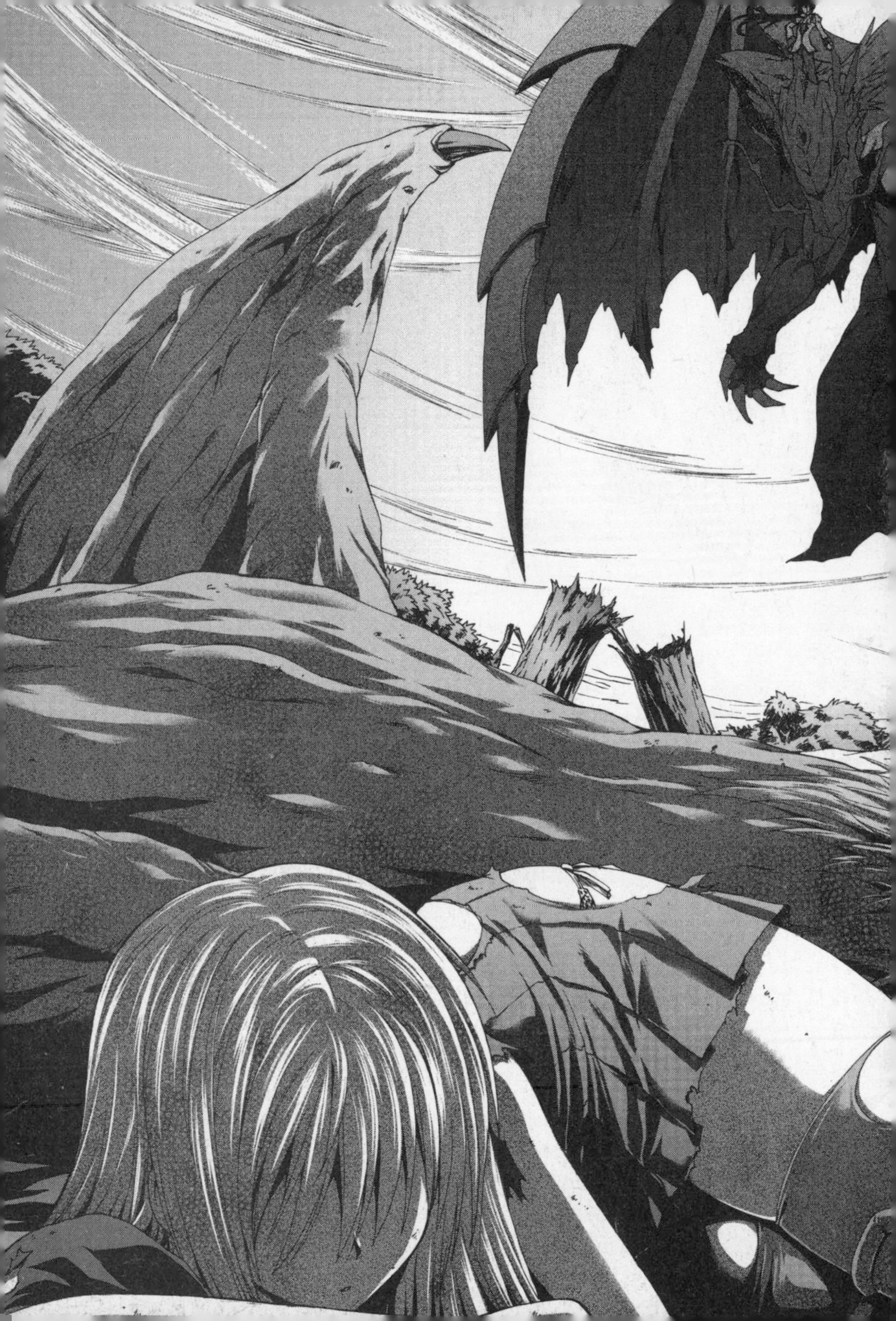

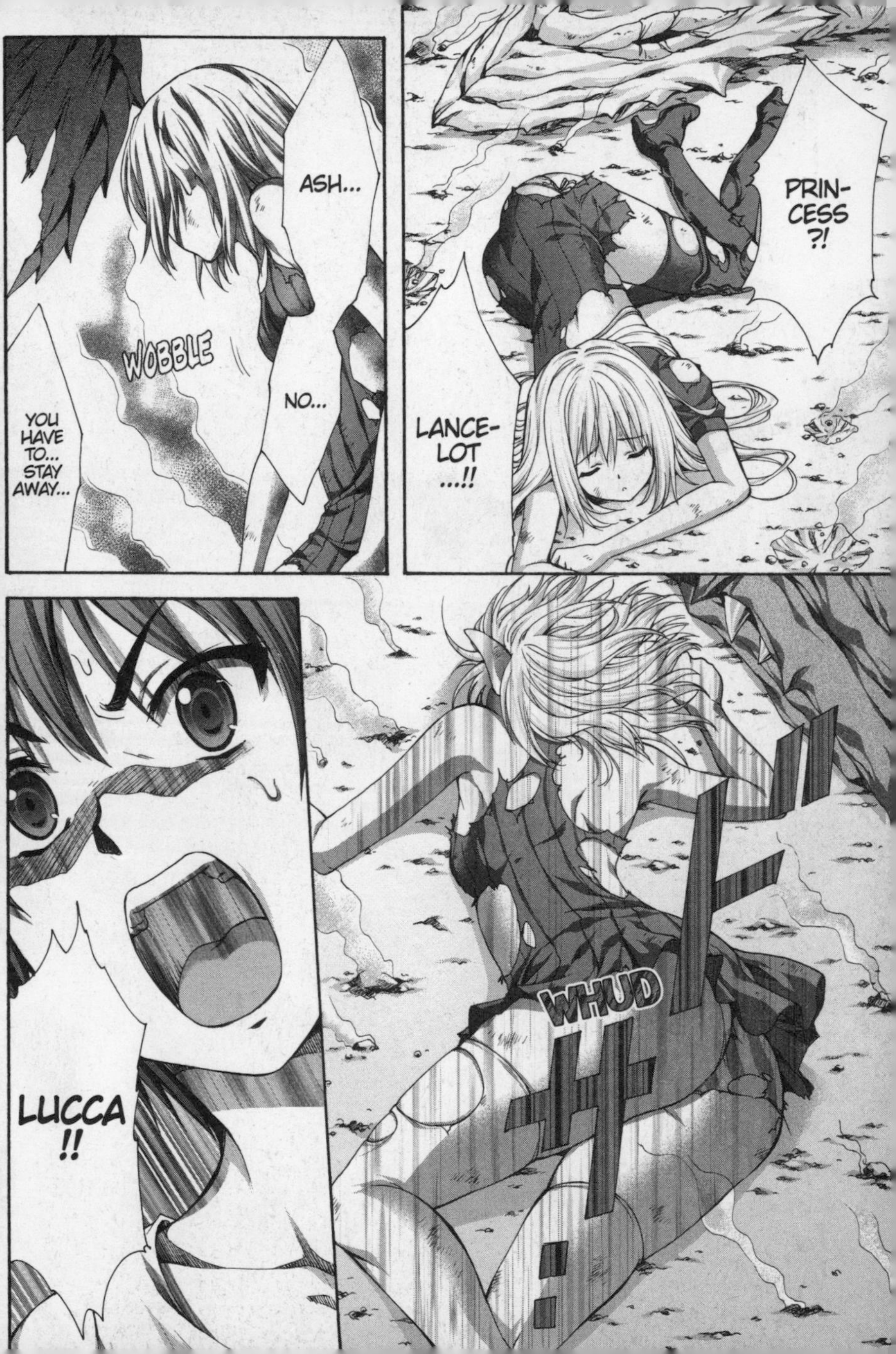

PRIN-CESS?!
LANCE-LOT...!!
ASH...
NO...
WOBBLE
YOU HAVE TO... STAY AWAY...
WHUD
LUCCA!!

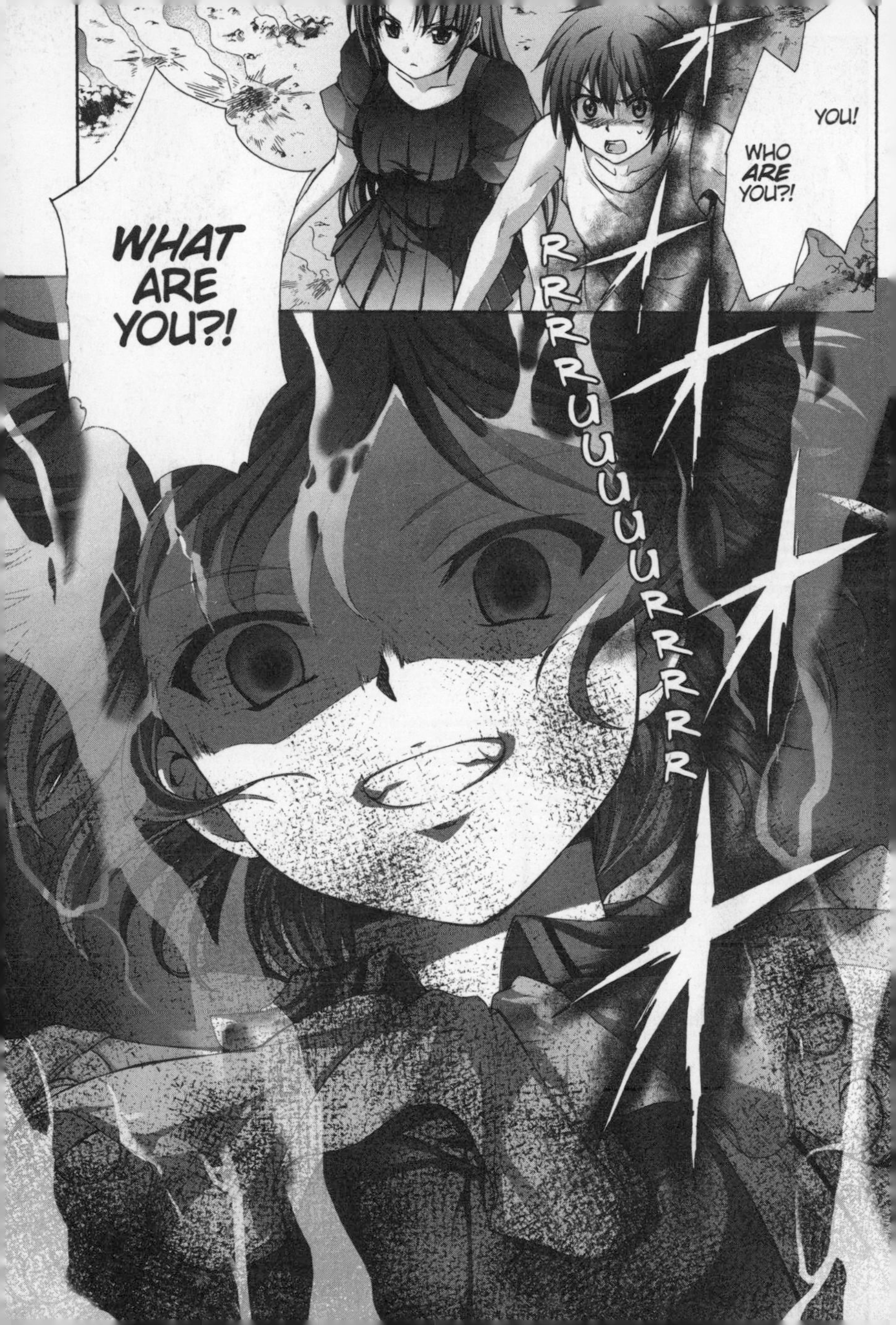
YOU!
WHO ARE YOU?!
WHAT ARE YOU?!
RRRRUUUUURRRRR

DRAGONAR
ACADEMY

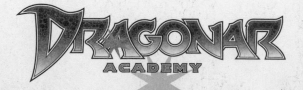

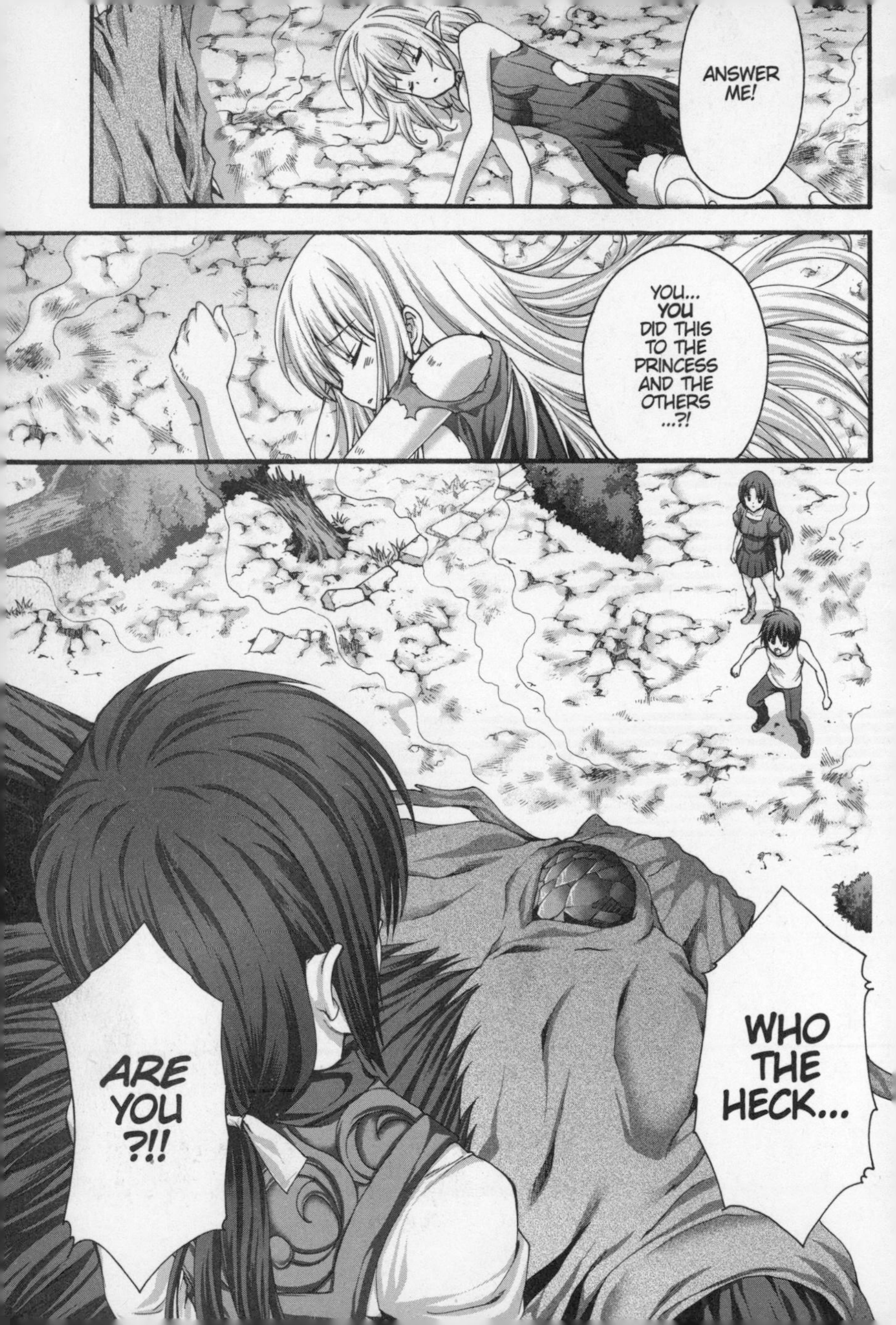
ANSWER ME!
YOU... YOU DID THIS TO THE PRINCESS AND THE OTHERS ...?!
WHO THE HECK...
ARE YOU ?!!

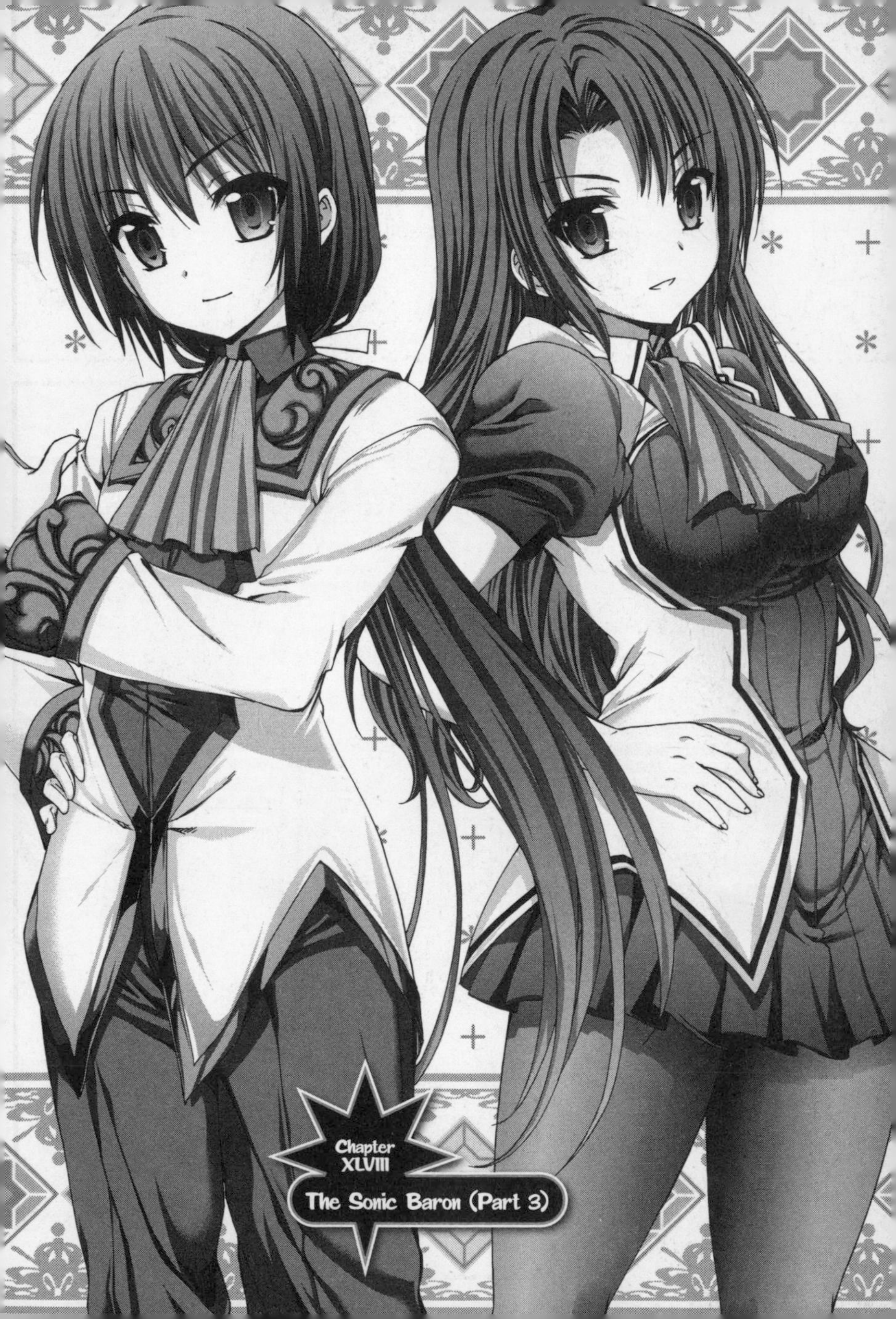
Chapter
XLVIII
The Sonic Baron (Part 3)

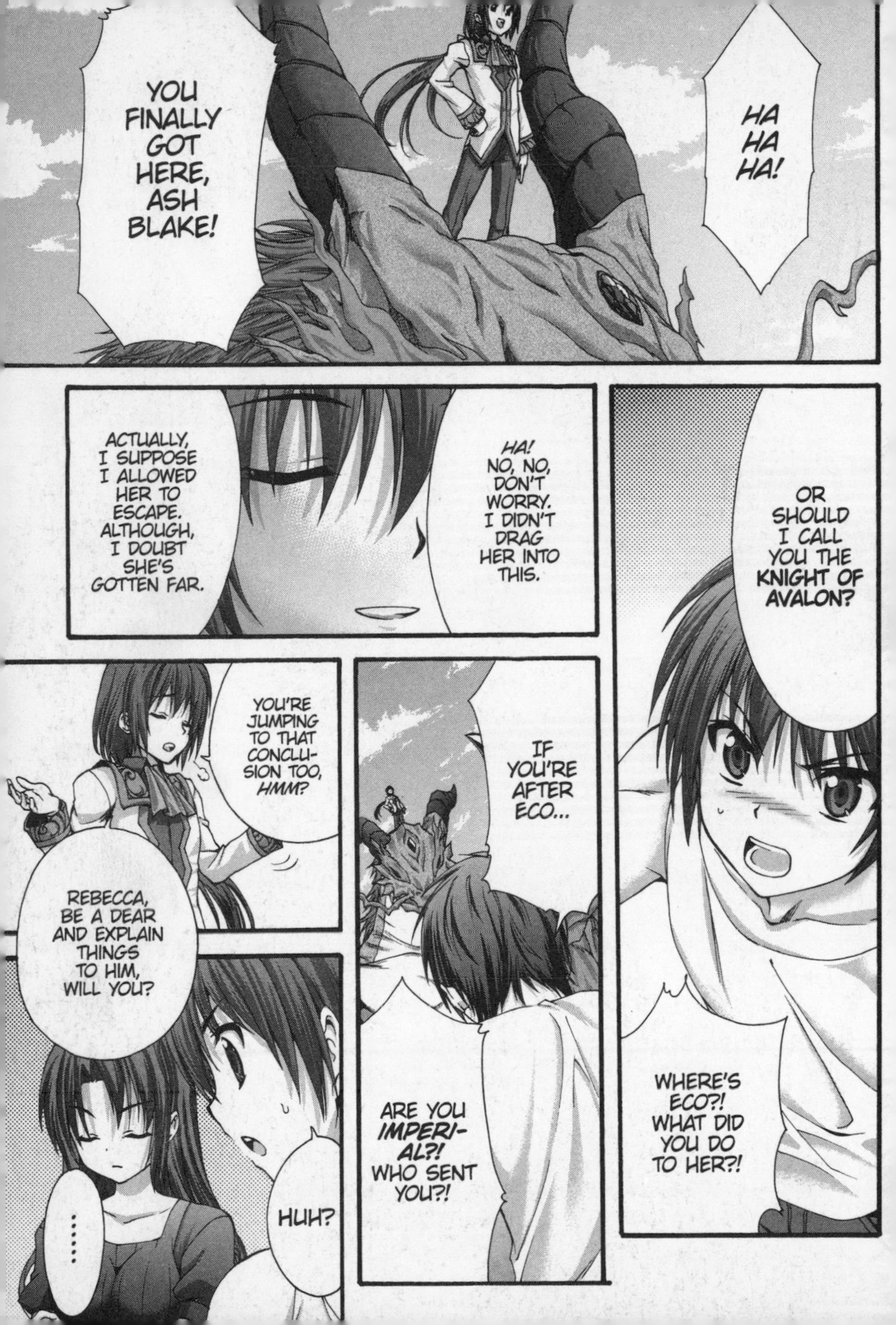
HA HA HA!
YOU FINALLY GOT HERE, ASH BLAKE!
OR SHOULD I CALL YOU THE KNIGHT OF AVALON?
WHERE'S ECO?! WHAT DID YOU DO TO HER?!
HA! NO, NO, DON'T WORRY. I DIDN'T DRAG HER INTO THIS.
ACTUALLY, I SUPPOSE I ALLOWED HER TO ESCAPE. ALTHOUGH, I DOUBT SHE'S GOTTEN FAR.
IF YOU'RE AFTER ECO...
ARE YOU IMPERIAL?! WHO SENT YOU?!
YOU'RE JUMPING TO THAT CONCLUSION TOO, HMM?
REBECCA, BE A DEAR AND EXPLAIN THINGS TO HIM, WILL YOU?
HUH?
......

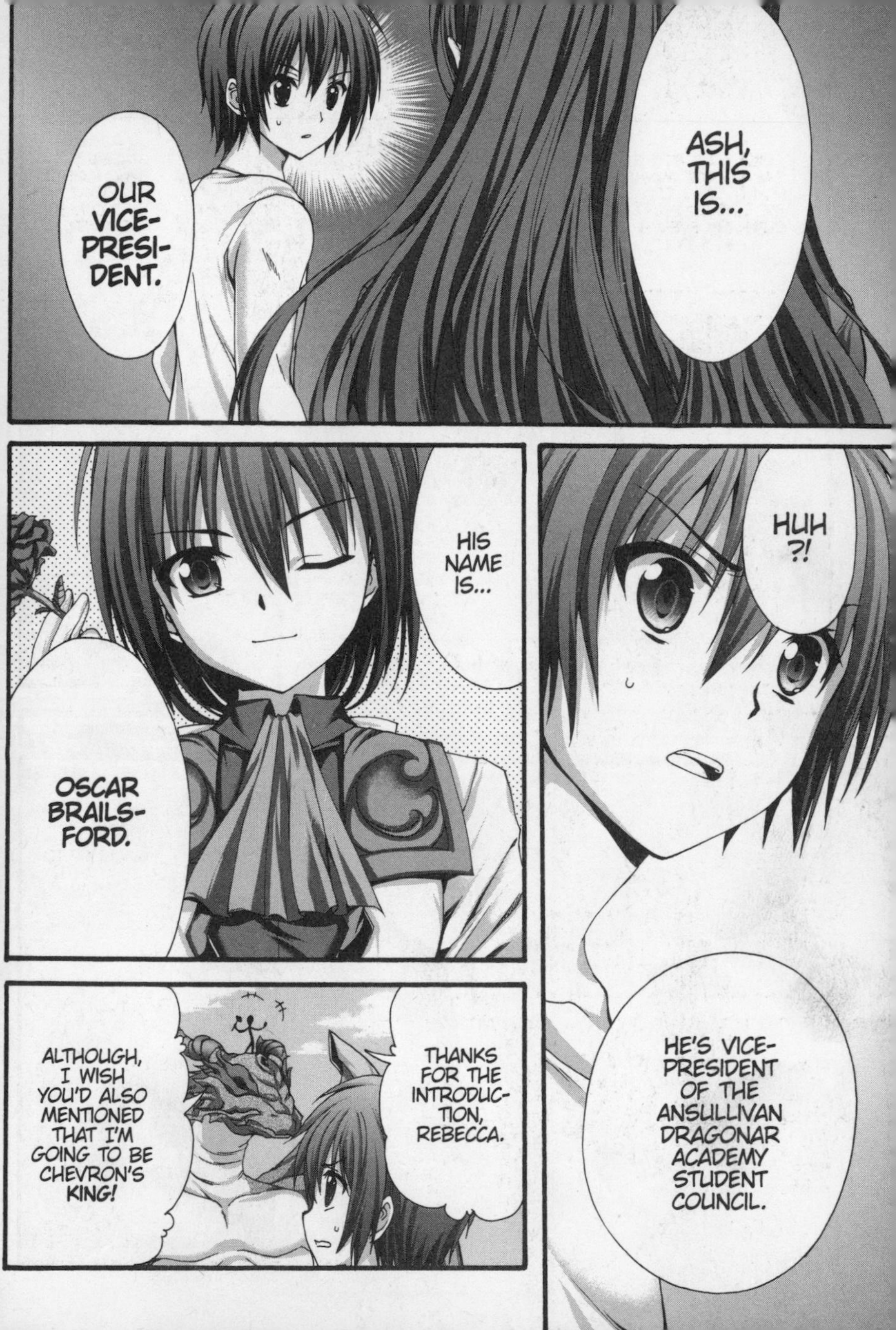
ASH, THIS IS...
OUR VICE-PRESIDENT.
HUH?!
HE'S VICE-PRESIDENT OF THE ANSULLIVAN DRAGONAR ACADEMY STUDENT COUNCIL.
HIS NAME IS...
OSCAR BRAILSFORD.
THANKS FOR THE INTRODUCTION, REBECCA.
ALTHOUGH, I WISH YOU'D ALSO MENTIONED THAT I'M GOING TO BE CHEVRON'S KING!

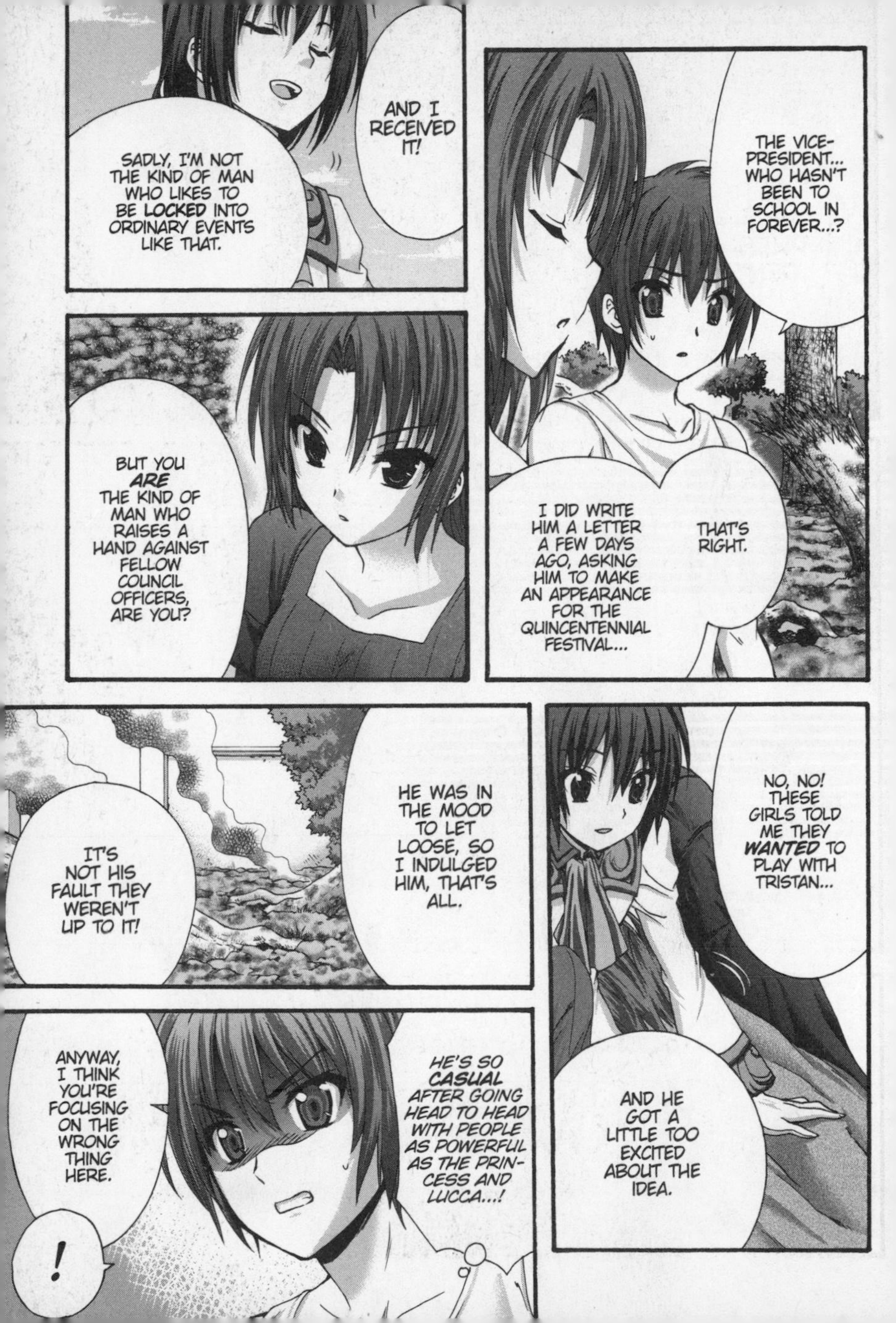
THE VICE-PRESIDENT... WHO HASN'T BEEN TO SCHOOL IN FOREVER...?
THAT'S RIGHT.
I DID WRITE HIM A LETTER A FEW DAYS AGO, ASKING HIM TO MAKE AN APPEARANCE FOR THE QUINCENTENNIAL FESTIVAL...
AND I RECEIVED IT!
SADLY, I'M NOT THE KIND OF MAN WHO LIKES TO BE **LOCKED** INTO ORDINARY EVENTS LIKE THAT.
BUT YOU ***ARE*** THE KIND OF MAN WHO RAISES A HAND AGAINST FELLOW COUNCIL OFFICERS, ARE YOU?
NO, NO! THESE GIRLS TOLD ME THEY ***WANTED*** TO PLAY WITH TRISTAN...
AND HE GOT A LITTLE TOO EXCITED ABOUT THE IDEA.
HE WAS IN THE MOOD TO LET LOOSE, SO I INDULGED HIM, THAT'S ALL.
IT'S NOT HIS FAULT THEY WEREN'T UP TO IT!
*HE'S SO **CASUAL** AFTER GOING HEAD TO HEAD WITH PEOPLE AS POWERFUL AS THE PRIN-CESS AND LUCCA...!*
ANYWAY, I THINK YOU'RE FOCUSING ON THE WRONG THING HERE.
!

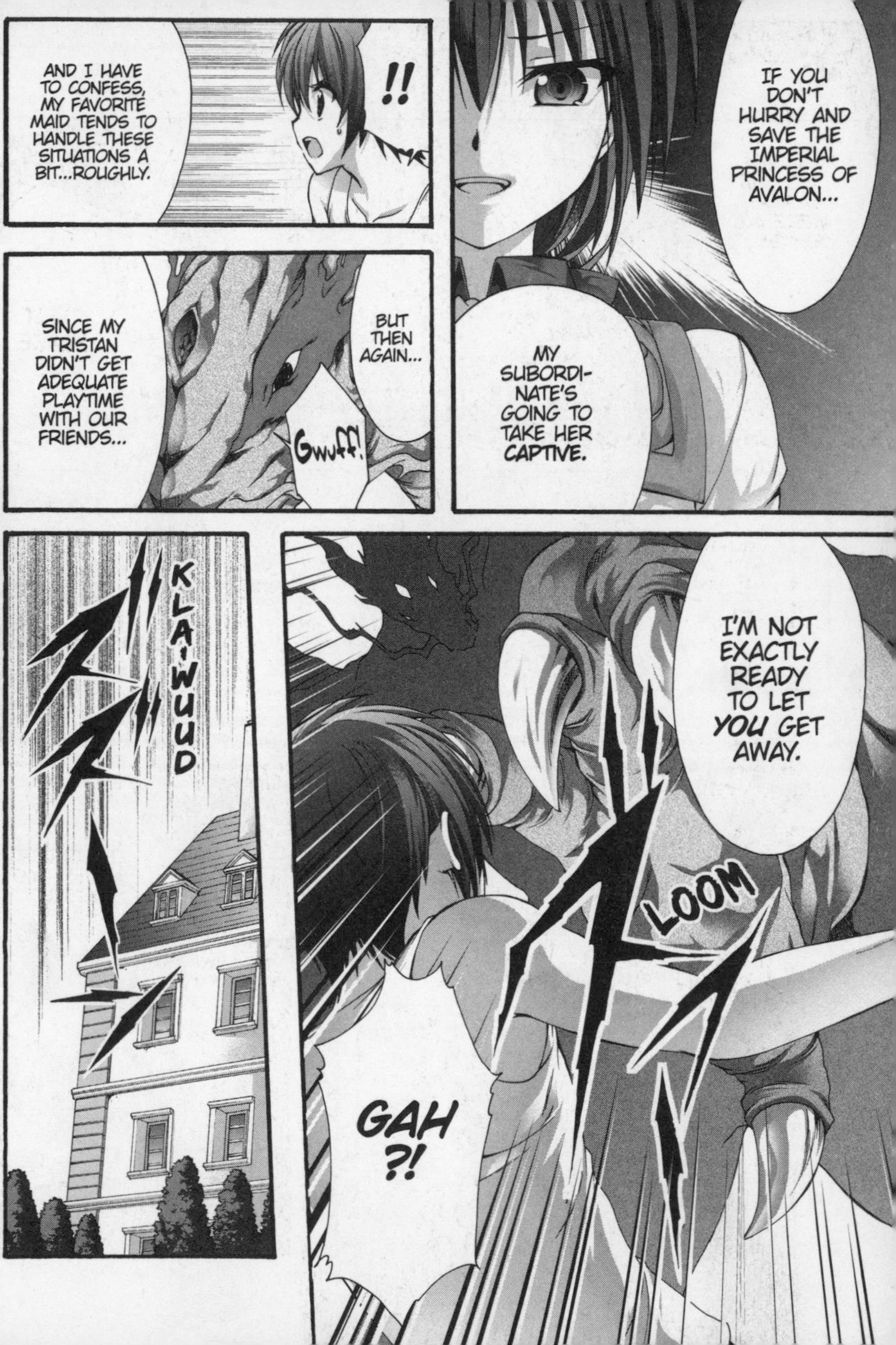
IF YOU DON'T HURRY AND SAVE THE IMPERIAL PRINCESS OF AVALON...
MY SUBORDINATE'S GOING TO TAKE HER CAPTIVE.
!!
AND I HAVE TO CONFESS, MY FAVORITE MAID TENDS TO HANDLE THESE SITUATIONS A BIT...ROUGHLY.
BUT THEN AGAIN...
Gwuff!
SINCE MY TRISTAN DIDN'T GET ADEQUATE PLAYTIME WITH OUR FRIENDS...
I'M NOT EXACTLY READY TO LET YOU GET AWAY.
LOOM
GAH ?!
KLAWUUUD

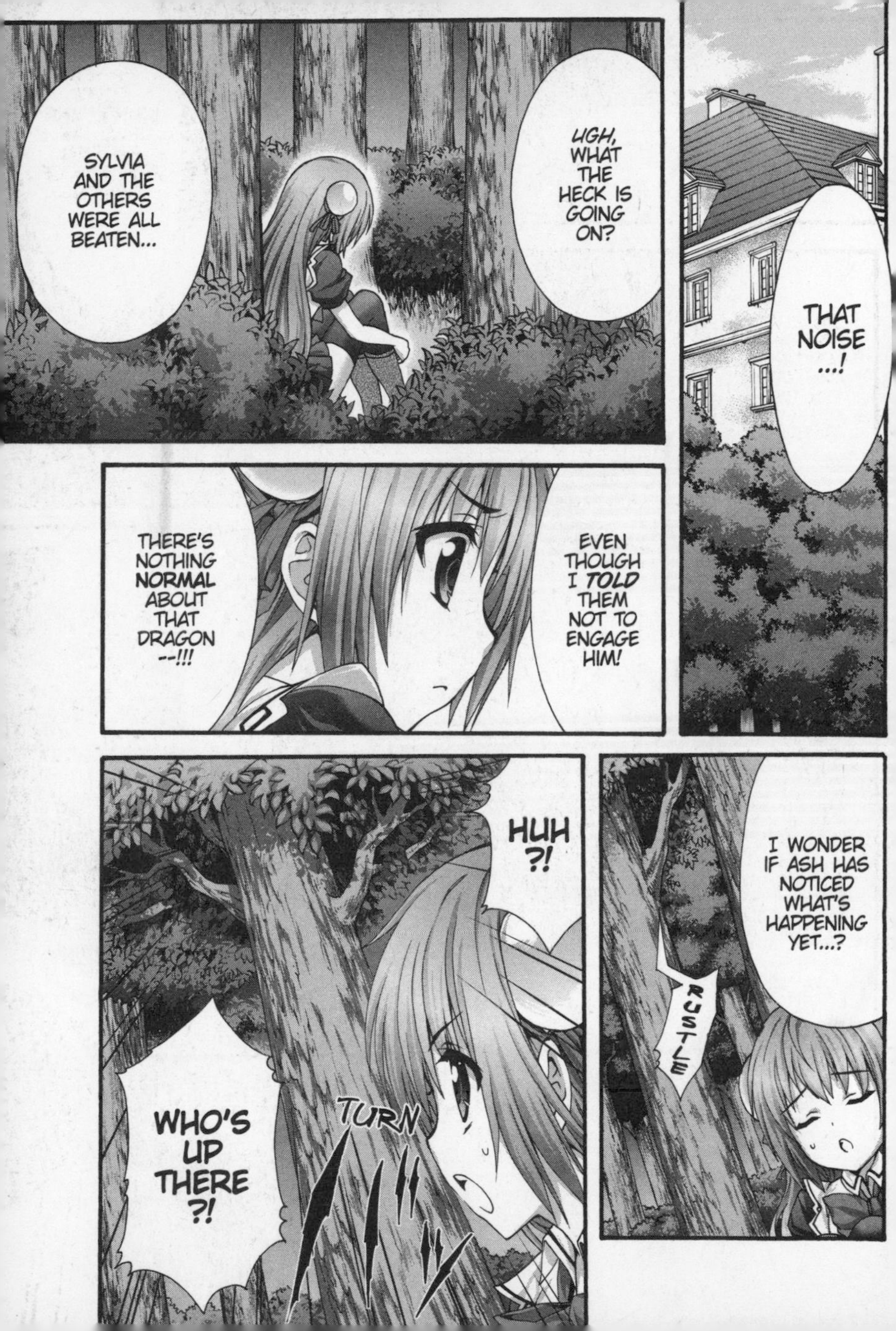
THAT NOISE ...!
UGH, WHAT THE HECK IS GOING ON?
SYLVIA AND THE OTHERS WERE ALL BEATEN...
EVEN THOUGH I TOLD THEM NOT TO ENGAGE HIM!
THERE'S NOTHING NORMAL ABOUT THAT DRAGON --!!!
I WONDER IF ASH HAS NOTICED WHAT'S HAPPENING YET...?
RUSTLE
HUH ?!
TURN
WHO'S UP THERE ?!

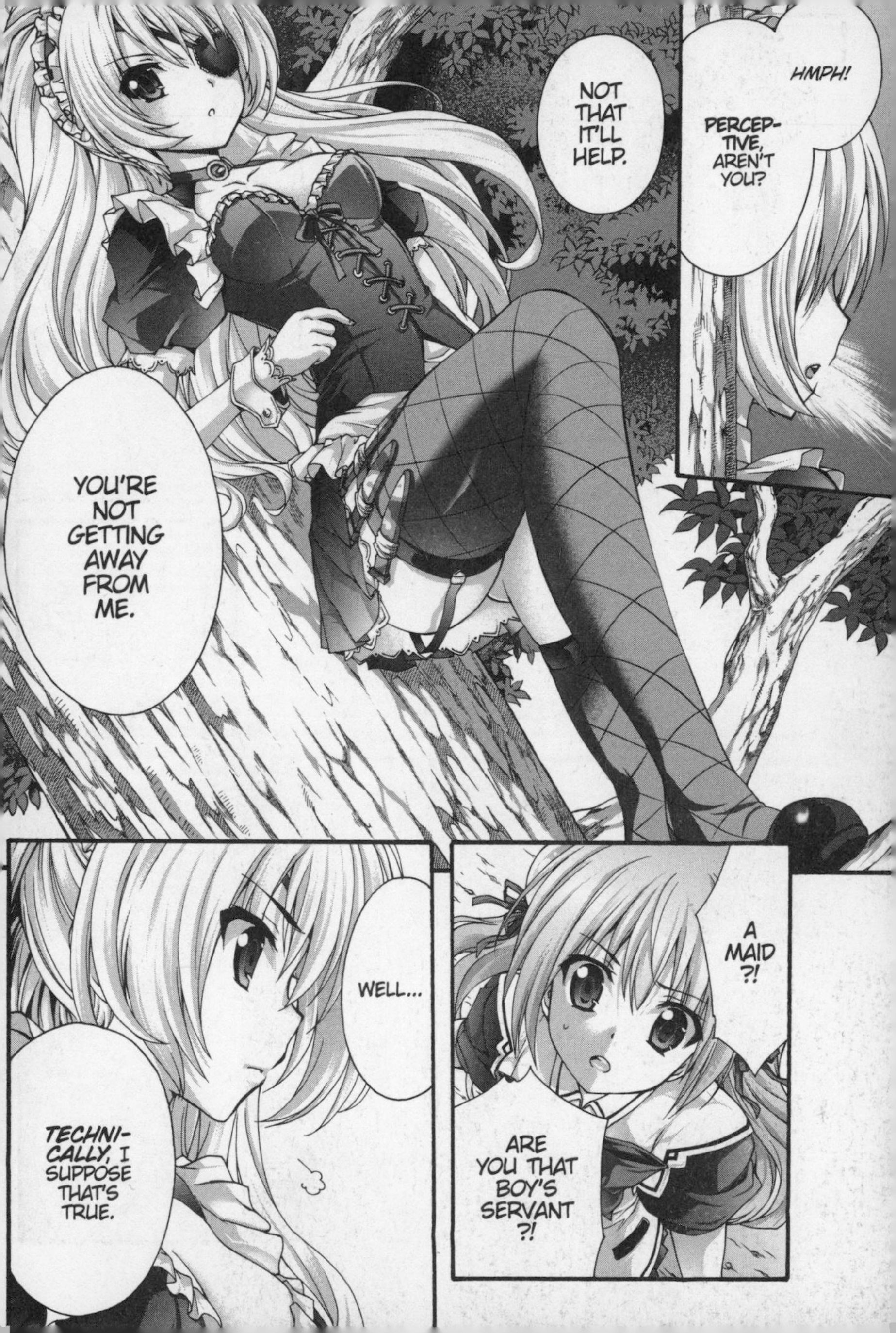
HMPH!
PERCEP-TIVE, AREN'T YOU?
NOT THAT IT'LL HELP.
YOU'RE NOT GETTING AWAY FROM ME.
A MAID ?!
ARE YOU THAT BOY'S SERVANT ?!
WELL...
TECHNI-CALLY, I SUPPOSE THAT'S TRUE.

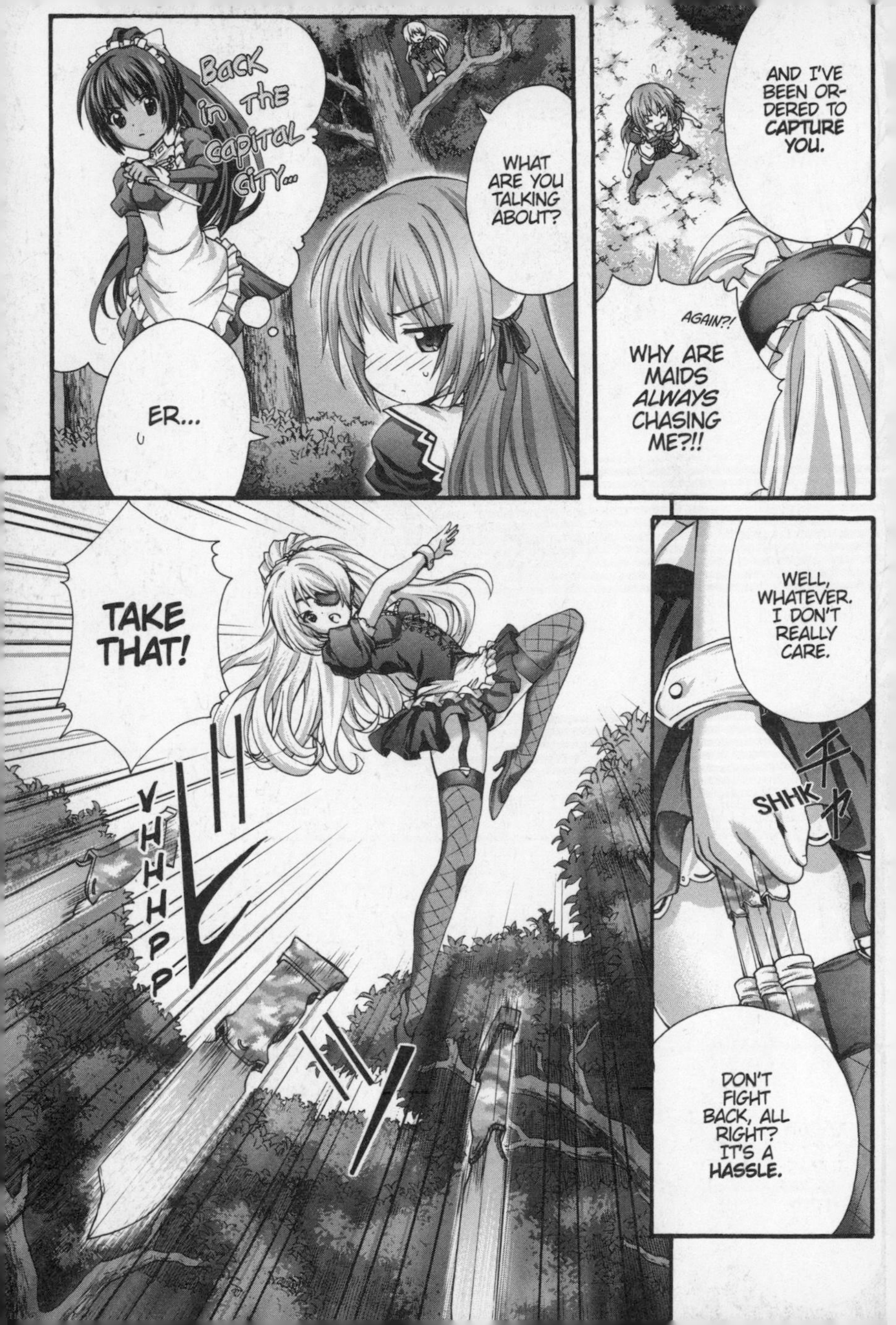

AND I'VE BEEN OR-DERED TO CAPTURE YOU.
AGAIN?!
WHY ARE MAIDS ALWAYS CHASING ME?!!
WHAT ARE YOU TALKING ABOUT?
Back in the capital city...
ER...
WELL, WHATEVER. I DON'T REALLY CARE.
チャ
SHHK
DON'T FIGHT BACK, ALL RIGHT? IT'S A HASSLE.
TAKE THAT!
VHHHPP

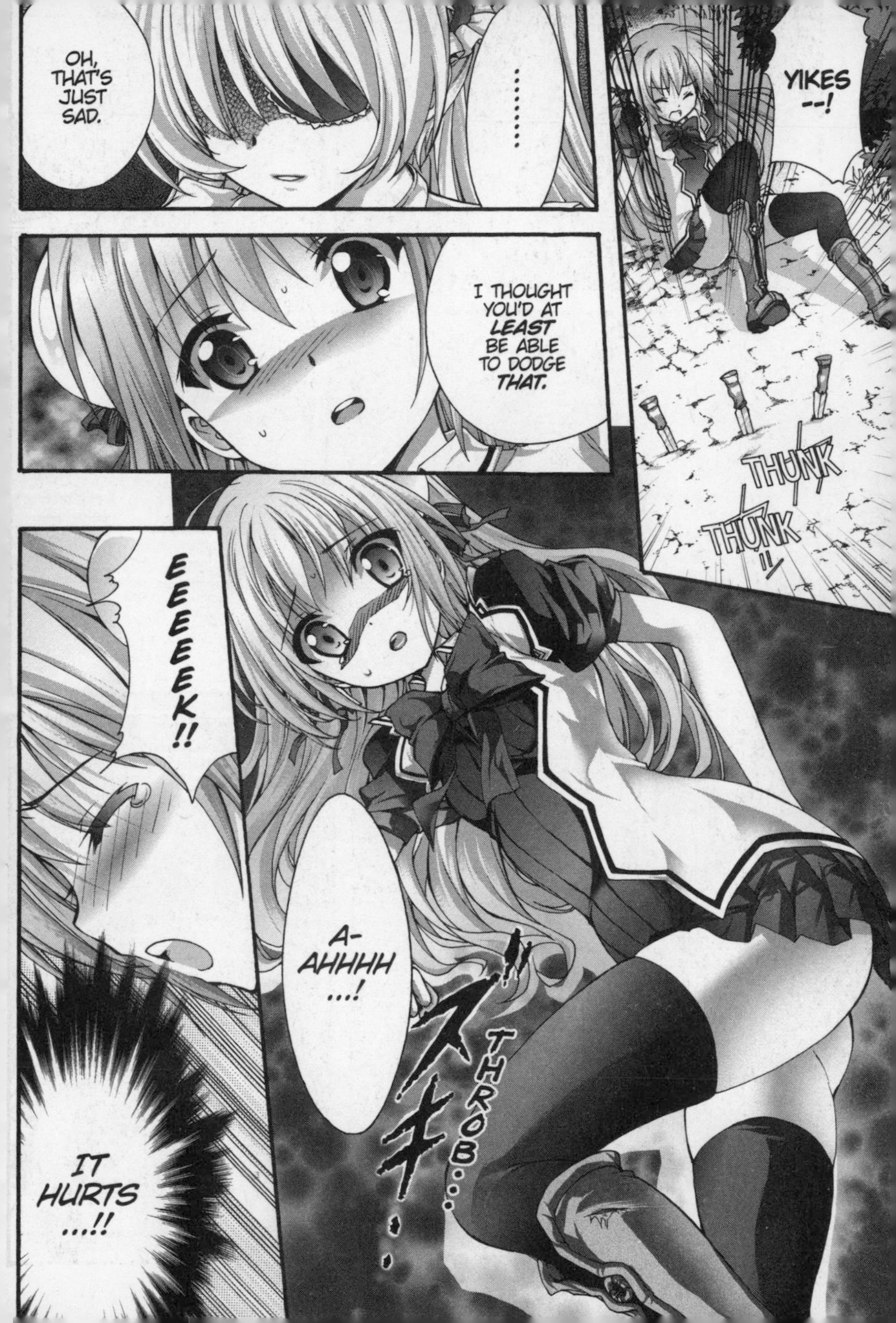
YIKES --!
THUNK
THUNK !!
......
OH, THAT'S JUST SAD.
I THOUGHT YOU'D AT *LEAST* BE ABLE TO DODGE *THAT.*
A- AHHHH ....!
THROB...
EEEEEEK!!
IT HURTS ...!!

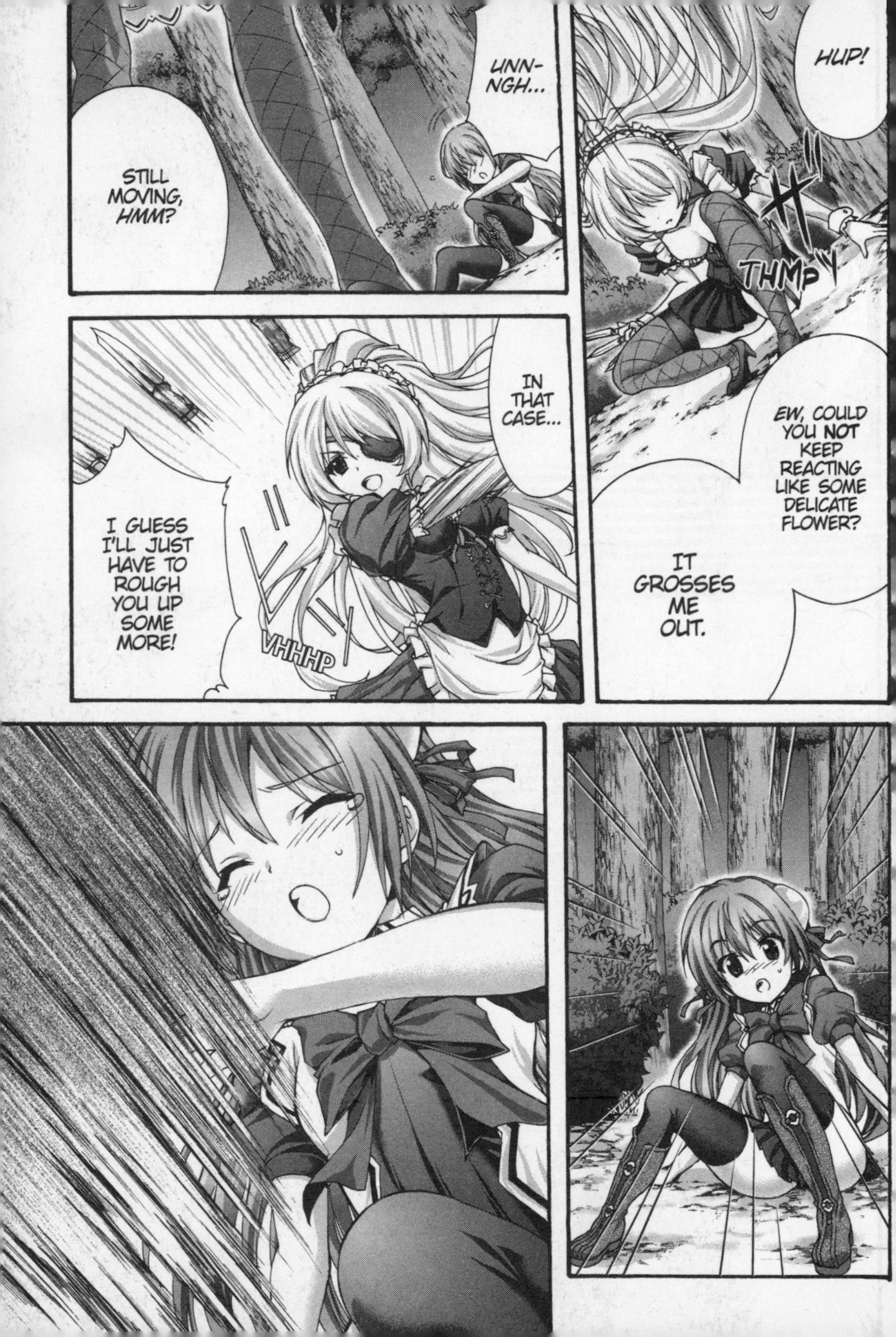
HUP!
THMP
EW, COULD YOU NOT KEEP REACTING LIKE SOME DELICATE FLOWER?
IT GROSSES ME OUT.
UNNN-NGH...
STILL MOVING, HMM?
IN THAT CASE...
I GUESS I'LL JUST HAVE TO ROUGH YOU UP SOME MORE!
VHHHP

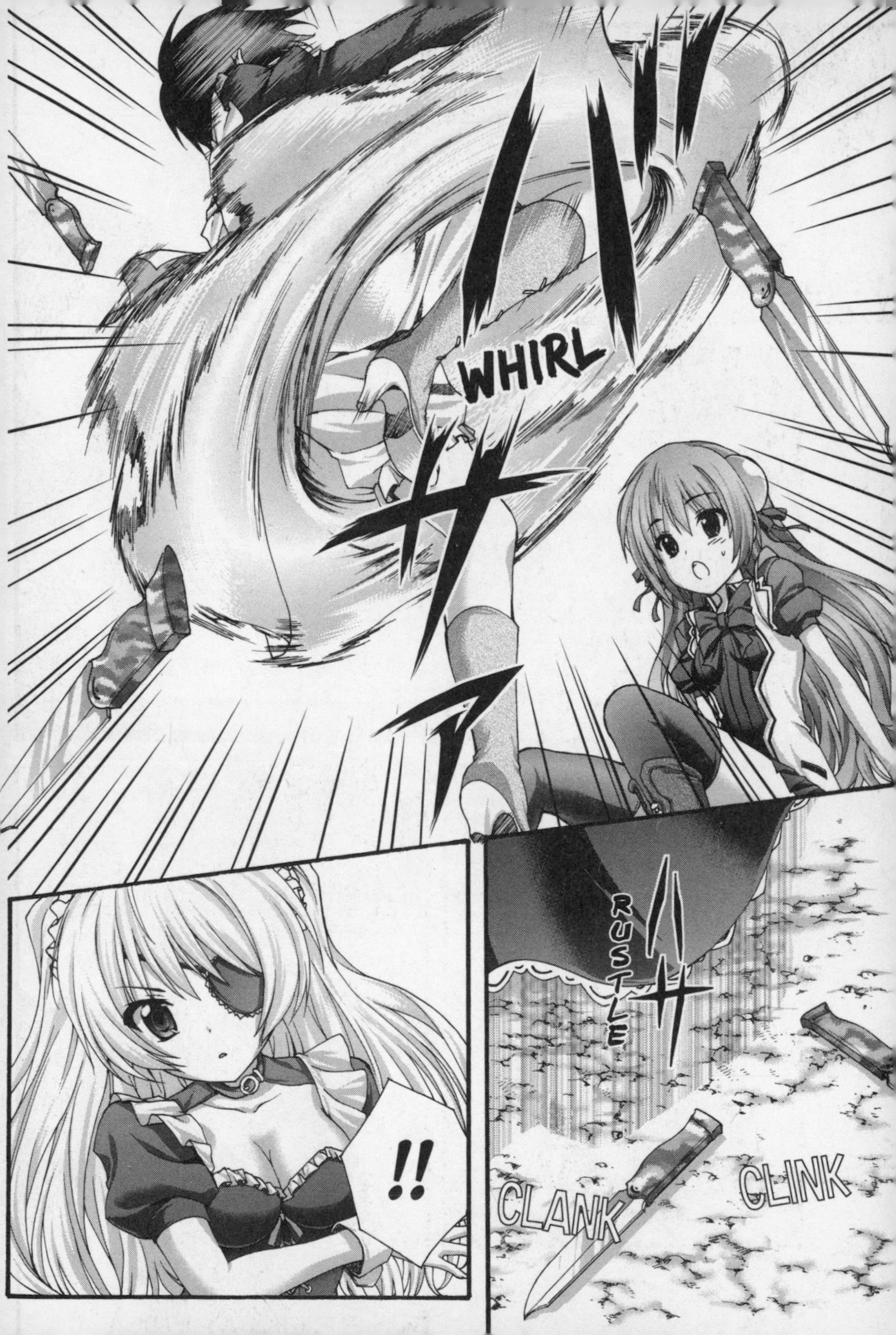
WHIRL
RUSTLE
CLINK
CLANK
!!

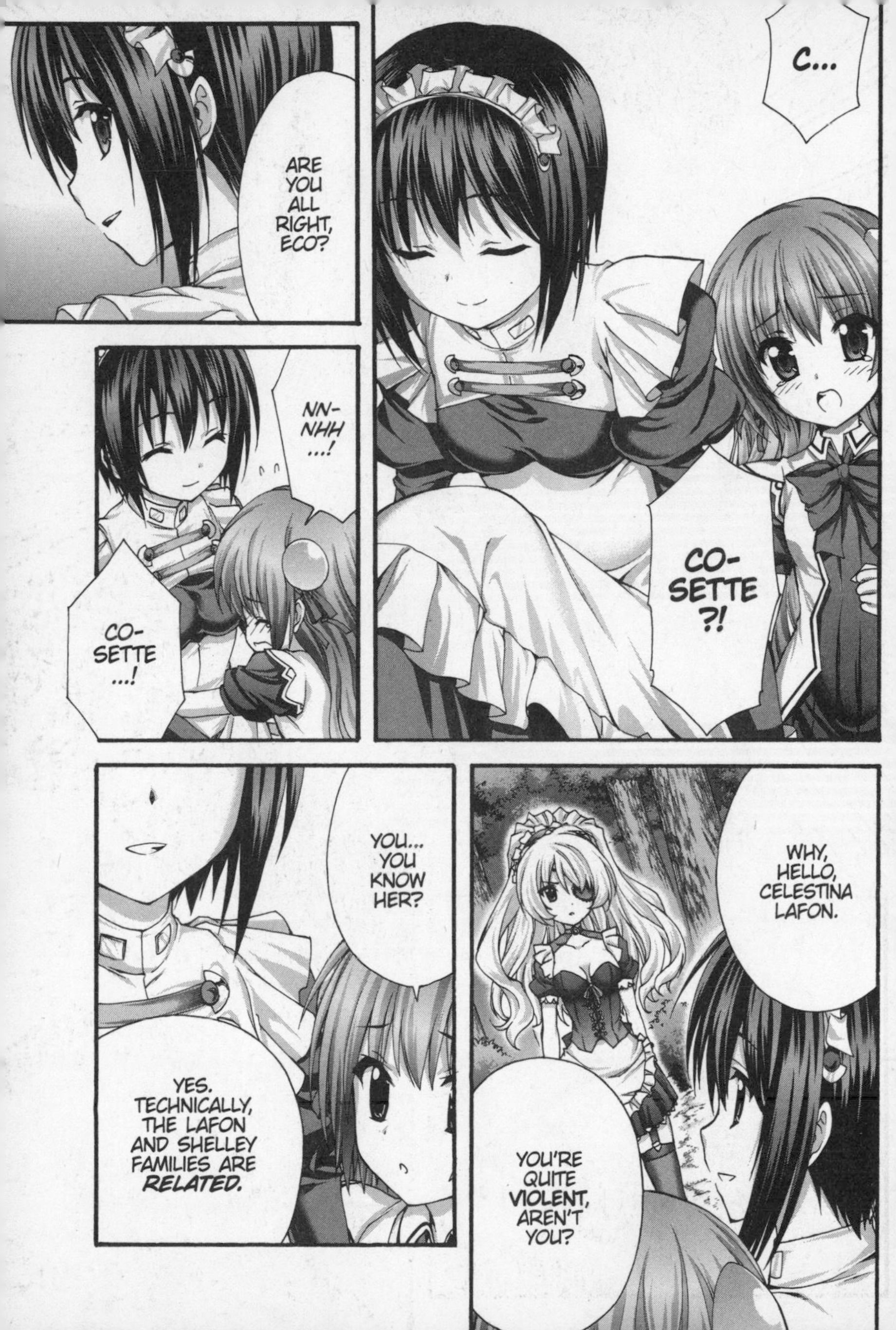
C...
CO-SETTE?!
ARE YOU ALL RIGHT, ECO?
NN-NHH...!
CO-SETTE...!
WHY, HELLO, CELESTINA LAFON.
YOU'RE QUITE VIOLENT, AREN'T YOU?
YOU... YOU KNOW HER?
YES. TECHNICALLY, THE LAFON AND SHELLEY FAMILIES ARE RELATED.

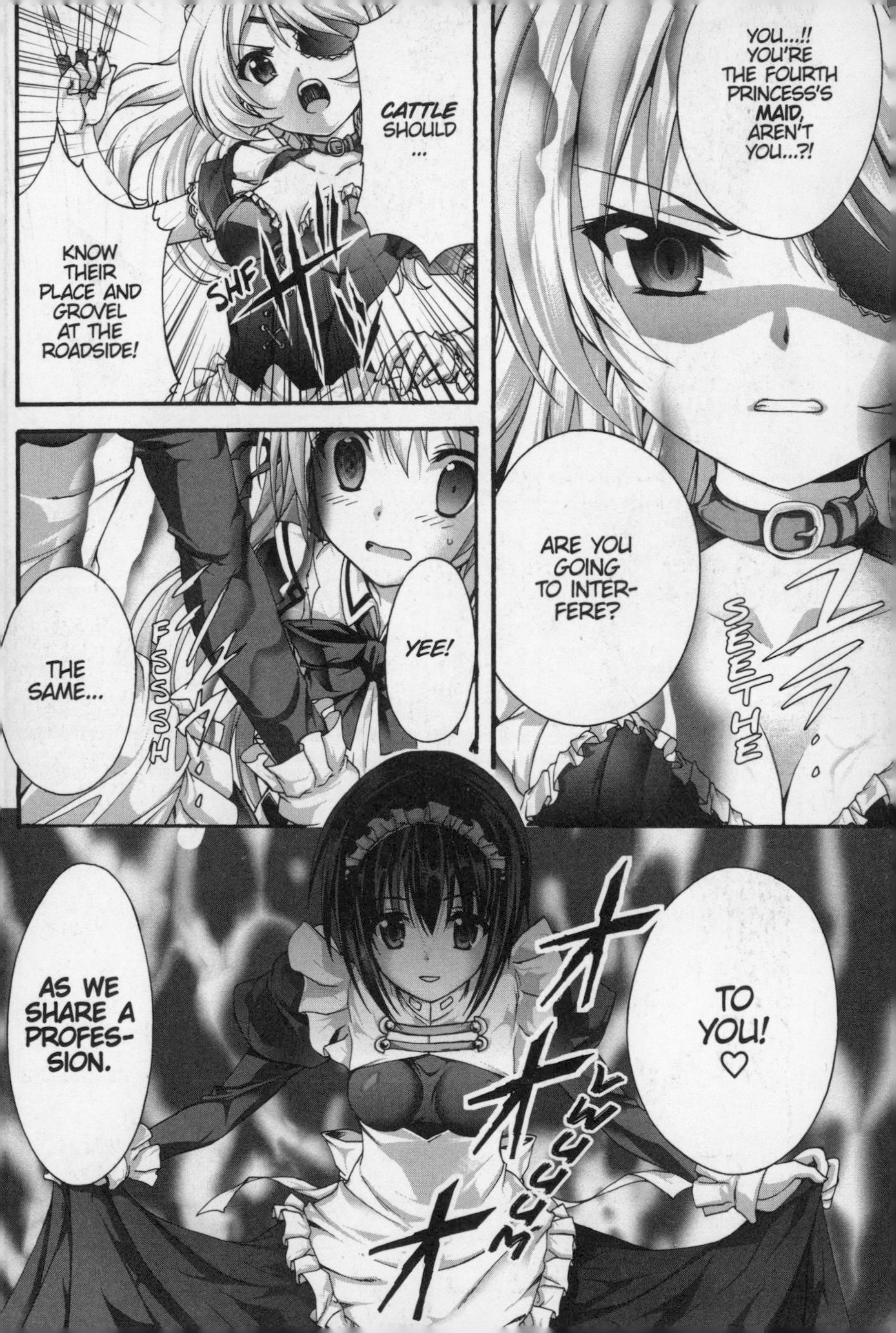
YOU...!! YOU'RE THE FOURTH PRINCESS'S MAID, AREN'T YOU...?!
ARE YOU GOING TO INTER-FERE?
SEETHE
CATTLE SHOULD ...
KNOW THEIR PLACE AND GROVEL AT THE ROADSIDE!
SHF
YEE!
THE SAME...
FSSSH
TO YOU! ♡
AS WE SHARE A PROFES-SION.
VWUUUM

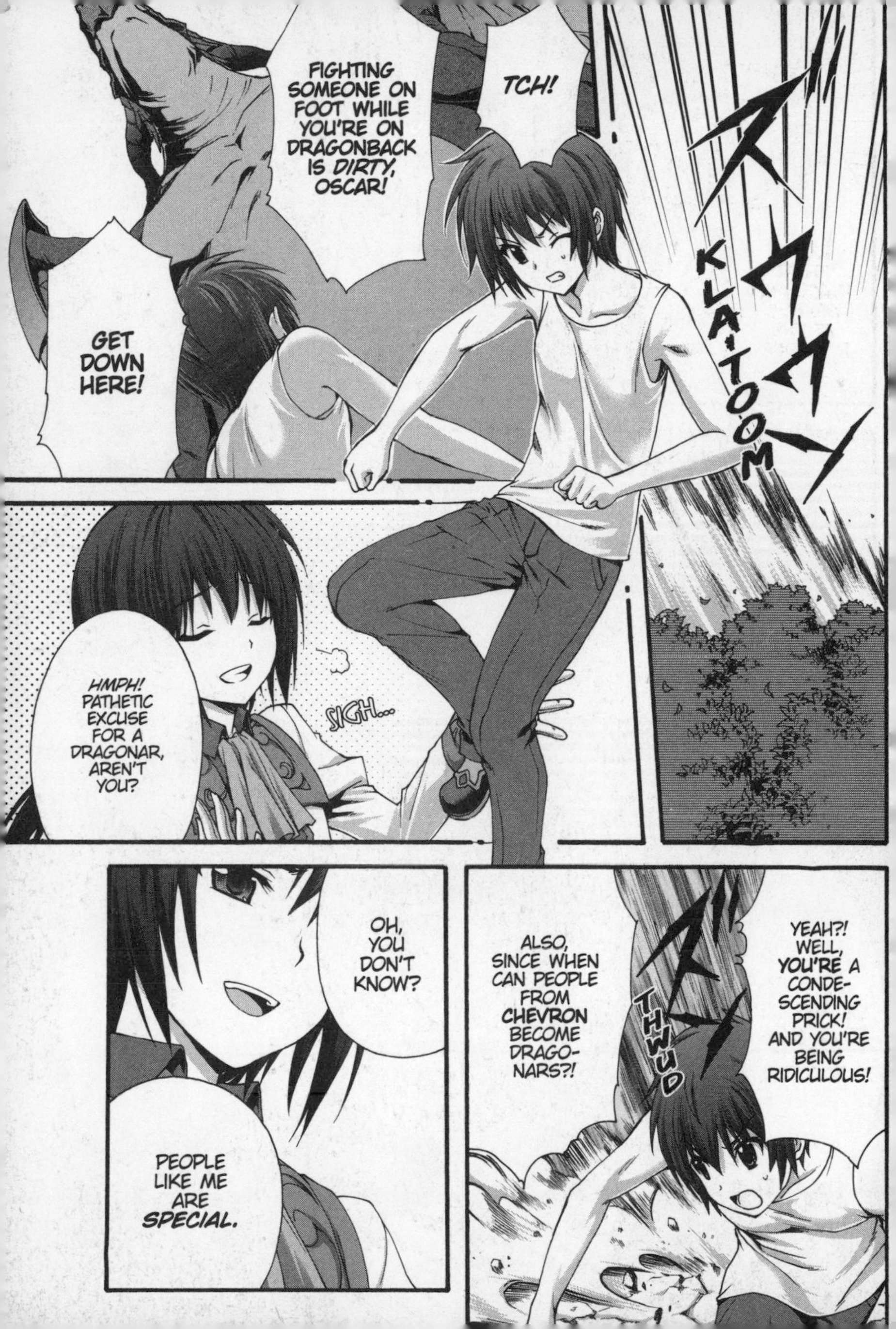
KLAITOOM
TCH!
FIGHTING SOMEONE ON FOOT WHILE YOU'RE ON DRAGONBACK IS DIRTY, OSCAR!
GET DOWN HERE!
SIGH...
HMPH! PATHETIC EXCUSE FOR A DRAGONAR, AREN'T YOU?
YEAH?! WELL, YOU'RE A CONDE-SCENDING PRICK! AND YOU'RE BEING RIDICULOUS!
ALSO, SINCE WHEN CAN PEOPLE FROM CHEVRON BECOME DRAGO-NARS?!
THWUD
OH, YOU DON'T KNOW?
PEOPLE LIKE ME ARE SPECIAL.

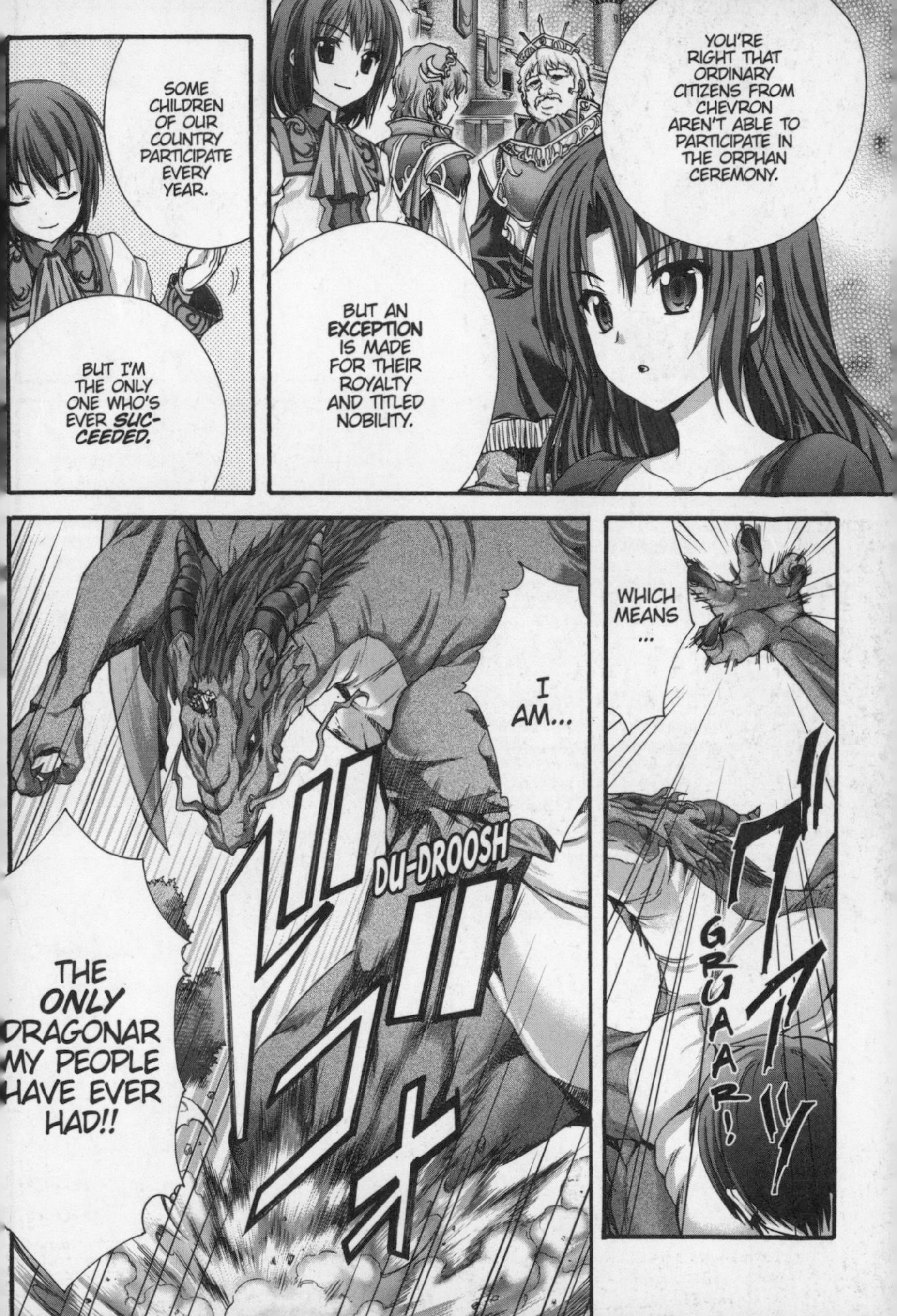
YOU'RE RIGHT THAT ORDINARY CITIZENS FROM CHEVRON AREN'T ABLE TO PARTICIPATE IN THE ORPHAN CEREMONY.
BUT AN EXCEPTION IS MADE FOR THEIR ROYALTY AND TITLED NOBILITY.
SOME CHILDREN OF OUR COUNTRY PARTICIPATE EVERY YEAR.
BUT I'M THE ONLY ONE WHO'S EVER SUC-CEEDED.
WHICH MEANS ...
GRUAAR!
I AM...
DU-DROOSH
THE ONLY DRAGONAR MY PEOPLE HAVE EVER HAD!!

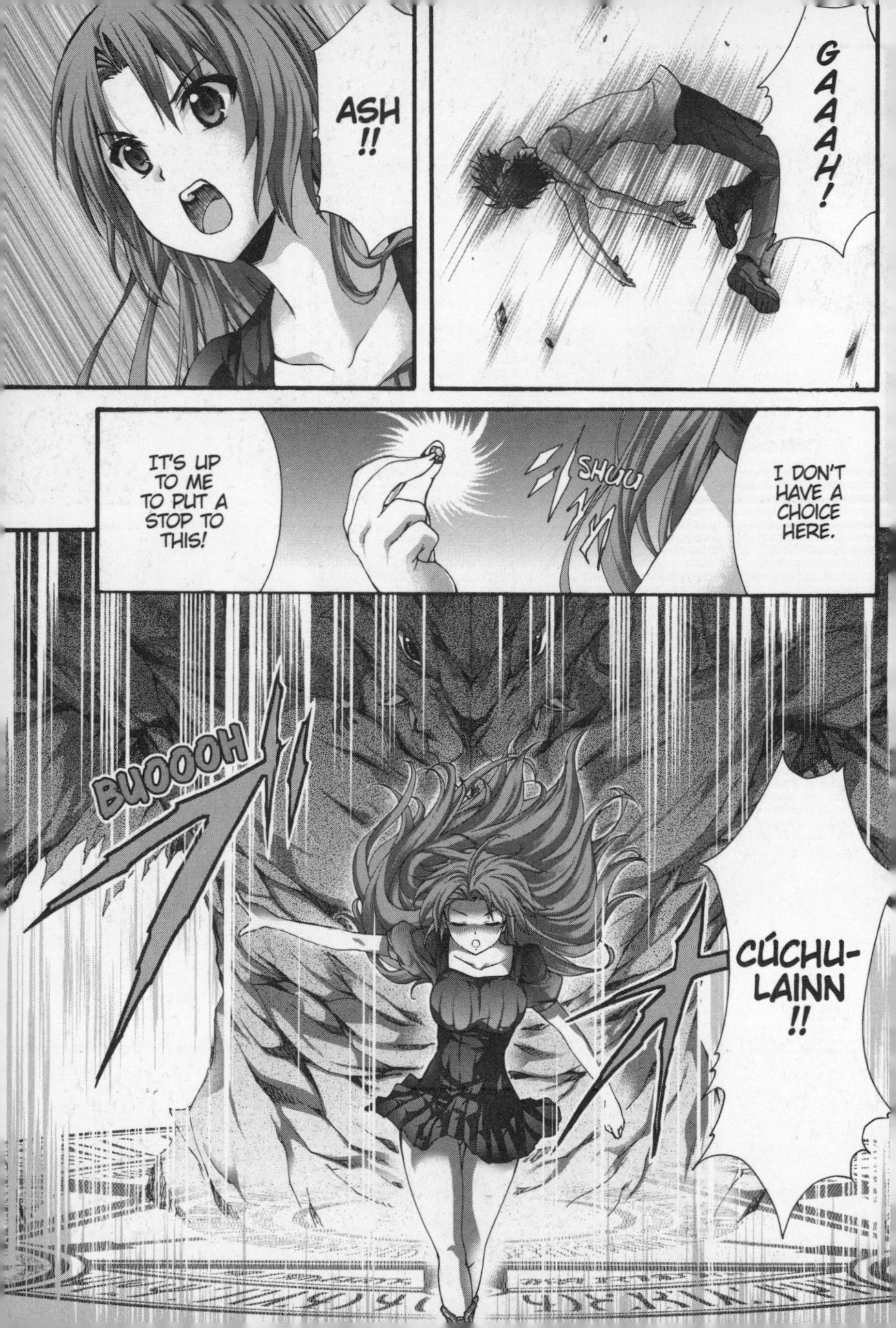
GAAAAH!
ASH!!
I DON'T HAVE A CHOICE HERE.
SHUU
IT'S UP TO ME TO PUT A STOP TO THIS!
CÚCHULAINN!!
BUOOOH

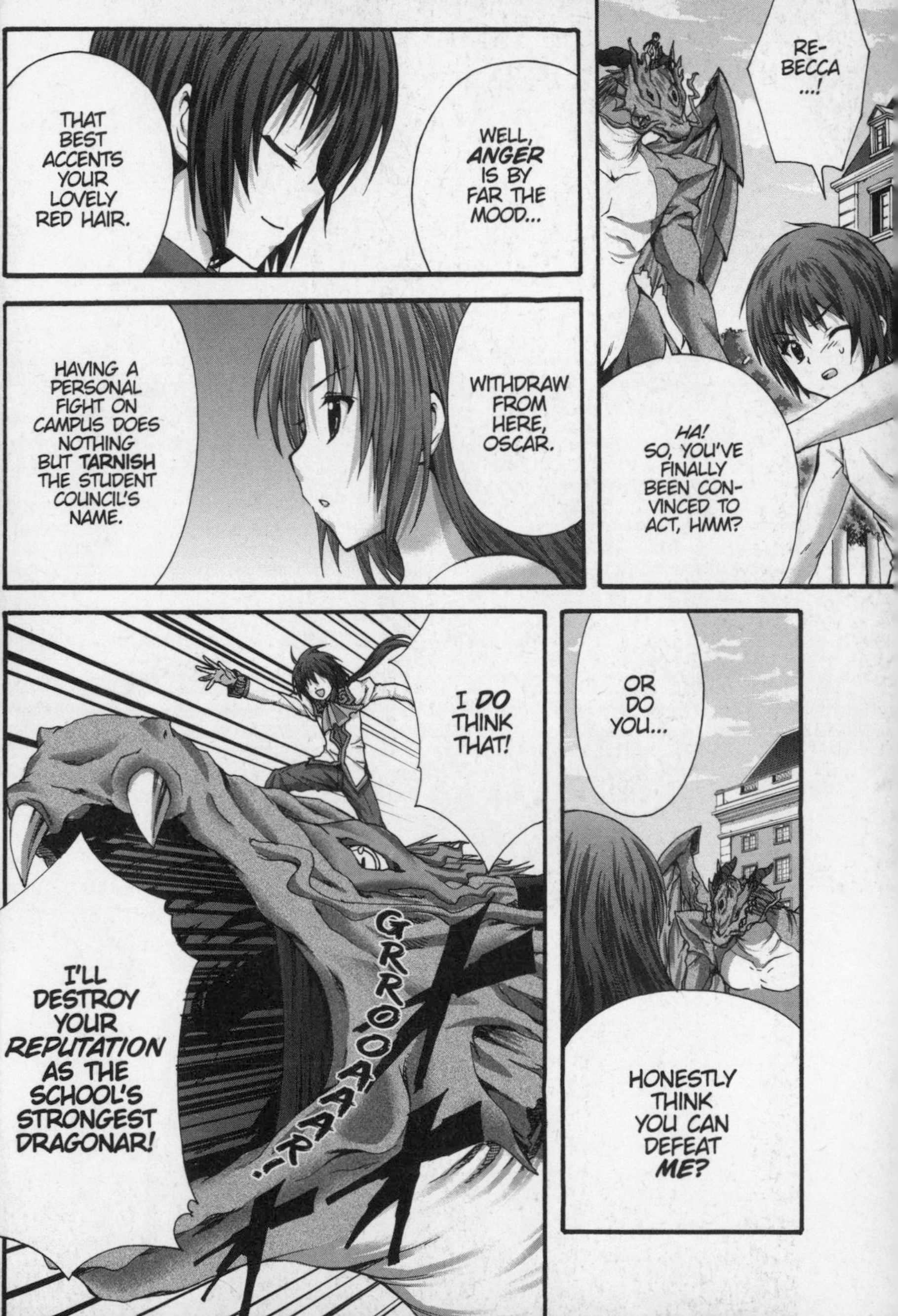
RE-BECCA...!
HA! SO, YOU'VE FINALLY BEEN CONVINCED TO ACT, HMM?
WELL, ANGER IS BY FAR THE MOOD...
THAT BEST ACCENTS YOUR LOVELY RED HAIR.
WITHDRAW FROM HERE, OSCAR.
HAVING A PERSONAL FIGHT ON CAMPUS DOES NOTHING BUT TARNISH THE STUDENT COUNCIL'S NAME.
OR DO YOU...
HONESTLY THINK YOU CAN DEFEAT ME?
I DO THINK THAT!
GRROOOAAAR-!
I'LL DESTROY YOUR REPUTATION AS THE SCHOOL'S STRONGEST DRAGONAR!

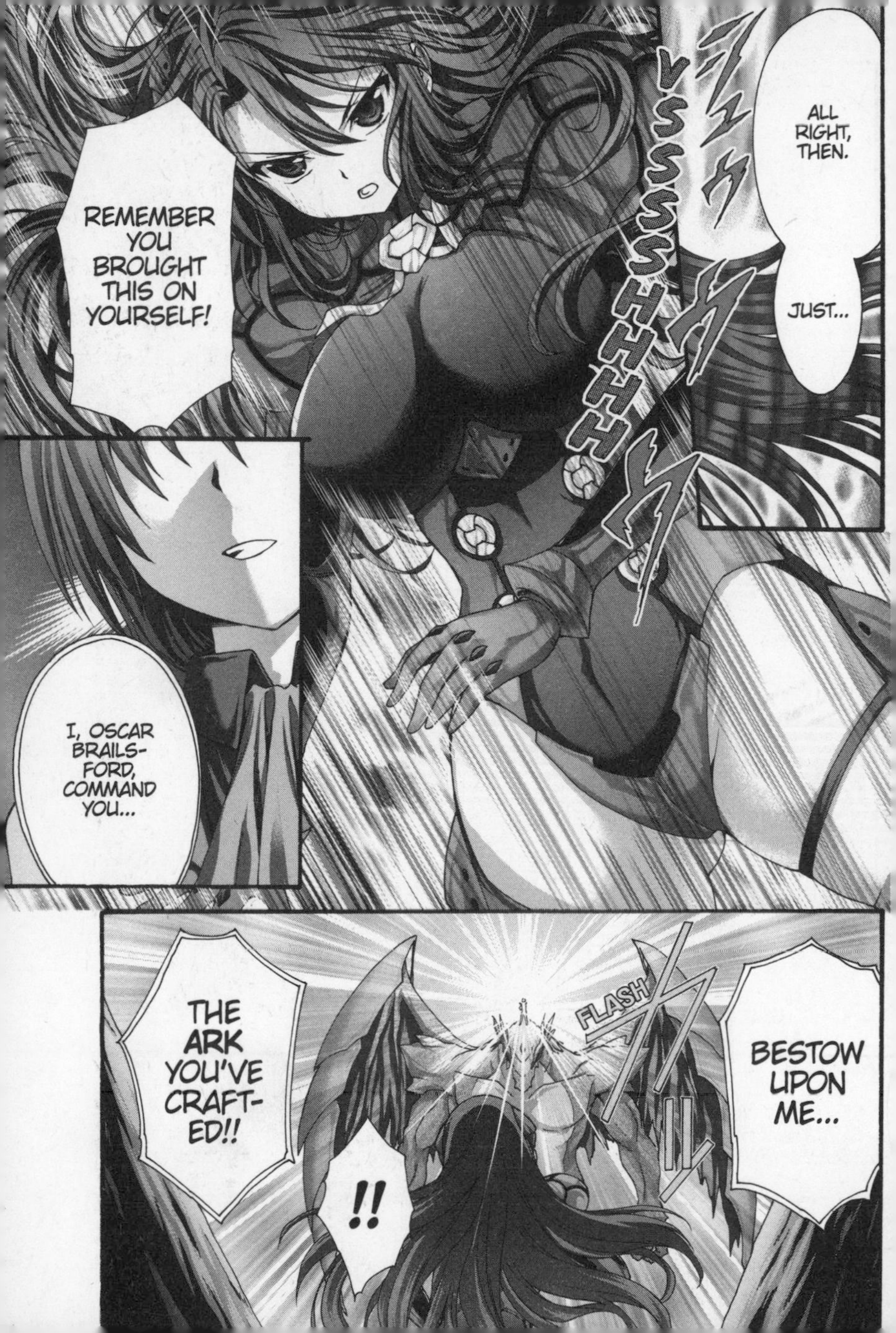
ALL RIGHT, THEN.
JUST...
VSSSSHHHHH
REMEMBER YOU BROUGHT THIS ON YOURSELF!
I, OSCAR BRAILS-FORD, COMMAND YOU...
BESTOW UPON ME...
FLASH
THE ARK YOU'VE CRAFT-ED!!
!!

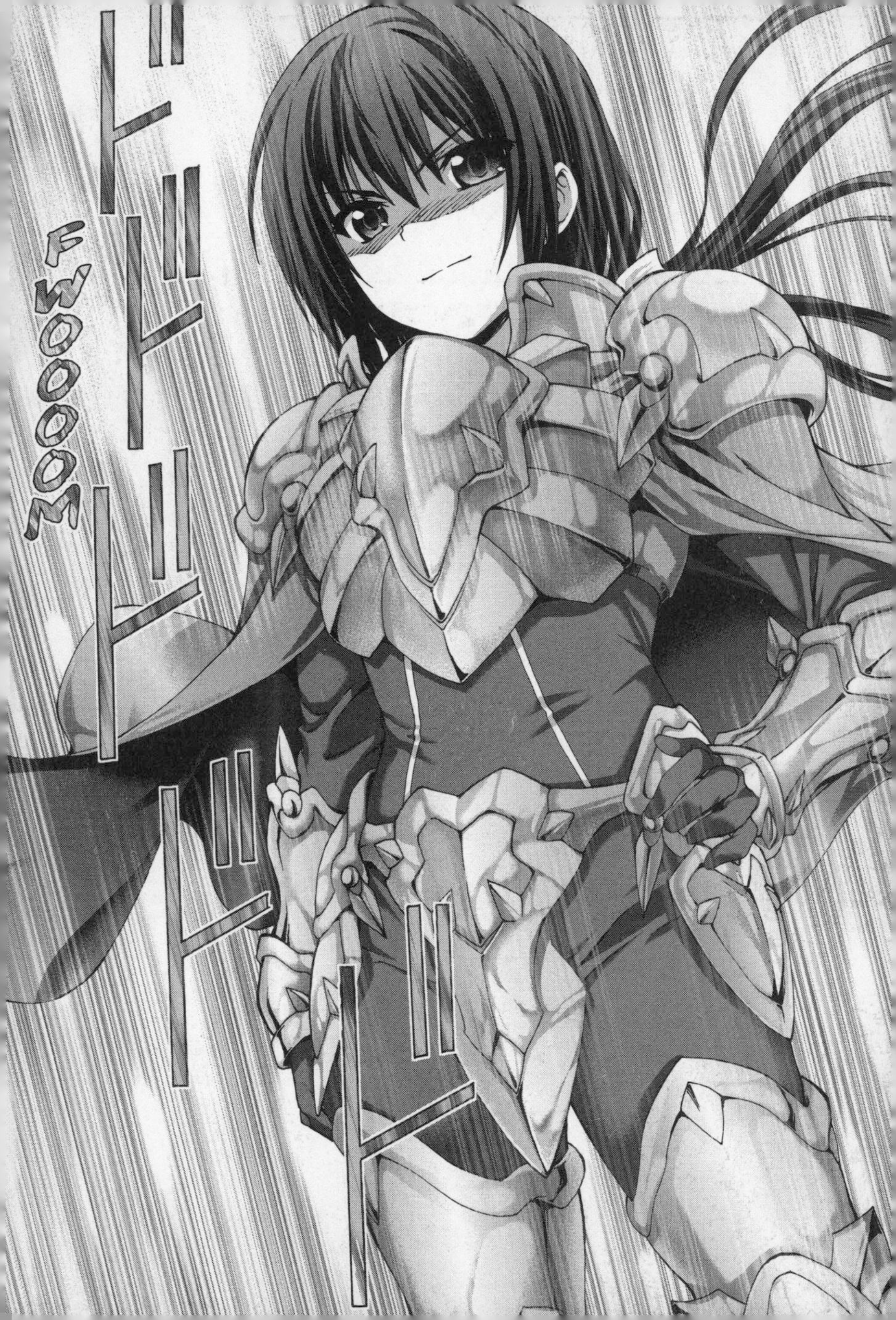
ドドドドドド
FWOOOOM

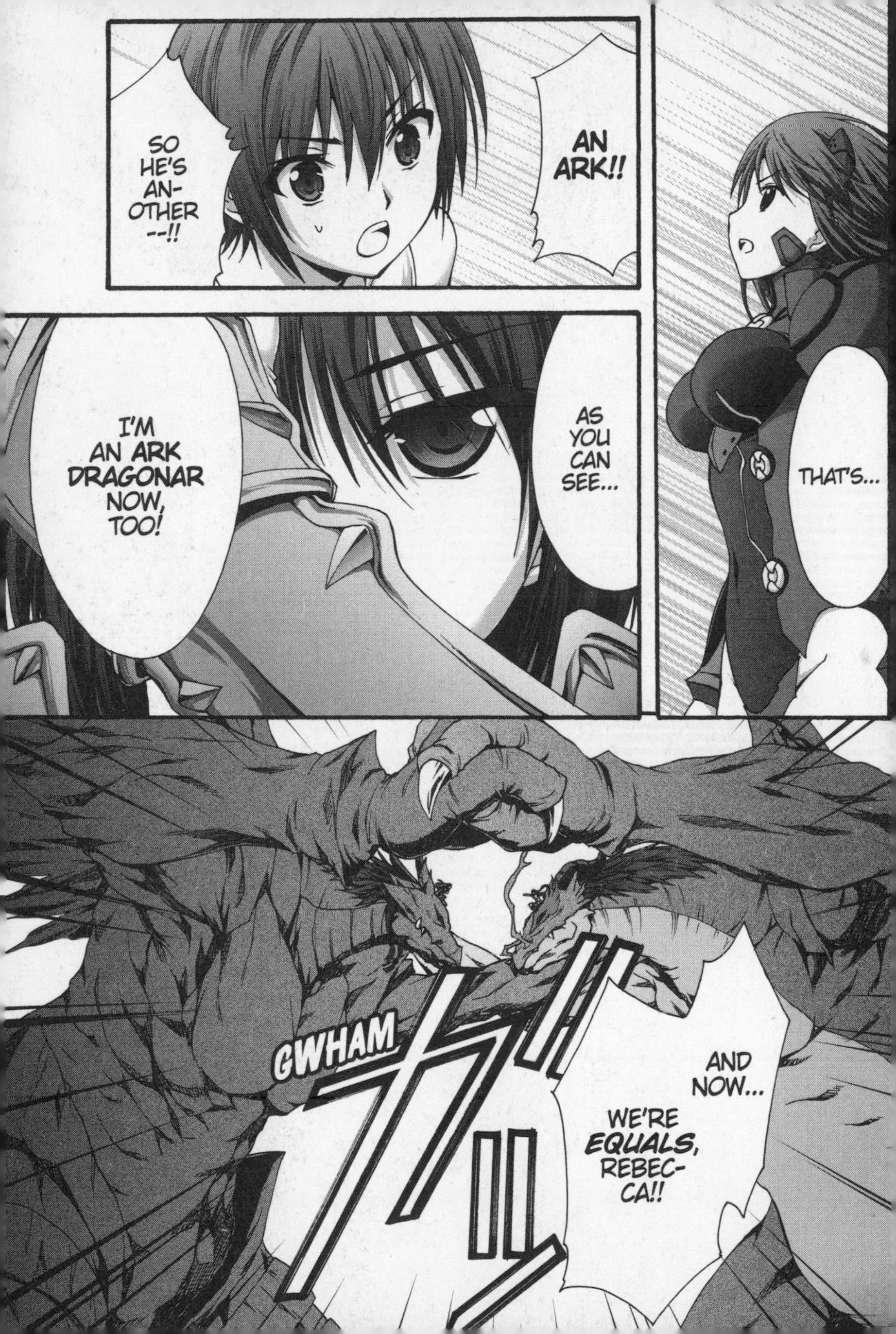
THAT'S...
AN ARK!!
SO HE'S AN-OTHER --!!
AS YOU CAN SEE...
I'M AN ARK DRAGONAR NOW, TOO!
AND NOW...
WE'RE EQUALS, REBECCA!!
GWHAM

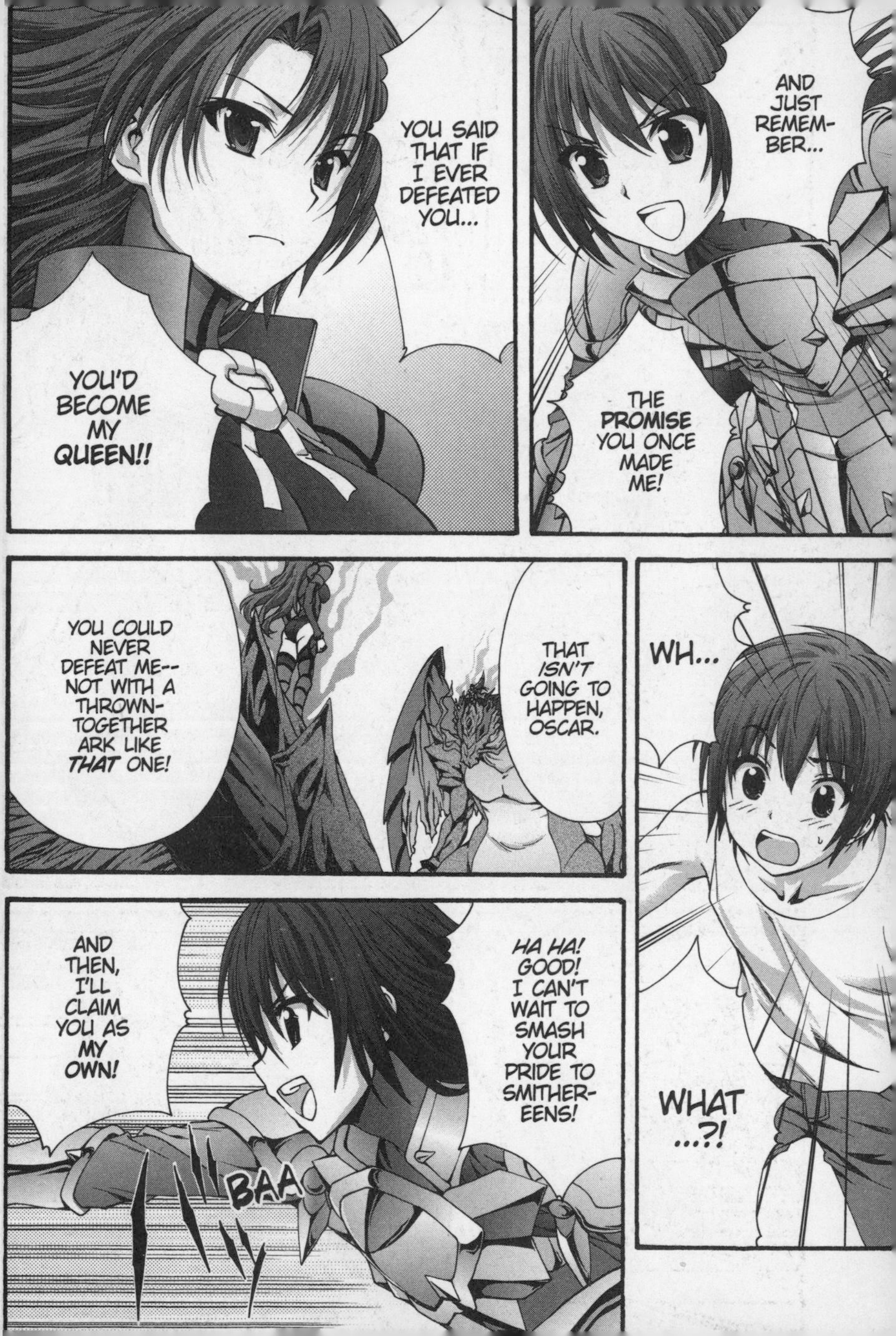
AND JUST REMEMBER...
THE PROMISE YOU ONCE MADE ME!
YOU SAID THAT IF I EVER DEFEATED YOU...
YOU'D BECOME MY QUEEN!!
WH...
WHAT ...?!
THAT *ISN'T* GOING TO HAPPEN, OSCAR.
YOU COULD NEVER DEFEAT ME--NOT WITH A THROWN-TOGETHER ARK LIKE *THAT* ONE!
HA HA! GOOD! I CAN'T WAIT TO SMASH YOUR PRIDE TO SMITHEREENS!
AND THEN, I'LL CLAIM YOU AS MY OWN!
BAA

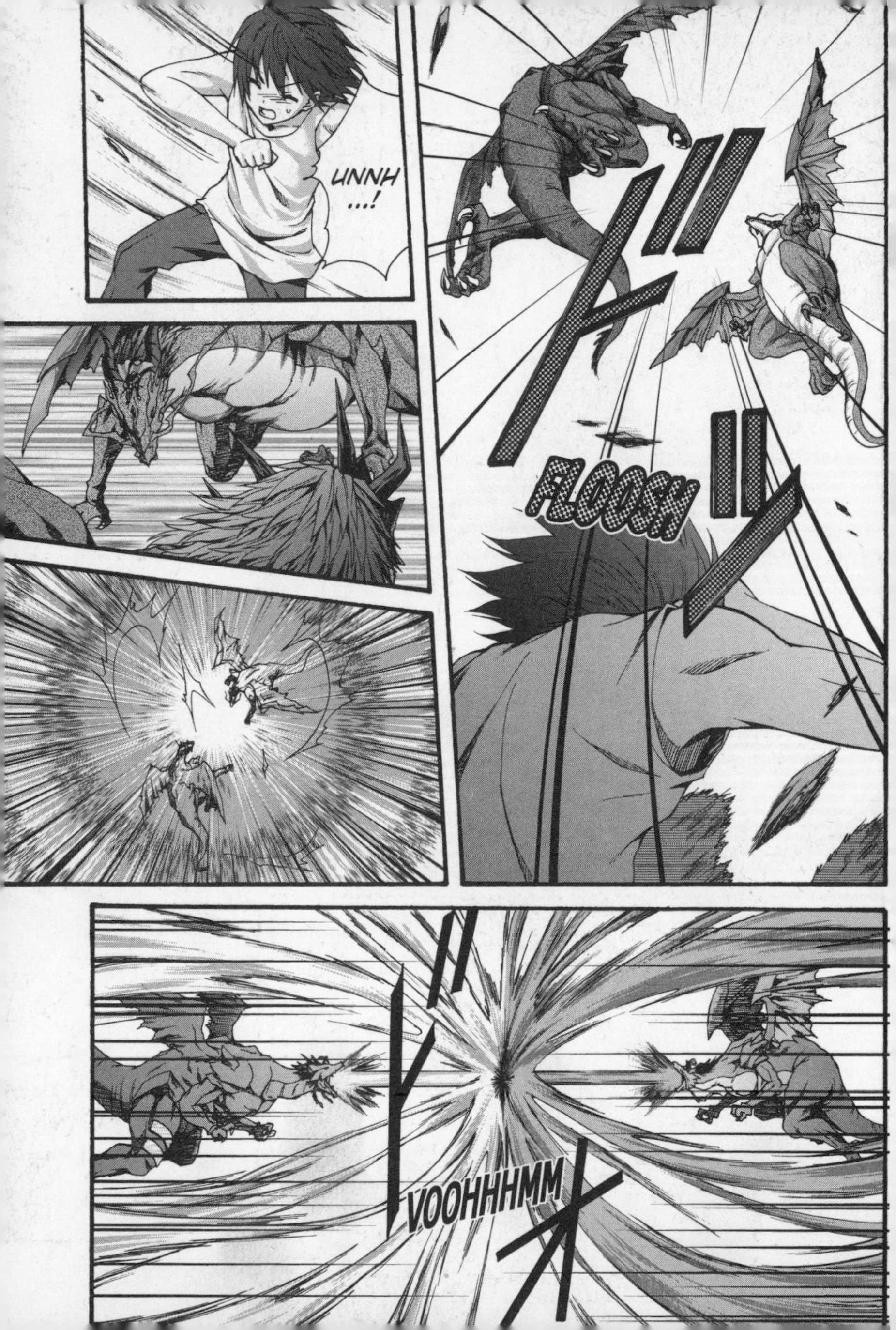
FLOOSH
UNNH ....!
VOOHHHMM

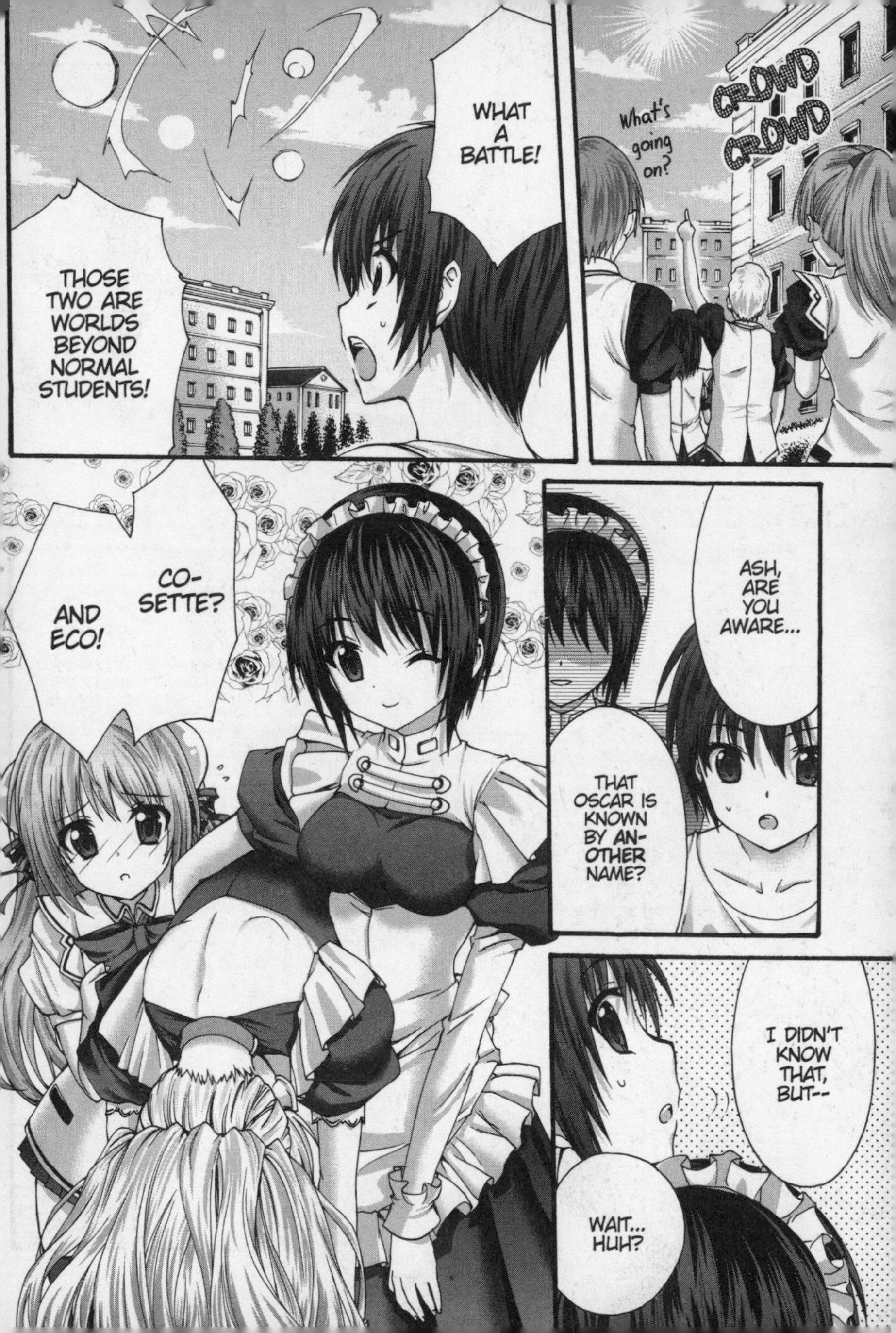
CROWD CROWD
What's going on?
WHAT A BATTLE!
THOSE TWO ARE WORLDS BEYOND NORMAL STUDENTS!
ASH, ARE YOU AWARE...
THAT OSCAR IS KNOWN BY AN-OTHER NAME?
I DIDN'T KNOW THAT, BUT--
WAIT... HUH?
CO-SETTE?
AND ECO!

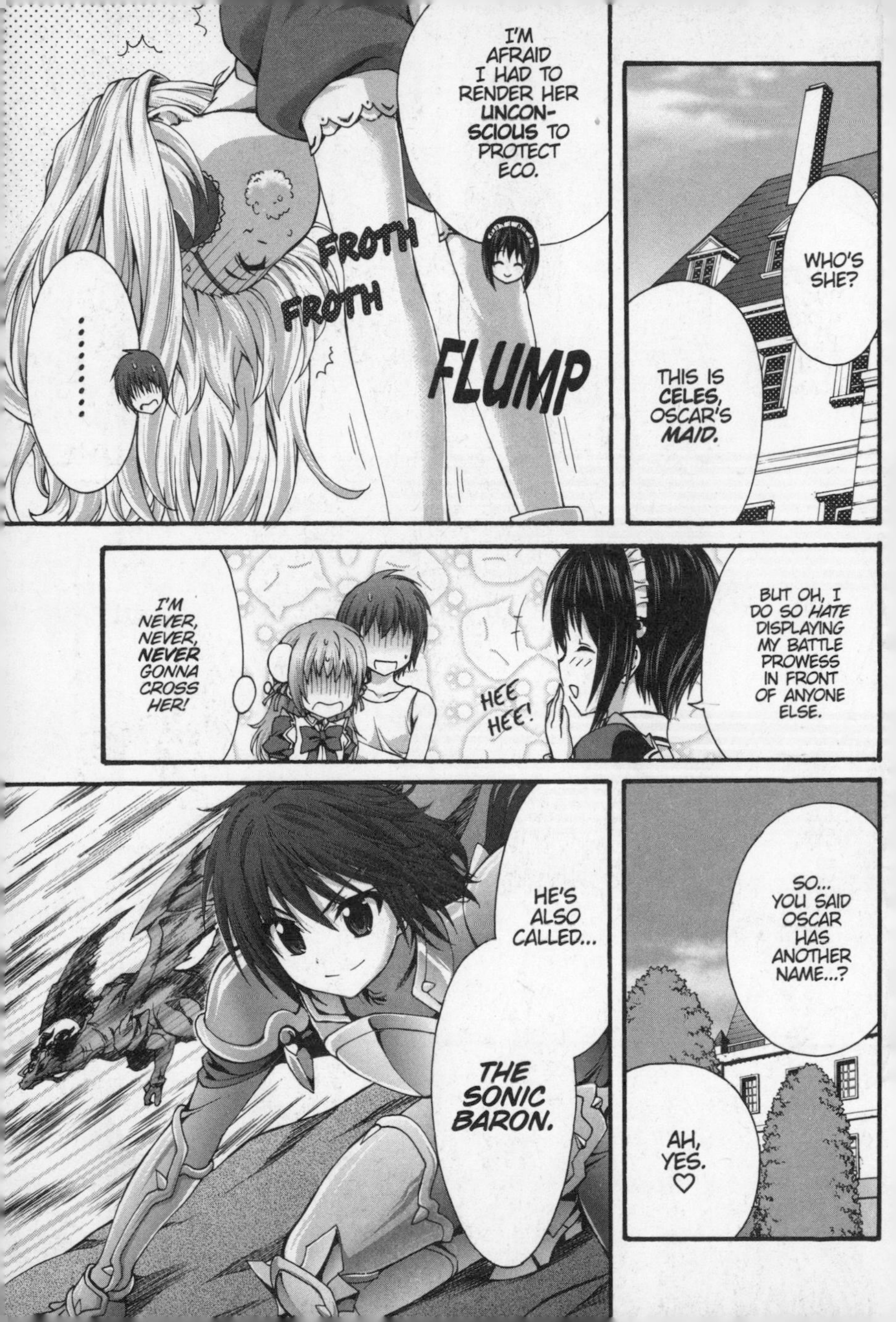
WHO'S SHE?
THIS IS CELES, OSCAR'S MAID.
I'M AFRAID I HAD TO RENDER HER UNCON-SCIOUS TO PROTECT ECO.
FROTH
FROTH
FLUMP
....
BUT OH, I DO SO HATE DISPLAYING MY BATTLE PROWESS IN FRONT OF ANYONE ELSE.
HEE HEE!
I'M NEVER, NEVER, NEVER GONNA CROSS HER!
SO... YOU SAID OSCAR HAS ANOTHER NAME...?
AH, YES. ♡
HE'S ALSO CALLED...
THE SONIC BARON.

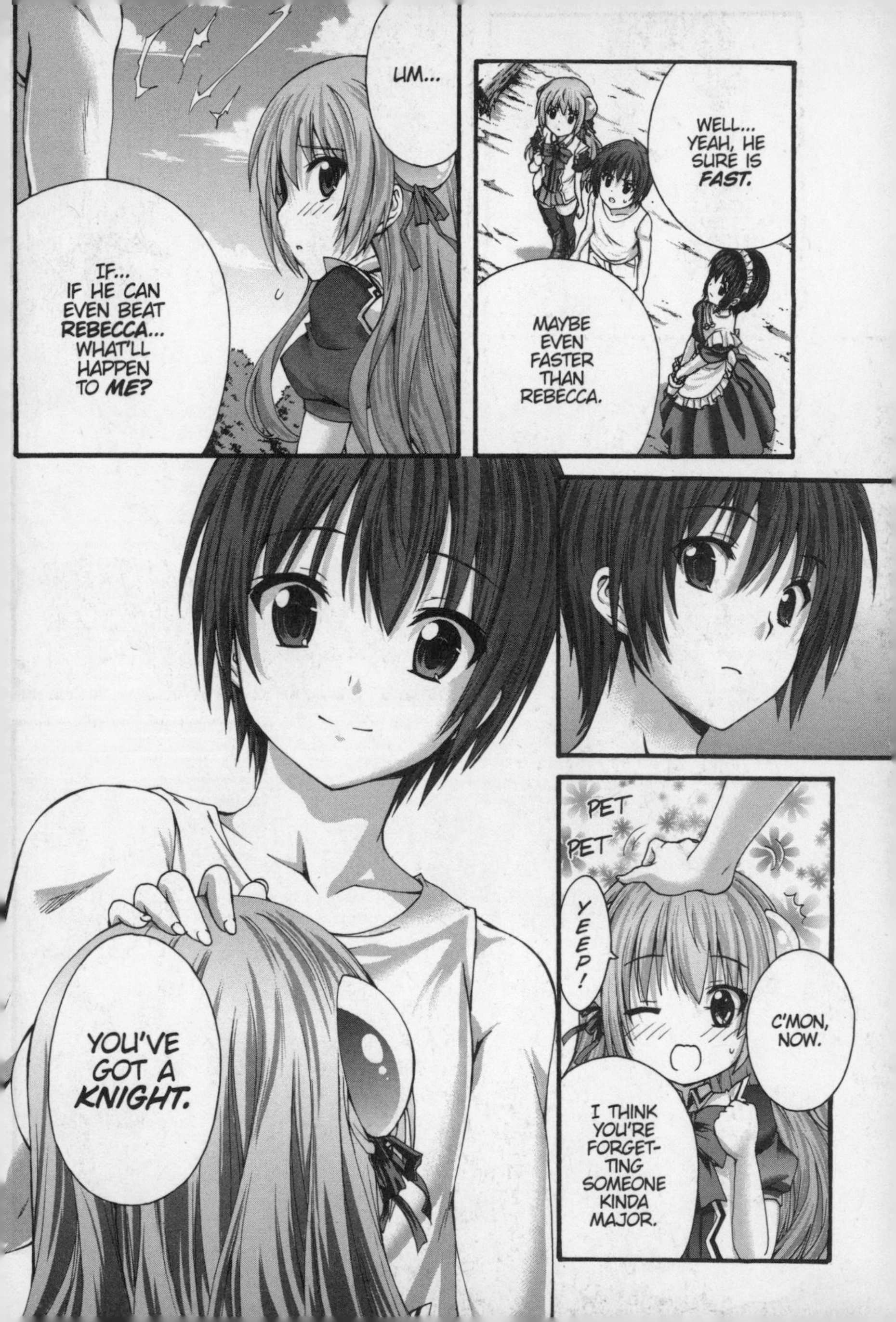
WELL... YEAH, HE SURE IS FAST.
MAYBE EVEN FASTER THAN REBECCA.
UM...
IF... IF HE CAN EVEN BEAT REBECCA... WHAT'LL HAPPEN TO ME?
PET
PET
YEEP!
C'MON, NOW.
I THINK YOU'RE FORGET-TING SOMEONE KINDA MAJOR.
YOU'VE GOT A KNIGHT.

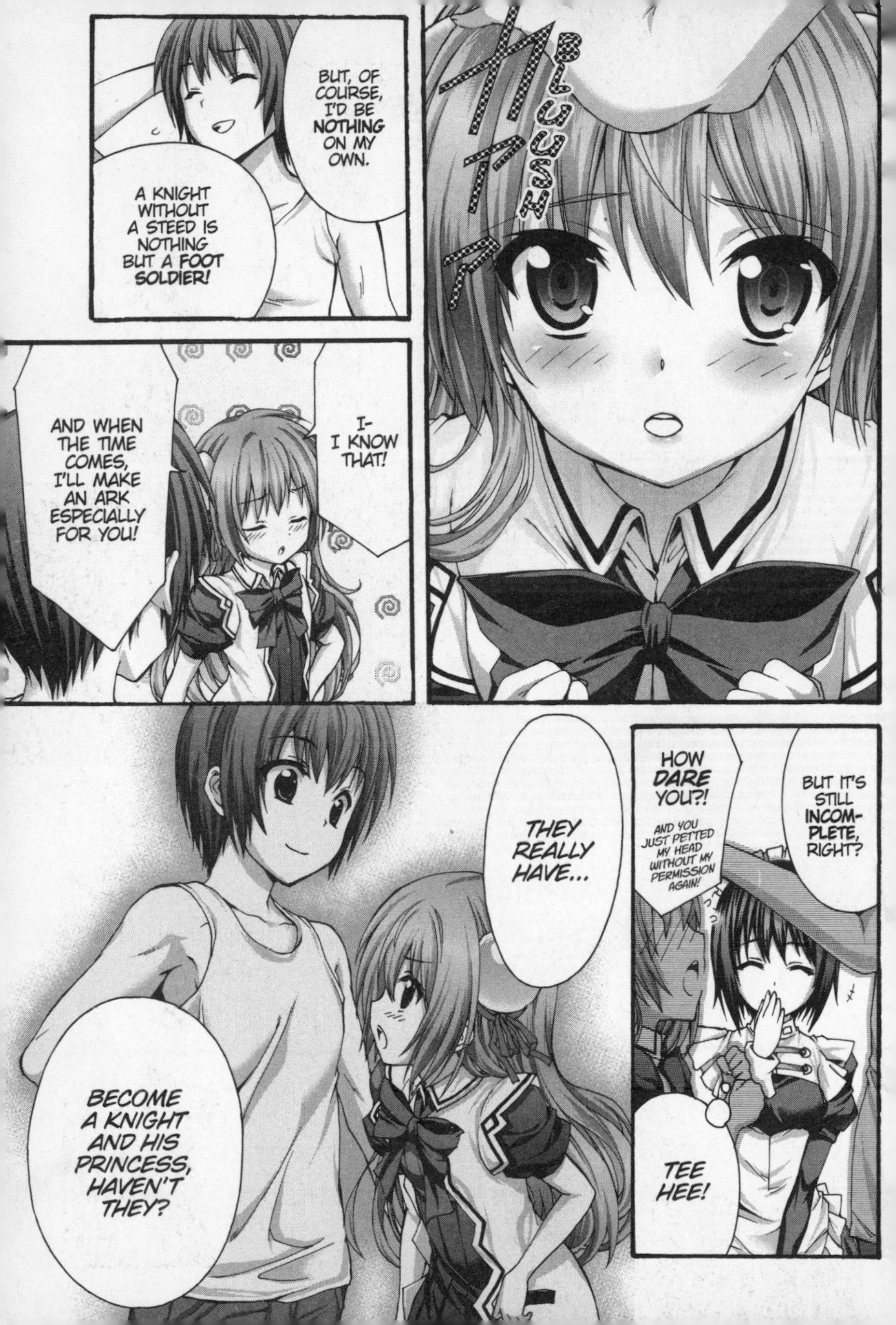
BLUSH
BUT, OF COURSE, I'D BE **NOTHING** ON MY OWN.
A KNIGHT WITHOUT A STEED IS NOTHING BUT A **FOOT SOLDIER!**
AND WHEN THE TIME COMES, I'LL MAKE AN ARK ESPECIALLY FOR YOU!
I- I KNOW THAT!
BUT IT'S STILL **INCOMPLETE,** RIGHT?
HOW ***DARE*** YOU?!
AND YOU JUST PETTED MY HEAD WITHOUT MY PERMISSION AGAIN!
TEE HEE!
THEY REALLY HAVE...
BECOME A KNIGHT AND HIS PRINCESS, HAVEN'T THEY?

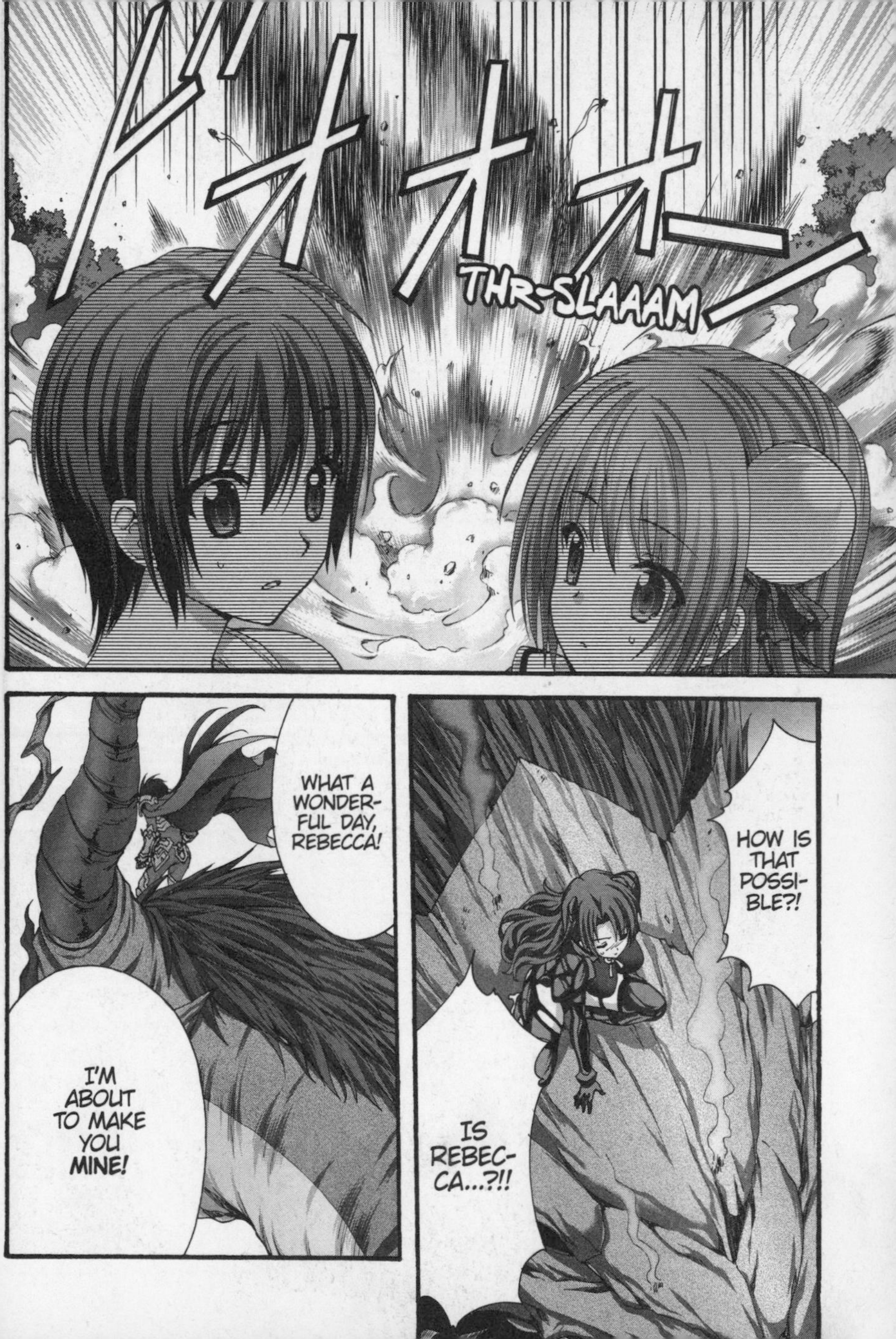
THR-SLAAAM
HOW IS THAT POSSI-BLE?!
IS REBEC-CA...?!!
WHAT A WONDER-FUL DAY, REBECCA!
I'M ABOUT TO MAKE YOU MINE!

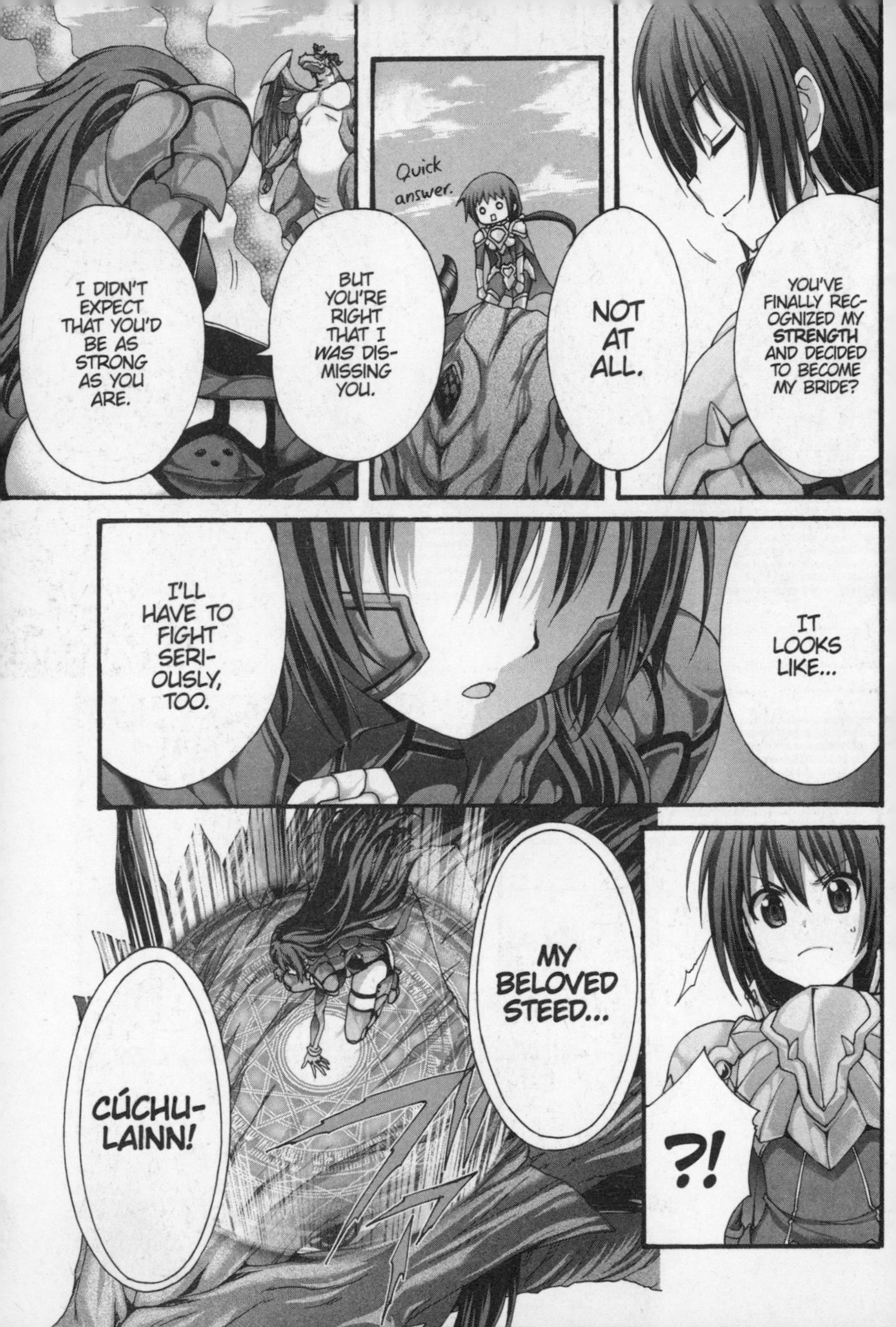

YOU'VE FINALLY RECOGNIZED MY STRENGTH AND DECIDED TO BECOME MY BRIDE?
NOT AT ALL.
Quick answer.
BUT YOU'RE RIGHT THAT I WAS DISMISSING YOU.
I DIDN'T EXPECT THAT YOU'D BE AS STRONG AS YOU ARE.
IT LOOKS LIKE...
I'LL HAVE TO FIGHT SERIOUSLY, TOO.
?!
MY BELOVED STEED...
CÚCHULAINN!

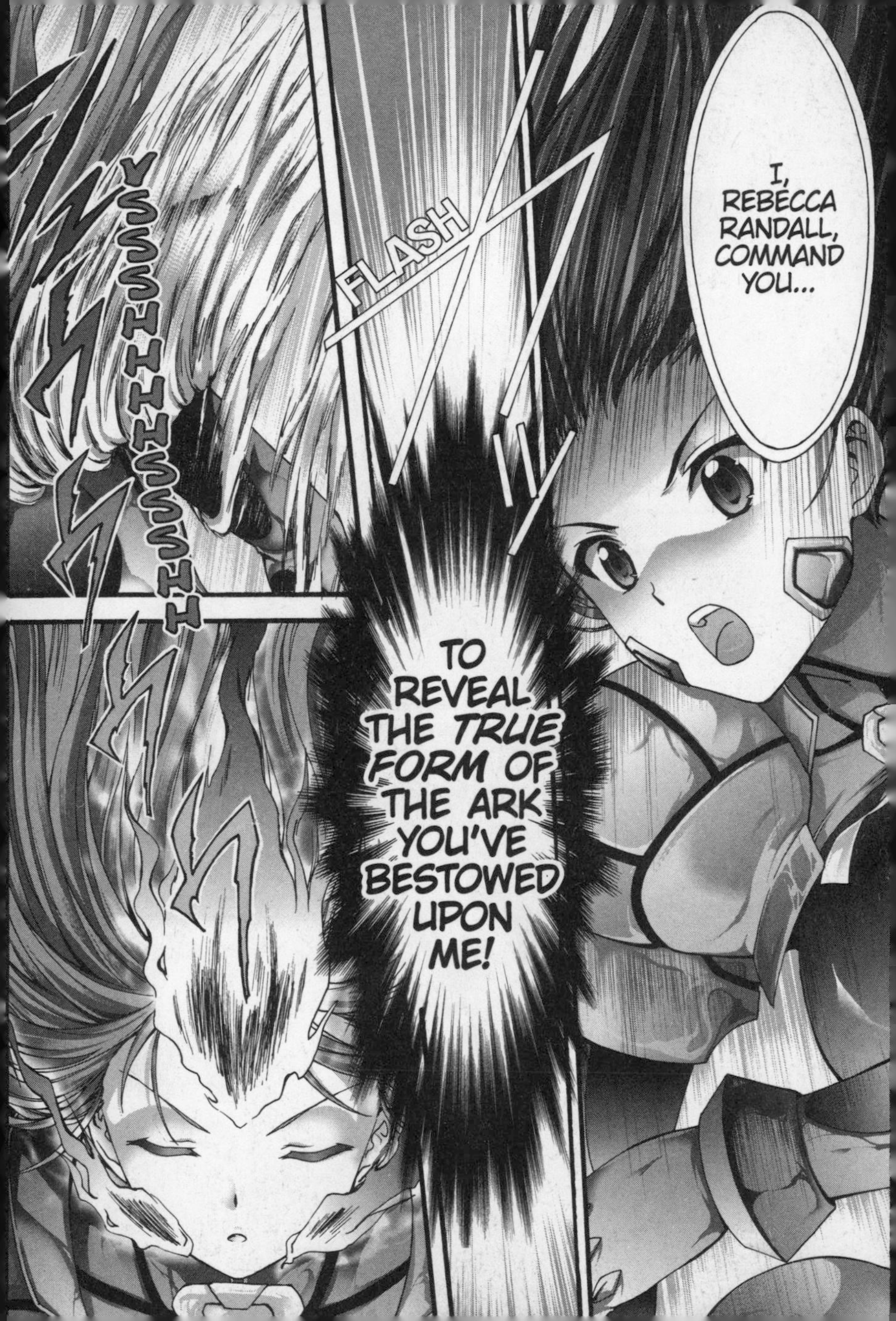
I, REBECCA RANDALL, COMMAND YOU...
FLASH
YSSSSHHHHHSSSSSHH
TO REVEAL THE *TRUE FORM* OF THE ARK YOU'VE BESTOWED UPON ME!

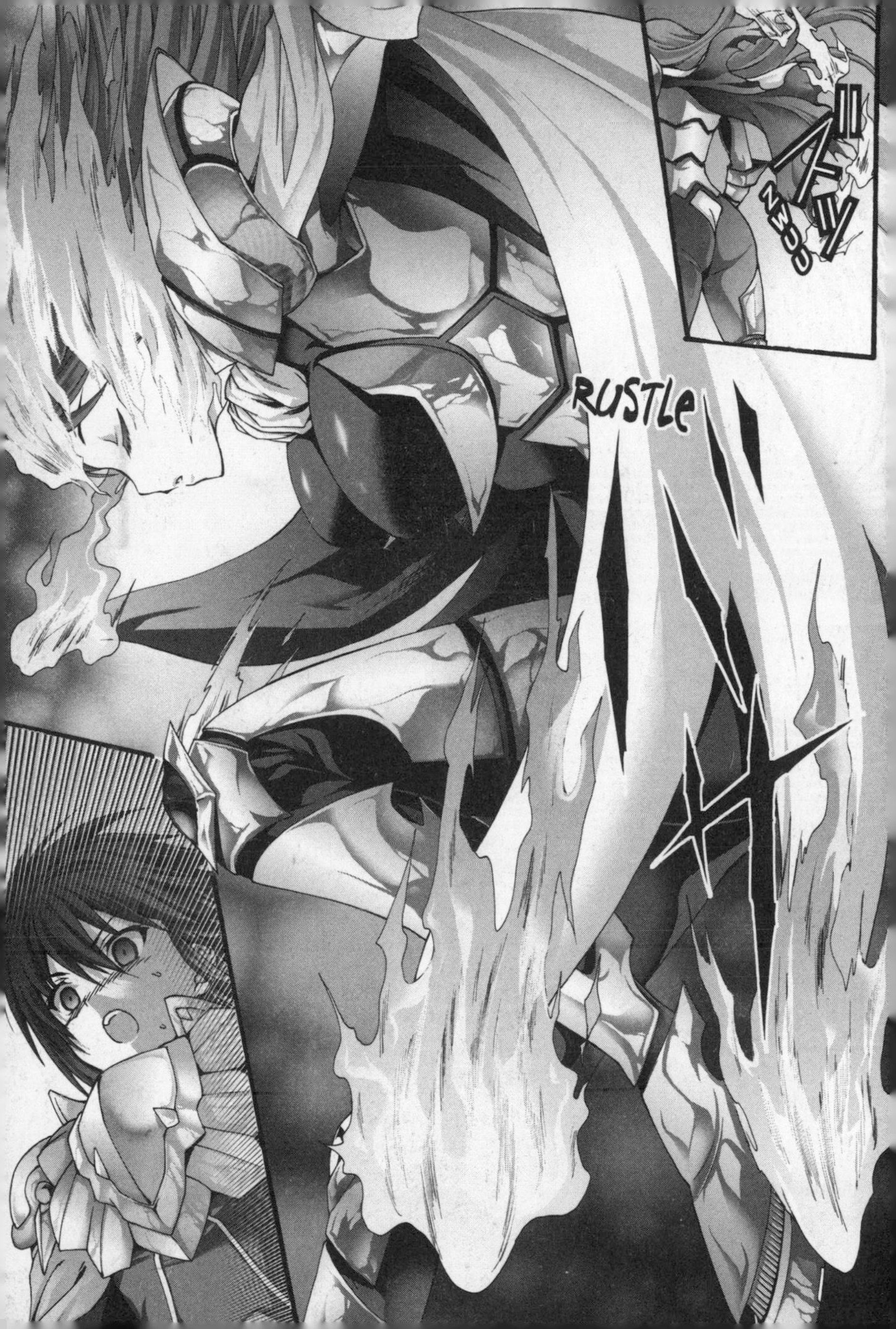
RUSTLE

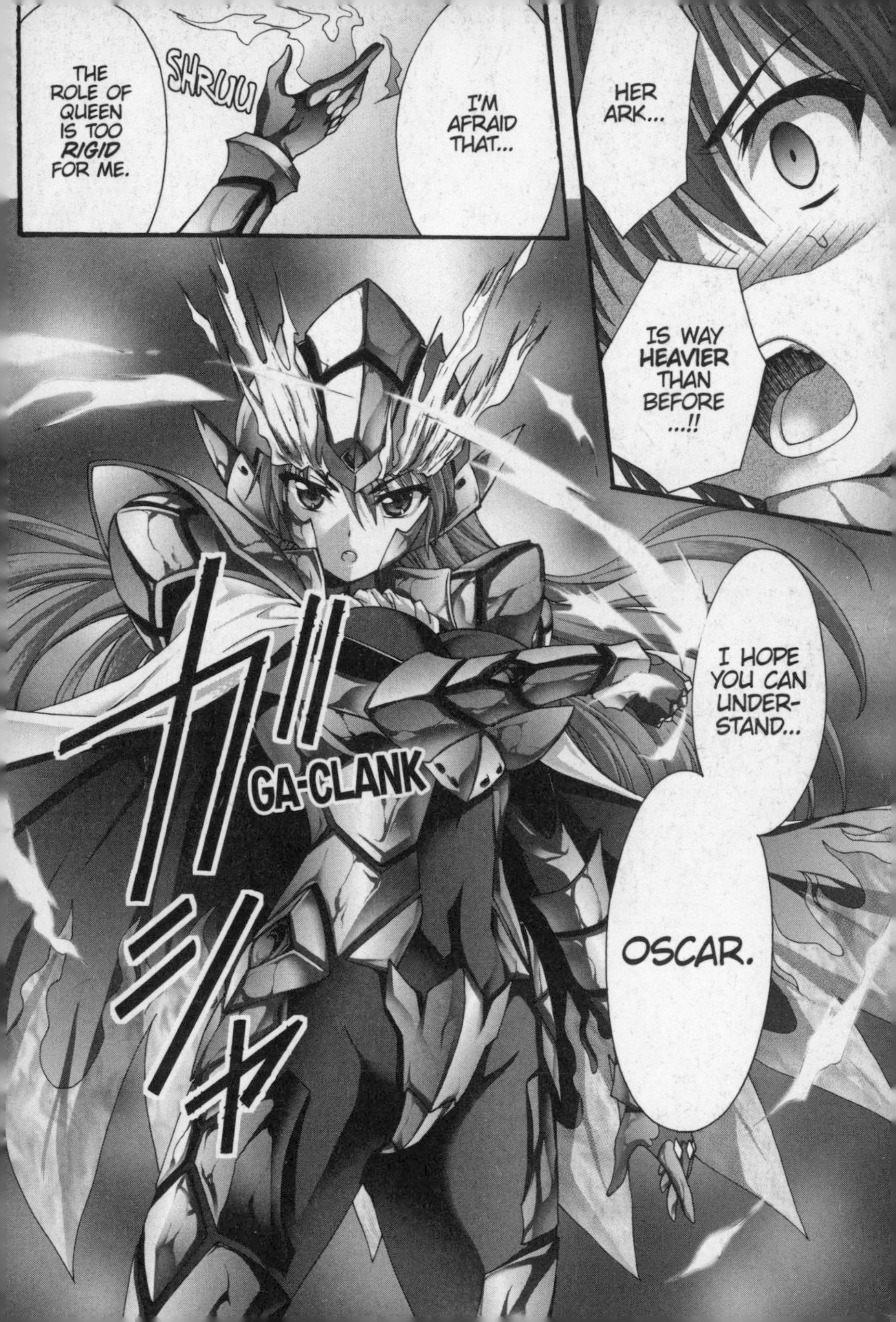
HER ARK...
IS WAY HEAVIER THAN BEFORE ...!!
I'M AFRAID THAT...
SHRUU
THE ROLE OF QUEEN IS TOO RIGID FOR ME.
I HOPE YOU CAN UNDER-STAND...
OSCAR.
GA-CLANK

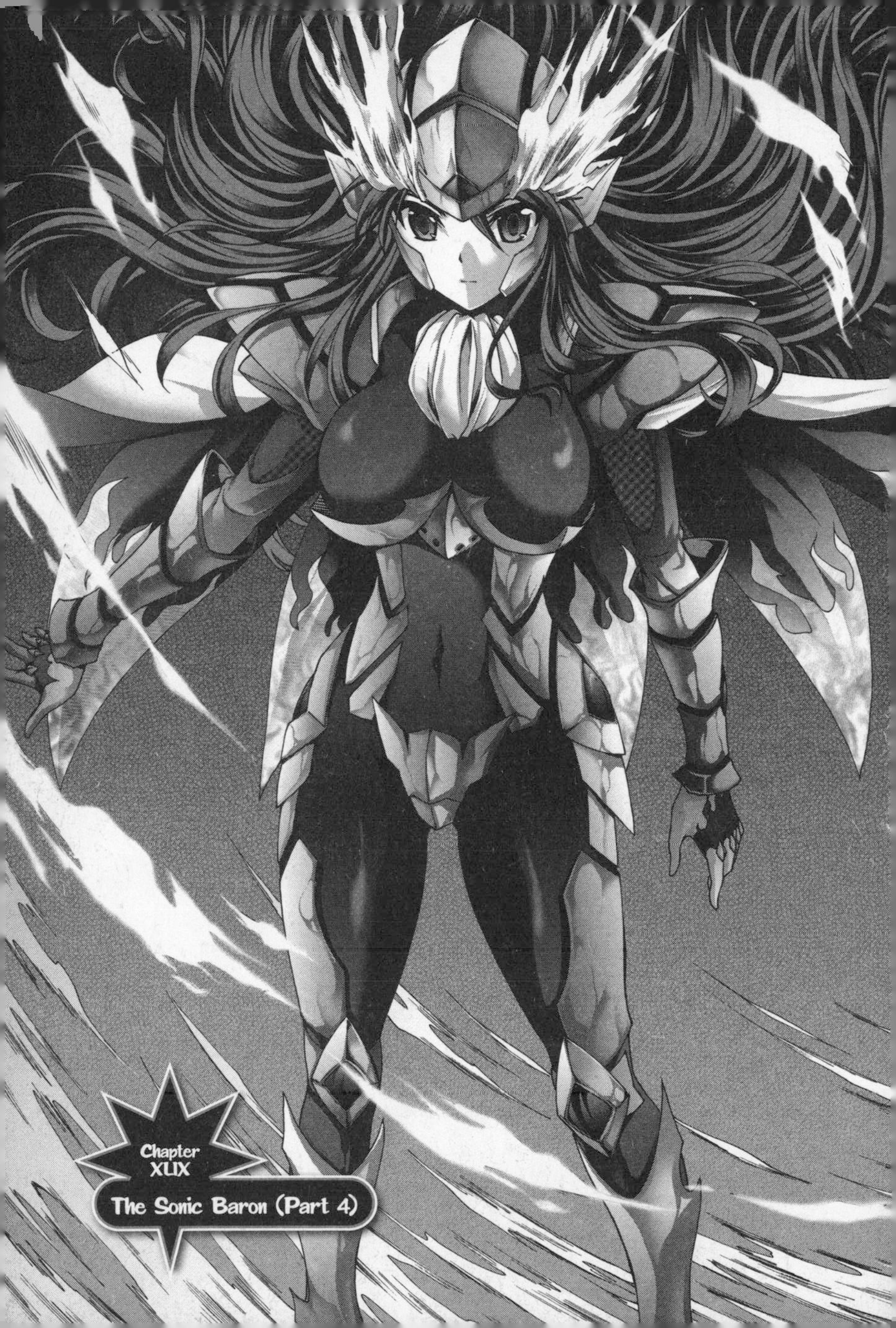
Chapter
XLIX
The Sonic Baron (Part 4)

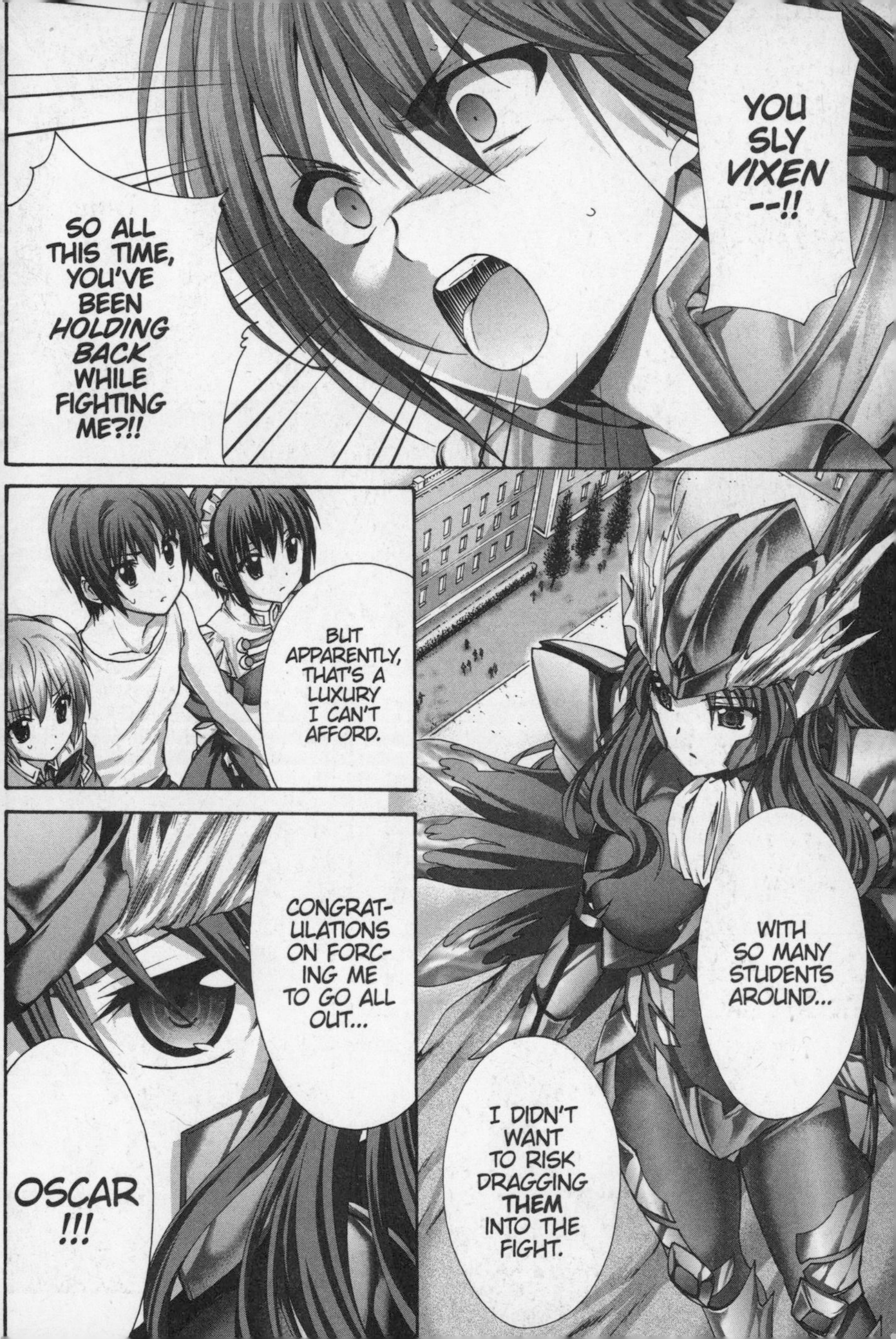
YOU SLY VIXEN --!!
SO ALL THIS TIME, YOU'VE BEEN *HOLDING BACK* WHILE FIGHTING ME?!!
WITH SO MANY STUDENTS AROUND...
I DIDN'T WANT TO RISK DRAGGING **THEM** INTO THE FIGHT.
BUT APPARENTLY, THAT'S A LUXURY I CAN'T AFFORD.
CONGRAT-ULATIONS ON FORC-ING ME TO GO ALL OUT...
OSCAR !!!

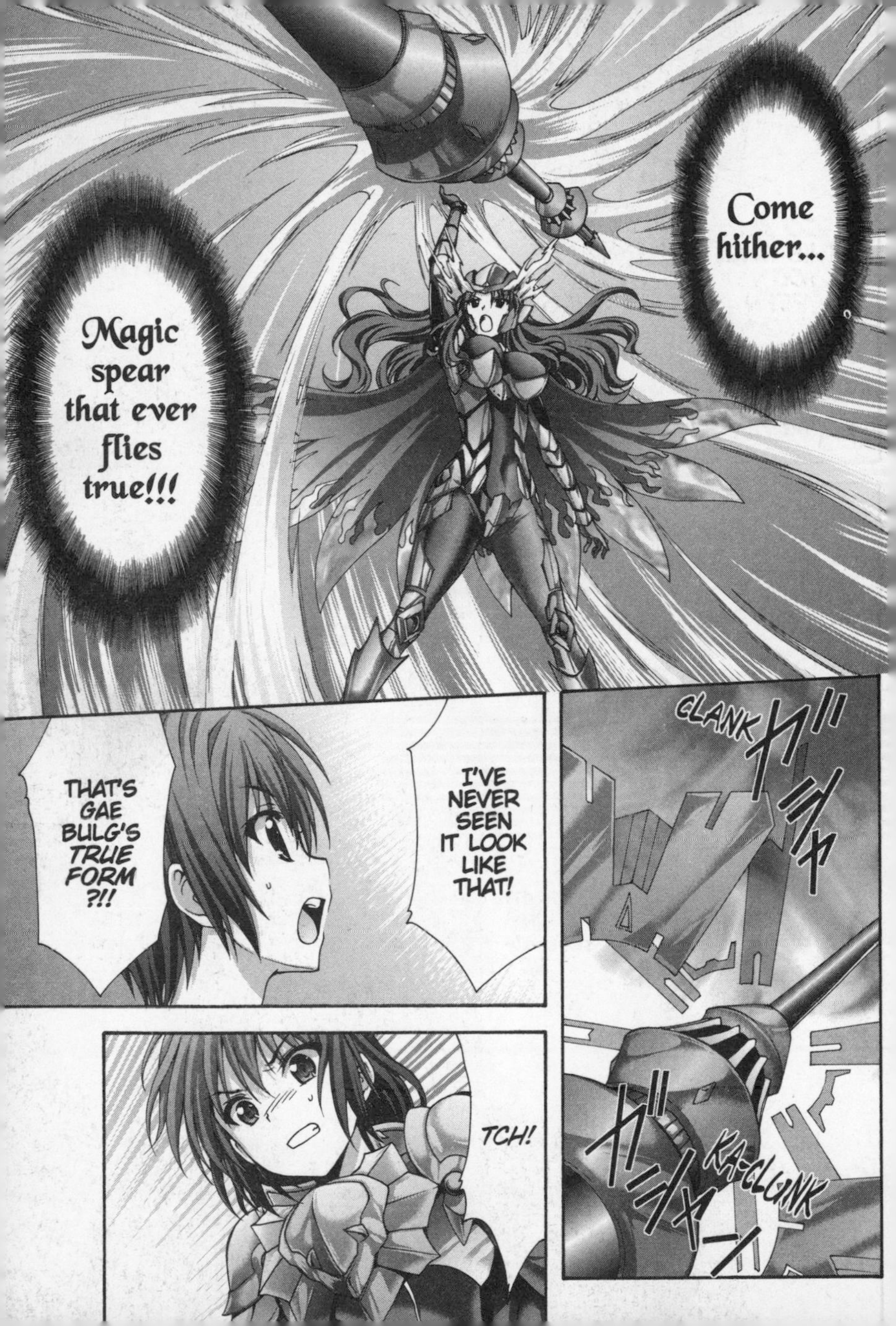
Come hither...
Magic spear that ever flies true!!!
CLANK
KA-CLUNK
I'VE NEVER SEEN IT LOOK LIKE THAT!
THAT'S GAE BULG'S *TRUE FORM* ?!!
TCH!

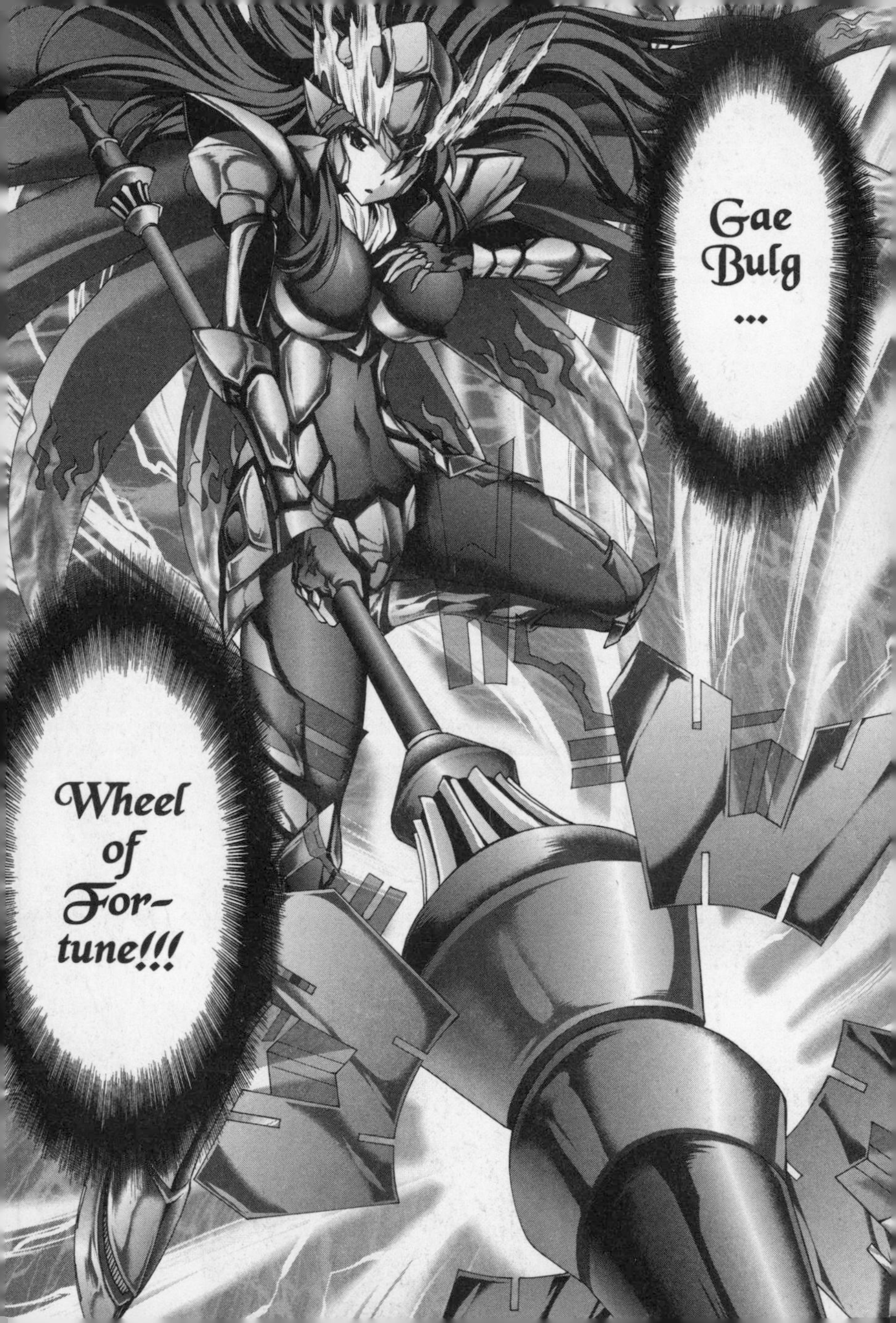
Gae Bulg ...
Wheel of For-tune!!!

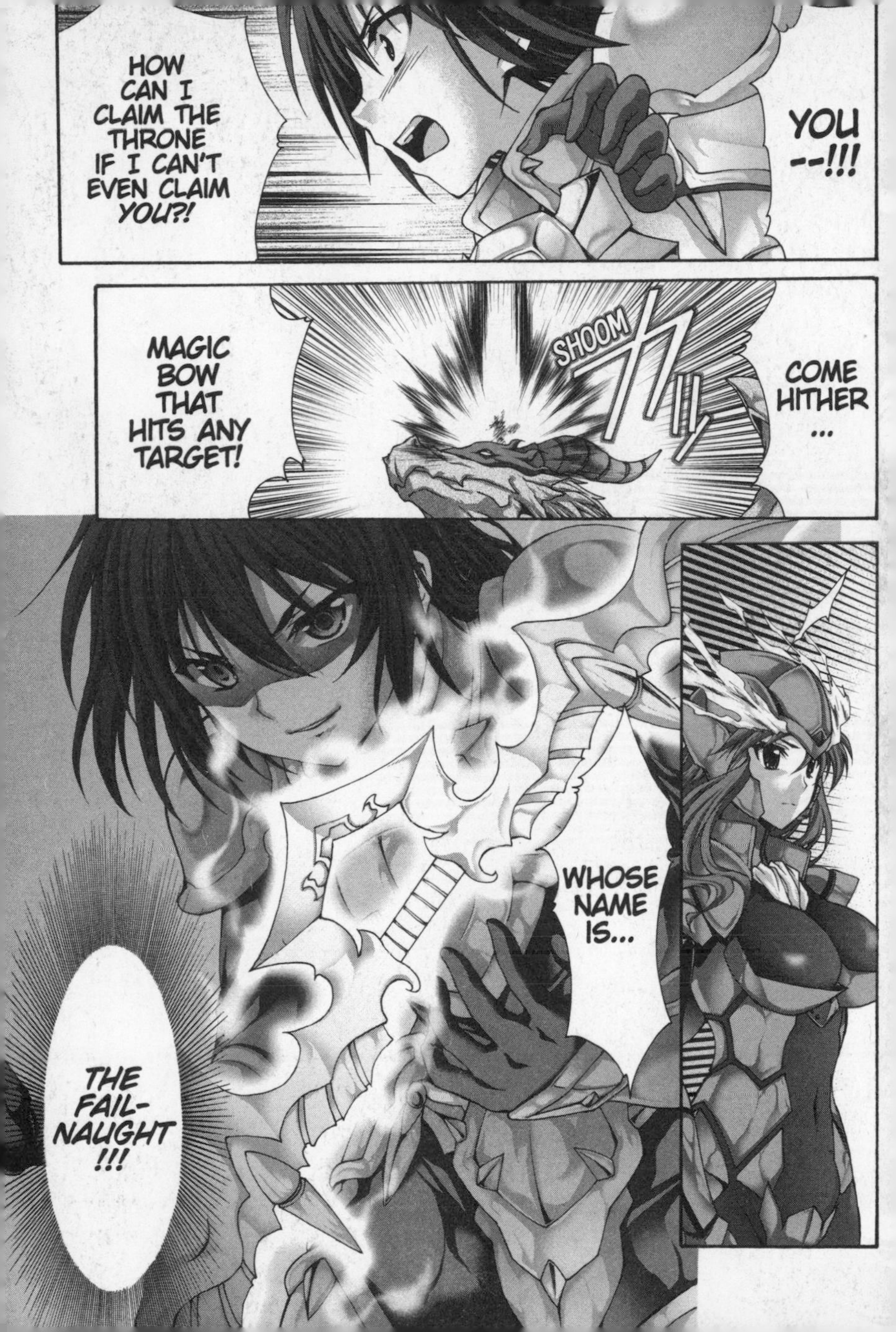
YOU --!!!
HOW CAN I CLAIM THE THRONE IF I CAN'T EVEN CLAIM YOU?!
COME HITHER ...
SHOOM
MAGIC BOW THAT HITS ANY TARGET!
WHOSE NAME IS...
THE FAIL-NAUGHT!!!

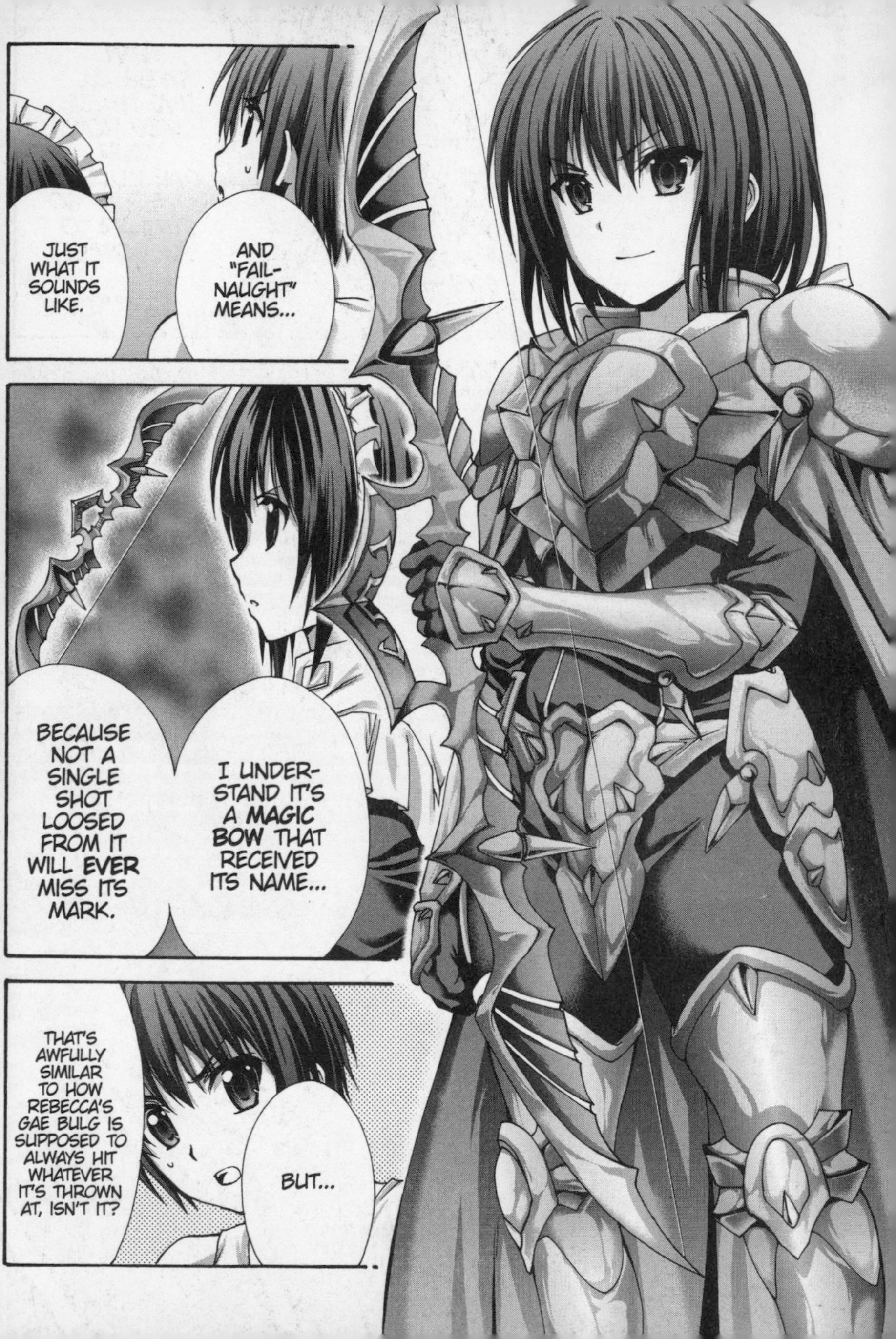
AND "FAIL-NAUGHT" MEANS...
JUST WHAT IT SOUNDS LIKE.
I UNDER-STAND IT'S A **MAGIC BOW** THAT RECEIVED ITS NAME...
BECAUSE NOT A SINGLE SHOT LOOSED FROM IT WILL **EVER** MISS ITS MARK.
BUT...
THAT'S AWFULLY SIMILAR TO HOW REBECCA'S GAE BULG IS SUPPOSED TO ALWAYS HIT WHATEVER IT'S THROWN AT, ISN'T IT?

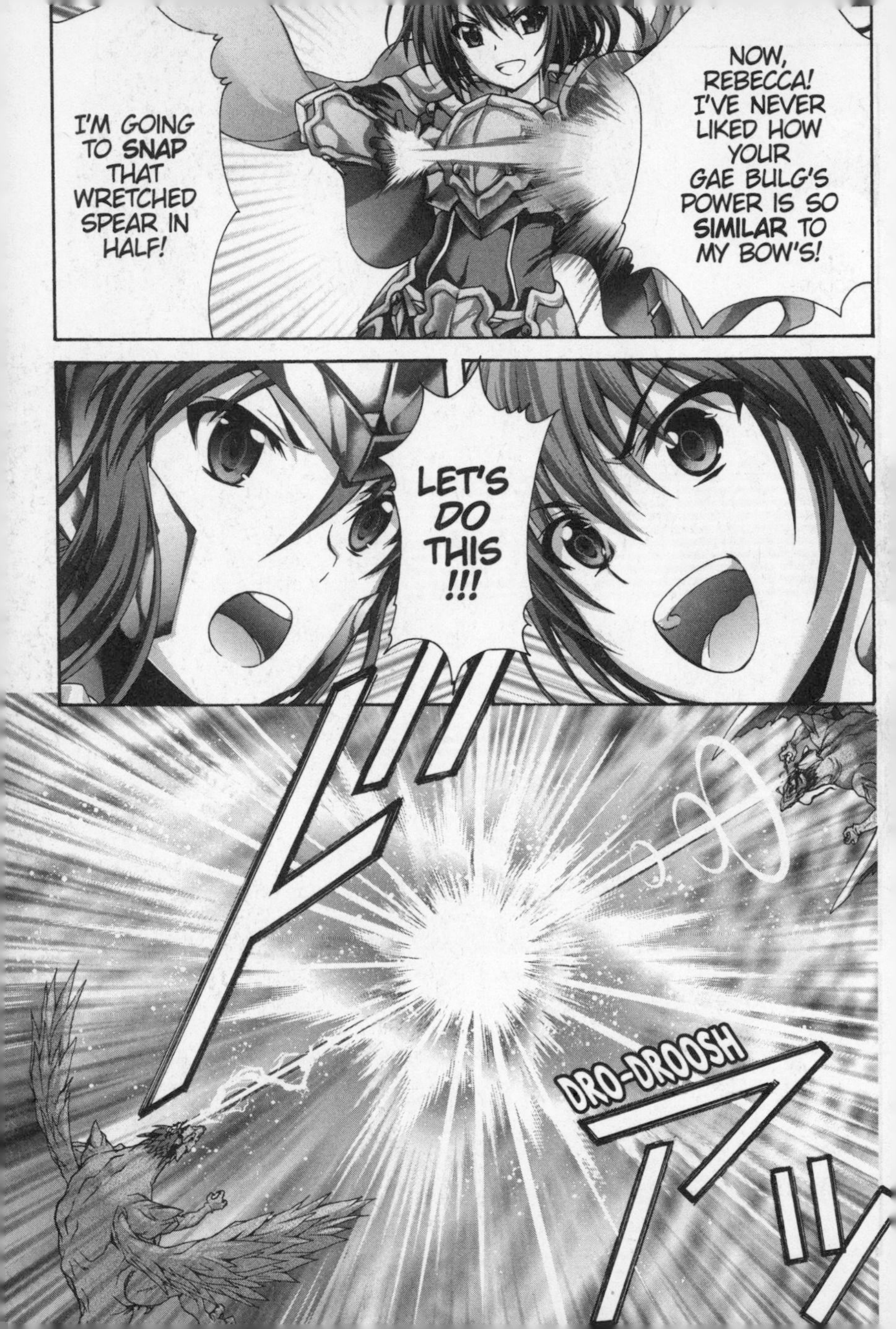
NOW, REBECCA! I'VE NEVER LIKED HOW YOUR GAE BULG'S POWER IS SO SIMILAR TO MY BOW'S!
I'M GOING TO SNAP THAT WRETCHED SPEAR IN HALF!
LET'S DO THIS!!!
DRO-DROOSH

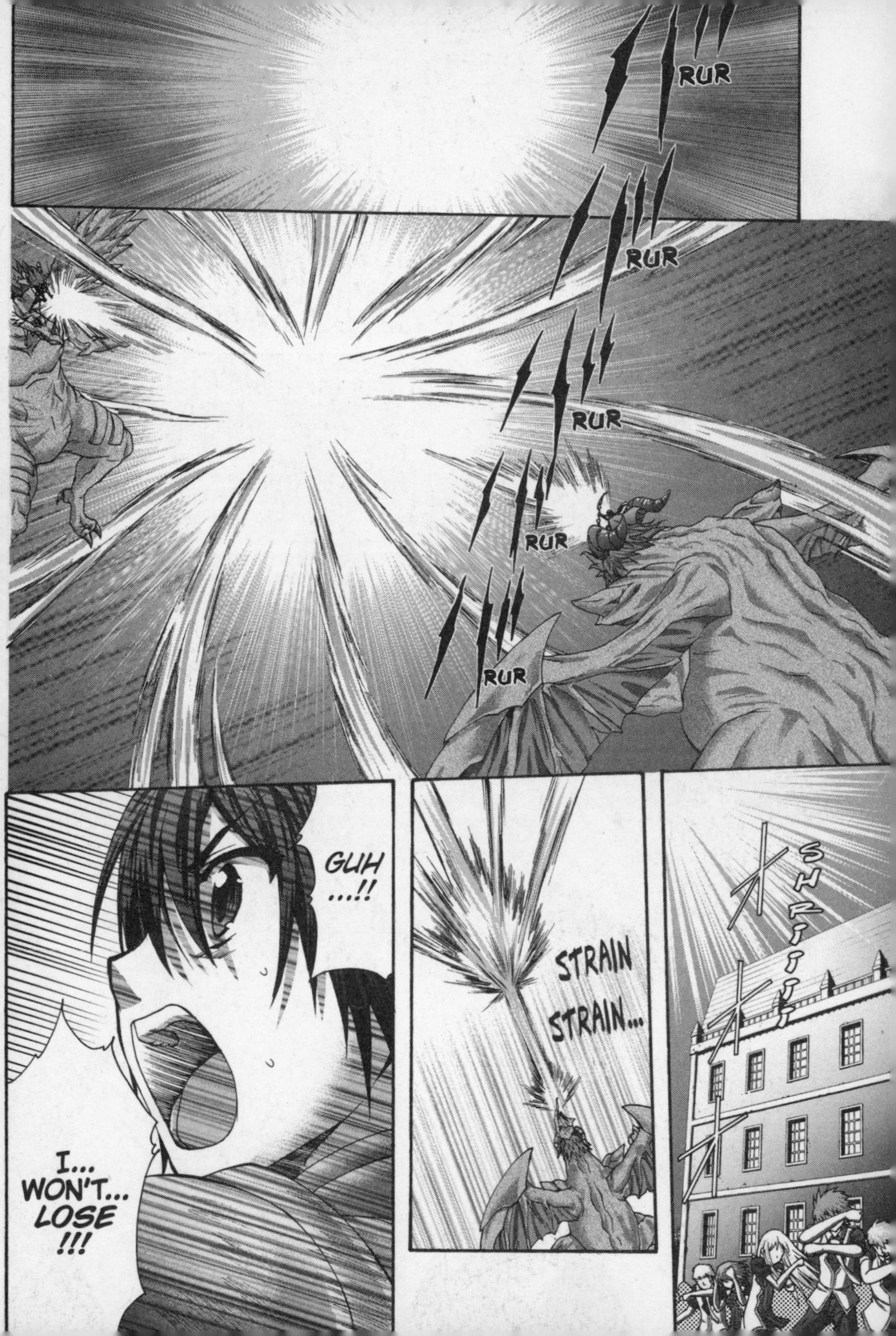
RUR
RUR
RUR
RUR
RUR
SHRIIII
STRAIN
STRAIN...
GUH ...!!
I... WON'T... LOSE !!!

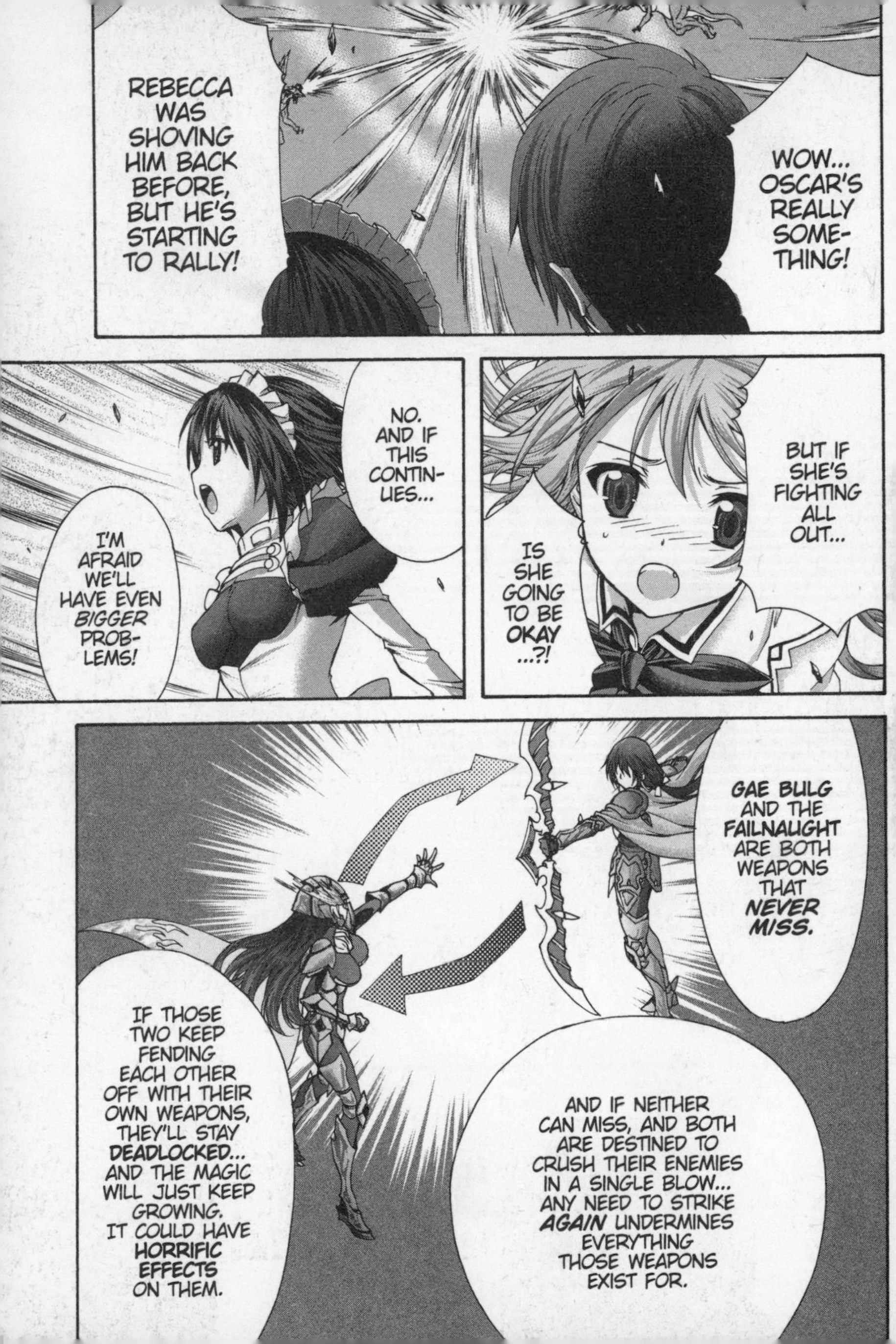
WOW... OSCAR'S REALLY SOME-THING!
REBECCA WAS SHOVING HIM BACK BEFORE, BUT HE'S STARTING TO RALLY!
BUT IF SHE'S FIGHTING ALL OUT...
IS SHE GOING TO BE OKAY...?!
NO. AND IF THIS CONTIN-UES...
I'M AFRAID WE'LL HAVE EVEN BIGGER PROB-LEMS!
GAE BULG AND THE FAILNAUGHT ARE BOTH WEAPONS THAT NEVER MISS.
IF THOSE TWO KEEP FENDING EACH OTHER OFF WITH THEIR OWN WEAPONS, THEY'LL STAY DEADLOCKED... AND THE MAGIC WILL JUST KEEP GROWING. IT COULD HAVE HORRIFIC EFFECTS ON THEM.
AND IF NEITHER CAN MISS, AND BOTH ARE DESTINED TO CRUSH THEIR ENEMIES IN A SINGLE BLOW... ANY NEED TO STRIKE AGAIN UNDERMINES EVERYTHING THOSE WEAPONS EXIST FOR.

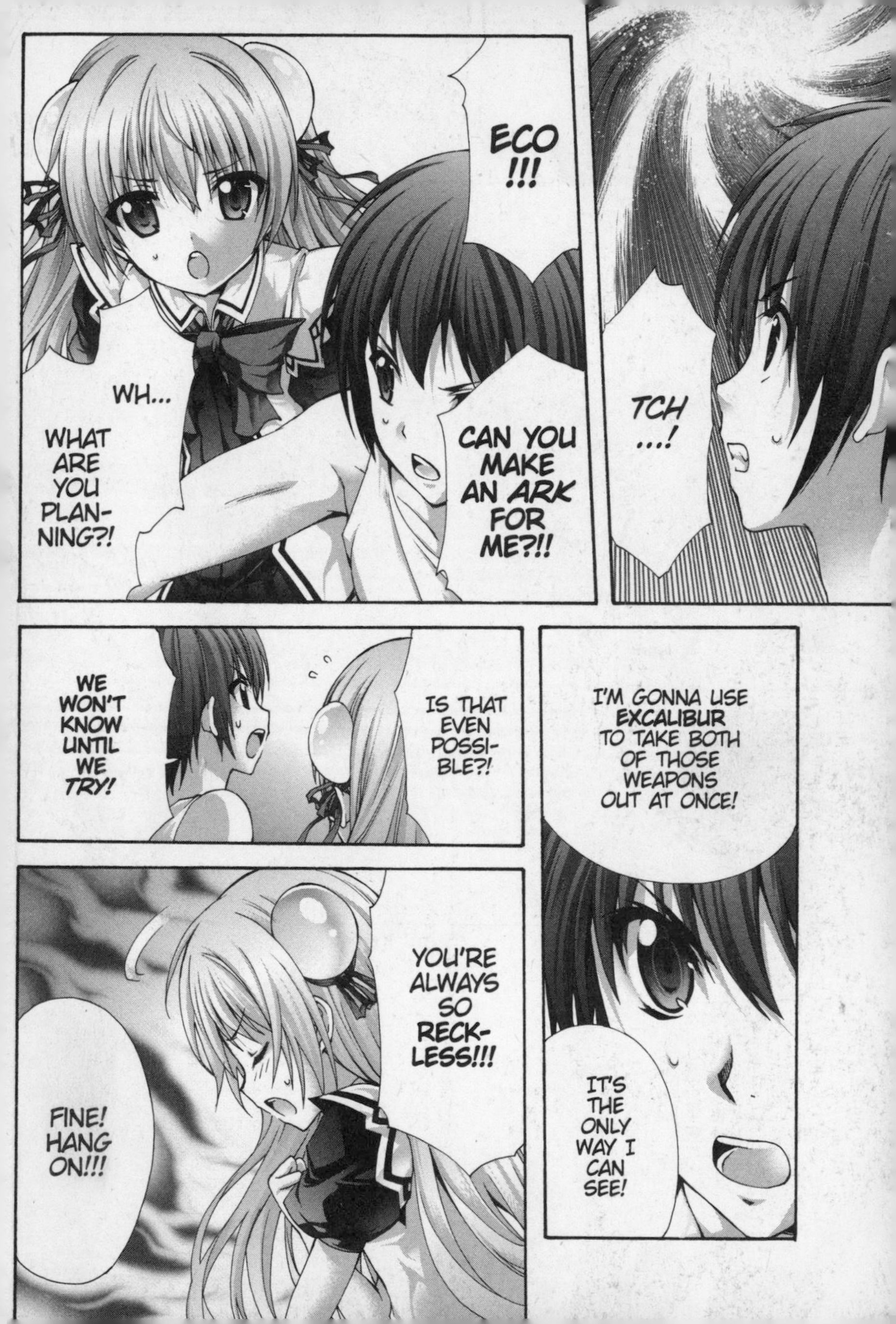
TCH ...!
ECO !!!
CAN YOU MAKE AN *ARK* FOR ME?!!
WH...
WHAT ARE YOU PLAN-NING?!
I'M GONNA USE **EXCALIBUR** TO TAKE BOTH OF THOSE WEAPONS OUT AT ONCE!
IT'S THE ONLY WAY I CAN SEE!
IS THAT EVEN POSSI-BLE?!
WE WON'T KNOW UNTIL WE *TRY!*
YOU'RE ALWAYS SO RECK-LESS!!!
FINE! HANG ON!!!

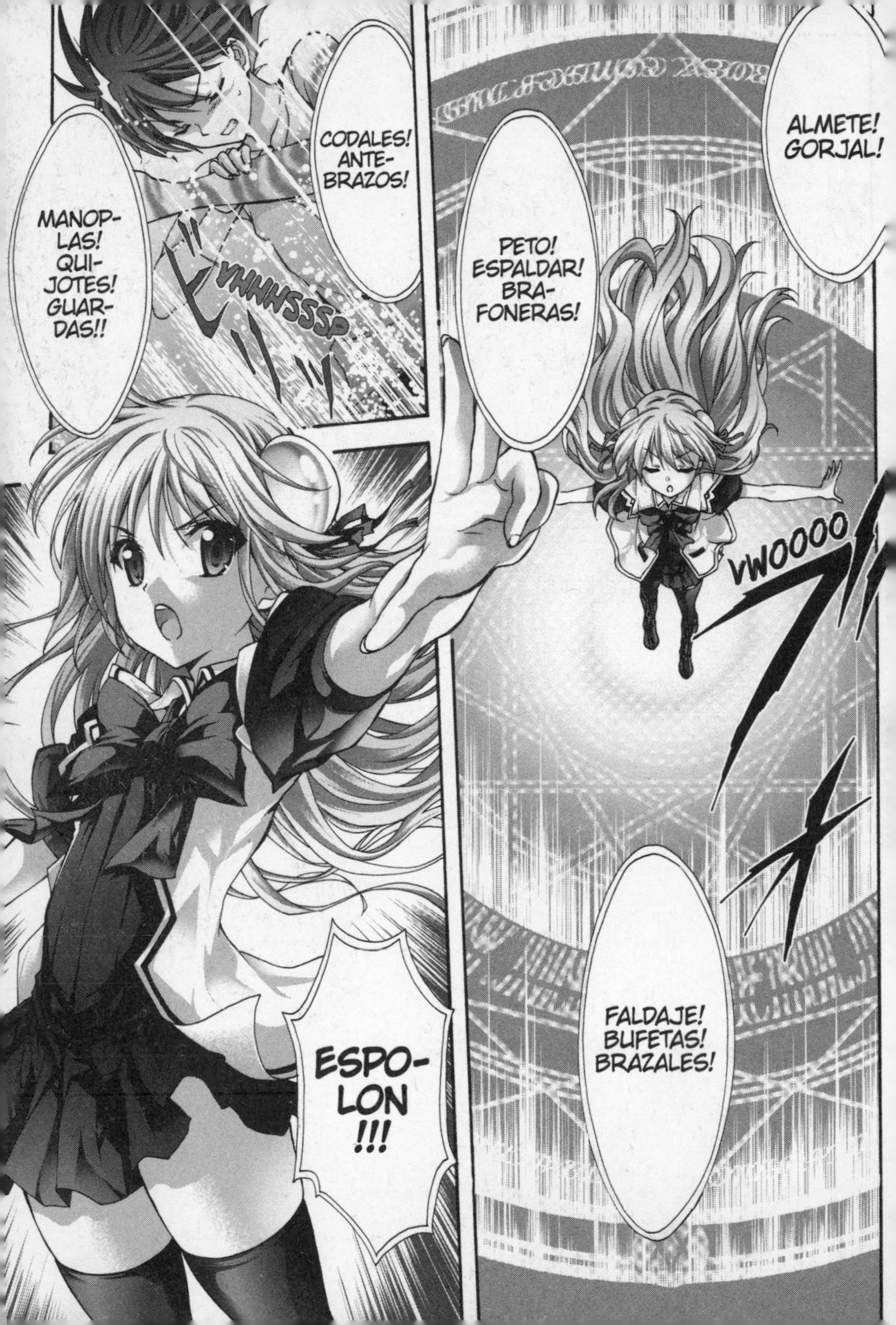
ALMETE! GORJAL!
PETO! ESPALDAR! BRA-FONERAS!
VWOOOO
FALDAJE! BUFETAS! BRAZALES!
CODALES! ANTE-BRAZOS!
MANOP-LAS! QUI-JOTES! GUAR-DAS!!
VHHHHSSSP
ESPO-LON !!!

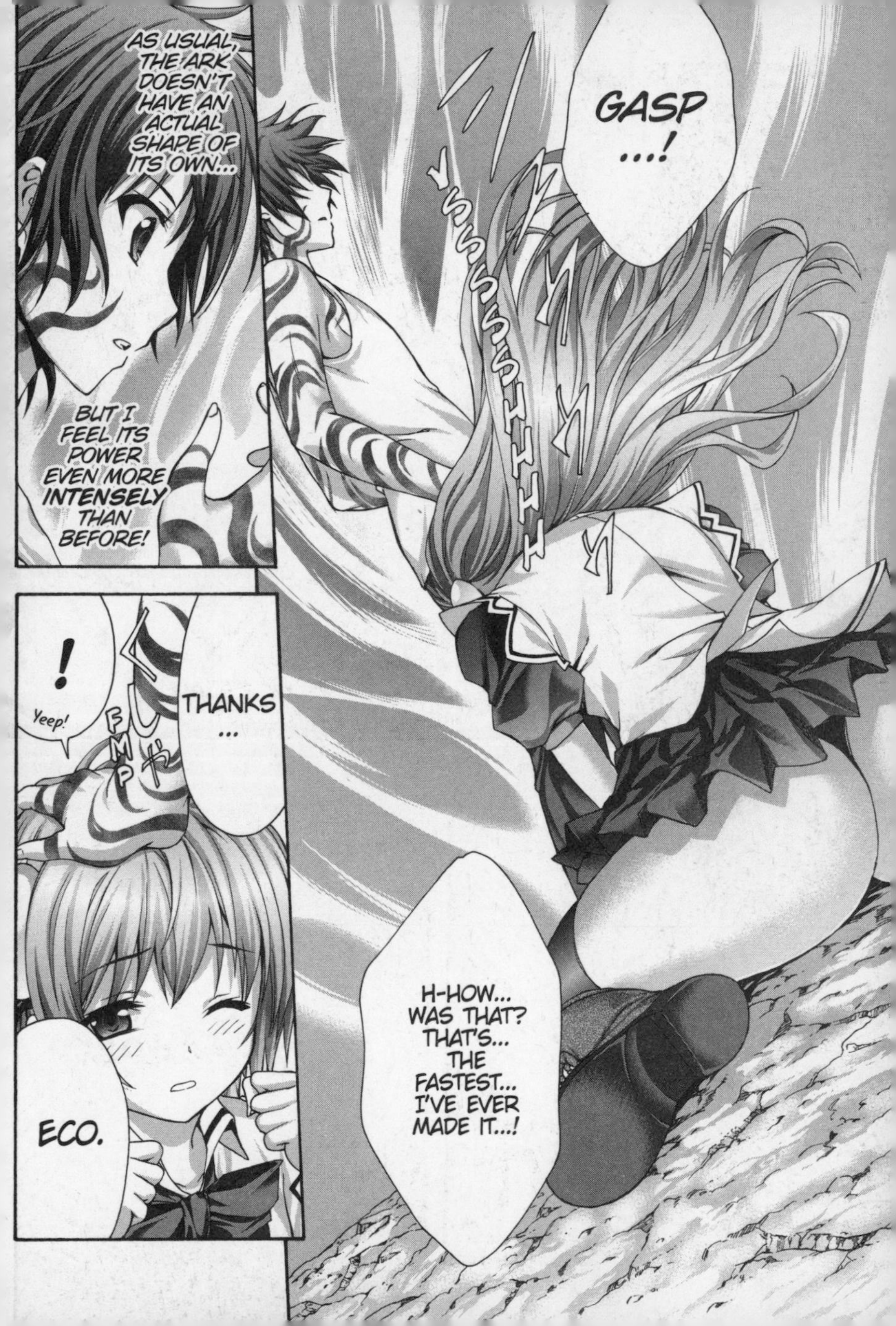
GASP ...!
VSSSSSSHHHHH
H-HOW... WAS THAT? THAT'S... THE FASTEST... I'VE EVER MADE IT...!
AS USUAL, THE ARK DOESN'T HAVE AN ACTUAL SHAPE OF ITS OWN...
BUT I FEEL ITS POWER EVEN MORE INTENSELY THAN BEFORE!
! Yeep!
FMP
THANKS ...
ECO.

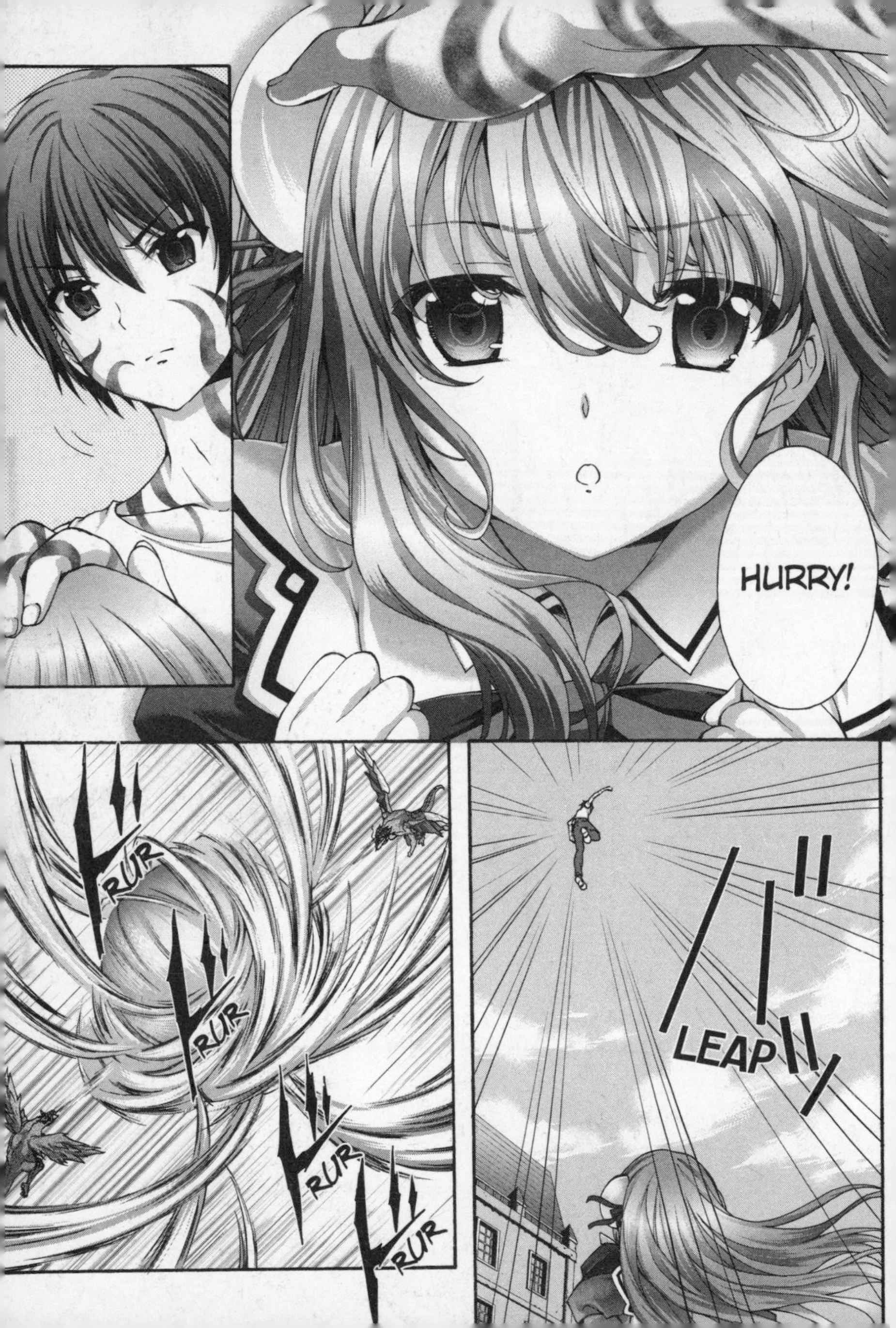
HURRY!
LEAP
RUR
RUR
RUR
RUR

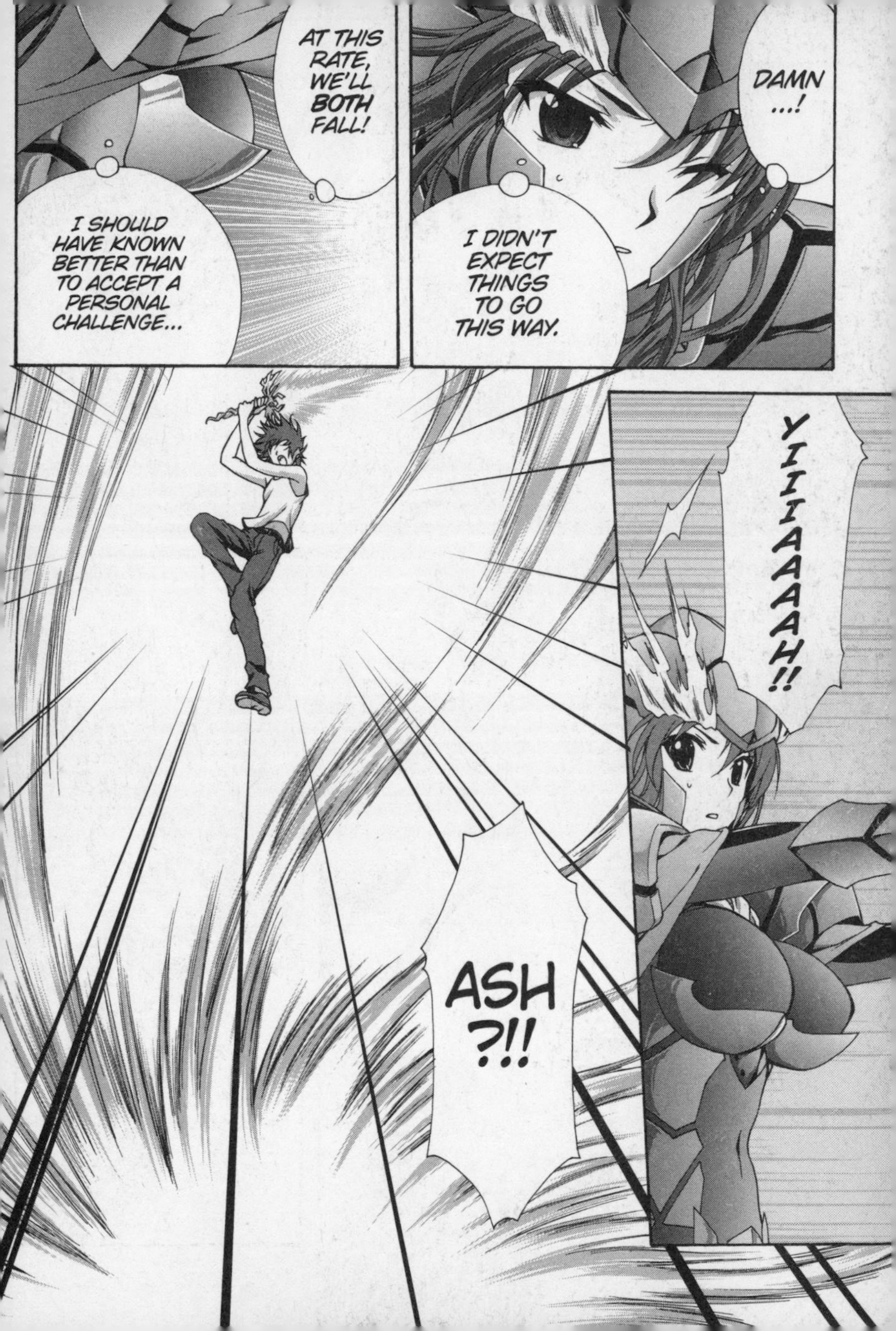

DAMN ...!
I DIDN'T EXPECT THINGS TO GO THIS WAY.
AT THIS RATE, WE'LL BOTH FALL!
I SHOULD HAVE KNOWN BETTER THAN TO ACCEPT A PERSONAL CHALLENGE...
YIIIIAAAAAH!!
ASH ?!!

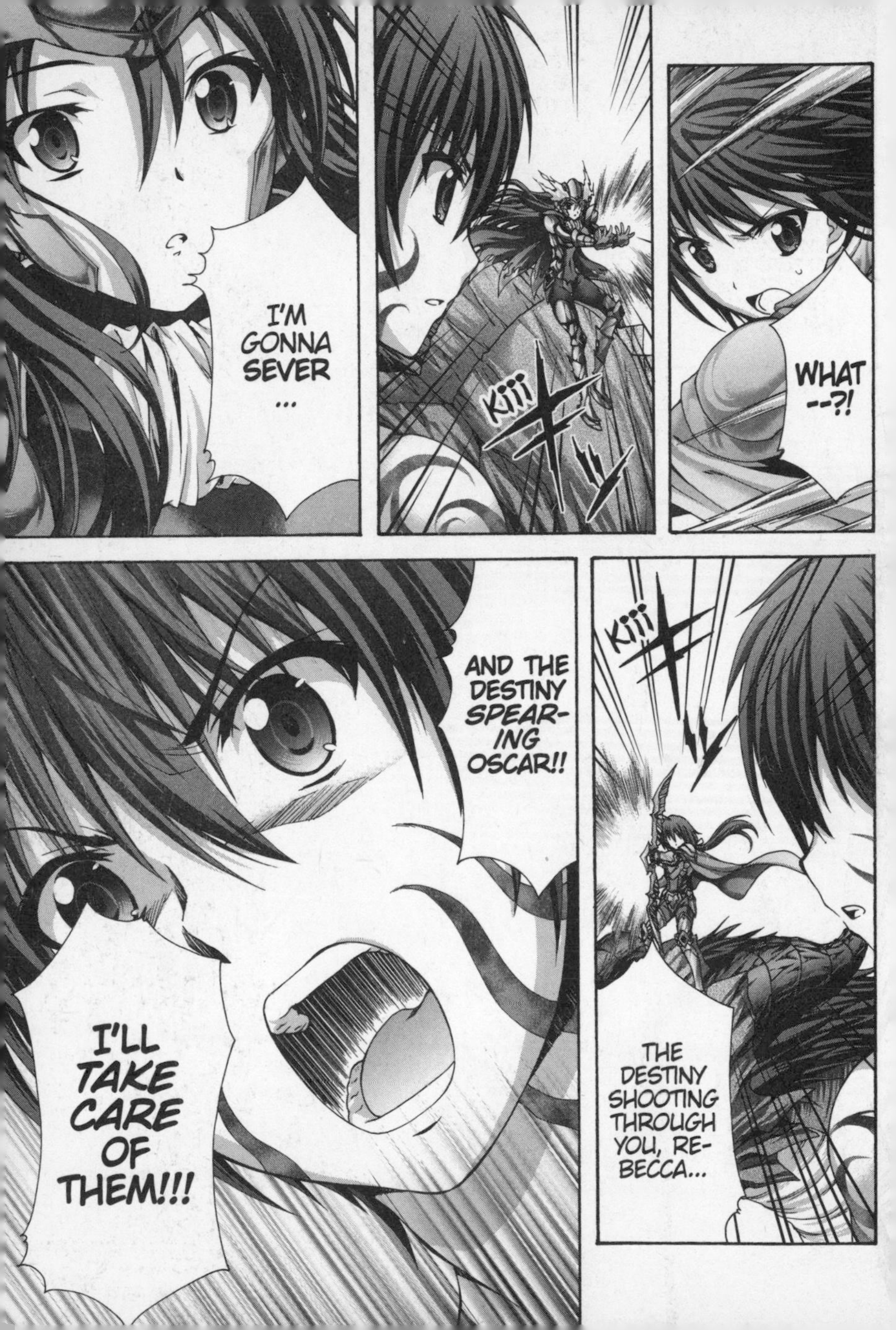
WHAT --?!
Kiii
I'M GONNA SEVER ...
Kiii
THE DESTINY SHOOTING THROUGH YOU, RE-BECCA...
AND THE DESTINY SPEAR-ING OSCAR!!
I'LL TAKE CARE OF THEM!!!

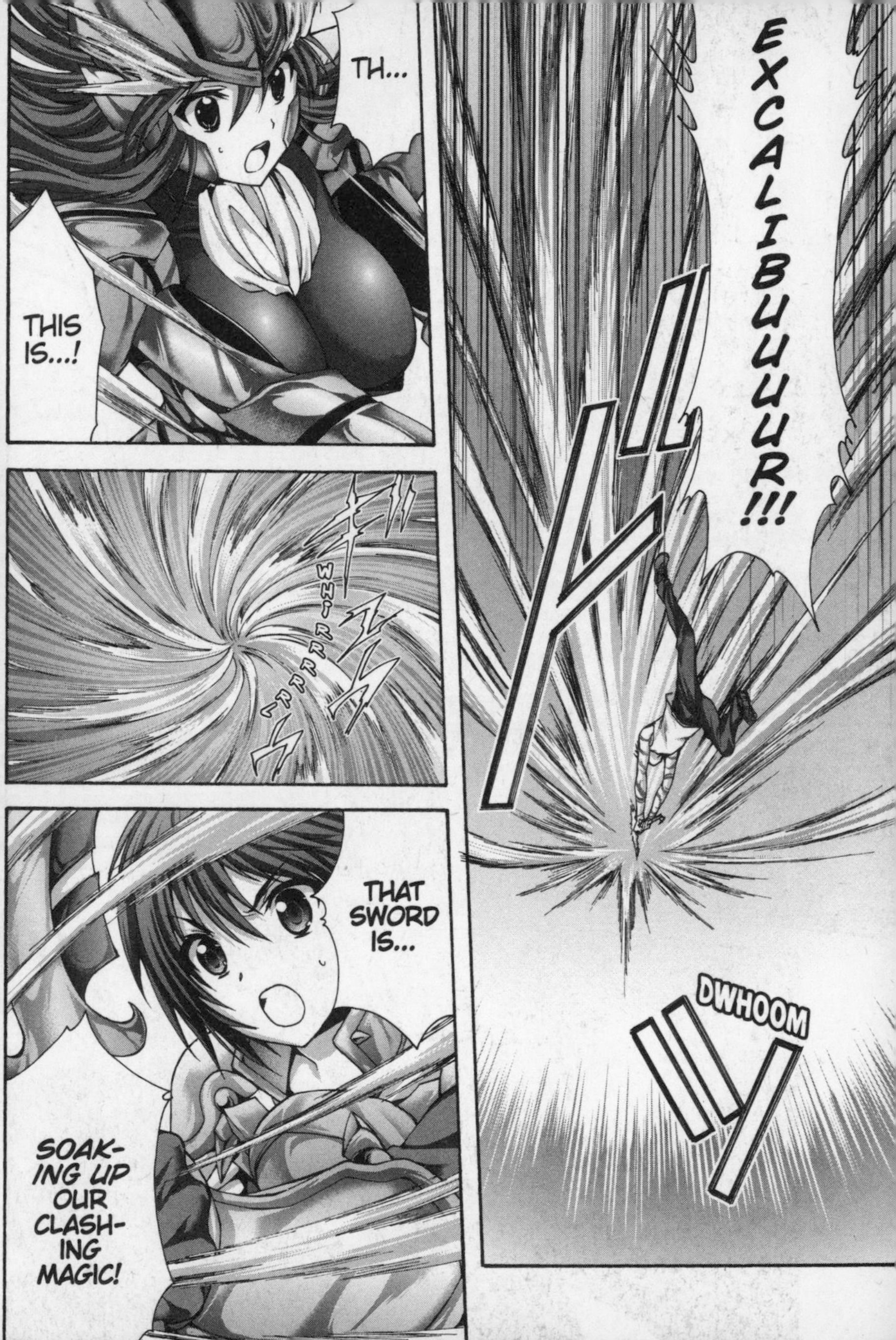
EXCALIBUUUUR!!!
DWHOOM
TH...
THIS IS...!
WHIRRRRRL
THAT SWORD IS...
SOAK-ING UP OUR CLASH-ING MAGIC!

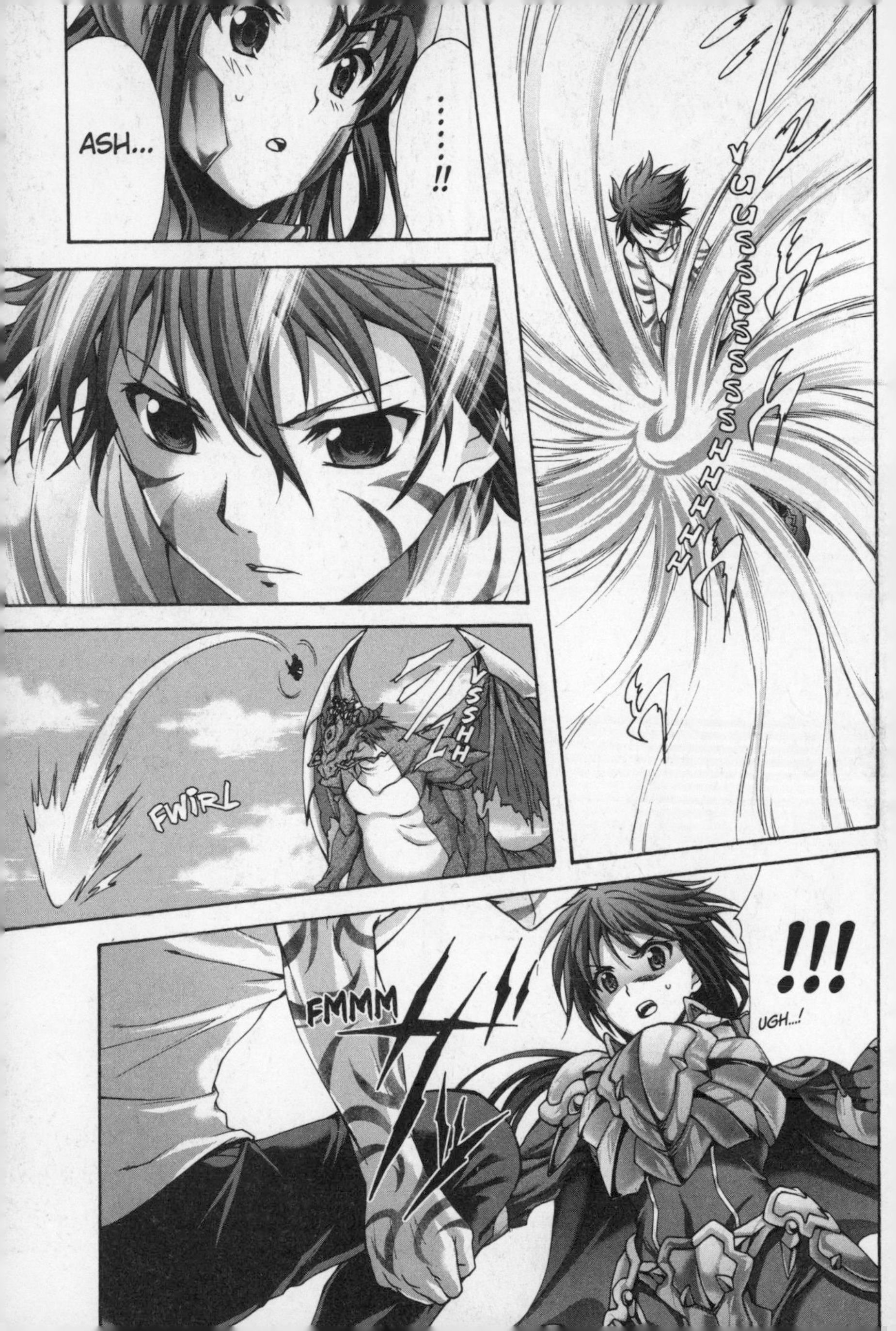
VUSSSSSSSSSHHHHHH
ASH...
......!!
VSSHH
FWIRL
!!!
UGH...!
FMMM

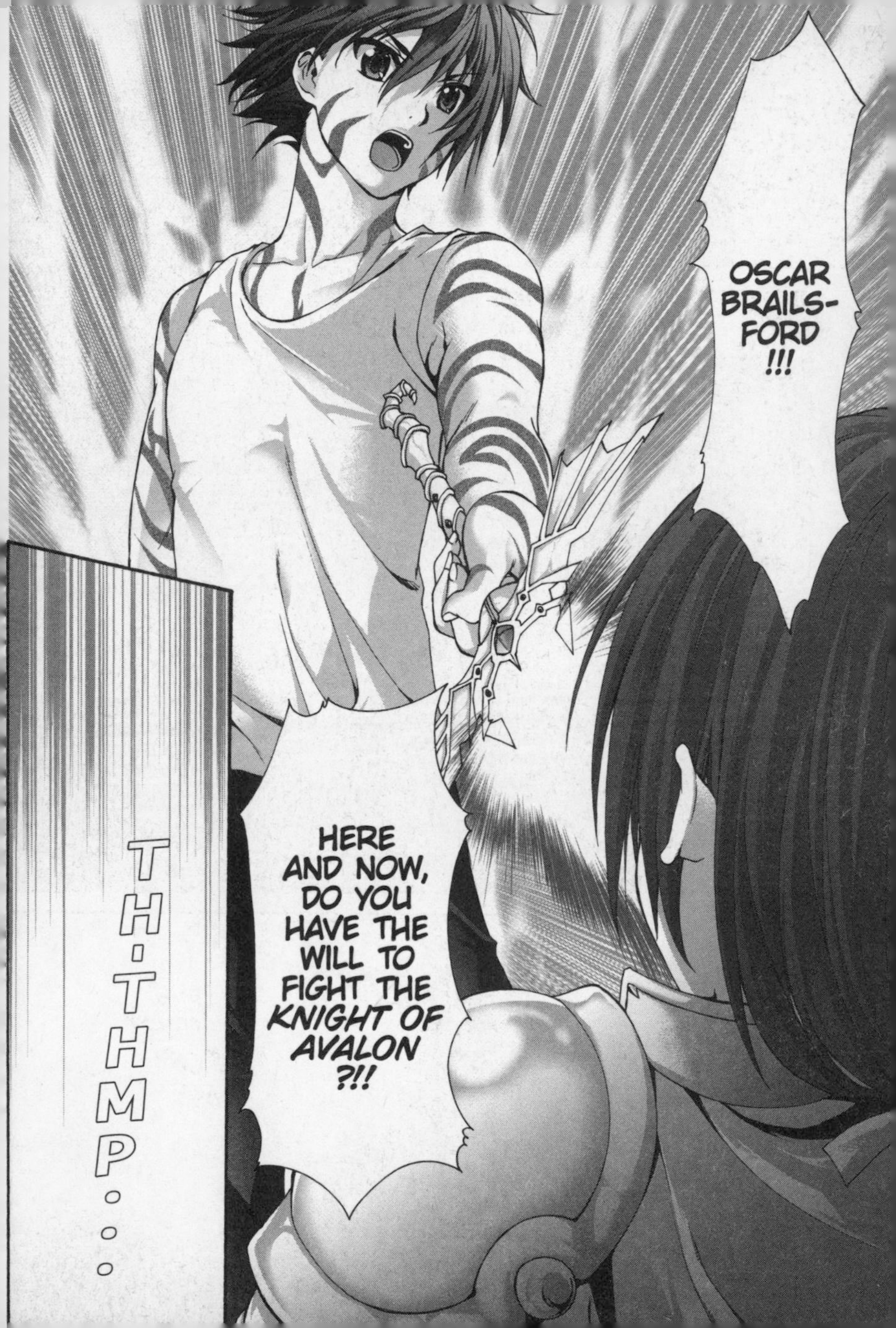
OSCAR BRAILS-FORD !!!
HERE AND NOW, DO YOU HAVE THE WILL TO FIGHT THE *KNIGHT OF AVALON* ?!!
TH-THMP...

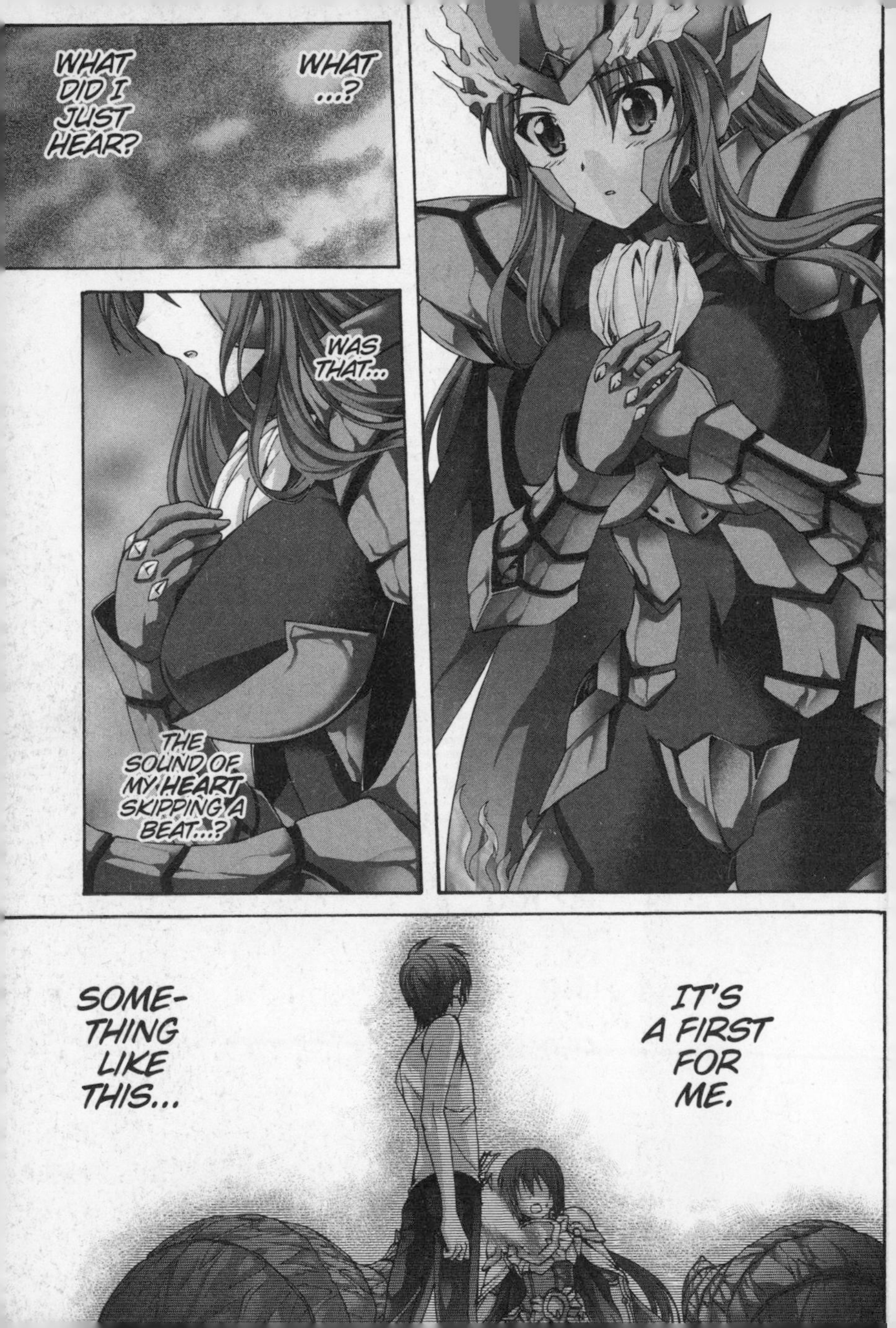
WHAT ...?
WHAT DID I JUST HEAR?
WAS THAT...
THE SOUND OF MY HEART SKIPPING A BEAT...?
IT'S A FIRST FOR ME.
SOME-THING LIKE THIS...

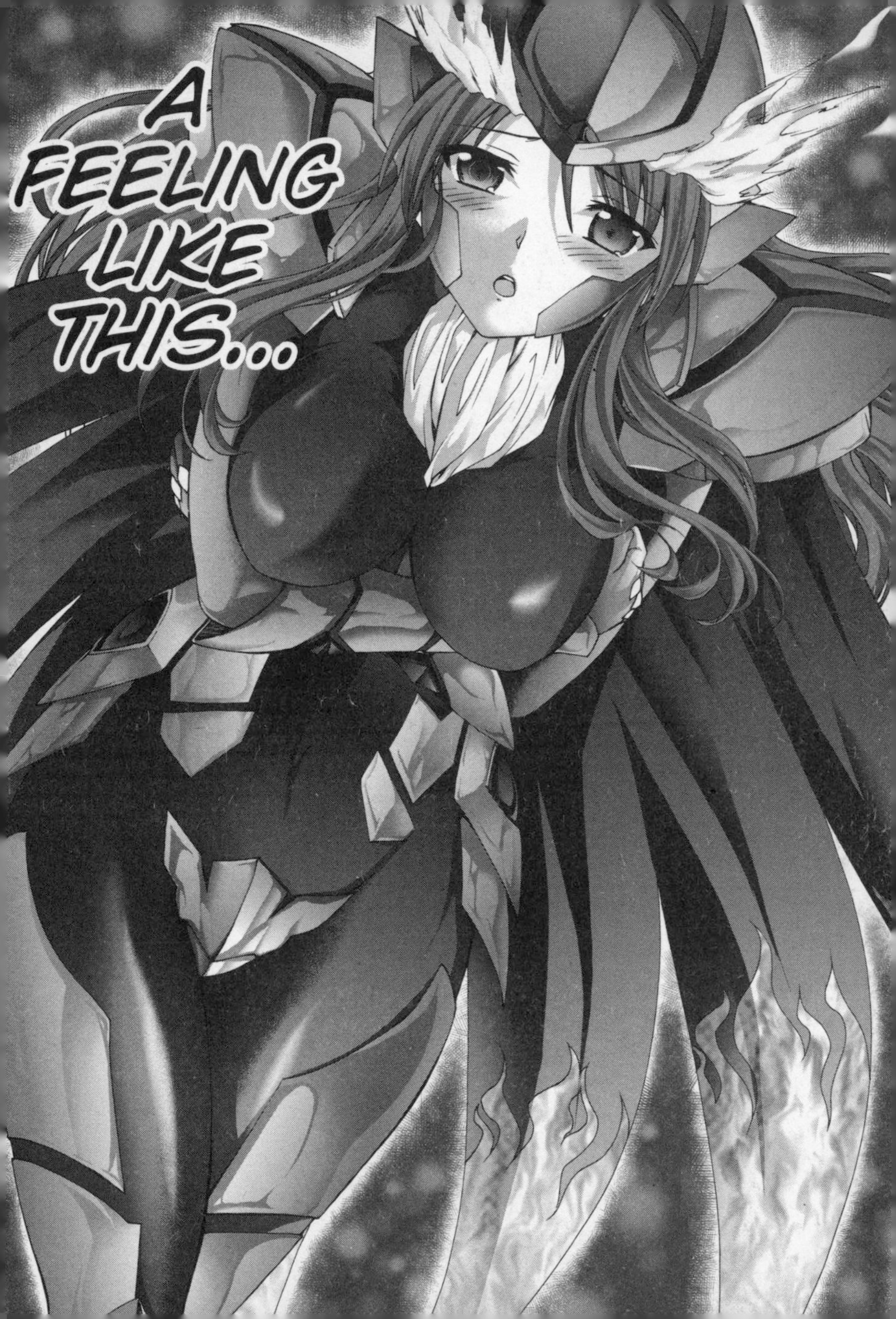
A FEELING LIKE THIS...

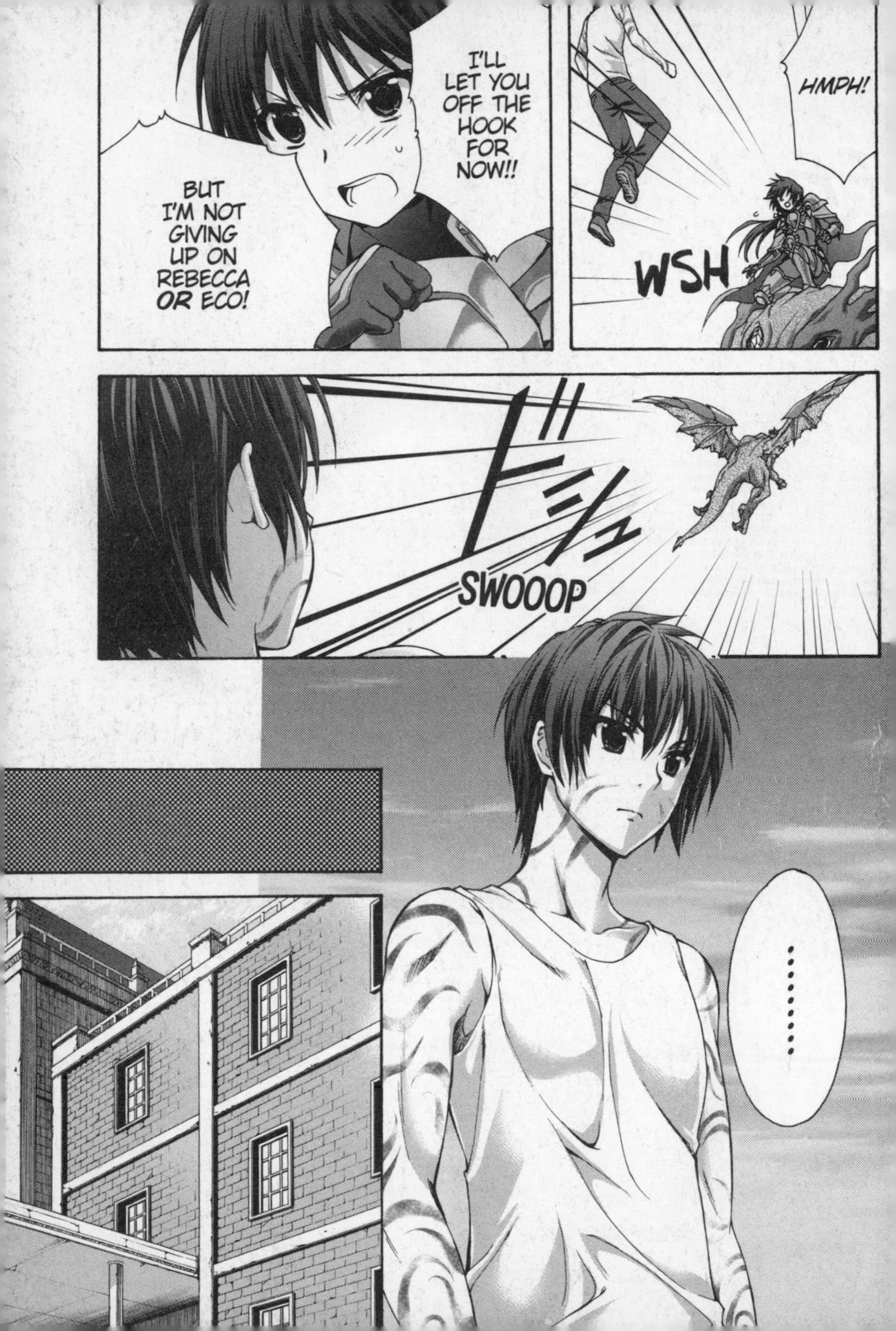
HMPH!
WSH
I'LL LET YOU OFF THE HOOK FOR NOW!!
BUT I'M NOT GIVING UP ON REBECCA OR ECO!
ドシュ
SWOOOP
......

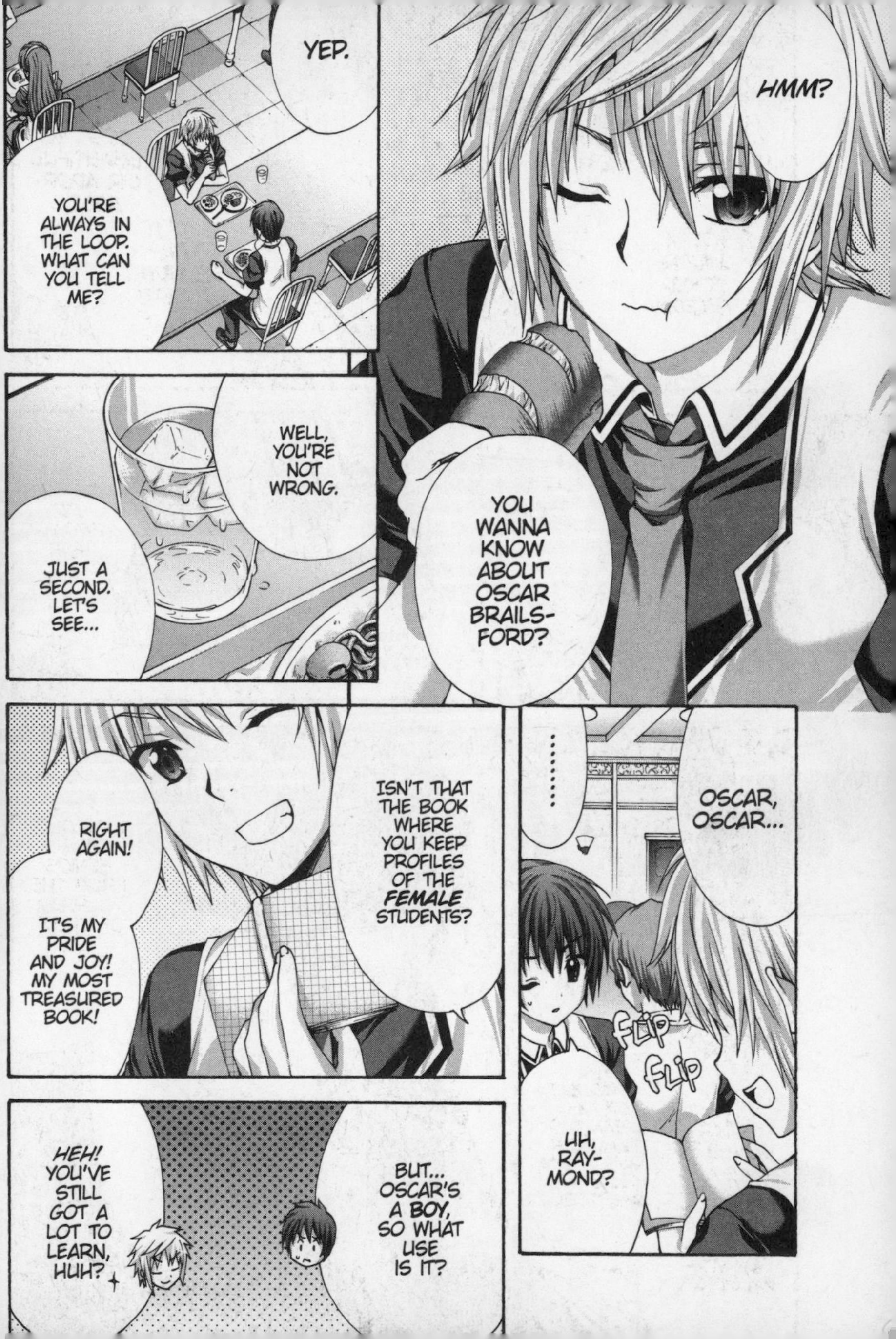
HMM?
YOU WANNA KNOW ABOUT OSCAR BRAILSFORD?
YEP.
YOU'RE ALWAYS IN THE LOOP. WHAT CAN YOU TELL ME?
WELL, YOU'RE NOT WRONG.
JUST A SECOND. LET'S SEE...
OSCAR, OSCAR...
......
FLIP
FLIP
UH, RAYMOND?
ISN'T THAT THE BOOK WHERE YOU KEEP PROFILES OF THE ***FEMALE*** STUDENTS?
RIGHT AGAIN!
IT'S MY PRIDE AND JOY! MY MOST TREASURED BOOK!
BUT... OSCAR'S A ***BOY***, SO WHAT USE IS IT?
HEH! YOU'VE STILL GOT A LOT TO LEARN, HUH?

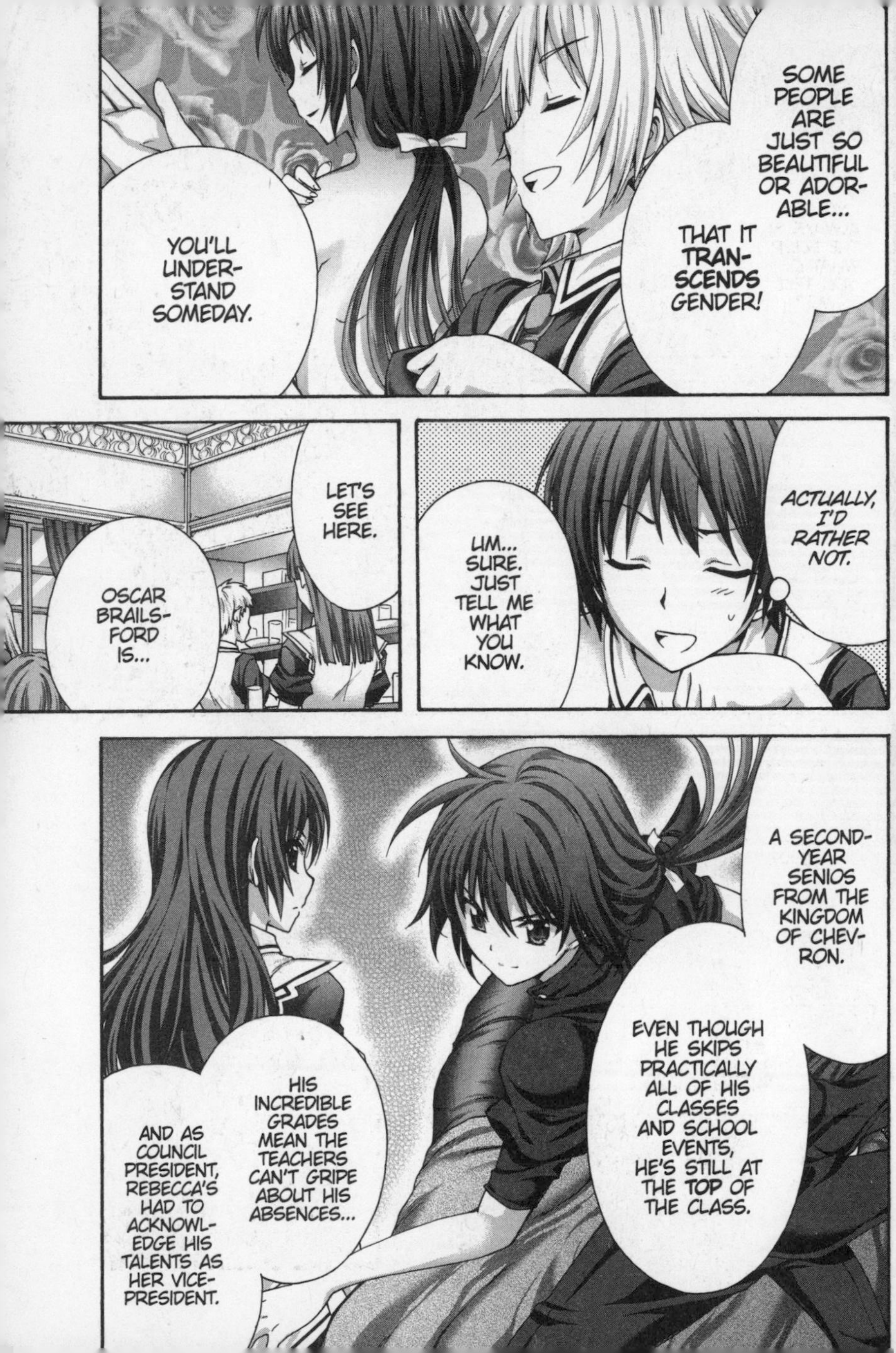
SOME PEOPLE ARE JUST SO BEAUTIFUL OR ADORABLE...
THAT IT TRANSCENDS GENDER!
YOU'LL UNDERSTAND SOMEDAY.
ACTUALLY, I'D RATHER NOT.
UM... SURE. JUST TELL ME WHAT YOU KNOW.
LET'S SEE HERE.
OSCAR BRAILSFORD IS...
A SECOND-YEAR SENIOS FROM THE KINGDOM OF CHEVRON.
EVEN THOUGH HE SKIPS PRACTICALLY ALL OF HIS CLASSES AND SCHOOL EVENTS, HE'S STILL AT THE TOP OF THE CLASS.
HIS INCREDIBLE GRADES MEAN THE TEACHERS CAN'T GRIPE ABOUT HIS ABSENCES...
AND AS COUNCIL PRESIDENT, REBECCA'S HAD TO ACKNOWLEDGE HIS TALENTS AS HER VICE-PRESIDENT.

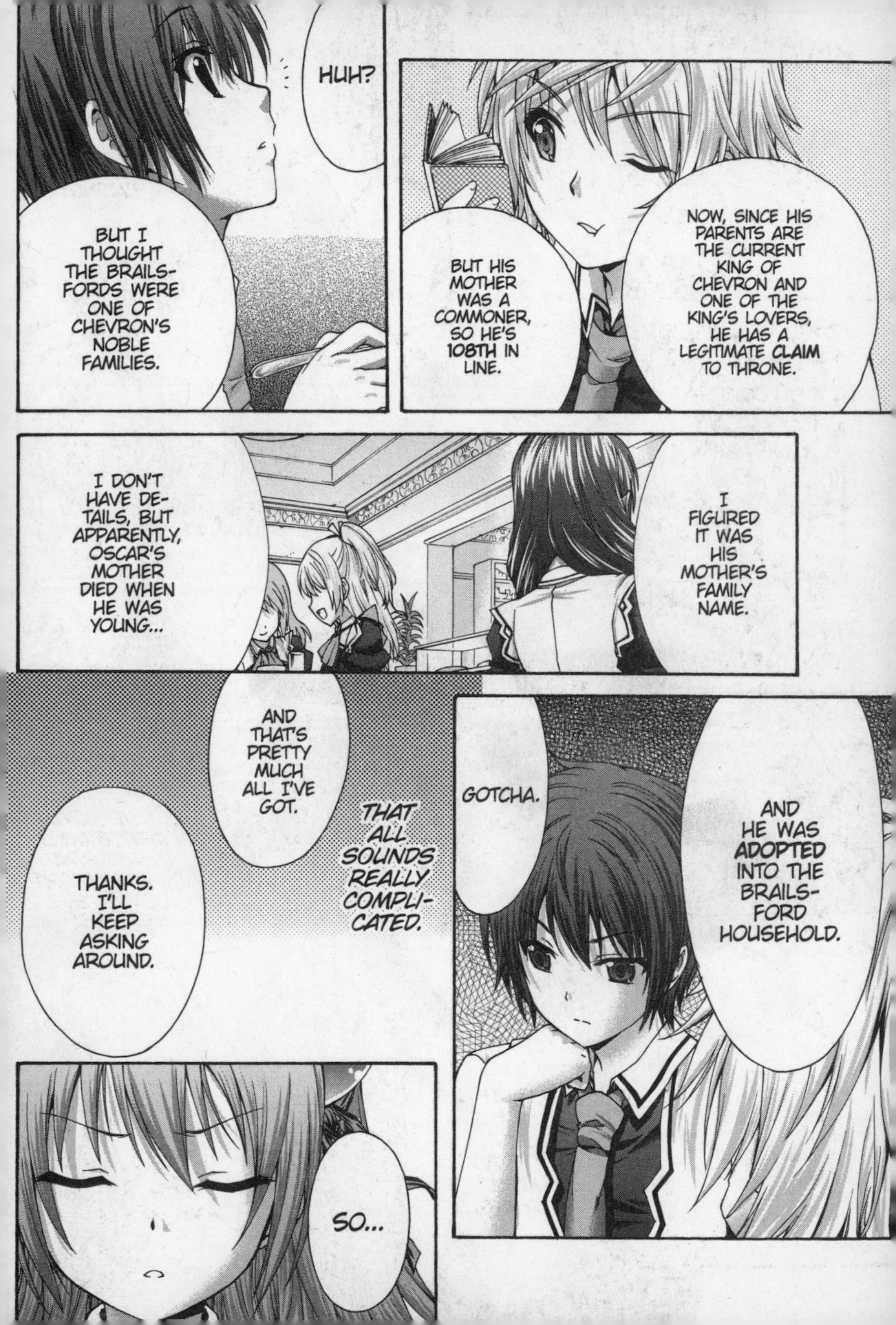

NOW, SINCE HIS PARENTS ARE THE CURRENT KING OF CHEVRON AND ONE OF THE KING'S LOVERS, HE HAS A LEGITIMATE CLAIM TO THRONE.
BUT HIS MOTHER WAS A COMMONER, SO HE'S 108TH IN LINE.
HUH?
BUT I THOUGHT THE BRAILS-FORDS WERE ONE OF CHEVRON'S NOBLE FAMILIES.
I FIGURED IT WAS HIS MOTHER'S FAMILY NAME.
I DON'T HAVE DE-TAILS, BUT APPARENTLY, OSCAR'S MOTHER DIED WHEN HE WAS YOUNG...
AND HE WAS ADOPTED INTO THE BRAILS-FORD HOUSEHOLD.
GOTCHA.
AND THAT'S PRETTY MUCH ALL I'VE GOT.
THAT ALL SOUNDS REALLY COMPLI-CATED.
THANKS. I'LL KEEP ASKING AROUND.
SO...

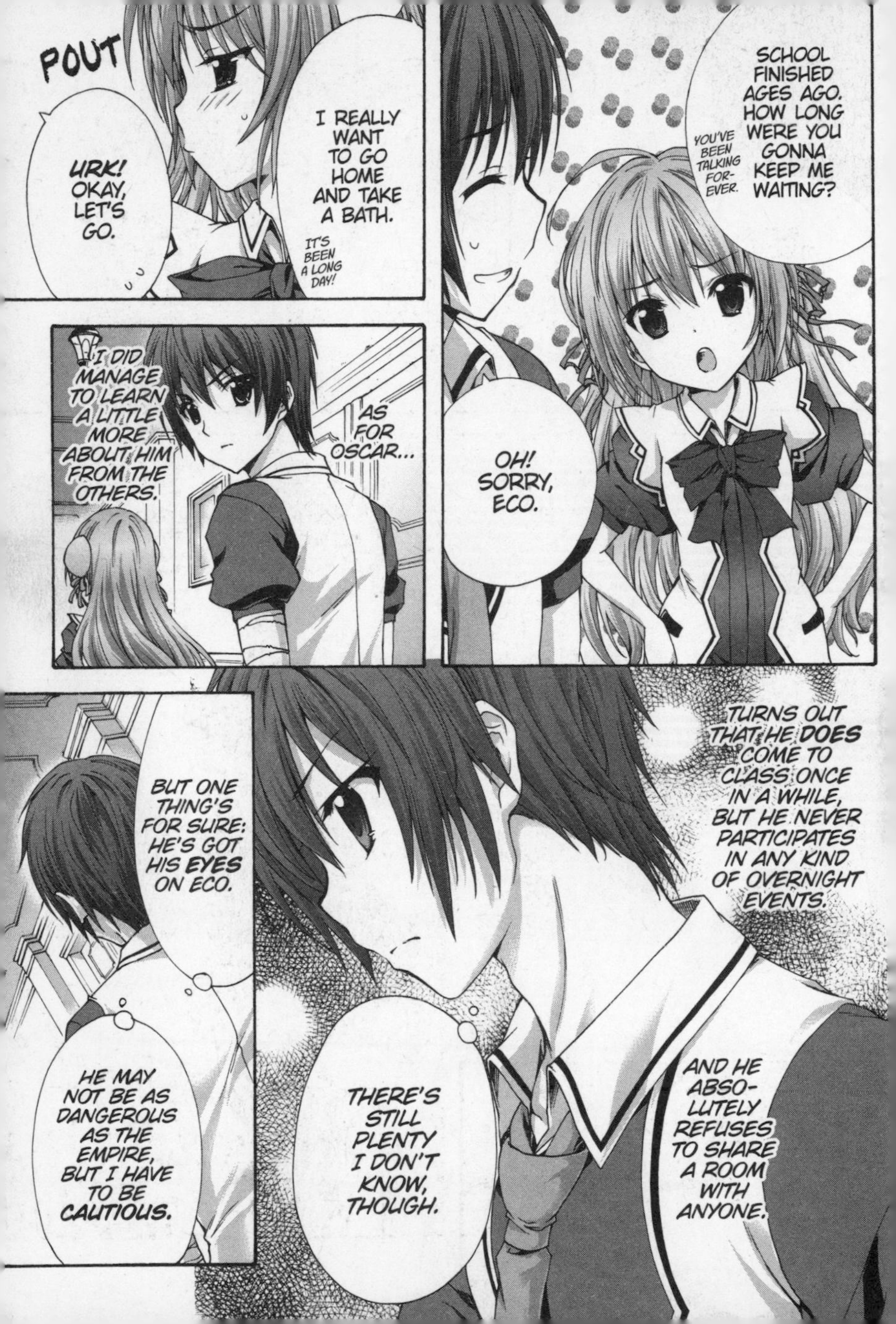
SCHOOL FINISHED AGES AGO. HOW LONG WERE YOU GONNA KEEP ME WAITING?
YOU'VE BEEN TALKING FOR-EVER.
OH! SORRY, ECO.
I REALLY WANT TO GO HOME AND TAKE A BATH.
IT'S BEEN A LONG DAY!
POUT
URK! OKAY, LET'S GO.
AS FOR OSCAR...
I DID MANAGE TO LEARN A LITTLE MORE ABOUT HIM FROM THE OTHERS.
TURNS OUT THAT HE DOES COME TO CLASS ONCE IN A WHILE, BUT HE NEVER PARTICIPATES IN ANY KIND OF OVERNIGHT EVENTS.
BUT ONE THING'S FOR SURE: HE'S GOT HIS EYES ON ECO.
AND HE ABSO-LUTELY REFUSES TO SHARE A ROOM WITH ANYONE.
THERE'S STILL PLENTY I DON'T KNOW, THOUGH.
HE MAY NOT BE AS DANGEROUS AS THE EMPIRE, BUT I HAVE TO BE CAUTIOUS.

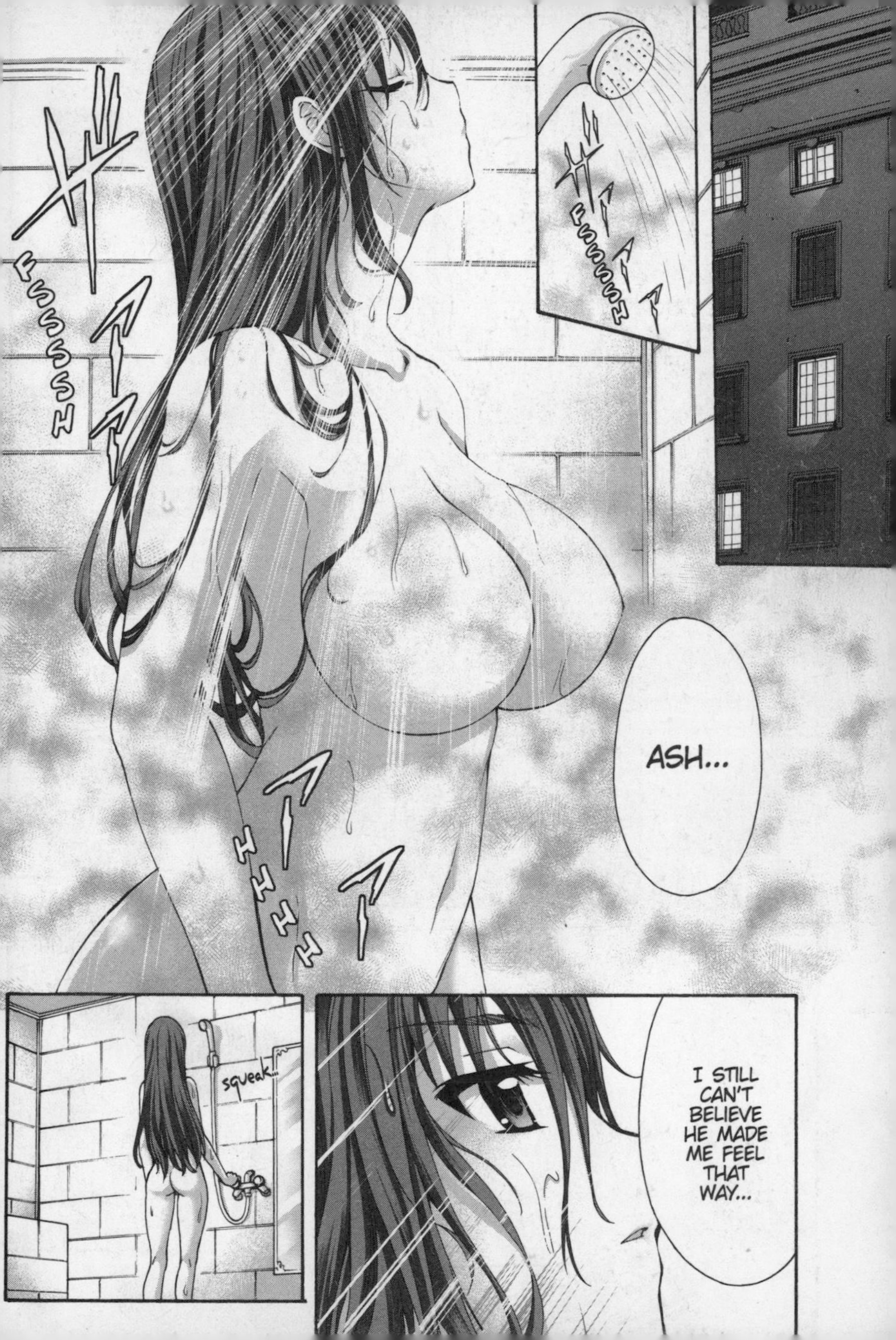
FSSSSH
ASH...
HHHHH
FSSSSH
I STILL CAN'T BELIEVE HE MADE ME FEEL THAT WAY...
squeak...

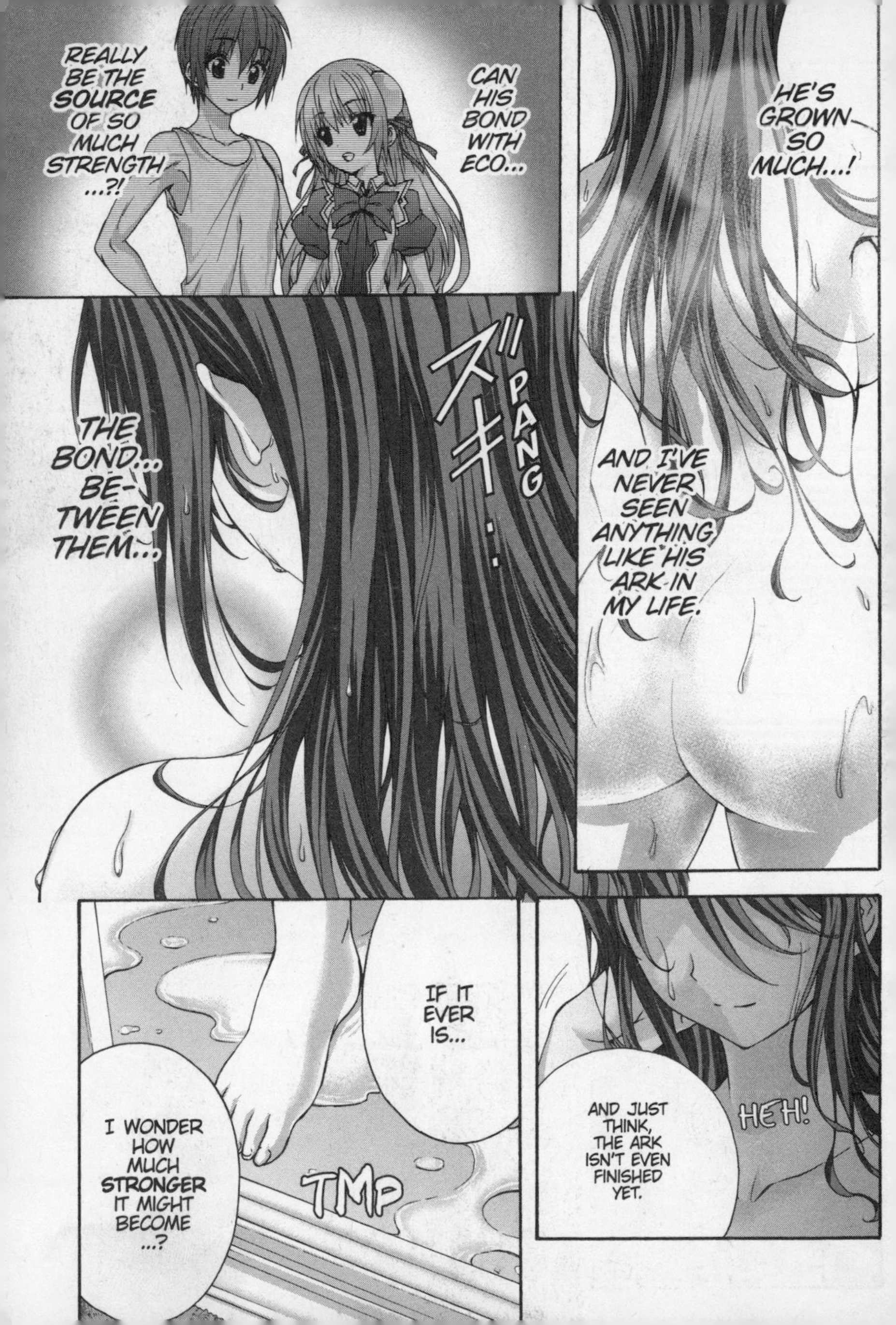
HE'S GROWN SO MUCH...!
AND I'VE NEVER SEEN ANYTHING LIKE HIS ARK IN MY LIFE.
CAN HIS BOND WITH ECO...
REALLY BE THE SOURCE OF SO MUCH STRENGTH...?!
ズキ…
PANG
THE BOND... BE-TWEEN THEM...
HEH!
AND JUST THINK, THE ARK ISN'T EVEN FINISHED YET.
IF IT EVER IS...
I WONDER HOW MUCH STRONGER IT MIGHT BECOME...?
TMP

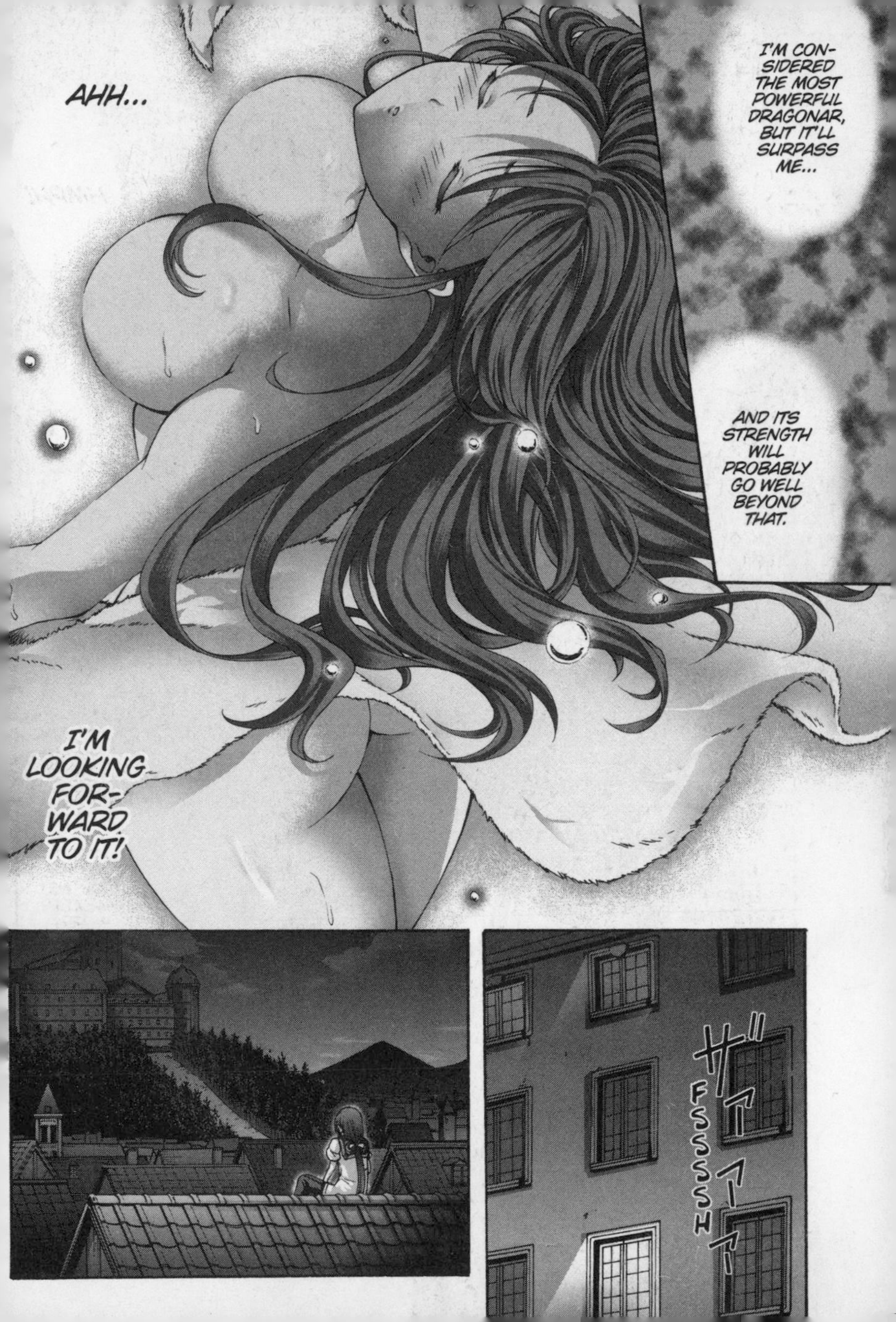
I'M CONSIDERED THE MOST POWERFUL DRAGONAR, BUT IT'LL SURPASS ME...
AND ITS STRENGTH WILL PROBABLY GO WELL BEYOND THAT.
AHH...
I'M LOOKING FORWARD TO IT!
FSSSSH

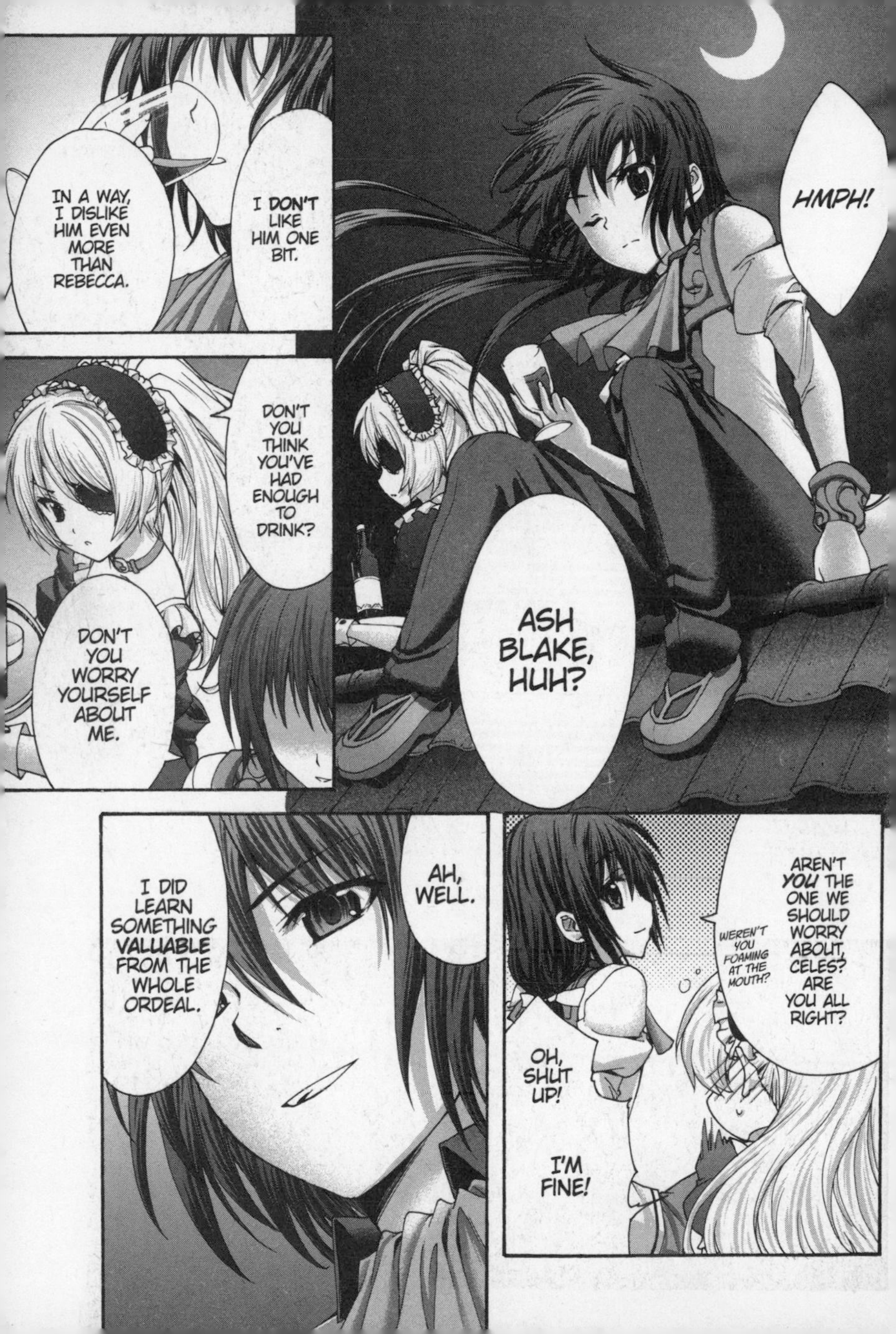
HMPH!
ASH BLAKE, HUH?
I DON'T LIKE HIM ONE BIT.
IN A WAY, I DISLIKE HIM EVEN MORE THAN REBECCA.
DON'T YOU THINK YOU'VE HAD ENOUGH TO DRINK?
DON'T YOU WORRY YOURSELF ABOUT ME.
AREN'T YOU THE ONE WE SHOULD WORRY ABOUT, CELES? ARE YOU ALL RIGHT?
WEREN'T YOU FOAMING AT THE MOUTH?
OH, SHUT UP!
I'M FINE!
AH, WELL.
I DID LEARN SOMETHING VALUABLE FROM THE WHOLE ORDEAL.

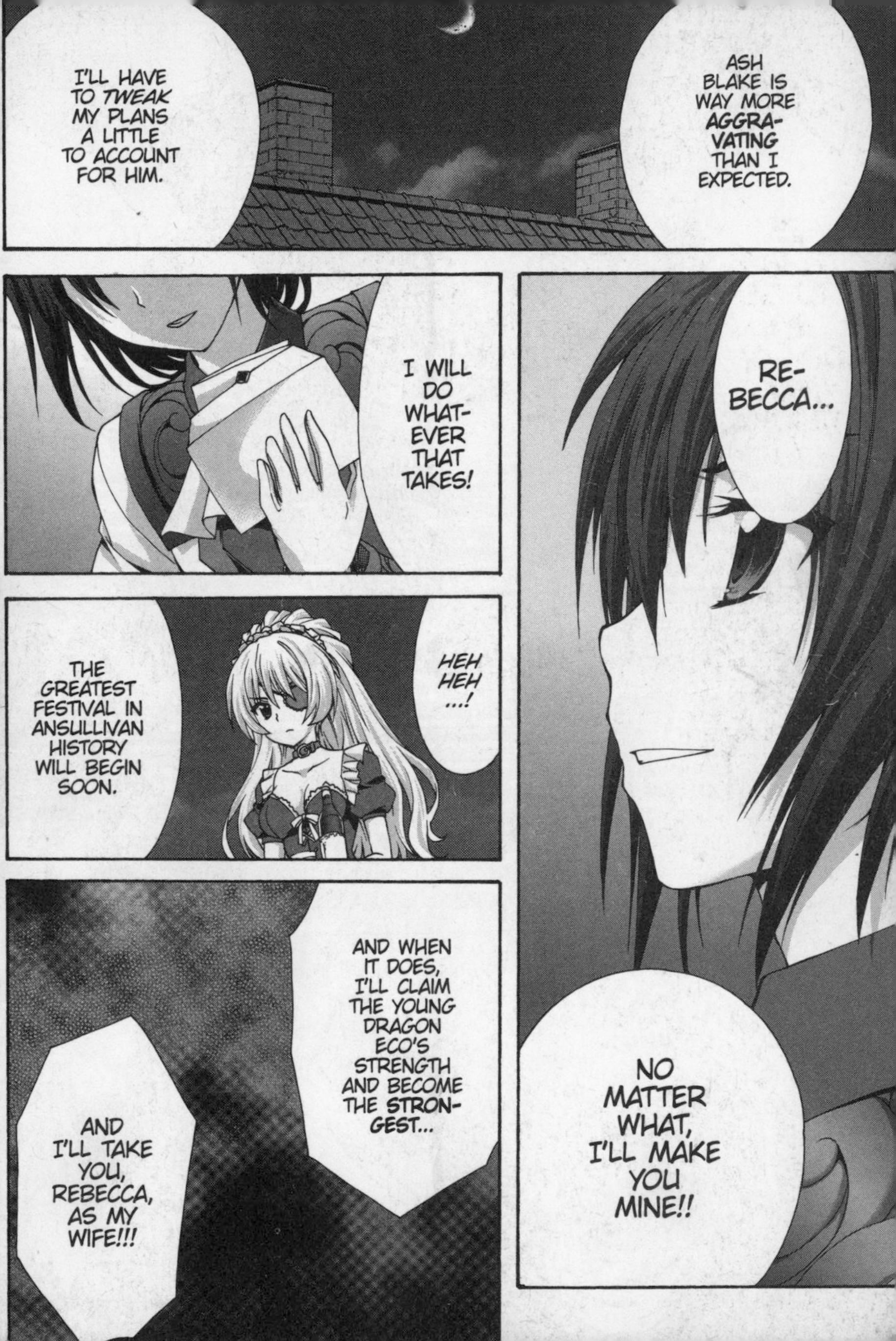
ASH BLAKE IS WAY MORE AGGRAVATING THAN I EXPECTED.
I'LL HAVE TO *TWEAK* MY PLANS A LITTLE TO ACCOUNT FOR HIM.
RE-BECCA...
NO MATTER WHAT, I'LL MAKE YOU MINE!!
I WILL DO WHATEVER THAT TAKES!
HEH HEH ...!
THE GREATEST FESTIVAL IN ANSULLIVAN HISTORY WILL BEGIN SOON.
AND WHEN IT DOES, I'LL CLAIM THE YOUNG DRAGON ECO'S STRENGTH AND BECOME THE STRONGEST...
AND I'LL TAKE YOU, REBECCA, AS MY WIFE!!!

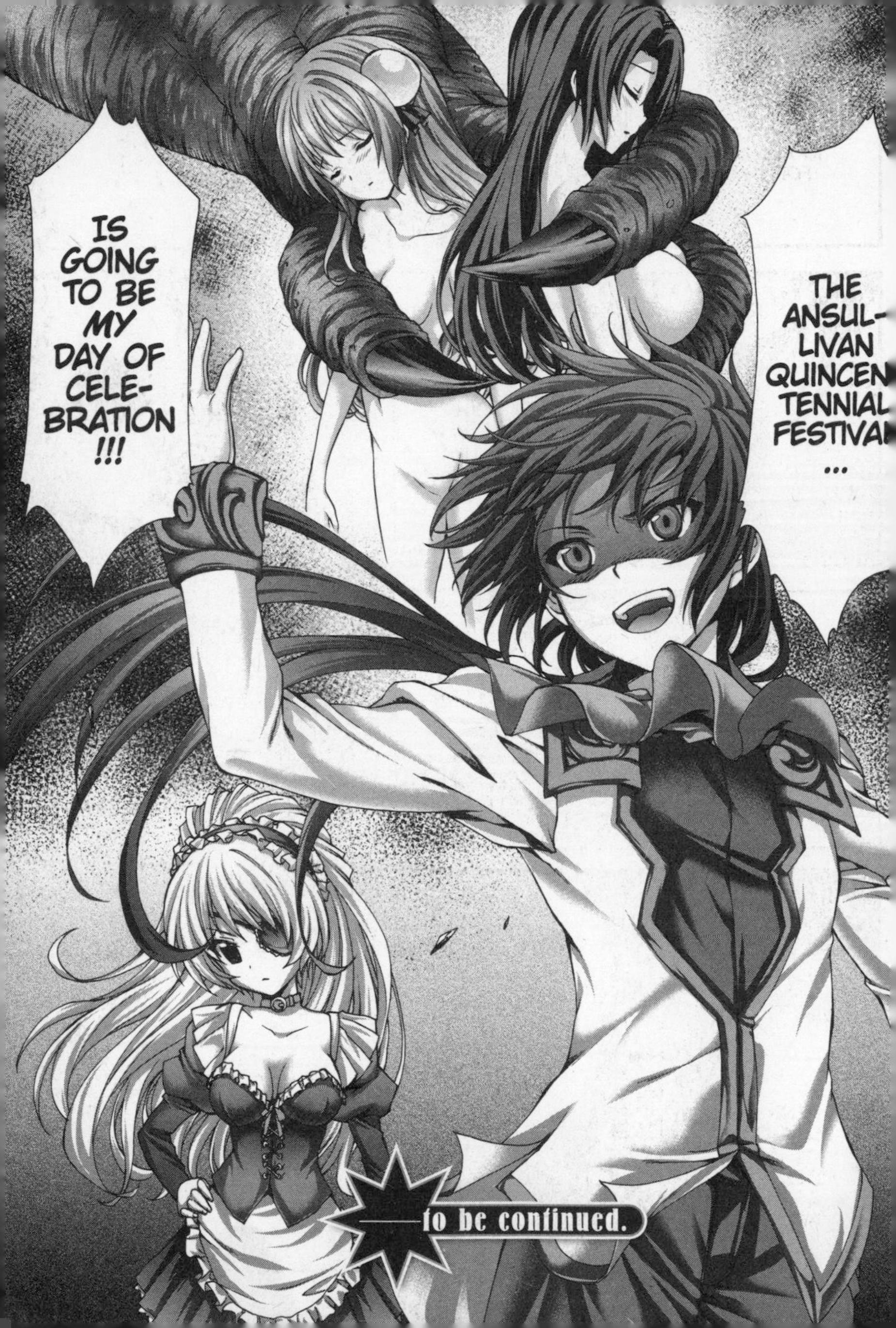
THE ANSUL-LIVAN QUINCEN TENNIAL FESTIVAL ...
IS GOING TO BE MY DAY OF CELE-BRATION !!!
to be continued.

DRAGONAR
ACADEMY

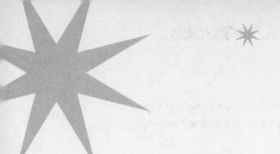

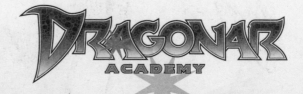

AFTERWORD

It's me, RAN.

Thanks so much to everyone who picked up volume 10 of the Dragonar Academy manga.

As we start this new arc, we're meeting a few new characters: Oscar and his people! Naturally, I'm thrilled to be drawing a new maid (laughs). I'm also ecstatic about illustrating Rebecca's true strength!

I hope you're all excited to see how things will unfold from here, and I hope to see you all again in the next volume.

Ran

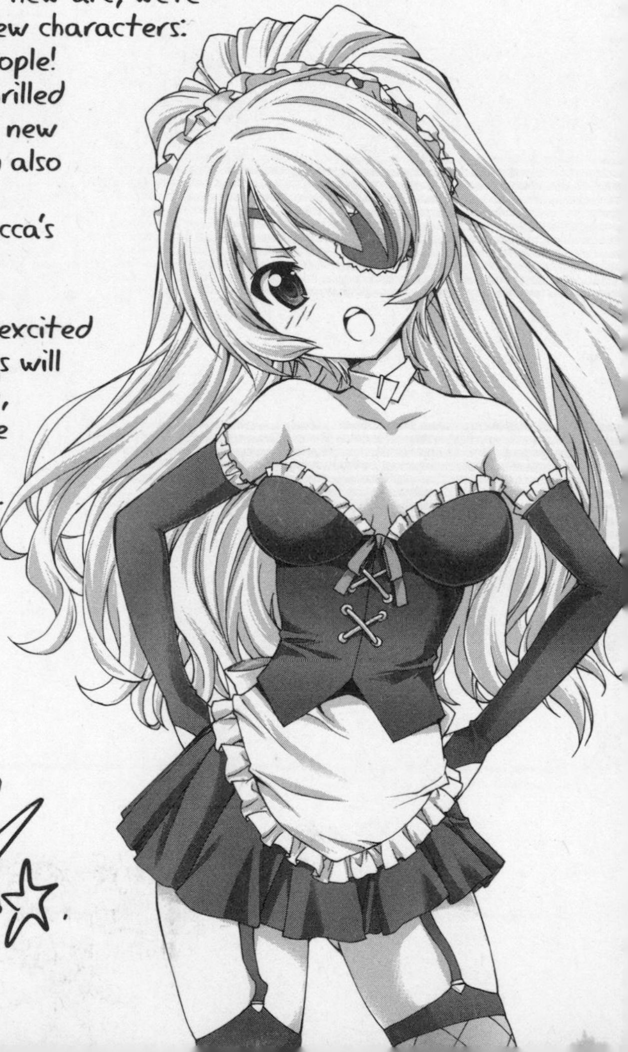

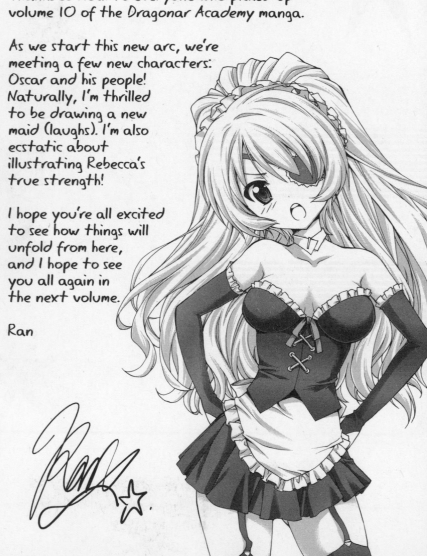

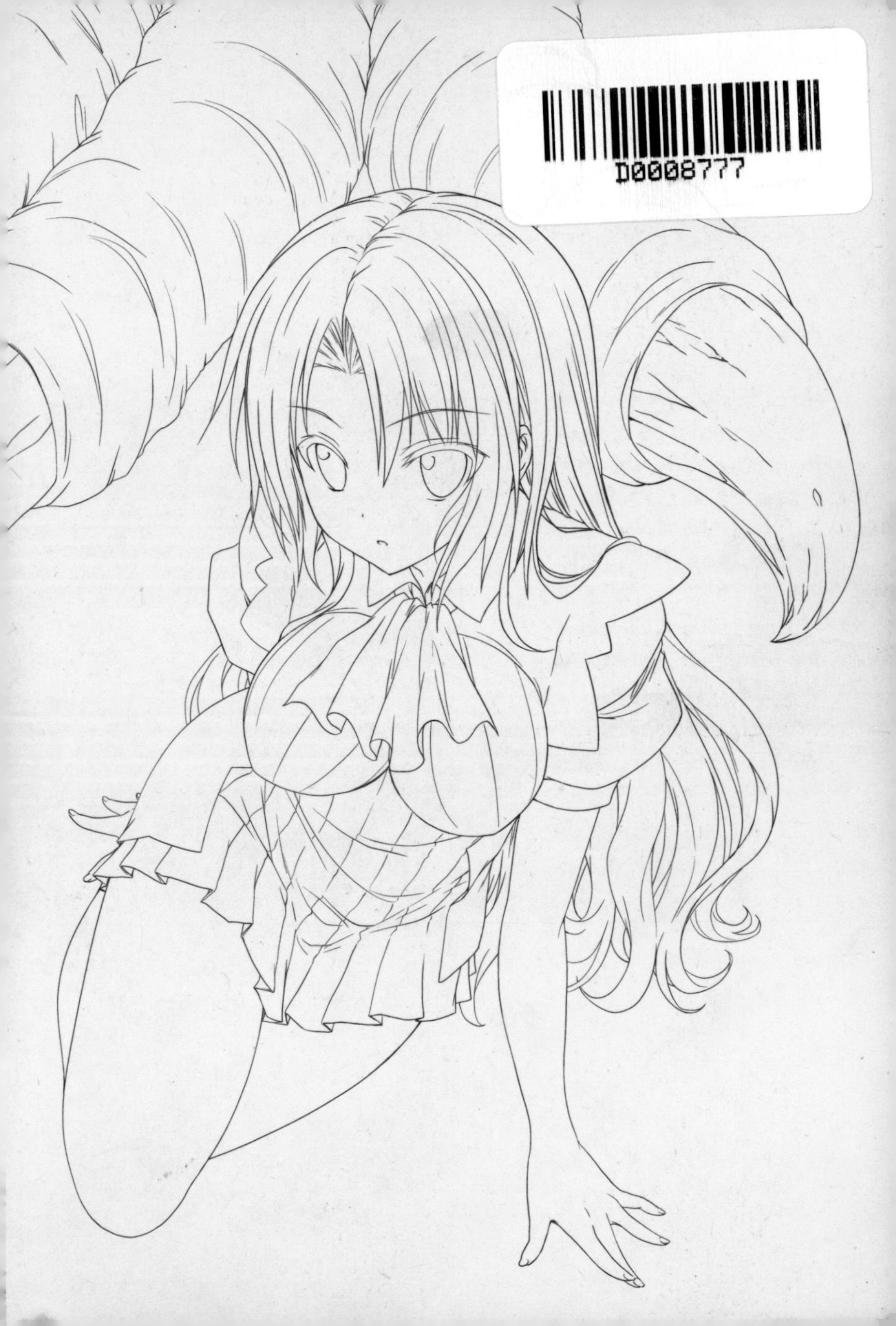